The Wild Marsh

BOOKS BY RICK BASS

The Deer Pasture

Wild to the Heart

The Watch

Oil Notes

Winter

The Ninemile Wolves

Platte River

In the Loyal Mountains

The Lost Grizzlies

The Book of Yaak

The Sky, the Stars, the Wilderness

Where the Sea Used to Be

Fiber

The New Wolves

Brown Dog of the Yaak

Colter

The Hermit's Story

The Roadless Yaak (Editor)

Caribou Rising

Falling from Grace in Texas
(Coeditor with Paul Christensen)

The Diezmo

The Lives of Rocks

Why I Came West

The Wild Marsh

The Wild Marsh

FOUR SEASONS AT HOME IN MONTANA

Rick Bass

HOUGHTON MIFFLIN HARCOURT

BOSTON • NEW YORK

2009

For Mary Katherine and Lowry

For information about permission to reproduce selections from this book,
write to Permissions, Houghton Mifflin Harcourt Publishing Company,
215 Park Avenue South, New York, New York 10003.

www.hmhbooks.com

Library of Congress Cataloging-in-Publication Data
Bass, Rick, date
The wild marsh : four seasons at home in Montana / Rick Bass.
p. cm.
ISBN-13: 978-0-547-05516-9
ISBN-10: 0-547-05516-1
1. Natural history—Montana—Yaak Valley. 2. Seasons—Montana—
Yaak Valley. 3. Yaak Valley (Mont.) I. Title.
QH105.M9B37 2009
508.786'81—dc22 2008049229

Book design by Brian Moore

Printed in the United States of America

DOC 10 9 8 7 6 5 4 3 2 1

© **Mixed Sources**
Product group from well-managed
forests, controlled sources and
recycled wood or fiber
FSC www.fsc.org Cert no. SCS-COC-00648
© 1996 Forest Stewardship Council

To inhabit a place means literally to have made it a habit, to have learned how to wear a place like a familiar garment, like the garments of sanctity that nuns once wore. The word *habit,* in its now-dim original form, means "to own." We own places not because we possess the deeds to them, but because they have entered the continuum of our lives. What is strange to us, unfamiliar, can never be home.

—PAUL GRUCHOW, *Grass Roots*

ACKNOWLEDGMENTS

I'm grateful to the editors of the following magazines, in which portions of this book have appeared in slightly different form: *The Atlantic Monthly, Audubon,* the *Bark, Big Sky Journal, Field & Stream, Los Angeles Times Sunday Magazine, Montana Outdoors, Narrative Magazine, O Magazine, Orion, Poets and Writers, Portland Magazine, Shambhala Sun, Sierra,* the *Southern Review, Tricycle, TriQuarterly Review,* and *Wasatch Journal.* I'm deeply grateful to my editor, Nicole Angeloro; my typist, Angi Young; my agent, Bob Dattila; to Lisa Glover and Alison Kerr Miller at Houghton Mifflin Harcourt for further editorial and production assistance; and to Brian Moore for the book's design and Patrick Barry for the cover design. I'm most grateful to my family and friends for their support of a writer who disappears into the dream-world for half of every day, and am grateful to the valley itself: grateful that such places of biological integrity, with the sometimes calming and other times invigorating reassurance of their breath, still exist.

CONTENTS

INTRODUCTION   1

JANUARY   10

FEBRUARY   40

MARCH   61

APRIL   80

MAY   129

JUNE   160

JULY   172

AUGUST   211

SEPTEMBER   265

OCTOBER   280

NOVEMBER   297

DECEMBER   349

INTRODUCTION

....

IT'S IMPOSSIBLE TO SIT in a cabin for a long time, musing in essay form upon the woods around you, without thinking occasionally of that most American of thinkers and spirits, Thoreau, and his own somewhat isolated residency at Walden Pond. Whether it's true or not, I find it wonderful that Thoreau's last words were reported to have been "Moose. Indians." More economical than even a haiku, the two words twine perfectly the occasionally but not always harmonious relationship between landscape and humanity. The moose requires the deep summer shade of the far north, exists on deciduous browse and meadow marsh grass, but also wanders up into the deep blue-green comfort of high-altitude spruce forests; and it stands stalwart too, with its strange and fantastic body, its incredible bulk, bearing testimony as well to the natural history of snow, deep snow, and long winters.

From that one word, *moose,* an imaginer could write a thousand pages describing the natural history of the landscape that a moose inhabits, and the way that landscape has shaped the moose; and likewise, and even more so, from the next word, *Indians,* a thousand pages would not begin to hint at the complexity and drama and steady challenges of the human experience upon a landscape — the attempts at the daily and seasonal integration of that most curious and complicated and often confused of species, humans, with any landscape of singular force and integrity. A snowy landscape sculpts, across the millennia, a species well suited to deep snow and long winters; a landscape wreathed in fire sculpts species well fitted to that dynamic force.

And a wild landscape, then, will elicit from the humans who inhabit it a certain wildness, a certain dynamism of spirit that, though ragged, strives for an eventual elegance of fit. We have not been in the world nearly as long as moose or so many other fitted species and citizens of the world, but we are trying, and wild landscapes of integrity — while we still possess them — urge us along.

The thing about *Walden,* though, is that it's an eastern treatise, beautifully written, deeply considered, and fully felt, but of-a-place, the East, even if the East in the 1850s was a hugely different kind of East from the one we know today. Reading *Walden,* I've always wondered what Thoreau would have thought of the West — a landscape he never inhabited though always wished to. How would the West have shaped those essays, and those values? Would there have been more tempering and refining, or more raggedness — or perhaps both? It's an unfair reading of *Walden,* to be sure, but every time I read it or look at it, I find myself wondering, *Can this be lifted and applied to a western landscape?* The answer for some parts is *yes,* for other parts *maybe,* and for still others, *no.*

But I think the idea of holing up and hunkering down against the larger forces of the world has not lost its allure since Thoreau's time. If anything that instinct, or impulse, continues to reside in almost all of us, sometimes activated or bestirred and other times dormant but always present. I'm not talking about out-and-out government-loathing misanthropy, not the survivalist's manifesto kind of hunkering down, but something more peaceable and searching. And from my home in northwest Montana's Yaak Valley, I've been extraordinarily fortunate to attempt to negotiate such a fit with the world, inhabiting an old homestead quarter-section that I went into debt to buy some twenty years ago, just before another individual sought to purchase it and clear cut it. I wasn't looking for a full homestead, but it found me; and the first thing I did was unearth the old falling-down cabin from the turn of the previous century, 1903, and scrub the logs with hot water and soap before dragging them down to the broad marsh on the property — a perfect clearing in the forest, reminding me of the eye of a hawk or eagle or raven — and reconstructing the old cabin there, like a child's toy, and putting a new roof on it.

And I went out to the cabin each morning, then — regardless of the weather — and sat at my desk and looked out the window at the marsh, perched so close to its edge that the swaying marsh grasses came right up to the window. The marsh grass seemed like a sea, and the cabin, a barge or ship, anchored. I stared out the window and daydreamed often, rather than writing.

The old cabin had been fitted between trees and bushes in such a way as to be almost invisible, even from the beginning, and subsequent years have enclosed it even further.

Butt-planted for four, five, even six hours at a time, laboring to make a few pages but often simply staring out that window and dreaming and listening to the sounds and silences of the forest all around me, and the marsh in its center, I have seen every creature imaginable up here, over the many years. They come and go, passing sometimes right by that window, eyeball to eyeball with me: marten, bear, wolf, mountain lion. Eagles have struck and felled geese right in front of that window, owls perch on the chimney, ruffed grouse drum and fan on the picnic table I have set outside, for those rare days that are neither too cold nor too hot, and when the marsh's — and the valley's — ravenous insects are temporarily dormant. Elk, innumerable deer in all seasons, coyotes, herons, cranes, and, yes, particularly moose, are drawn to the marsh's fecundity.

The Yaak's Indians are the Kootenai, a tribe from the Columbia River basin, who are now confederated with the Salish. Largely a fish culture residing along the Kootenai and lower Yaak rivers, the Kootenai people, I am told, came up into the Yaak's mountains to hunt mountain goats and woodland caribou in the summer and fall, though they did not — I am told — inhabit the upper Yaak all year long. If this is true, then the Yaak is a remarkably young place, with whites moving in year-round only around the beginning of the last century. The 1900s were possibly the first century of full-time human habitation. I find this astonishing, and redolent, in some way I cannot explain, with mysteries, and lessons for the future.

In other regards, however, the Yaak is ancient. There are outcrops of mountain here that have etched in their strata wind-lapped ripple marks from the great inland Cambrian Belt Sea of roughly a billion years ago — and then yet again, the valley is new, for as recently as only seven or eight thousand years ago, the Yaak lay sleeping beneath more than a mile of blue ice, even as higher peaks in this corner of the world were emerging from that ice, being carved and shredded rather than compressed and sculpted. To my eye, at least, the Yaak possesses an elegance, and a calm, for this compression.

It's gloriously remote, snugged right up against the Canadian border. It was one of the last inhabited valleys in the United States to get electricity, and even today, in twenty-first-century America, there are many parts of the valley that are not electrified, and others that do not even have phone service. (Needless to say, there's no cell service here.) Whereas Thoreau lived famously only a few minutes away from his mother, able to join her for midday tea after only a mild saunter, folks up here live miles apart. Sometimes a path through the woods on foot, or on horse, gets one to where one desires to be more quickly than a roundabout trip in a car, and other times, of course, quickness is not the desired outcome anyway.

There is still an incredible raggedness of spirit up here, a scrappy, Yaakish way of doing things; of improvising, often, and the merging of two ways of thinking. Duct tape is paramount.

The Yaak is still very much a hunter-gatherer society, and at times still possesses elements of a barter economy. Five miles back in the woods live a couple with a team of sled dogs that they can't leave untended. They've got a snowplow, and I don't. Sometimes in the summer when they go camping up in Canada for a couple of weeks, I'll go and check on their dogs, and then in winter, they'll come now and again and plow my driveway. Eggs for firewood, old horse tack for studded Subaru tires. An old truck for a new solar panel. And on and on, around and around.

Something it took me a while to learn, through those slow and close observations out the cabin window, is that always, the Yaak is a beguiling mix of two stories, two ways of being; that part of its power or spirit comes from its geographical positioning, and that ecological fecundity. It's where the fire-dominated natural history of the mountain West grades into the rainforests of the Pacific Northwest, and it's where Canada's great legacy of boreal forest, and the immense Purcell mountain range — Canada's largest — just barely tips a finger down into the United States.

And in that finger resides all manner of species, and interspecies relationships, and vegetative assemblages not found anywhere else in the United States. The Yaak is its own place, but it is also a critical gateway from the United States into Canada, and vice versa. (For wildlife, that is; there's no border crossing for people, thank goodness, only rugged mountains and deep forests.) And likewise, the Yaak is a gateway east and west, between Glacier National Park and the vast Bob Marshall Wilderness — country known as the Northern Continental Divide ecosystem — and the Pacific Northwest, beginning in the Colville country of northeast Washington and continuing on across to the Cascades, and then the ocean. (The Yaak River rushes straight down out of the mountains into the curve of the Kootenai River, joining it like an arrow fitted to the arc of a bow — "Yaak" is the Kootenai word for "arrow" — and the Kootenai River, in turn, is far and away the largest tributary to the mighty Columbia.)

The Yaak is also the major ecological turnstile between Yellowstone and the Yukon; it's the rarest and most singular, if not largest, jewel in the great crown of remaining North American wilderness, and yet none of it is protected as such, even forty-five years after the passage of the Wilderness Act.

Because of all this ecological mixing, this feathering of various ecosystems, the Yaak has more species diversity than any other valley in Montana; and although it's the northernmost valley in the state, it's also the lowest elevation. The Yaak enters the Kootenai, for instance, at an elevation of only 1,880 feet above sea level. It's lush despite the long northern winters; and it is in the stippled chain, the glittering necklace, of the Yaak's boggy marshes and buggy wetlands that some of the valley's and the region's greatest biodiversity is to be found.

But about those bugs: the Yaak is a biological wilderness, not a recreational wilderness. Parts of the valley have been hit hard by the previous century — it's laced with thousands of miles of old logging roads, many of which are infused with weeds, and large sections of the valley are riddled with thousands of clearcuts — some old and regenerating with dog-hair thickets, and others still new. But other, farther parts of the valley are still pristine and possess an ecological integrity — whether they burn or rot — and a wildness that is qualitatively different from those places that have been roaded and logged.

I have spent the bulk of my adult life advocating for the permanent protection of these wilder, farther places in the Yaak through the congressional designation of wilderness areas. But right here, right now, is — in this book — the only time you'll hear me carry on about any of that.

This book, unlike so many of my other Yaak-based books, aims to be all celebration and all observation, without judgment or advocacy. I'm not sure why I made that choice, with this book; perhaps in order to simply stay sane a while longer. One of the dreams and hopes I have for the Yaak is the establishment of an intricate biological survey, a series of ecological transects and measurements aimed at identifying the presence, distribution, and, if possible, population counts of as many different species as possible, to serve as a baseline data point for the coming century. As a natural historian, I wish very much that such a foundation of ecological knowledge had been established at the beginning of the 1900s, and I cannot help but believe that natural historians and scientists who fall in love with the Yaak in the year 2100 will wish just as intensely that there was some sort of usable record about the condition of this ecosystem — the nuts and bolts of it, and how it all worked — in the year 2000. I envisioned, and still do, some kind of multiyear, quasi-private, quasi-public expedition in which some of the country's, or the world's, finest scientists — lepidopterists, mammalogists, herpetologists, ichthyologists, and so forth — lead little seasonal bands of data collectors and surveyors along their transects, utilizing easily replicable scientific methods and protocols.

In the meantime, I reasoned, I could lay down a similar if not easily replicable transect across the year in a journal; though rather than bisecting the million-acre valley north to south, or east to west, I would let the valley come to me, flowing past me, and I would make notes, observations, markers embedded within the new century, beginning a few hours before the first day of the millennium. And though a fan of wilderness, I would seek also to chronicle the characteristics, movements, and patterns of the humans who inhabit this remote valley, here at one century's end and another's beginning.

Not quite Indians, really, living amid so many moose, but still, quite a bit different from the rest of the world: different enough that when you mention to someone in Montana that you're from the Yaak, he might look at you as if a hundred years ago you had said *Kootenai* or *Blackfeet, Assiniboin, Crow, Flathead,* or *Arapaho,* the questioner taking a step backwards, even, and reassessing the one thus questioned, with traces of both fear and longing, and searching for a radiant, remnant wildness.

It still surprises me to consider where I came from and how I got here: growing up in the petrochemical suburbs of Houston in the 1960s, spending weeks at a time in the summer up at the edge of the hill country, at my grandmother's, who was born in 1898 — before making it out to the mountains I longed for intuitively and attending school in northern Utah, at Utah State, then being pulled back to the South, to Mississippi, where I worked as a geologist for some years before getting in my truck one day and simply leaving, striking out back west, partly drawn and partly seeking, and aiming for the biggest, blankest spot of green on the map I could find, wandering all the way to the literal end of this country to do so. Falling in love with it at first sight and settling in, in fits and starts: a newcomer at first, but all of a sudden, or with what seems a suddenness, having become an old-timer as others fall back and away. It's always been a hard place to make a living, and to live year-round.

I remember when I was a small child, perhaps six or seven, riding with my mother in the car, in Houston. Let's suppose it was 1964, or thereabouts. For one reason or another, the topic of the year 2000 came up, and I asked her if I would still be alive. "You will be," she said, laughing. "You'll be forty-two" — a number that of course seemed at that time depressingly, impossibly, old. "You won't be a young man anymore," she said, "but you'll have seen some things by that time" — and I remember asking her how old she'd be, and whether she'd still be alive then. *Maybe,* she said, *hopefully. Probably.* Sixty-six.

She would have been around thirty at the time of this conversation, and still a long way even from forty-two herself. She died several years ago, and as the millennium approached, she was much on my mind. I was filled with a feeling both large and hollow, crossing over that not-insubstantial line by myself — or rather, without her. Of the two of us who began that conversation, only one has continued it; though in my heart, as that date appeared, it was a small solace to know that even nearly four decades ago she took the time to consider it, and I can recall the thoughtful look she gave the subject as she answered my child's questions.

It's not just for the scientists of the future that I've profiled the passage of a year, here in a northern land still fortunate enough to have four full seasons despite the rising tide of the world's increasing heat, the ever-increasing global exhalations of warmth and carbon. I like to imagine that this record has value, in a scrapbook sort of way, to my family, and to others who will in the future inhabit, and love, the Yaak. Often, particularly as I grow older, I am aware of wanting to share with my children little secrets, little points of interest, about the valley — where the huckleberries are best in a dry year, or late in the summer; where the elk are in November; where the wolves dig their dens; where the grizzly claw marks are on the old cedar — and that the passing on of such knowledge constitutes a transfer of some of the most valuable currency, other than love, possible; that the transfer of that kind of intimate and place-based knowledge, the knowledge of home, *is* a kind of love, and rarer and more valuable now certainly than silver or gold.

Some days I worry that there is a sand-through-the-hourglass effect to such observations, and the passing on of that knowledge; that though the knowledge might be passed on to the next generation, and the next, so rapid now are the ecological changes in the West, so severe the dissolution of various biological underpinnings as one piece after another is pulled from the puzzle, the map, of previous integrity, that the future will render such knowledge irrelevant: as if, already, I am describing things that are gone-away, or going-away.

But one of the key components of love is hope — enduring hope — and to let fear replace hope would be a bitter defeat indeed, a kind of failure in its own stead.

Already, nearly a full decade has come and gone since I set out on this project, undertaken when Mary Katherine was eight and Lowry, five — after much anticipation, the millennium got here so quickly, and then passed, even more so — and it is with no small degree of wonder and bittersweet reflection that I look back now across the unknowing divide of then and now, to a pre–September 11 time when we thought we were ready for the future, and possessed what already, in near retrospect, appears to have been a phenomenal, if unsustainable, pre-millennial amount of innocence.

I'm struck also by the prevalence of euphoria in these pages — the exhausting, exhilarating cycles of ever-ascending, as the seasons, and the valley, deliver more beauty, and more bounty, with each passing day. Who was the young man, or younger man, who wrote those pages?

I like to believe he was the same one who reads these pages now: who had the luxury, there at century's turn, of slowing down for just a moment, and paying attention. That he was an observer to whom innocence was not an impediment, nor wonder and unknowingness a liability. As if each day, no matter what the season or century, we each and every one stand always on the other side of such a divide.

JANUARY

WE'RE HAVING FRIENDS OVER for New Year's Eve, as we usually do. Not a lot — just the Janssens, the Dailys, the Linehans. The Janssens' two children, Tyler and Wendy, as well. There's food and music, and, hellions that we are, we're playing Pictionary and Scattergories. We've got apple cider for the children, and beer and wine and margaritas for the adults. There's a lot of food, and it's all incredible. We joke about the sign that was out on the marquee in front of the Ben Franklin store down in Libby: SHOP NOW, THE END IS NEAR. All year long we've been amused by the flurry of activity, nationally — folks buying generators (as if the supply of the gasoline required to run them would not be disrupted) and hundred-pound bags of navy beans, and fifty-gallon barrels for rain catchment. Gold bullion, extra ammo, and that kind of thing. It's so strange to see the rest of the world scrambling to prepare for an attempt, a possible attempt, to live, for an indefinite and frightened period, the way we live day in and day out. I'm not quite sure how to explain the feeling. For a fact, we take both pleasure and pride in feeling set aside from the rest of the world and the confusions of civilization — *it's why we're here* — and it's slightly disconcerting to feel the world rotating as if to assimilate itself, even temporarily, to our worldview and practices. It makes us feel less an island, less isolated. Less independent, even as we understand, upon any kind of examination at all, that there is no absolute independence, that it is all only relative.

What it feels like, in a subtle way, is that the world is joining up with us, when we do not *want* the world to join up with us; it's why we left the world.

Around ten o'clock, the lights go out, just as everyone has been predicting they would when the new century turns over and all those computers freak out. Power grids collapsing, satellites falling from the sky, bank accounts spinning to zero point zero. There's no punch line, no alarm or surprise for even the briefest and most delicious of moments — we all understand that because we're off the grid, there's no way this power outage can have anything to do with any computer in the world. Or can it? Are even the generators wired somehow to acknowledge this computerized doomsday meltdown? But still, the darkness is sudden and absolute, and, laughing, we light the candles and pass out the flashlights that are always a staple in any of the homes up here. The main propane generator is down, and we've been using the backup gasoline generator, and it's run out of gas, is all; I walk out into the silence of hard-falling snow, away from the party and my friends, and visit with my mother above for a while before refilling the generator and starting it back up. She's been gone nine years and still it doesn't seem right; still I see things almost every day that I think how much she would enjoy or be amused by. Sometimes it even seems that I will see her again.

When I go back inside, my friends are visiting with great animation. There's just something about candles, and though I announce that the power's back on, there's no rush to turn the lights back on, and indeed, we realize that we prefer the candles.

It's snowing like a son of a bitch. We haven't had much snow yet down in the valley, just rain (though up in the mountains, for the last couple of months, it's been snowing steadily). Today however it's been coming down all day: almost a foot and a half so far, and it's still coming down harder than ever. There's the slightly intoxicating feeling that accompanies the largest blizzards — the realization that there's a chance, increasing by every second, that you are about to be trapped by beauty. It's quite possible our guests won't be able to get out of the driveway when it comes time to leave, but so what? That's what the holidays, and the end of the century, are for.

It seems like something from a fairy tale — such a soft, heavy, calming snow, one of the heaviest and most beautiful snowfalls I've ever seen. And how wonderful it seems, if this evening is somehow near the end of the old world as we knew it, that that end should come not in fire or chaos but with silent, beautiful burial. We're all becalmed. We all feel joy. All the year's despairs — and there have been many; who among us does not carry them in great quantity, these days? — feel swept clean, or even better than that, not merely hidden or absolved but transformed, covered with beauty, converted to beauty. As if all failure or disappointment or hunger or absence has been redeemed.

I go back out to check on the generator and then stand in the falling snow for a long time. I haven't felt this happy in a good long while — and best of all, I'm happy for no reason.

I go back inside, with an inch or more of snow on my shoulders from just the brief time spent outside. We continue to browse on the bounty of food, to drink and joke and visit. All of our discussions are of the future: our hopes, our certainty of joy. We play board games, games of skill and chance, all night, and on toward the gray morning.

The children wander into the forest with sparklers in the last hour before light. It's still snowing hard. We set off a single firework, a large one, hissing and sputtering and smoking upward into the illuminated sky of falling snow, sparks and traces of light streaming and clattering in incandescent blossoms. Our friends embrace us and then drive home, their trucks all but buried beneath the mounds of snow, and even after they are gone, we do not feel alone, can feel them lingering, and we clean the dishes and wander up the steps in the morning light, to rest for a while. The century has ended, the century has begun.

It keeps snowing; it just keeps pouring down, not like any meteorological phenomenon but as if some dense and infinite reservoir above has been opened with a knife and the snow is pouring out through that rip as fast as it can, falling like feathers — snowflakes falling so hard and steady that it seems they are stacking up on each other even as they are falling. No such collisions occur, however — each snowflake shifts and slides, does whatever it takes in that falling curtain of snow to keep from merging with the others. Standing out in such snow, you can watch any of those ten thousand flakes, and any one of them will reveal to you how isolated and independent it is; but it's no matter, you need only to take one blink and refocus on the whole to see what a vain and ridiculous myth that is; one blink, and a slight step backwards, will reveal the truth to you, that it is all but one wall of sameness, in the end, and that the much-vaunted structural differences of any two crystalline flakes are of no real importance, in the end; it all becomes compressed and molded into sameness once the flake has fallen to earth.

Still, we watch, soothed and lulled, and unable, for long moments, to turn away. It's more mesmerizing than fire. You feel that you can stare at it forever. You feel it binding you with its stillness, pulling you down and into that sleeping sameness, and yet you are not afraid.

It snows without pausing for ten days. A week into the blizzard, my friends Tom and Tim and I travel down to the big river that bounds the valley to the south, to drift in Tim's boat, to hunt ducks and geese one last time before the season ends.

I'll never be able to explain the hunter's paradox. It's one of the most wonderful feelings of the season, to shoot and take with skill a bird from flight — to have your dog plunge into the icy, mist-steaming river and retrieve that beautiful bird, and to take it home and pluck it and clean it and prepare it for dinner — and yet even that really matters not at all, compared to the truly important thing of being out on the open river with your friends, deep into the new heart of winter, winter still only beginning, and the forest and the mountains shrouded with the stunning brilliance of all that snow; to be drifting around each new bend, early on a cold morning, watching and waiting for the explosion of wings — mallards, usually, or goldeneyes, or, once or twice a season, Canada honkers.

To be drifting, visiting with your friends in low voices, with the dogs shivering both from the cold and the anticipation, and the bald eagles lined up like soldiers in the giant cottonwoods up and down either side of the river, and the great blue herons gliding through the fog with prehistoric grunts and croaks as they leave their morning rookery, the dawn sky aswarm with fifteen, twenty giant birds at a time, coming and going in all directions.

The bird — the duck, or the goose — doesn't matter, any more than one of those snowflakes matters. All that's important is being out on the river with friends, and strengthened by that, in the heart of winter, at the end of one year, and the beginning of another one.

The scent of old Tom's little cigar. The sight of him and that winter cigar as familiar as his old-fashioned straw rucksack. The way Tim, a fishing guide, rows so expertly, so effortlessly. The sunlight on the snowy hills above Rainy Creek. The sharklike dorsal fin of a trout swirling in the steamy river, just ahead of our bow. The cold iron of the guns in our hands, and the anticipation, and the silences.

This year I'm rowing when we spot, in the fog ahead, and on the far side of the river, the high arched necks of a sentinel goose, and then beyond that goose, the huddled shapes of half a dozen more, resting off the point of a gravel island that is shrubbed over with young cottonwoods and willows.

All year long, Tim guides for a living. He rarely, if ever, gets to hunt or fish for himself. But now the season's over; this is his time, his one hunt. He's the world's nicest man. He would never put himself before anyone. But as his friend, I'm able to insist that for once he consider himself, and his dog; that he take pleasure in hunting, and for his own sake, rather than forever leading others to the hunt.

Maybe I'm making too big a deal out of this, but it's like this is his big chance finally. The guiding season is over; this is the busman's holiday. In some sense, this is what he's been waiting for, and working toward, all season long — though he would never tell you that, or even admit it to himself; truly, he loves to guide.

But now we've got seven geese stationed downstream of the point, and they don't know we're coming. It's Tim's one chance.

We drop Tom off at the head of the little island so that he'll be able to get a passing shot at any birds that might fly upstream. Then Tim and I ease downstream, with me laboring to row as quietly as possible — each stroke a prayer, water trickling quietly off the blades of the oars, and the half-submerged cottonwoods sliding past, the current carrying us down toward that point where the geese are tucked away, unsuspecting, on the back side. I very much want Tim to get a bird — to take something, after a season. Two seasons — summer and fall — of nothing but giving, and because I'm a poor and inexperienced paddler, I'm taking extra care to be quiet, and am concentrating extra hard on making the right strokes and aiming the boat properly.

Up in the bow, as we draw nearer, Tim is beginning to allow himself the pleasure of anticipation; he crouches lower and lower, grows more serious, and I can see him entering that zone that hunters enter in the last moment before the final engagement with, and taking of, their quarry. The place that defines them as hunters. That place inside them intersecting with the place of their quarry. A ritual, a ceremony, an act more ancient than the hammering of steel against stone; as ancient as lifting one's hand to one's mouth with food.

What we'd planned to do was drift right on down to the point, snug to the shore; and upon passing the point, Tim would rise and fire at the geese, which would have leapt into flight at the first glimpse of us. But just before that point is reached, we change our strategy. There's a little slot leading in to the island, and it occurs to us that we can pull the boat in there, get out on foot and skulk to the other side, and flush the birds in that manner. Tim points to the slot, whispers to me, and I change course and start in toward that slip, just as he shakes his head to say, *No, never mind*.

But I'm not proficient enough with the boat to change course so quickly or easily; I'm still struggling to maneuver it into the slot, and it turns out I'm not even successful with that; instead, I row us up over the stump of a beaver-chewed cottonwood, scraping our hull and stranding us high-centered atop that gnawed stump; and at the sound of our misfortune, the great birds honk loudly and leap into flight on the other side of the island. From a distance, we can just see glimpses of them passing upriver, flying low across the water and bellowing their dismay.

I signal to Tim to charge on through the young cottonwoods — perhaps not all of the geese have left yet — and he splashes through the water, waist deep, gains the island. His dog Lily is leaping along beside him — they're making a huge ruckus — and he crashes through the young whips of cottonwoods, but it's like a bad dream: he can't close the distance in time, they're gone, I've let him down, and a few seconds later, we hear Tom begin to shoot, upriver: *pow pow*, reload, *pow pow*.

Now a swarm of goldeneyes comes wheeling past us, flying ninety to nothing, and Tim turns on those birds, fires twice, misses, reloads. In the boat, still stranded atop that stump, I pick up my gun, load, and get a shot at one of the trailing ducks, but miss. Tim fires twice more as a new batch wings past, misses twice, and up-river, Tom fires again, once, then twice, and then all the birds are gone; and when we wander, embarrassed by our poor shooting, up to where we've left Tom at the top of the island — dead-eye Tom, who never misses — we find that he's embarrassed also: not a bird has fallen, not a single feather cut.

There's nothing to do but laugh. We stand there in the fall-ing snow and laugh, even as I've got that hollow feeling of having fucked up. I almost got Tim in on the birds. He doesn't care that it didn't work out, but I do. I really wanted him to get a bird. It's the end of the season, and that was his one good chance.

They stand there in the snow, laughing, and then we wade back out to the boat and continue on down the river, watching for more birds, though we see none. It's snowing so hard now that we can't see either shore, and the sky is the same color as the river; all is a swirl of falling snow, so that it seems as if we're falling sideways, fall-ing from the sky, being blown through the sky, and it is the river, or time, that is standing still.

A patch of sunlight, an opening, appears in the storm. Ducks are flying through it — a flock of goldeneyes. Tom, the good shot, stands up and fires, and hits one. Lily leaps into the current, swims out, and retrieves it. Then we reenter the curtain of snow: snow fall-ing so wet and hard and fast that it's an inch high on the barrels of our guns. We're just rowing blindly. Tim and I won't get a duck that day, but it doesn't matter. Maybe next year.

Work — writing — is hard, in January. The words come no more or less easily, but the physical act of hunkering next to the dull-glowing fire in the pissant wood stove out in the drafty log cabin where I work, candles fluttering in the cold, hands and feet chilled so much that often I prop my feet up right by the flames, and have to stop and tuck one bare hand or another under my armpit, or hold it per-ilously close to the flame, midsentence, before being able to con-tinue on with the sentences, is just plain hard.

During the deepest of freezes — generally anything colder than ten below — the cabin's uninhabitable, even for a few minutes at a time, and so then I'll arise at two or three o'clock each morning so I can work in the warmth of the house, downstairs, before anybody awakens, finishing by daylight, in time to make the school run, before returning home disoriented and weary to nap for half an hour or so.

Out of such irregularity, a rhythm eventually develops. It is a rhythm of fatigue, as you're stretched thinner and thinner by the odd hours. This couples with the natural insomnia that plagues many of us in winter and combines with the brilliant full moon to lure you into another world entirely different from the one most of the rest of the country's engaged with. Add to this the fact that you're frequently working on short stories or novels, in which that part of your world, though believed in deeply, is entirely made up, and the results can be very disruptive to your grasp on reality. You become convinced that the bears, who for the most part don't fight January but instead sleep straight through it, have it right; and that the animals that migrate are also wiser than us.

Like a prisoner, or a puppet, or some brute utterly lacking in imagination, you reel on through January, enraptured by its beauty, but always, it seems, unmindful of the cost: spending energy in January that will then not be present in February.

Not every day is frigid. There are some, many, when I can and do work out in my cabin, out at the marsh's edge. On the warmest mornings, the mornings when it has snowed the night before and the new snow rests atop the cabin like the warmest quilt in the world, I'll often work for two or three hours before the sheet of snow above me — warmed by the faint heat of my old stove, and the candles, and my own breath — begins to creak and moan — the ice-skin between tin roof and snow becoming slick, viscous, and then suddenly the whole shittaree releasing, with the beautiful curve and arc of a whole rooftop of snow cascading past my window, followed immediately by a sparkling shower of smaller ice crystals in the big slab's wake, crystals shimmering like fairy dust. And then more snow still falls from the highest reaches of the sky, ready and able to begin replacing again, replenishing immediately all that just slid down the roof, and more . . .

The only thing that keeps me from exulting fully in this nearly complete burial of the old world is my concern for the deer. (The same deer that, make no mistake about it, I love to hunt and eat.) In this kind of weather, amid so much snow, the deer will ease into the shelter of the last groves of the oldest forests, which, with their closed canopies above, provide much-needed refuge from the deep snows that pile up in the younger forests. As these large groves of old growth become fewer in the world, however, and farther between one another, the deer (and elk and moose) have less sanctuary in times of such acute stress, and they sometimes take shelter in the smaller groves of old growth, where the mountain lions can then target them easily. In this manner, it is as if the deer have wandered into a trap and become more vulnerable than ever: doomed by the thing they are relying on to save them.

Often, I wish I could let go of my worries for the wild world, letting go in the same manner as the snow sliding from the steep roof of the cabin. I wish I did not have a sense of duty; I wish I were oblivious to the feeling of obligation toward these last wildlands tucked here and there in the national forests, and could instead only glory in them, without almost always feeling the need to argue, and fight, for their continued existence.

I wish I could simply drink in this landscape like a glutton: gulping it down, simply taking it, without having to return anything.

I don't know. Maybe I don't wish that after all.

My sociability, limited though it is, hits full peak in January; at its apogee, I might go and visit a friend, or friends, two or three days in a row, or four times in a week. I love how frail and lonely I get under January's great snowy claw; we all do. My friend Bill is a master telemark skier, and for these past couple of winters he has been giving me lessons in the backcountry of our favorite mountain. We ski up through the forest, and carefully across the avalanche slopes, keeping to the edge of the forest for relative safety, climbing sometimes for two hours, sweating like horses, in order to gain a ten-minute ride down — but what a beautiful climb it is. And though the ten minutes whiz past on our way down, such is the amount of beauty and joy that's compressed into that little wedge of time that it almost doesn't seem to matter how ridiculously short it was.

Your mind slows way down, in winter, up here, in January. You find yourself thinking at great length about useless or insignificant little things. Memories from far away and long ago seem to ascend to the surface unbidden, as if in a dream. One such memory I have, while skiing one day — total silence, save for the creak and rasp of my wooden skis, or "boards" as Bill calls them, across the tight skin of the frozen snow — is from my childhood in Texas. I find myself remembering what a big deal it was back then — thirty-five years ago — to put on long underwear. How strange the sensation was, to be wearing one set of clothes beneath another, and how exciting, almost dangerous, for it meant that dire weather was coming — a norther, with raw sleet and ice, and temperatures that might drop into the teens, or even, once every ten years or so, into single digits. *Drama.* Once or twice a year, we'd need to pull on those long white thermal tops and bottoms, to brace ourselves against nature's rawness.

How quickly we adapt! Now I cannot imagine not wearing long underwear, in every day of the heart of winter, and a much warmer material than those heavy old white cotton suits. It's almost as if I've been given the opportunity to live two lives. As a boy, pulling on the novelty of that long underwear once or maybe twice a year, I would never have dreamed that one day I'd be wearing it every day, that wearing it would become as common as lacing up shoes or boots.

Such are the kinds of thoughts you find yourself dwelling on, contentedly, mindlessly, as you ski your way up the mountain through the hypnosis of falling snow, curtains of it everywhere, and the whisper of your blood not like the waves of some gentle ocean but like the sound and rhythm of that steady-falling snow, hushed and quiet and calm and ceaseless.

I love driving the girls to school each morning; I love traveling the same route through the snowy woods, watching the days grow incrementally longer, and seeing the same stretches of woods each day.

Anything's possible. We've seen mountain lions bound across the road in front of us, and elk, and coyotes; once, a weasel. Always, deer.

Always, crossing the river in town and looking upriver, we seek out the snowy mass of Mt. Henry, with the line of its 1994 burn traveling halfway up it, neat as the faint scar from some old surgery.

The river is almost always frozen by January, and glancing at it as we cross over the bridge, we can see, and are almost momentarily mesmerized by (in the manner that one can be hypnotized by a fire), the strange lunar patterns in the whorls of ice: stress fractures and rifts that have sealed back in over themselves like broken bones knitting themselves together again, the frozen skin that is a blanket for the sleeping river stretching and contracting, cracking, splitting, yawning. The script that remains behind after each night's flexions exists either in long, sweeping arcs stretching in radii across the entire river, as perfectly carved as if transcribed by some giant compass, or as an odd assemblage of perfectly straight lines, like those in a game of ticktacktoe; or as if a pile of spindles has been spilled onto the ice in a game of pick-up sticks.

In either instance, whether arced curves or straight lines, the impression you get — the impression you cannot shake from your mind — is that each riverine marking in the ice, remnant and residue of the previous day's and night's thermal variation, is not random but exists in this world under the auspices of some mathematical formula, some reason for being: not yet known by us, and as alien as some language never before heard.

Reading, or rather, looking at, the riverine etchings, one easily imagines that the elegant, unknown formulas are pursued vigorously by mathematicians and physicists in universities far away, that these men and women pursue the formulas like hounds; but it's easy to believe too that they will never gain on or capture the river's crackings, that always, like some animal that's able not only to stay ahead of their pursuit but to cover its tracks each night, the knowledge, or the formula, will always evade them, and instead there will remain only each morning's new glory.

Looking at the inscrutable elegance of the ice patterns' strange geometry, one is reminded of the children's story in which the spider spins in her web the words "Some Pig."

Punctuating too the river's flat crust of snow are the stippled tracks of deer, their hoofs sometimes as small as coins, hundreds of coins spilled the evening before. Knowing deer as we do, it's no problem at all to recognize an interpretation for the snowy sentences of their passages. *Here* is where they crossed the river to get to the browse of the hawthorn bush. *Here* is where they came down off Hensley Mountain in search of morning sunlight. *Here* is where a doe with two fawns wandered along shore's edge, nibbling the dried stubble of last autumn's wild roses.

Horrific, sometimes, will be dark ovals, shadowy lozenge shapes in the snow about the size of a deer's body, where the stippled tracks vanish. One imagines that though the deer for the most part are equipped with vast reservoirs of instinct, refined and accumulated across the millennia, so too is there chance and error, mistake and uncertainty in the formulas of their own passages; and it seems that over the course of a winter — the river thawing and freezing, opening and closing, thawing and freezing again — the river must become as filled with the bones and bodies of deer as were the fields of the pilgrims said to be filled with the fertilizer of fish, as taught to them by the natives of Plymouth Rock. One imagines the frozen river as possessing a hundred or more hungry mouths, secret and yawing, anxious for the taste of a deer; or that the river beneath the ice is thirsty and must drink of the deer, whose pale bones come in time to decorate its stony bottom like jewelry, the jewelry of chance or carelessness.

By mid-January, the deer are already beginning to look tired. They are not yet thin or gaunt, but to a close observer, and one familiar with their daily appearances, the weariness is clearly evident; and though it must have been building, it seems to me that their fatigue has appeared from almost out of nowhere, in the same manner that sometimes, early in the fall, after a hard south wind and heavy overnight rain, the ground is pasted and littered with the red and yellow leaves of the season and the trees' branches bare, whereas only the previous day the trees had retained their brilliant, burning colors and the ground its somber brown. You know intuitively that whatever has arrived on that overnight wind has been a long time in coming, but what it looks like to our sleepy eyes is that all was one day a certain way and then different the next. As if a hundred small things make no difference to the world, really, and are unobservable, but that one hundred and one small things do, and are.

Sometime in January, that one extra inch of snow arrives, or that one extra unit of *something*, and though I do not believe it breaks the wild spirit of the deer, things are different that next day, and a certain burning light is gone from their dark, wet eyes. There is a new slowness to their movements, and a pause, a studied gathering of energy before they commit to any one movement. It's particularly noticeable in an animal in which such gathering or hesitancy had not been previously witnessed.

This is the only thing, the only one, that tempers the rich feeling of bounty, of joy and beauty and peace, that accompanies a heavy January snowfall: the awareness that what to me is simple, exquisite, calming beauty — a blizzard piling up — spells trauma and hardship for another.

It's going to snow, whether you want it to or not. And it's going to be beautiful, whether you want it to snow hard or not. And there is really just only that one temperance, the concern for the deer, that keeps you, in January, from fully embracing the heaviest snowfalls, and walking out into the forest and looking up at the boughs of the snowy trees and asking for more, please more, even as it seems already that all the snow in the world is falling — still more, please.

It closes in. You stare at things longer, in January. Seen from the window of my writing cabin, the frozen gray bare limbs of the alder bower are like a screen, a maze, that transfixes the eye, and hence, the brain.

The picnic table right outside the window, beneath the arc of those bare limbs, is piled high with snow. The same pattern, same variation in shelter provided by the arrangement of those branches, has resulted in a differential of snowfall that's landed on the picnic table's top so that now, several feet into winter, it appears as if there is a person sleeping on top of that table, a young person, warm in a down sleeping bag or beneath all those many blankets, with his or her head tucked down into the bag for warmth. In the loneliness of winter, such a thought is comforting, and I like looking up from my pages in the morning to see that sleeping form, comfortable, resting, just on the other side of the window.

The simple pleasure of brute tasks, vitally efficient, and utterly requisite in January. As one who can fail to execute almost any specific mechanical assignment, leaping instead too often to the impractical dream-world of the abstract, I possess steadfast envy for those to whom such chores seem to come easily, naturally. Perhaps I take far too much pleasure in completing even the simplest task successfully. I once built a crooked clubhouse for my daughters, and every time I look at it, it astounds and surprises me more than any book I ever wrote, or any job I ever held, any task I ever completed. I am not a skill guy, or a closer, a finisher. I'm an ideas man, a big-picture dreamer; I become so easily distracted by all the intermediate steps that lie between, say, A and D, or A and F, much less A and Z. There was never a grilled cheese sandwich I couldn't burn; I don't know how to use the microwave ovens in hotel rooms.

Perhaps it is for this reason, among others, that it fills me with such joy, on a cold night when the stars burn so fiercely that they seem to moan and whistle, to take armloads of dry, clean hay and stuff it into the dogs' kennels so that they will be warm and clean through the night, warmer than you or I beneath our blankets.

For the night to be so frigid yet the dogs so dry and warm, without any fire or electricity — and for my arms to smell of the sweet scent of clean hay as I go back into the house, and to be able to go to sleep knowing that all is well, that the task has been completed, tucking in tight and successful — well, each night, this pleases me inordinately. It's almost as if I've warmed myself against the great cold, out there with the stars burning bright. I can lie down in my own bed afterward and be pleased by it — the act of putting new dry hay in the dogs' kennels — for five, sometimes ten minutes, while the stars glitter.

Just as warming to the chilled soul in January can be the dutiful act of removing snow from the roof of your house and any outbuildings — generator shed, woodshed, barn — lest the winter weight of all that wet snow, compressing steadily into glacial blue ice, might one day or night as if for entirely mysterious reasons suddenly fracture or crumble that structure as surely and completely as would a meteorite.

For days, even weeks, you watch the snow building up on your roof, watching it in somewhat the reverse manner of a sailor who stands at the bow of a ship watching for shore that never appears. This shore, this landfall, however, is imminent from the first day, draws closer with each hour, each beautiful storm, and finally one day if you have waited too long, you will be startled by the ice-breaking crack of the first timber groaning from deep within the eaves, or the creaking twist — a sound like a big branch snapping from some staunch and upright support.

These sounds at first aren't the sound of the real thing, timber breaking — it's only the music of the twisting, mounting stress, like the cracking noise your knees or back or elbows make occasionally when stiff — but the sounds do not cease or abate, through the night or into the next day, and soon enough — it can be put off no longer — you are hauling out the long extending ladder, and the snow shovel, and homemade roof rake (a stick of wood nailed crossways to the end of a long, limber pole, which will act as a cross between a long broom and a bulldozer blade), with which you can push large piles of snow over the edge of the roof without having to get too near that edge.

For safety, and because I have two young daughters, I fasten a rope to the chimney, or double-belay off the frame of a window jamb, though there are souls up here hardier as well as more foolish than I who do not use ropes for this annual activity but instead wade through the drifts of their roofs, on a sixty-degree pitch and steeper, like mountaineers up to their knees in snow; and there are souls up here, hardier and more foolish, who every year slip, in their gathering fatigue, and tumble down that slope and over the edge, falling ten, twenty, sometimes thirty feet or farther. Sometimes they are unhurt, though other times they break legs and arms, ribs and collarbones; and at that point their snow does not get shoveled and they, now one-armed, or one-legged, must depend on the vagaries of the weather — a warming spell, to trickle the snow off drip by drip, and a long stretch of days without new snow — or the kindness of a neighbor to perform for them that back-bending labor, as well as all of winter's many other labors, for at least a few months. And so I use a rope, like a sissy; like a middle-aged man who is trying to relearn daily the return of his limitations, after having been almost entirely free of them for what seems like only a very short while.

There is a wonderful, purgelike mindlessness to the rhythm of shoveling snow off the roof — pitching it wantonly out over the edge, into the great beyond — listening to the three seconds' silence, and then the soft, sifting *thump* of it landing far below; a feeling of gain, of accumulation, even as the reverse is true, with each patch you clear, methodical and rhythmic, up there on the mountain peak of your home, defending your home, protecting it against the future. It is very much a feeling like that involved with the laying-in of a season's worth of firewood, or more — a feeling of bounty, when what you are doing is ridding yourself of a thing rather than gaining a thing.

Perhaps the feeling of accumulation comes because you are gaining space, and distance — shoveling your way out of winter's depths, shoveling your way toward spring.

You lose yourself in it. The sweat on your brow, and down your back, is a kind of currency — you are rich, in this kind of labor, and yet cannot afford to cease — and there is a unique quality to the sweat you evoke, shoveling snow so far above the ground, a different humidity about you and different heat reflecting off the vast white slope of the roof. Your mind rids itself of all images save the color white, and of all movement save for the one, the steady arc of the shovel, again and again.

The sweat, the salt, continues to bleed out of you. One of those NASA thermal-image-gathering satellites would pass the picture of a small red devil working slowly across the cool white slab of the roof: blazing, but very much at peace.

Lovely is the deftness of cut the blade makes — the machinelike demarcation, row by row and lane by lane of where your shovel has been. Great mounds of snow accumulate below you, from where you've tossed it over the edge: entire new mountain ranges being born, far below. You slice the snow from the roof as neatly and efficiently as if carving it with a giant knife. You become obsessed with both the beauty of the labor and the totality, the cleanliness, of the result. Something wonderful snaps within you, and you keep on shoveling, on past the red distant sunset through the tops of the trees and into electric blue dusk, and on then into the rising light of the moon.

The mountains beyond are visible in a way you do not usually see them from the top of the house. Sparks drift from the chimney as your family below settles in for the evening, warming themselves. Stars are all around you, and still you work on, scraping and shoveling, and loving the privilege of being able to do so.

The deer are everything: they anchor us, and they tell us when to sail. We notice everything about them until we notice nothing about them, until they have become a part of us, their rhythms and patterns as incorporated into the subconscious of our lives and the pulse of our own blood-rivers as the sighing of the wind high in the canopy of the old larch and pine forests beneath which we live, as incorporated into us as is the grind of each one and singular day, in the sometimes sinuous, other times restive, units of time with which we bide and mark our days, separating these living sections of shadow and light into months and seasons, as might a skilled butcher cleave and render in preparation for a great banquet the lean and exquisitely fibered muscles of a deer or elk.

Cut as neatly as if with a knife through the snow in the forest are the trails of the deer's passages. Their hoofs cut the ice as if with razors, so that all throughout the forest there are these startlingly clean and precise lanes, which, as the snow piles higher and higher, are cut ever deeper, in the manner of some grand river sawing its way down through the mountain itself.

These hoof-cut rivers will disappear soon enough (leaving only a strand line of the high concentration of deer pellets, and the shining silver hairs that were shed, and the occasional burnished mahogany antlers, each as magnificent as a candelabra) — but in January they are a dramatic part of the landscape, the only place that either you or the deer can walk without sinking up to your belly in snow. The deer use these constant compressed-ice thoroughfares of their own making to stay alive — to save their lives — with each few calories saved possessing some equivalent of time, measured in minutes or hours if not days, moving them that much closer to the end of winter, and survival.

The lanes, with the sharpness of their relief, look exactly like the straight-line cuts you made up on the mountain of the roof with your snow shovel. If, as it often seems up here, there is but one story, one pattern to all movements and paths and events, how then can the world be so infinitely mysterious and diverse — so wonderful — even in the silence, the almost maddening silence, of deepest sleeping winter?

I try to calculate how many tons of snow are shoveled from the roofs — estimate the weight of one shovel, estimate the number of shovel tosses per hour, count the hours. A hundred tons? Surely there's a flaw in my math. Call it even half of that and it's still an alarming amount. Working on into the night again, working by the moon. Working close enough to the edge sometimes to see the glistening columns of snow separate and stratify by weight, following each sifting toss over that edge.

Inside, then, drenched with sweat, in time to kiss the girls good night and read them a story. A quick hot bath first, two aspirin, a glass of cold water. What's it going to be like to get old, too old?

A phenomenon occurs, a great phenomenon. What I love most about the passage of the year is the tininess and slowness of its uncountable exquisite gears, each turning upon another to produce what seems to be the labored miracle of whatever it is you happen to be looking at, whatever it is you happen to notice. But it's good for me to remember that those tiny gears, the ones we notice and care for, are even more minute than we can imagine — their own whirrings, like ours, composed of a gear works of even more numerous, and smaller, practically invisible, cogs below. Though occasionally above us, above it all, there is a far greater and vaster conspiracy of truly immense miracles, universe-size — the birth of a star, the collapse of a galaxy, the death of a planet — some of which are observed or noticed by us, while others we surely never even glimpse.

Collisions of miracles, collisions and designs and meshings of gears so outlandishly large and powerful as to render us less than even the dust from their turnings: though still, occasionally, we look up and witness some of these vast movements.

Such as this: the world has scheduled a full lunar eclipse for late on the evening of the winter solstice, beginning in the first hours of darkness and increasing until cresting shortly before midnight. The rarity of it is more delicious to our minds than would be the most wonderful meal on our palate. We did not ask for this wonder, and again so vast is it that there exists even the question of whether our participation is deserved or not, marveling that we're even able to observe it.

The scientists — astronomers and physicists — have predicted it with a brilliancy and precision nearly as exacting as would have been the prophecy of any poet. For weeks beforehand, we have been anticipating it — there will not be another event like it in the lifetime of any but the very youngest of us: another eighty years to wait if this one is missed.

Like some wild and ostentatiously confident, even swaggering animal, the path, the column, of ancient light emanating from the sun — light that was born before any man or woman ever strode the earth — will be blocked by our presence, rerouted from its accustomed path toward the mirror of the moon, so that our existence, the bulk of our small blue planet, will be revealed against the shining face of the moon as a shadow, plunging the full moon into a total darkness that will last several minutes. In that darkness, that blindness, we will know that what we are seeing is both the physical evidence of our presence as well as the physical evidence of our invisibility, our vanishing.

In the rarity of the full lunar eclipse (if the weather holds) we will be able to witness what looks like our disappearance — our moon blinking out, as well, though our consciousness will remain, hanging suspended in space — but then we will emerge on the other side, with the gift of our moon and our shadowlessness — our world of floating light — being returned to us.

In the aftermath, as well as in the short time preceding the eclipse, the moon will glow an odd color — perhaps green, perhaps red — as the oblong rays of the sun strafe the membrane of our dusty atmosphere, illuminating the night air into a corona that bends and skitters the bands of light (mingling with the prisms of myriad sky-borne dust particles) to paint our silver moon its strange new, brief color on this one night unlike any other.

There was an extraordinarily dramatic full lunar eclipse in 1883. Rumor, folklore, or history — take your pick — has it that the beleaguered tribe of Sioux Indians used that eclipse to stage a counterraid on the U.S. cavalry.

The story sounds, to my Western-benumbed ears, apocryphal or, at best, coincidental, though again, who can say that the leaders of that deeply religious culture did not possess a depth of science and oral history as full as our own, aided further by the prophecy and nuances and sensitivities of their prophets and visionaries?

For this one, the scientists have it scoped down to the minute, even if the spirit side of the equation seems somewhat lacking.

For days beforehand, the newspapers have been running articles informing us about the miracle to come, and in any given paper you can find an updated weather forecast for that coming evening. It's touching and refreshing to see the hunger and — how to express this? — the *cleanliness* with which many in the world prepare for this event like no other. It's also refreshing to see an event in which nothing is for sale; no money awaits to be "made," and the influences or opinions or reputations of one person or another will not be altered or strengthened or weakened by the moon's momentary disappearance.

It is a coming act of absolutely no ego. For a moment, we will all be hanging equal, breathless, pure, floating.

The world is not all any one way, is not all our way. You can forget that, and forget it easily, as an artist; you can become accustomed to bending imaginary iron bars, like a circus strongman, and pounding your chest and making the tides roll in and draw back out, reuniting (and again rending asunder) lost lovers, revealing fortunes made, kings and princes riding to war, entire worlds being born, mountain ranges disintegrating, and skies filled with thunder and lightning.

As an artist — unlike an astronomer — you forget that it's not all real. You forget that you control nothing and that almost everything you do, as either an artist or a human being, is as shadow, if even that.

With three days left before the winter solstice, and the eclipse, luck seems to turn away from us. The week's forecast calls for clouds, clouds, and more clouds. The valley labors beneath that dismal, beautiful, socked-in panoply of boiling gunmetal clouds, an eternity and infinity of purple and gray reefs and shoals. *Let the rest of the world have its sun,* one thinks. *There is something noble about our lightless winters* — even if they do, over the long course of the silent season, hammer your spirit deeper and deeper into submission and then, later, despair.

The weather forecasters are calling for more snow and clouds on the solstice. Other places around the state, and around the world, will have clear skies — each day, we look at the weather map and covet, for the day at least, the clearness of sky they'll experience, and which they doubtless take for granted, or even believe (as all are wont to do with good fortune) is their due. With regard to the coming miracle, the scheduled miracle, the best we are going to be able to do is hope for a lucky break — a momentary and perfectly timed break in the clouds through which we might be able to view it.

Which is precisely what happens.

With only minutes to spare before the eclipse is to occur, a warming south wind begins shoving the several days' accumulation, layers and strata of cloud-scud, quickly past, revealing to us, in glimpses, the great moon, so perfectly round and waiting, and seeming to me surprisingly low in the sky — barely above the mountaintops, barely above the top of the forest. As if it is in the design of the moment to be sure that the seeing world can observe this strange brilliance, strange phenomenon, and yet as if that same plan or design or pattern too possesses or desires an equal part of secrecy, or privacy.

We stand at the upstairs window looking east and watch, through the gapped shutterings of fast-moving cloud streams, the silver moon begin to glow dull red; and we watch as the moon merges slowly with our shadow.

It's alarmingly like a feeling of responsibility — knowing that it is we, or rather, the mass of the place we live, that are blacking out the sight of the ever-present, ever-loyal moon. (And it is a panicky feeling, also, to realize that of course the moon is still present, still astronomically loyal — that it is only our vision of the moon that has disappeared, that nothing else in the world has changed. Though still, you can also feel the brief suck or lag or lull in some unknown pull of energy, a disorienting feeling of free-floatingness, as if some part of the mind or body or spirit is suddenly bereft of a connection, a relationship or association, it never knew it had.)

We are afforded no long, unfettered views of the vanishing moon, but it doesn't matter; each time we catch the new glimpse of it, further swallowed, we're grateful. That the clouds seem to be moving faster and faster only adds to the drama, and there is further disorientation when, as the moon becomes almost completely obscured by our shadow, we can't tell if its disappearance is due to the final and ultimate height of the eclipse or just another shoal of dense clouds. Several times we'll relax (not having realized we'd been holding our breath), thinking the eclipse had peaked, only to be almost startled by one more fleeting revelation, like an encore: a summoning, and then a resummoning, that seemed somehow heroic — as if the moon is resisting even this brief vanquishing, as if it is not merely a reflector of light but possesses its own and seeks in some urgent fashion, like a living thing yearning for breath, to keep that light from being extinguished for even a few moments, even for once in a century, or once in a millennium.

The four of us stand at our upstairs window, watching the darkness, hanging in the darkness of blind faith — waiting for another gap in the clouds to reveal the moon coming back out on the other side.

The thought occurs to me that what we've just witnessed is like something one might have seen in a movie, in some Hollywood sleight-of-hand spectacle — that it's all been but an illusion — and yet there remains to the event some residue of realness, an authenticity that goes beyond what our visual senses tell us we have just witnessed. Standing there at the window with my family, I can see that there is a finite distance between the sublime and the representation of the sublime, and the four of us stand there in the shadow, in the darkness, knowing firmly and fully the space between the two, and residing comfortably between them: our back turned toward the one and facing the other.

Soon enough — in perhaps fifteen or twenty minutes, though it seems like only some tiny fraction of that time — the moon reappears, emerging from the other side of its shy darkness, and when it does, we experience a feeling very much like warmth. I'm surprised at how good it feels to have the moon back in our sight again, if only through the ragtag portal: clouds hurtling past, so that it seems we are all moving at great speed, as if summoned perhaps to some challenging or noble or simply necessary endeavor.

The curtains close once more.

An hour later, a new storm system moves in, dropping more snow, and the moon and stars are hidden from us again for three more days, blanketing the world in whiteness and silence. We saw it though, and will remember it, for as long as we are in this world, and — who knows? — perhaps longer.

The girls and I wander out onto the marsh to go for a ski not too many evenings later, while the moon is still fullish; and because the clouds are gone, the night is cold. Due to some inexplicable and doubtlessly entirely random sequence of the frost-thaw cycles — warming snow, followed by repeated nights of intense cold and perhaps even influenced by the solstice, the eclipse, and other rare phenomena — the snow out on the marsh has rearranged itself into a flat skiff of broad plates, each snowflake recrystallizing into a perfectly planar structure so that the entire snowscape before us appears to have been converted to a land of fish scales, three feet deep of fish scales, and each of them silver-blue in the light of the big and aching moon.

The re-formed flakes are tilted in all directions, brittle in the cold, leached of all moisture — dry as fossil fish scales — and though most of them are lying one micron thick, parallel to the ground and the pull of gravity, enough of them have tilted upward too, as if in strange geological yearning, so that they sparkle and glint like huge sequins in that blue light. The entire world, or rather, our world, is ablaze and asparkle with the strange shimmering coronas and prisms cast by these new fish-scale flakes.

As we ski and skate through them, they make a delightful, musical tinkling. They are as loose as dry sand. Our skis cut them, these fish scales, making a music that sounds like glass wind chimes.

We ski into and through the blue light. I hold my breath, hoping that the girls will remember the strange sight — though, perhaps better still, the conscious part of them might forget it, might take it for granted, assuming such wonder to be a daily occurrence in the landscape up here. That would be all right: would be more than all right. Nonchalance and wonder, right next to each other.

On the way home, Mary Katherine stoops and picks up a handful of that strange micro-flaked snow and tosses it up at the moon, and we watch as the large metallic-looking flakes come sifting back down in sprinkling silver shining columns, flashing and fluttering, swirling like shafts and beams of blue electricity, thrown by our hands, by our hearts. *Yes,* I think. *Take it for granted, please.*

Such is the silence of January, on later into the month, that we grow excited, several nights afterward, at the sound of the neighbor's snowplow truck coming down our driveway, audible long before it's visible, coming with a thundering that sets the dogs to howling even before we humans can hear it, or know it consciously: the ice-skimming blade drumming and skittering across the frozen earth, with sparks flying through the night, rooster tails of bright cinders and ingots flying up from either side of the blade, and our deep pleasure in knowing that in the morning when we drive out to school we'll have a crisp new-cut path through the snow, that we will not have to earn ours, step by labored step, red muscle by muscle, as do the deer and other forest creatures, but waking instead to a simple, silent grace. Sometimes amid such beauty you can't help but wonder who gave each of this life, and perhaps more important, why?

January is the social month. On Tuesdays, after school, the children from the little school (nine students this year, covering grades kindergarten through eight; one teacher; and one teacher's aide position, shared among three different aides) bring their sleds to the big hill outside town, and the adults join them. For a couple of hours, until the dimming blue dusk sinks down from the tops of the trees, we skitter down the hill on big inner tubes and plastic-slickened sleds, shouting and whooping in the forest, trudging back up, then, only to slide down again, leaving, across the course of the afternoon, as dense a skein of tracks as if an immense elk herd had been wintering on that slope, cutting with their hoofs the myriad trails of their daily comings and goings. All in a day, however; and again, what would be survival for them is merely play for us.

Afterward, with the children soaking wet from their exertions as well as their snow tumbling, we picnic; we stand around a crackling campfire as dusk thickens into true night and sort through all the loose and extra scattered jackets, caps, gloves, and mufflers as we visit. Parents have brought cookies and cakes, crackers and cheese and lunch meats, and, always, hot chocolate.

We visit about the most mundane and trivial things, and in the ease, the safety, of that mundaneness — against all odds and logic — we grow slowly closer — awkward at first, but then gradually across the winter, into a deeper elegance of fit. What is community? I submit that it is not people of similar intent and goals, or even values, but rather, a far rarer thing, a place and time where against the scattering forces of the world people can stand together in the midst of their differences, sometimes the most intense differences, and still feel an affection for, and a commitment to, one another.

Am I dreaming? Perhaps. But January is as fine a time for dreaming as any.

I sense that January is getting overlong, in this narrative, this testimony, this witnessing. I want to close it, for the reader's sake: there is almost an entire year left to experience. But I want it to be understood also, fully, that even though wonderful, it is one long damn month for almost everyone and everything but the wolves and the ravens.

January is the isolate month, and January is the social month. We go skiing with other adults, our friends, regularly (like almost everyone else in the world, it seems we're too busy in the other months of the year — that even here time hurtles past and neither cunning trapper nor stalwart engineer can figure out a way to slow it here, either — not even here). After dropping the children off at school or having secured a babysitter for the younger ones, we'll set off on an adult ski, starting right behind the school, striking off up a snow-covered logging road in a long safari-like train, brightly clad, cheery, vigorous, living. We move through the dark woods sometimes in silence, other times garrulous, and gawk hungrily skyward whenever the sun appears briefly through the clouds. On one such occasion, a friend of ours, Joanne, is so thrilled to see the sun that without irony she whips out her pocket camera and takes a photo of it, of the sun amid the clouds only, with no foreground or background, and no human characters in it — photographing the rare and elusive sun the same way one might hurry to snap a picture of an elk or a moose crossing the road in front of her.

I love the pace and rhythm that's involved in skiing through the woods. I love how slowly your thoughts reveal themselves to you, and I love, in the loneliness of January, the blurring of the lines between the animate and the inanimate. On this one ski, for instance, the one I am thinking of, it seemed that everywhere I looked in the forest I saw a snag, a dead tree, that had been carved and sanded and sculpted into the same shapes as the animals that lived in these same woods, that the same winds and rains and snows and fires that sculpt and influence the animals' shape also even the outline of inanimate materials such as stone and deadwood.

I think there might be more to this idea, this coincidence or observation, than meets the eye — some vast law of physics existing far beyond coincidence, though on a scale so immense as to be beyond our comprehension, beyond our ability to grasp and measure and count. In a month like January, one is free to ski along at a leisurely pace, hypnotized by the landscape of snow, and hold such a thought, or any other, comfortably in one's mind for long moments, if not hours, and to savor and contemplate the ultimate solitary essence that resides somehow in the core of each of us.

One night late in the month — that big moon on the wane, though still huge and swollen in its misshapenness, blue-silver washing out all the stars, filling the forest with its breathless, eerie, metallic light — I step out into the garage to get a piece of venison from the deep freezer, to take inside to begin thawing out for the next evening's meal. It's dark inside the garage, though the world beyond is alit in that blue fire. It's frigid. All sounds have a clarity and density to them not noticed at warmer temperatures, or in the daytime. I hear a scuffling sound out on the ice and look out into the bright moonlight to see a herd of deer standing by the dogs' kennels, nibbling at the tufts of loose hay that are sticking out of the kennels' doors.

The moon is so bright, I can see the gleam of the deers' eyes. I recognize one of them as the doe who lured in the buck for me on the last day of the season; the same buck whose antlers are drying in the garage, between her and me. The same buck whose backstrap I am taking out of the freezer — am holding now in my hand — for tomorrow's dinner. The muscle that had powered the animal that had chased her.

Does she carry his progeny within her? Who will outlast whom?

She, and the others, just stand there looking at me, dark silhouettes in that amazing blue light. It's too cold out for them to run back off into the woods; they're seriously intent on pawing at that hay.

I could take ten, twelve steps and be out among them. They can't see me, back in the darkness, the blackness: they can only sense and scent me.

It's so cold. They're shivering. It's so cold that the dogs aren't even coming out of their kennel to bark at them but are instead remaining inside, shivering also.

After a few moments, the deer lower their heads and go back to eating.

I should comment briefly on the strangeness of the phenomenon that occurs in this tight-knit little valley, deep into every winter, every January: a preponderance of extrasensory perceptions among and between all of us. I don't want you to think we're all whacked out and cuckoo, believing overmuch in that kind of thing, but neither can I deny that it exists, late into January. I'm confident that someday far into the future (or perhaps not so far), scientists will have found an easy and credible explanation for it; but in the meantime, we dream it, we live it, it's present.

It comes in waves and spells: rises, surges, crests, then fades away, as if summoned in egress or regress by the moon's tides.

During the last week of January, I am involved in three startling incidents, one right after the other.

All occur in the out-of-doors.

The first one happens while driving home from duck hunting with Tim. It's a sunny afternoon, and I'm tired and weary from paddling, and feeling good because I've got a couple of ducks, mallards, in the back of the truck, and I'm thinking how good they'll taste.

In my fatigue, the unbidden thought occurs to me that I'd very much like to see a flock of wild turkeys crossing the road. I don't know where the thought comes from: the nearest turkeys are over on the Idaho line, more than twenty-five miles away. I've never seen, or heard of, turkeys over by the dam, where I am now. But I have not driven more than a mile than I look up and see, indeed, a flock of wild turkeys pass through a stand of open ponderosa pine.

The second incident occurs the next day. My friend Bill and I are driving up into the mountains to go backcountry skiing. We're just riding along, shooting the shit — way up in the high country, past where any game should be found, at this snowy time of year — and I have the thought — actually, it's almost like a craving — that I'd like to see a lynx or a bobcat.

We round the corner, and a young bobcat is standing in the middle of the road, standing where I have never seen one before. The bobcat stares at us for a moment — is it my imagination, or does it seem to be hesitating, as if to be sure we see it? — and then bounds off the road.

Every day is a gift.

The third incident occurs later that night. I dream, again completely unbidden, that I am writing a letter to a friend of ours, discussing how much she and I love the short stories of Alice Munro.

The next day, in the mail — it's as eerie as if I have written the letter, or read it in its entirety, before its inception — there is a letter from this friend, detailing why and how very much she loves the short stories of Alice Munro.

* * *

Some people get depressed up here, in the long, lightless winter. I've talked to some of these folks, and they say that it's the strangest thing: that when it, the depression, hits, they're still fully capable of recognizing beauty, but that such recognition almost makes the depression even worse, for they can no longer take pleasure in the recognition. As if there is a disconnect, some error in internal wiring, separating beauty from joy, or, worse yet — or so they say — connecting beauty to sadness.

The scientists say it's all really only about sunlight: a function of the shortening and then lengthening days. As if we are but machines in that regard, or solar cells, fueled by the sun.

Can you imagine what it must be like for those folks, year in and year out — entering each year the dark tunnel of winter, knowing that it is going to knock them down, pick them up, knock them down, pick them up — stretching and pulling then compressing and darkening them, making them a little wearier, a little more brittle, every year?

What I think it must be like for these people is as it is when you are walking along a river and encounter a submerged piece of driftwood, so water-soaked that it no longer floats. The years and miles drifted have hollowed out intricate seams of weakness, have scoured out all the knots and replaced those pores with river sediment, clay and gravel, jamming and packing it in between the pores and then polishing it further, as the club — half wood, half stone, now — tumbles farther downstream.

You can no longer call it a branch or a stone; it is something in between, something altered, and beautiful and unique, even daring, for that alteration: between two places, two worlds. I would think that a person who had survived winter's almost inevitable depression of spirit — the violent euphorias balanced by the dark, even black, troughs — might hold such a piece of wood in his or her hand and feel a brute, physical kind of connection to the beautiful pattern of it: that once soft wood made all the tougher by the enduring, and by the filling in of erratic loss with a grit of gravel that is both of the world's making, and the branch's.

I would imagine further too that the hiker might run his or her hand over that time-polished object and in the sameness of it all not quite be able to tell anymore which is stone and which is wood.

I imagine that this walker would place the stick back down into the icy river, buoyed, if even briefly, by the stick's beauty, and walk on.

Because it's still January — the latest, last, deepest part of January — that person might be on skis rather than on foot. It might, with luck, be the first sunny day in weeks, brilliant and frigid, the sky cracked open with blue and sunlight, the world breathing in full color again rather than black-and-white. Pushing on into that bright clear winter light that has been missing for so long, the skier might marvel at his or her returned happiness — the happiness coming back upon and within as suddenly as a float, an air-filled ball, released from far beneath the surface and rising quickly, and unencumbered, finally, to the surface, the return of happiness (or — who knows — one day, perhaps, even joy) coming back like a migration of something in his or her blood, some rare and wild and elemental herd or flock of a living, traveling thing that is always in the blood, shimmering, hopeful, even yearning, but which travels in some seasons far away, only to return, always, with force; and the skier might, in the onrushing return of this mysterious migration of happiness (or even joy), marvel at how utterly strange it is that we are here, marveling not even at the *why* of our existence, but at the mere fact that we are.

An awakening. Not every day such an awakening, or in every moment — but always, hopefully, again and again, and again and again.

FEBRUARY

....

SOME YEARS FEBRUARY is the hardest month, and the longest, while other years the traveler clears it with ease, hurdles it with barely a hitch in stride; but always, the traveler respects February, and the cold, dark, somber snowy corridor of its passage, and accepts without shirking the end-of-winter weight of its accrued darkness.

Some years, a traveler in this landscape, this life, will have paid his or her northcountry dues in December or January — will already have passed through the blood's helpless Sludge-O-Rama of tired and lightless winterheart. Call it the blues, call it depression, call it seasonal affective disorder: whatever name you give it, it's a real thing, and cumulative through the years, like the effects of too many concussions, each long dark winter a biological hammer blow to the pituitary or some other important gland, irrespective of how much one loves backcountry skiing, or beautiful snowy skies at dusk, or snowshoeing, or sledding, or any of the other infinite wonders of winter. Or if each February is not like the cumulative effects of one concussion after another, then they are like a sustained diet that has for too long been lacking in a certain vitamin or mineral.

There's a part of any northern resident that wants to believe, in the early years, that being affected by this winter heaviness indicates a character flaw, that if you succumb to February or are even slowed by it, this signifies a character weakness, a flaw or soft spot in one's force of will.

But it's not that way. It — the February effect — is far larger than our puny abilities to either accept or resist. At least as much as any other, this most compact of months is a force of nature, and it packs a wallop. I've had it, the heaviness, come upon me without warning, lasting several weeks — like a rude guest — arriving when only days earlier I'd been on top of the world, and I've had it come creeping in slowly, preceded days or even weeks by sinuous and then later erratic rumblings and palpitations.

The heaviness just comes when it comes, and it comes as best as I can tell whether you're a strong person or a weak one, a happy one or a sad one. After you've lived up in this wonderful landscape long enough, it comes almost every year — sometimes in October or November or December or January, other years not until March, but most years — as best as I can tell — in February.

This happens to be a good year for me, on that count, and a good February. Who can say why? The older I get, the more I believe those downturns, those sluggish periods, have nothing to do with character, or uncontrollable external or internal circumstances, but are instead governed by some hand-from-above, or some wave-from-below, and that we are only but storm-tossed bits of twigs and leaf, or tiny insect striders, riding those huge swelling waves of mood. And yet even in a good year, and a good February, in which that lead-hearted torpor does not return, even then there are days in February when I can feel those swells trying to build far below, or when I can hear the faint rattling clack of the puppeteer working his or her strings and crossbars, which, for one reason or another, this year at any rate, are simply and mercifully unattached to the marionette of myself. Still, in February, I sense those distant swells below, and venture forth into the world cautiously, not cockily. I advance in the manner of some ground-hugging upland bird, a grouse or quail, that pauses and then freezes anytime the shadow of a hawk passes overhead.

This year, the hawk is passing on. But still, out of habit, I move carefully in February, and I do not take my happiness for granted. Neither am I convinced, despite my love for this place, that human beings are designed for or capable of dwelling here all year long, year after year.

Or perhaps I've simply got too much invested personally in the issue: the rises and plummets of my own heart. What's a little sluggishness, a little malaise — or even a lot of it — in the long run, in the arc of a life, really? Just because a tree is consumed by a forest fire, or falls over and rots, or is eaten slowly by beetles and woodpeckers, it would be silly, wouldn't it, to hypothesize that that tree didn't belong in this landscape?

Still, there's something about February, even a good February, that tries and tests and threatens to darken the soul, and brings a bit of hesitation to even the boldest of hearts.

February is when the ice comes, and with it, the slippery falls. January has been dry powdery snow; but February, with its warmer, damper breath, its short and lightless days, and its scudding clouds — a fantastic beauty of clouds, a full twenty-eight days of the fantastic beauty of clouds — brings the sore-throat cough and cold and dampened feet. And each day, under the warming breath of February, the top layer of snow thaws and melts, and each night, as the sun scuttles away like a coward, a traitor, and those February puddles freeze back into a glaze of ice, so that the forest is coated with a translucent crust, a shell of ice, and the roads glint, it becomes necessary to drive slower and walk slower, and to keep one's center of gravity hunkered down lower, this month, whether one hears those puppet strings above or feels those swells and surges below, or not.

There are days too in February, short dark February, and cloudy white February, when despite your knowing better, you never get out of the house. The morning begins, you putter around lazily with paperwork, you eat lunch, you work an hour or two more, you go to pick up the children at school, you come home and feed the dogs and make a phone call, and suddenly dusk has eaten the day and you tell yourself, *Tomorrow* . . .

The trees are starting to get their blood back; the sap is stirring, and the terminal and axial tips of the larch branches, previously winter brown, are glowing gold. The branches of the aspen are breathing as if pulsing blood red, fire red, and best of all, the slender limbs of the willow and alder are turning bright yellow, a living yellow that is rich enough in the sunlight, yet seeming even richer and more alive in the falling snow or, on some foggy days, in the drizzling, hissing rain. The sight of the yellow and gold branches attaching themselves to the backs of our winter-starved retinas is so welcome that while skiing around the marsh and passing near those willows, resurrected one more time, at least one more time, we come to a full stop and simply stand there, drinking in the color with our eyes, color in a landscape where for more than three months there has been almost none at all.

It's not over, not by a long shot. Most of us will have spent all our energy loving, and climbing over, the high, long, snowy wall of January. And now here it is February, with nothing left, energy-wise. It's real good, at this point, if you've got someone to love. You're falling, by this point, whether you mean to or not, and whether you even realize it or not. There is an old winter part of you that is melting to slush and falling away, for better or for worse, even as the heated breath of the earth below is tickling the cap of snow that blankets it. Sheets and dribbles of water are beginning to trickle beneath that blanket of snow and ice, and fractures and crevasses are appearing up at the surface — and in your own falling, which again may be good or may be bad, it's nice if you have someone to hold on to.

And you try to enjoy it for what it is, *February*, whether it is a joyful one or a darkened one, but make no mistake — be honest — what you're really holding on for is March, and the return of the geese, and dirt and mud, and all the other months beyond.

February, as much or more than any other, is a time for quiet, steady work, work with very low and attainable goals, or, best of all, work with no goals, work that is simply work.

The light is softer and prettier, when it appears — which is still rare and infrequent — and, as with the blushing limbs of the softwoods, seems to somehow be alive, which is an odd concept indeed for a thing as abstract as light. And yet it seems as alive as an animal, so strong and beautiful a presence is it; and you know that any day, or perhaps even any hour, any minute, a bird is going to begin singing again, though still you don't dare to hope or dream yet after so long a trudge through the snows and lightlessness of the other months. Still you lay low, if you are wise, or experienced, and you wait patiently, waiting for February to move past and behind you, rather than your endeavoring to push on, floundering, through it.

And beyond the return of those first slender fibers of color, and the first few patches of living sunlight, there is something even more wonderful.

There is the first hint, once again, of warmth: faint brushings of warmth, light as the touch of a handkerchief against the back of one's neck, or against an upturned face — faint, but enough, at first, after such an absence; for now, enough.

Appearing all throughout the woods too are the shapes and textures of old buried things, emerging as if from beneath shrouds — some ragged, as they were before they had the blankets pulled over them, though others sleek in their emergence, with a thinning glaze shining over most of the world, as the days warm the snow to the melting point only to have the nights freeze it back again, until that world's shell is more transparent than glass and seems to magnify the objects that are beginning to reappear beneath that lens of thinning, clearing ice.

There is something now that looks sharply different about the woods each day, and if it is one of those Februarys when you are feeling good, you can understand and see, in your joy of the approaching spring (even as you milk, with pleasure, the last of winter's goodness and silence and beauty), how the world is being made ready quickly for the return of the birds and all the other sleeping things. And if it is one of those Februarys when you are feeling low, you marvel at the brute tenacity and determination of life and are humbled by the onrushing force of it, even as you, supposedly a superior being, possess no such force and perhaps, even in February, feel defeated — though by what you cannot say.

More and more sun drifts into the valley, and the snow melts and trickles in the daytime, then contracts again beneath night's bright stars, scrunches back up: but each next day there is a little less of it.

On a walk, the old blind dog, Homer, passing through a sunlit opening in the woods, one which possesses that clear hard glaze of the previous night's freeze, is delighted to be capering across the taut frozen surface of that ice rather than punching through the snow as she usually does: scampering now as if in once more the freedom of her youth rather than her sixteenth winter. Tail wagging. One more winter behind, or almost behind. Can she see, in her near blindness, the brilliance beneath and above and all around her? Or is she aware only of the spaciousness of it — some vast and delightful emptiness everywhere, near the final end of winter's hard story, and with a little pause in the world now, as the world, this northern world, begins to prepare to receive all its characters, and the jumble and speed and complexity of life, once more?

Even though the temperatures are warmer, you feel colder, sometimes — as if your resistance has been worn down. Or perhaps it is because of all the moisture that is being released by the melting snowfields, or the return of the winds and the stirring breezes; but in the mornings and again in the evenings, you're chilled, and a fire still feels good in the wood stove, even though the cold bright sun is shining and even though the water is dripping from the eaves.

Bald eagles soar in pairs high over the open bowl of the marsh, almost out of sight. It's cozy to visualize the column of shimmering updraft, the pillar of it, rising from the reflected perfect circle of the snowy marsh below, the dark woods all around absorbing the sunlight but the snowy marsh reflecting the heat straight back up into the blue sky and the eagles riding, as if on waves, the pulses of that one pillar of marsh updraft, spinning and soaring nearly a mile above the marsh, tracing the perimeters of it with their wingtips.

And while splitting wood one evening with the girls, loading the wheelbarrow to ferry the wood up to the porch, it comes, winter cracking open like a perfect gem being tapped by just the right blow. The sound of it hurtles past us, the whistle of duck wings near overhead at blue dusk, ducks headed hard and fast for the opening upriver just beyond, flying so hard and fast that it gives one the impression they're late for spring, rather than early — and I stop midswing with the maul and look up into the dusk, in the direction of that already-gone-by sound, and cry out to the girls, "*Listen!*"

Four little patterns that I notice, every February, as familiar and in their own way as methodical as the turning of the pages of a calendar:

First, the incredible compressed cobalt-mercury color the snow takes on as the warming days melt it and freeze it, melt it and freeze it, compressing and then supercompressing it, and sculpting the snowy hills with that clutching, body-draping, new tighter fit, the tightening body cast of dense ice contracting tighter and tighter upon the land, and the curves and shapes of flowing water halted midmoment everywhere, each cold starry night, before beginning to soften and loosen and flow again, the snow a little bluer each time, each next day of freezing and thawing — *stop, start, stop, start,* like some ecological rumba and rhythm, and the promise of the things to come — the accruing strangeness of that mercury color is invigorating . . .

Second, the delicate filigree of black lichens, old-man's-beard, *Bryoria,* embossed within the curves of that so distinctly February snow. The returning breezes, and, some days and nights, true winds (both southerly and northerly, and all the earth warming, beneath that dying death grip of the blue-blackening snow, the ice cap of winter now in fierce rigor mortis) toss the black lichen down onto the snow, where, absorbing more warmth, the lichen-moss sinks slightly into the colder snow, then is further ensealed each night beneath the refreezing. It is a February sight, a mosaic that speaks to the coming end of winter.

About those winds: the old-timers — both of them (by and large, this is a valley of newcomers, ten-year and twenty-year men and women being the oldsters; seed-drift colonists come and go here, as it's a hard place to make a living, and in many respects it's a new place, and a young place, as if itself only recently emerging from beneath the snow) — claim that the valley is a lot windier now, since the Libby Dam was built in the early seventies, creating the giant reservoir of Lake Koocanusa, bounding the valley on its entire eastern edge and effectively cutting it off from the rest of the world, including the Glacier and Whitefish Ranges, just as the town of Troy as well as Libby along the arc of the Kootenai River cut it off to the south, and the Purcell Trench, a great chasm running along the Idaho border, cuts it off from the rest of the world to the west

Though it's never been measured or monitored or proven locally, I believe them, that the new lake has created what scientists call "lake effect" and that the spring and autumn wind shiftings, particularly, possess greater turmoil, and that the valley, the forest, is still adapting to this new aerodynamic turmoil . . .

In any event, the winds of February and the returning sunny days — sometimes, in February, miraculously, we'll have two, even three days in a row, of sun and blue sky — create a distinct embossing, wherein the tendrils of old-man's-beard are blown onto the new snow, black upon white, landing in what can only be called random drift.

And the next day, the return of the winter-long-exiled sun heats the black lichen with differential vigor, while that warmth is deflected away from the bed of white snow in which the lichen has landed, so that by comparison the lichens resting in that snow at day's end are as hot as the new-burnt tips of match heads; and those warmer lichens settle down into the snow perfectly, like veins wrapped in flesh, sinking down into the snow like the ancient cliché of the hot knife into butter, the lichen chilling sufficiently to slow its descent only when it has sunk to a depth of being level with the snow rather than resting atop it, sinking that millimeter downward, powered by its own warmth, like a swimmer submerging.

And then night comes again, and the melting snow freezes taut to a shiny cast, with that filigree of lichen embedded by the cooling clutch of the night; and sealed down in the ice like that, the lichen seems like some elegant signature, or like a valuable thing preserved and embossed for all time in that cast. In December and January, the lichen just kind of blows around and drifts here and there and is buried by new snow upon old snow; but in February, the lichen saws its way down into the snow and ice, trapped there and fitting each tendril into each groove of its heat-seared cast so perfectly that the indelible signature of each lichen cannot be pried out of its embossed slate but will remain there, housed in the ice until the snow has melted completely and the sodden lichen rests on the bare forest floor, where it might wait all spring and then into the summer, growing drier and drier, as if waiting for the drift of some loose July or August spark to catch in its nest and ignite . . .

The third thing that speaks to me of the pattern of February is the pawed-up snow at the fringes of the previously serene marsh: vast excavation of snow where the herds of deer and elk have ventured from out of the jungles of alders and willows at marsh's edge to claw at the snow with their hoofs, each dainty hoof and slender leg scraping away the snow to get to the dry grass and reeds below as if operating a miniature backhoe, on a cold morning after a heavy snow.

After such storms, in which a foot or more might fall, the marsh is where the deer go to find their for-certain feed; the place where they can always count on something being there for them, in those vast bent-over dry-hay swaths of autumn-dead reed-grass, even if relatively low in nutrition, by February.

In February, after one of the big storms, the deer can wander out into the marsh and not have to worry about picking and choosing through the snow to find this or that preferred food item, all vanished beneath the new snow now like the needle in the haystack, and instead can merely lower their heads and like poor dumb brute animals paw steadily, mindlessly, and almost ceaselessly at the new snow overlying the marsh, no matter how deep, and they know they'll be rewarded with something.

In a few days, some of the snow back in the woods will melt again, and new trails will be cut by the herd's wandering passages, leading to one food source after another, and the *Bryoria* will continue to fall from the trees, blown by the wind; but in that first day or two following the big wet snowstorms of February, the deer and elk come out into the amphitheater of the marsh, the place where they know they can always find something, and with that strange backhoe digging motion begin scraping away the snow, excavating their way down to the dead and colorless stalks of autumn, and nibble away: chewing that dry grass as much for the heat generated by the digestion, the fermentation, as for whatever leached-out nutrients might linger in the cell walls of those stalks. It is a sobering sight to see them doing this, one that always only increases the respect we have for the deer.

Sometimes after such a big storm, we don't see them out there pawing at the snow but instead will see, while out on our skis, only where they have been; and the disparity between the perfect smoothness of the untouched snow and the shredded terraces and canyons they have cut frantically, desperately, with their sharp hoofs — eight or ten deer working long and hard in a concentrated area, pawing and pawing, like salmon pushing upstream through the rapids — reveals to even our soft and comfortable lives a sharper and fuller and fairly horrifying glimpse into, if not understanding of, the true nature of hunger: the ceaseless, nearly volcanic forcefulness of it.

Those new-cut canyons and terraces look exactly like the land-forms of the desert Southwest, where violent rivers crossing magnificent spans of time have carved similar features not over the course of a single day or evening but across millions of years; and in either instance, what we are witnessing is nothing less than the signature of hunger; and we ski on past.

The fourth thing, every bit as delicious as the first three: the way the ground, the wonderful bare ground (I'm speaking now of the extreme end of February, and that only in a dry year, such as this one), first opens up around the trunks of the largest trees, umbrellas and ellipses of bare earth, first amid the snow, where each tree's branches (particularly the spruce) have trapped the day's heat and held it there for a little while, into each night, thinning that ice further and further until it is there that the earth first reappears, around the bases of those trees.

The darkened trunks of the trees likewise absorb, with differential vigor, the heat of the sun, mild though it is, while the snow everywhere else reflects and diffuses it back into the atmosphere; and again, on into the night, the absorbed heat in those blackened tree trunks radiates slowly back out across the snow, warmest on the west side, which is the part of the tree trunk that received the last and most intense heat of the day. The bare earth appears here first, in that west-canted ellipse that makes it appear as if someone or something has been buried at the base of that tree, at the base of every tree, feet pointing west, the soil appearing so recently excavated that no snow has yet fallen on the gravesite.

It is, of course, no death that is being marked, but birth, first birth; and in late February, when the earth first begins to show itself again, the hungry eye of the winterer lingers on these open patches first, and marvels at the random, intricate beauty of last autumn's cache of twigs and leaves and pine needles revealed once more: a miracle of delicious specificity after so long a sameness of white.

You watch those grave-shaped patches of earth grow from hamster-size plots into something larger, day by day and night by night, more and more earth appearing in that same west-southwest cant, like a sundial of the waking dead — the patches of earth shrugging off more and more snow until now the earthy openings at the base of each tree are nearly suitable for something the size of the family dog, and then larger, able almost to fit a human beneath them. (On some mild days, with the return of the sun, you're able to recline on some drying gentle slope of earth, upon such a plot, and stare out at the snowy marsh and listen to the south wind and the barking of ravens — no other birds yet, but soon, very soon.) Still, even when there is enough earth available to house a full-grown human body, even when there is enough earth available to house such a creature, such a specimen, as yourself, it's not over yet.

It is still fully winter — a glance at the tracks of deer, which are leaving blood in their prints from where they occasionally punch through the weakening ice, cutting their hocks, will provide as graphic an example as any that it is not over yet — and it's important not to disembark yet, in your overeagerness, from the slow-unfolding wave of winter, important not to be lured too far out into the open, yet, important not to rush or be rushed. It's important to honor the shortest month with caution, and to ride it all the way in to shore, rather than getting overanxious and leaping off early and swimming in choppy, awkward strokes, ill timed with the slow and powerful unfurling of the wave that is still behind you now.

Seeing the smudge of the distant trees of landfall, while invigorating, is still not the same thing as seeing the sandy beaches of the actual shore itself. You still have to wait a little while longer.

Sometime in February, the great four-week cough sets in — a maddening and seemingly ceaseless cycle of hack and phlegm, the accrued effect of too much wood smoke, too much fog and dampness, and almost no sun for three months now. For all of winter's wonder, you have to question, at this point, whether humans, or at least your race of humans, were meant to live year-round in such a dim and lightless land. What of the geese, the hummingbirds, and the monarch butterflies, all that flee thousands of miles south at the first vanishing of the sun? What of the swans, which also leave, and the bears, which descend into sleep? What of the snipe and the mallard ducks, the warblers, vireos, and kinglets?

Writing by candlelight in the cabin one cold dark night, I cough my February cough — as familiar to me by this point as the act of breathing — and a jet of visible frost-air, rime-breath, bursts from my mouth and snuffs out, with startling alacrity, the entire row of candles, the wavering light by which I am working.

I sit in the darkness for a moment, waiting, and then relight them using the coals from the fire in my wood stove, and go back to work.

While out backcountry skiing yesterday, practicing my awkward beginner's telemark turns in new powder, I lost my keys on any one of a couple dozen head-over-teacup tumbles — a fact I discovered only upon reaching my truck at the bottom of the mountain. I was due to pick up the girls after school and had allowed only a few minutes of buffer time for this operation — it was a good fifteen miles to the school, still, too far to ski and get there on time (and in February I could not count on another truck passing and giving me a ride to the school; in winter's depth like that, you can sometimes go the better part of the day without seeing another vehicle on the road). But fortunately, in the gravity of the wisdom gotten by my experience and my advancing age, I had guarded myself well against my own distractedness and had wired an extra set under the bumper so that I was able to retrieve those keys and start the truck right up without a hitch. I felt proud, if you can imagine that — losing all my keys in the snow and still I was pleased with myself, pleased with having outwitted even my own crafty self — and I went on up to the school and picked up the girls, right on time.

I decided however to go back the next day, if it didn't snow, and look for those keys, for a number of reasons. I knew it was a long shot that I'd find them, up on the huge mountain, in all that snow, but so great is my reverence for that mountain that I felt the obligation to play it out, to make at least one search, out of respect, to try to avoid littering the mountain with all that steel; and I wanted to look too because there were a lot of keys on that ring, some of which were the only key I had for this or that padlock, and because also attached to those keys was a wonderful little multipurpose knife Elizabeth had gotten me for Christmas one year. And I wanted to look too because I had a strange and utterly illogical feeling that I might be able to find them, against the odds.

This mountain has fed my family across the years with its berries and has been the place I go in times of joy, and in times of sorrow too; and it has given my family, over the years, numerous deer and elk. Finding a set of keys deep in the snow in the backcountry is nothing, really, compared to finding an elk, sometimes, in this valley — or rather, having that elk delivered to you via the mountain and via the elk itself — and so I set off the next day up the trail, carrying a shovel in my right hand instead of a ski pole, backtracking my way up the mountain. (I had called down to Libby to inquire about renting a metal detector, but as is often the way of such things, the cost was prohibitive: the heck with the detector, I decided, resolving to rely instead on grace and luck.)

Only the faintest skiff of snow had fallen in the night; I'd gotten lucky in that regard. And it was easy enough to follow my tracks from the day before; and easy too to find the places where I'd biffed, huge snowy volcanic craters of clumsiness and spasticity.

It was good exercise, going back up the big mountain for the second day in a row, and at each crash site I dug and dug, excavating an even wider pit. (What would those who came this way later in the week think, encountering such mammoth excavations?) After I had exhausted a ten-foot abyss around each tumbledown marker, listening intently, keenly, for the light and telltale clink of metal shovel blade against steel keys, muffled beneath the snow, I would move on farther up the mountain, retracing the previous day's falls in reverse, reliving my spectacular ignominy in such slow and studied fashion as to approach penitence — noting, as I moved in reverse that way, how the tight twin tracks of my skis had begun to wobble and separate just above each crash site, analyzing coldly, impassively, the slope and angle of terrain and the skier's approach that had led to each of the numerous miscues.

And even after I failed to find the keys with each new pit I dug, I didn't give up but instead sketched on the back of a scrap envelope the approximate location of each spill so that I might come back again in the spring and search in the absence of snow, and before the vegetation greened up, for the bright metallic sparkle of my key ring glinting in the sun — assuming a squirrel or pack rat had not carried the shining treasure off to its nest, or that a sharp-eyed, curious raven had not found the keys first and carried them off jangling in midair to a distant and secure stick nest even farther into the backcountry; and assuming too that the sliding sheets of ice in the spring would not transport the keys too much farther downslope, or in too erratic a pattern, carrying them hopelessly away from the origin like the distant detritus of some clattering moraine.

It was all but useless. Still, I had a good feeling about it; and in any event, it was a fine day to be up on the mountain digging holes in the snow. Blue sky, a bright sun, and good exercise.

Like some mad golfer, I counted the holes as I worked my way upward — dogleg left, hook right, slice left, dogleg right — weaving in my backtracking the same story of the fall line, not in the animal grace of a traverse but in the speed-thrill bombing run of the skier, carving only the most slender of *s*'s — and punctuated too often with those explosive craters — and my map grew more complex, noting this tree and that. I know the mountain so intimately that it would be no problem at all for me to return to those exact spots in the spring or any other season, snow or no-snow. And finally, near the top, after having nearly finished my bizarre cartographic project, I spied a strange-looking bump in the snow that was just about the size of the clump of keys, and though the clump was coated with an inch of snow from the night before, it looked to me as if there might be a sixteenth of an inch of metal key tip sticking up through the snow.

I climbed straight on up to that spot, not daring to take my eyes off it, and daring to hope, daring to believe, all the way up — and sure enough, there they were, on the seventeenth crater — or the third, if you wanted to count your way down from the cornice at the top. The familiar sound they made when I picked them up and dusted the snow from them and dropped them in my pocket was a kind of music extraordinarily sweet, and on the ski back down the hill to my truck, I wondered, and not for the first time, at the silliness with which we fill our days, at the passing of the hours that end up composing a life.

Nothing sleeps forever. That there are stories, out upon the land as well as in our own hearts — the ceaseless reordering of patterns and events to create stories, whether in the script of pen on paper or by the elegant calligraphy of fires and glaciers, and natural selection, succession, evolution and devolution — proves, I think, that all things will rise again, that there can be no permanent sleep, and that even the stillness of geology, or death, is temporary. In *The Snow Leopard,* Peter Matthiessen writes,

> In the book of Job, the Lord demands, "Where wast thou when I laid the foundation of the earth? Declare, if thou hath understanding! Who laid the cornerstones thereof, when the morning stars sang together, and all the sons of God shouted for joy?"
>
> "I was *there!*" — surely that is the answer to God's question. For no matter how the universe came into being, most of the atoms in these fleeting assemblies that we think of as our bodies have been in existence since the beginning.

I do not think we would have been gifted with the ability to observe stories, much less create them, if this background movement, this narrative momentum, were not one of the underlying forces or currents of the world itself. For what other reason would the world have instilled in us such a proclivity or talent if not for use — even if that use is but to celebrate, observe, replicate, the larger patterns?

Nothing sleeps forever. The river reawakens first, in February, stretching and cracking and groaning and glowing sapphire green as the ice softens and fills with warming water from below, the ice acting like a magnifying lens through which that returning sun strafes; and after the rivers begin to break apart and stir and then flow once again, the land begins to awaken — and after the land awakens, then the plants begin to stir, the trees and grasses and forbs, and after the vegetation awakens come last the animals that had been sleeping within that sleeping earth, spilling from their burrows and caves like boulders loosened from the frost's grip on a frozen hillside, warmed by the climbing sun, and tumbling downslope and back out into the world. If that in itself is not the grand pattern of story, the progression and movement of some larger narrative, some larger meaning gotten from the assemblage of the many individual parts and scenes, then what would you call it instead?

Nothing can sleep forever. No matter how rock-hard the frozen earth was in January, in February the ground begins to soften, right after the rivers open and begin to move again, and right after the first ducks and geese return, looking for those early patches of open water, quacking and honking and braying like donkeys, so that to one who did not understand perhaps the cant of the sun and the incredible power of that increased angle of its incidence, and the increased force of radiation, it might seem that it was the powerful stride of the geese's honking alone that was softening that frozen ground to jelly, to mud — the ground softening finally, and loosening, stretching and bending up into sluggish oceanlike waves, swales and troughs that oscillate like the living thing the earth has become, not just across fields and pastures but up and down the dirt roads, bunching them up into corduroy washboards.

As the land awakens, coming back to life, these swales and troughs pitch our trucks so that we bob up and down like small boats in the crossing of them. The loads of firewood we carry in the back for added traction on the ice fly up into the air, crossing each swell, before raining back down scattered and repositioned, thumping hard when they land. You can hear such thumping anywhere in the valley, at any time of day, in February — new swales appearing almost anywhere overnight to surprise the habituated and inattentive driver. Those falling-back-to-earth loads of firewood (it's fun to watch in your rearview mirror when such a wave catches you by surprise: you feel the lift and rise, the sudden weightlessness, and glance in the mirror, and sure enough, it's like a magic trick: all your firewood is up in the air behind you, hanging and floating for a second), when they finally land — settling right back down into the bed of your truck, in only slightly rearranged fashion — set up a tympanic clattering that echoes through the woods and drums loudly on those very same warped and frost-heaved roads that first gave rise to the drumming.

(Later in the year, when the awakening is complete, the softened roads will finish their yawn and will be stretched back out all the way flat again; and again you will understand that almost everything has some sort of life, or the semblance of a life, through story, and that almost everything has some sort of motion, and as such, some sort of narrative . . .)

And though the bears, off in the distance and still asleep in the earth as if entombed, are not quite reawakened in February, these bumpings and thunderings must surely be communicating themselves to the bears' dreams, the pitched and jouncy loads of our firewood and our bang-hollering trucks drumming down through the tight skin of icy earth, the bears picking up on those sounds with the sonar of their sleeping bodies, as the enormous whales are said to be able to hear the ocean-stirred vibrations of distant drilling rigs and buzzing motorboats hundreds or thousands of miles distant, or even, perhaps, the oar of a single kayaker as the blade enters the dark water, a distant whisper spoken in a language that is a complete mystery to our own slack-bodied selves.

To those sleeping underground, perhaps the sounds of the stirring world above enter their dreams in a jumbled state and incorporate themselves into the bear's dreams in such fantastic reassemblage as to create the most amazing dreams and stories imaginable. Perhaps the bears and other earthbound, sleeping creatures dream of a sky filled with floating pieces of firewood, neatly sawn stumps hanging in the air, drifting, waiting to come back down to earth, waiting and waiting . . .

More sounds, on the eighteenth and nineteenth of February, this year: the air as aswirl with sound as the buried earth, with the strange raucous chitterings of the pileated woodpeckers calling out as they fly from ailing tree to ailing tree, searching for the ants and beetles that feast on those trees, as the pileateds, with their long anvil bills, feed on those insects, so that — again, another marvelous equation — a forest grove of dead or dying trees, rotting or burned, equals the sight and sound of a great pileated woodpecker, three feet from bright red head to tail and with an even larger wingspan, flying through these forests with wild whoops and wails and laughs. And while it is an equation beyond our ken to completely measure or replicate or even fully understand, it is not one that lies beyond our ability to observe and celebrate, which is, to paraphrase the poet Mary Oliver, exactly what I have been doing all day.

And again, the sameness or similarity of the equation and its patterns expresses itself across the different media; as the shouting, laughing giant woodpecker is in many ways but a miraculous blossoming of the dead-standing spars — little more than a leap of thought, as if the dead-standing spar had all along desired to become such a bright and flightworthy and attractive bird — so too does the sound of the great pileated woodpecker carry within it the same energy and pattern, the vibrancy, of the silent sap that is beginning to stir in the living trees, and of the overwintering insects that are beginning to stir in the dead or compromised ones. It all seems to be attempting to merge, once winter starts to lift.

Unerringly, it seems, the woodpeckers swoop to the trees that contain the stirring insects. (How do they know? By sight, by sound, by odor, by intuition?) Tentatively at first, they begin to tap at the chosen tree, probing it, until, within the first few trial excavations, the tender and delicious insects are revealed to the uncurling tongue, and further excavation begins now in earnest. A rapid, concussive drumming issues throughout the forest, the pileated hammering out its deep and distinctive rectangle-shaped cavity, chips and slivers of bark flying everywhere — the bird, it seems to me, preferring to test the green bark of still living trees, in February. (Do the woodpeckers mark with anticipation, visually or otherwise, those trees each autumn that are or might possibly be newly diseased?) There could be ten thousand reasons, ten thousand related connections, dependencies, and advantages for such an intricate seasonal preference, some acute and exquisite forest balance — but all I know is that in February one notices with far greater frequency the new-peeled slivers of green glistening bark resting atop the new snow, new wood pale and bright as new-milled lumber, and chips scattered about wildly, looking at first like the residue from where some sawyer passed just hours before with ax or chain saw . . .

And in the drumming sound of those excavations, despite the falling snow, one can hear another of the first sounds of spring returning, and in those glistening chips and slivers that the woodpecker has carved from the trunk one can see that the sap is beginning to move, and just like the river, and just like earth, and just like the braids and ribbons of ducks and geese overhead. The butter-colored wood chips are sticky with living resin, and revealed like that, resting upon the open snow, it is as if the blood within the blood, the sap within the sleeping tree, and the sleeping tree within the sleeping forest, are beginning to awaken; and again, whether the woodpecker is drawn to the first few signs and clues of that awakening, or perhaps participates more actively, helping to accelerate that awakening, not just with the booming cannonade of its drumming and its wild and strange calls but with the actual cracking open of those new-stirring trees, I could not say for sure; neither do I need to know.

Again, I really need only to know that I like to walk across the diminishing snow, in February, usually on snowshoes, and notice, and celebrate, those bright new-peeled ribbons of bark resting fragrant upon the snow; and to know that there are forests where I can do this, that there are forests where I will always be able to do this.

And another new bird! My God, a ruby-crowned kinglet perching cold upon a bare alder branch outside my cabin, on the twentieth of February, peering in at me through the frosted window and cheeping quietly, while in the spruce thicket behind the kinglet the chickadees are foraging this bright morning, with the sun higher than it has been all year. Even the owls are calling, courting, midmorning, and it doesn't matter that it's eight degrees today: the sun is higher than it's been yet, the light upon the world is fuller and richer than we have yet seen it, and all the birds are more active than they've been all year.

Watching that kinglet watch me through the thick frost of cabin glass is proof again that spring's coming soon now. The first of February is far too soon to lean forward in your traces, as is even the seventh, or even the fourteenth — but I would estimate, based on my own experience, that if you want to get really reckless about it, you can begin to dream of spring on this date, the twentieth of February. There's still a good three to four weeks of rutted ice and snow cover remaining, but if you're tough enough, you can go ahead and begin dreaming now.

Three to four weeks is still a long time — especially after so long a trek — and like the deer back in the forest, you'll want to conserve yourself, and your strength — don't sprint for the finish line yet, and, in fact, don't sprint at all — but on or around the twentieth of February, it's all right to begin to dream.

I was skiing again yesterday, noting the new angles of light upon the forest, and found myself thinking again about the cant of this valley. You would think that for neatness' sake, and symmetry and balance, February light would have the exact qualities of August light, that each would be balanced against the earth evenly, cleaved six months apart from each other, half a year, like the severed halves of a pear, an apple, or some other round and balanced fruit. But again, because of the valley's cant — this one sweet and specific place on earth — it's not that way at all. Neither is April light like October light.

Instead, early March is more like early October; April, more like late September.

Somewhere in between these two parts — their variance from the perfectly cleaved half — lies a rough outline of this valley's formula of cant, based on angles of and amounts of light alone. The formula — the secret — could be further studied and refined by examining temperatures, wind directions, and innumerable other physical or biological processes, but to begin with learning about this place, the sheer tilt of the earth-meeting-the-sun could first help derive that formula, even if crudely: enough of a working model, perhaps, to begin noticing and understanding other patterns falling under the same governance of the laws established for the territories within the shadows and rhythms of this one place, or any one place.

And isn't it an error right from the beginning to desire or even expect an easy-to-understand, perfect bipolar cleave of symmetry — the apple, the avocado, the strawberry, the orange, halved so cleanly? The mistake in such a wish, it seems to me, is to assume that there cannot be balance in asymmetry. Who knows? Perhaps it is even that slight tipping, that subtle leaning of the specifically asymmetric — and the slight tension and effort required to compensate and balance that tilt — that provides, in some way, the generative forces and rhythms that attend to any one certain place, and which are nothing less than the driving force of life for this or any place: a thousand or ten thousand such cants then braiding, elliptically, asymmetrically, and in that convergence, the world easing forward with its peculiar and powerful surges and pulses.

Chickadees swarming now as the blood within all of us begins to thin and stir beneath the returning light, tree and bird and man alike — the chickadees singing and swarming and chittering, buzzing and tweeting, calling and squabbling, some singing their sweet two-note courting song, singing it so relentlessly that I can't work, can't concentrate, after so long a winter's silence.

The dull sunlight bouncing off the marsh's snow, a glare pushing through the woods-fog, is nonetheless intense enough to throw shadows from my hand and the pen across the page as I write, further distracting me, as do the flitting shadows of the birds themselves, passing back and forth before my window.

I can't work today; I'm edgy, pacey, antsy. I'll get up and go for a walk, a ski. These are not the things a writer does, normally — usually a writer writes — but I can't help it. It's as if I'm trapped on a raft or island of ice that is breaking free from all the other ice, and the cold black current is pulling it, spinning now, down the river, and if I sit here any longer I'll get so dizzy, I'll fall off. I have to get up and go for a walk.

It's the shortest month, and yet in many ways the most convulsive. It's too soon to begin leaning forward, sometimes too soon to even begin moving at all, and yet even in the midst of all that stillness, things are falling away. At dusk on the last day of February, while I'm walking up the icy driveway, a band of seven elk crosses in front of me, six cows and a one-antlered bull, like golden horses in the blue foggy gloom and mist. They pass from right to left, heading down farther into the woods, and I turn to the right and begin backtracking them, trying to find where the bull might have shed his mahogany-colored antler, like some great burdensome sword or scimitar laid down in the snow, with the war finally over.

MARCH

....

AT NO POINT of the year are we more incorporated into the seasons, more completely owned by the world, and the woods. Summer and autumn, and even the first holidays of winter, are traditionally the seasons we think of as most easily summoning the joy of the human condition; and yet in February, March, and April, the Slog-O-Matic mud season, the long brown night of the soul, never are we quite so owned by the beautiful world. Beaten down, made malleable as if by the accruing weight of the ivory snow itself, we become tempered to the very shape of the land itself, and by its rhythms and processes, as surely as if we were buried by that snow and lay pressed flat against the darkened ground, our bellies spooned against each curve and hummock of soil, each swell of stone, and the snow above pressing down, kneading and pressing and sculpting us physically, while at the same time impressing upon us somehow some deeper, unspoken counsel of rhythm and pace.

On the surface, there's very little difference; in fact, the sameness seems to be spreading, as the snow — which initially mimicked the sleeping shapes of every humped and curved and buried thing — becomes deeper, smoother, more homogenous.

But down below, things are moving, being reshaped by the mounting pressure, even if only a tiny bit each day. The bears and frogs are sleeping, letting the season pass on by, largely undisturbed by its slow but powerful dynamics, and the songbirds, and so many others, have fled south, likewise disengaged from the snow's incremental but forceful grip. But for those of us who remain, whether buried by the snow or shrugging off each day's mantle, we are always emerging, changed and sculpted a little more each day. The valley owns us as surely as it owns any of its rocks or rivers, forests or fields, or any of its other animals.

Everything still seems the same, in March. But beneath the snow, and within our blood, there are stirrings that tell us that the land too is stirring.

The stems and branches of the willows have begun to glow yellow — seeming incandescent, particularly in the falling snow, with the willows the only color on the landscape, so that the eye is drawn to them, mesmerized, almost with the intensity or focus of one in need of rescue or salvation, physical or otherwise. They burn there, at the far edge of the snowy marsh, glowing and waiting, unchanging, it seems, against the same joyless gray sky: a dendritic spread of color looking like our own veins and arteries, which — we can only hope — are filling likewise with that same gold light.

Nothing else is different, and yet for (perhaps) the first time, you sense the movements. Change — dramatic change, the kind our species is better at noticing, and paying brief attention to — seems closer now, if even only through the gap or difference between the two words *February* and *March,* one long and backward-moving, the other shorter, brisker, and more forward-moving: as if the force of our nouns can be almost enough to help nudge a thing into motion — as is said to be the case, sometimes, with even our dreams, and their bold summons of a thing much wished for, much desired.

Our little nouns, *February* and *March,* as plaintive against the gray sky as the faint cries of the birds that are no longer here, and yet their own part of the world, helping — along with all else — to ease along and urge along the chain of the seasons.

In March, it would be hard to say whether one is witnessing the end of winter, the beginning of spring, or some strange and dreamy land between the two, wherein some of the world awaken and rise while others in the world remain suspended — summoned, perhaps, but not quite awakened. And even for those fully awakened, in March — Pisces, and the fish beneath the ice, unblinking — perhaps the world is still half dream. And in that half-dream, then, surely the yellow glow of the willow is a beacon in the storm, a signpost and candelabra lit, or a conductor's baton, encouraging all to rise — to dare to rise, reshaped by another year's passage — and to move forward toward that curtain of falling snow, and through that curtain, with faith and confidence that a bright and joyful, explosive world of color and life lies waiting just on the other side.

*   *   *

Some years — not every year, but some — the snow will begin to finally grow lower, in March, or will lower for a while, only to fill back up in April, which is another matter entirely. (It amazes me, the way each month has such a separate identity. We think of time as a river, and know intuitively that it is. But if one pauses to look back almost any distance, the months might seem as discrete blocks, chunks of stone, all stoved up and jagged against one another, like the spines and teeth of glaciers, gnashing at the sky and both devouring and yet creating the mountains and, in the mountains' dissolution, creating the dusty plains below.)

And perhaps it is this way, with the months not any ethereal river braid but rather devourers and creators of time — the individual months gnawing away at some bedrock of time.

And as these stone blocks of the months exist sometimes jagged, other times smoother, above the bedrock form of a God-made landscape, a Creator-made core of the irreducible, then so too might there exist a third and higher level, something more graceful and seamless — something truly more riverlike — flowing just above those jagged blocks, jagged devourers. Though I suppose it's just as possible, if not more so, that this is all there is, the months above and the bedrock below, and that we, and our lives, our little histories, are the glacier dust, ground fine and sifted as flour, caught eternally between the two.

And in those years when the snow melts a bit, in March — regardless of whether it fills back up in April or not — only as the snow level begins to drop a little bit, finally melting slightly on the rare and warming sunny day, do you start to really understand how deep the snow has been. The tops of fences and rock walls begin to emerge from beneath you (even as you still are walking above them, looking down upon their emergent shapes as they begin to crown, popping up through the snow — just a dark shape beneath the translucent thinning at first, but then, barely, the real thing, like the heads of crocus bulbs), and you understand how, for a few months, you might already have been up in that higher, even celestial level, up in the more graceful place where the laminar flow of time moves with less friction — moving around in your winter life at some significant distance above, elevated several feet above the "true" world; though if that is the case, why has it still been so damned hard, at times, so gray-blue leaden, sludge-blood hard?

And yet, whether trudging five feet above, or down on terra firma, navigating one's way through the rocks — whether asleep and dreaming, or wide awake and fully sensate — it is all still always pretty much the same world, regardless of the gnawing blocks of months, or centuries, or millennia, or eons; and in the close examination of a single month, I often feel a kinship with all who have ever lived before me.

Are we still sleeping, or are we awakening? Change is dramatically imminent, eternally poised for its grand entrance, and yet there are still, particularly in March, I think, these long moments when *it is all the same*. The frilled and braided lace of wax forming runnels from the lip of the candles at my writing desk, out in my cabin as I work far into the night, at the edge of the winter-silent marsh, is the same as the crenellations of ice that creep down over the eaves of this same cabin (warmed by those candles, and my breath, and the dim little glow of the wood stove); it's the same translucent, moonstruck filigree of ice, not wax, leaning in past the frost-spangled window.

Everywhere I look, some months, and particularly, it seems, when in the womb of ice, the womb of winter, it is all almost the same, both pattern and image, dream and sensation. As if we are not quite ready for the furor and clamant wonder of the "true" or living world, the green world of living and dying, and must emerge into it slowly, like crocuses ourselves, or chunks of stone in a rock wall, reappearing above the surface and only gradually becoming enspirited, and animated.

What dreamer dreamed us, that we might begin dreaming? Thank goodness that in these moments of our realization of a shimmering background *sameness* in the world there is so much beauty too, or we might all get incredibly bored with so much unity, really, at the heart or core of all things.

Faced with the recognition of such sameness, our souls and spirits might abandon us, no longer needing the specificity of us; might fly right out the window if one day we lost the ability to look around and perceive the individual beauties attendant — like lace or fringes — to all this other sameness — the rest of the world's unchanging core or essence.

On the seventh of March, my birthday, the woods are all but silent. The laugh-out-loud sound has not yet returned: the sound of water running through the forest in sheets, water dripping from every branch, water dripping from the roof, a laughing, awakening sound. There is still only the nighttime hooting of owls, which begin their nesting so much earlier than any other bird. The bears are still sleeping, and all the forest's other creatures have not yet returned from their southward migrations, or have not been born yet — though it's very close now, with those first bare branches of the willows beginning to glow gold, like the upraised wands of so many orchestral conductors: the last moment of deep silence that builds and swells before the conductors stir their wands and summon that music.

The golden orange wands are lifted and poised along every creek and river and beside every marsh, and at night, back in the forests, the owls are calling to an audience not yet arrived. I like to think that in the bellies of their mothers, the elk calves and deer fawns can hear these first summons and can understand too from the all-else stillness that surrounds them, the last of the stillness, that their time is coming soon, and that a world, a whole new world of song and movement and color and warmth, is being made for them; and that in their mind's eye, perhaps, or their other ways of knowing, they can already somehow see those uplifted bare branches, burning in the falling snow and spring rain like beautiful candles seen across a great distance.

Who knows how these things work, or where the dream begins? My grandfather, father, and one of my brother's sons all have the same birth date, October sixteenth. My oldest daughter came into this world only six days after my birthday. Is there a fraternity and sorority of time — of the days, seasons, years? The birth dates for me and my best friend are but two days apart. It goes on and on, such accountings, far beyond random coincidence. There are patterns all around us, above and below us — of that there can be no dispute. The only real question that seems to me worth wrestling over is whether they are designed or not.

How could they not be?

And here, perhaps, is blasphemy, though it is not intended as such. In the genius of the design, perhaps the beauty and elegance of the initial or developing organic system is what gave rise to the designer — demanded a partnership, a designer, for such beauty and elegance of fit to continue, and be carried further. Perhaps the world's beauty and intricate desire for order produced a god, or a God, through all of that relentless fit, relentless adjustment and readjustment: a god or God being formed from the very clattering of rocks and rivers, the swelling and sanding down of mountains, like the terminus of such a process, such a long and wondrous and breathtaking work; and that that god, that God, then produced us.

It has to begin somewhere. Perhaps it is linear rather than circular, and there was nothing — no order, no design, not even any dream or dreamer. Or maybe the dreamer dreamed the rocks and rivers, the forests sweeping in the wind; dreamed the near silence of winter, and the awakening sounds, beyond that. We're here. It's wonderful. And from it, who could possibly *not* dream a dream, then, of this or another life eternal?

Soon enough, the laughing dream returns. Often, in this country, it comes in the form of rain, rain on top of snow, weakening the snow so that as you walk across it, it opens up to bare ground with each step. You can hear the water running just beneath the skin or crust of snow, the water warmed by the awakening earth, even as the snow above is still chilled by the wintry nights. The rain falling through the trees makes a hissing sound as it lands on the slushy ice. There will be more snow, but this is the first sign of weakness, if one chooses to look at it that way.

Through it all — the silence, and the waiting — the deer are trudging down the icy latticework of the trails they've been making all winter long, their hoofs compressing the snow into dense, hard-packed ice that will remain long after all the rest of the surrounding looser snow has melted away, the remaining latticework of their passage as white as bones cast randomly across the dark floor of the forest. The rain drenches the hanging black moss, the lichen, *Bryoria,* that they feed on whenever they can reach it. The lichen absorbs the March rain until it looks like a woman's long black hair after she has just stepped out of the shower; and becoming heavier still, the super-wet lichen pulls free of the branches and lands on top of the fading-away snow, to where the deer hurry over to eat it, so that it is as if the deer are being nourished directly by the rain, like a crop rising from the earth, even though they have always been here, loyal to this place through hardships as well as the rewards of the softer seasons.

When Mary Katherine was born (I can barely remember the days and years before, as if they were in some ways their own form of sleep), she emerged stone-faced, as we all seem to — stone-faced, or snarling — and though we had been up all night, it seemed to me that she was bathed in a strange sheen, strange light. Then immediately upon her full arrival, her face relaxed, and she smiled this wide, beautiful smile and slowly brought her hands together — it seemed to be occurring in slow motion — and clasped her fingers together, interlocking-style, without a single hitch. I knew nothing about babies, but knew enough to be astounded.

It was an early spring that year, and when we came home with her, the ice in the pond beside the cabin we were renting had already opened up, and though the mornings were still below freezing, the Canada geese had already returned. There was a big wide plate-glass window looking out onto the pond, and when we walked into the cabin with her that first time, bright early morning, the sun was just clearing Waper Ridge and coming up the valley.

It was a blue-sky day, and the new gold sun was coming right through the window, lighting nearly everything in the cabin. A flock of geese came flying up the narrow river valley, honking loudly, and we stood there with her in our arms, watching and listening as the geese kept coming closer, descending, their braying honks growing ridiculously loud until it seemed they were in the room with us, or we with them.

It looked as if they were going to keep on coming, right on through the big window, but they set their wings into a glide and landed on the pond's surface and coasted all the way in, right up to the window's edge, clucking and grunting and braying, and the ripples from their splashing cast shimmering disks of bronze and yellow that reflected in wavers across the cabin walls and ceiling, bathing the three of us in that rippling pond light, and Mary Katherine just watched and listened to it, as if it were all the most normal and regular thing in the world.

I think that when you save someone, you become saved. I think something passes between you and the rescued person, something almost entirely unnoticed, so that it is as if some thin and perhaps artificial barrier that gives each of us a bit of necessary distance from all others, and a place in the world, and a place in time, has been pulled away, as if all along it was nothing more than a curtain of gauze no more substantial than a veil or a dream: as if such distance, believed to exist at the heart of all things, might sometimes really exist only in our imaginations — again, even if only for a few moments at a time.

Mary Katherine stopped breathing the night she was born. Elizabeth had delivered her, and we were in our hospital room, had spent the first night there; she was still in her first twenty-four hours of life. All of her vital signs had been perfect at birth — seven pounds, nine ounces, nineteen and three-quarters inches, etc., etc. — and remained fine. But only a few hours into having moved to our hospital room (there was only one other baby in the entire neonatal wing, several nurses per baby), she just stopped breathing.

She didn't care for it at all. Her face scrunched up and turned red as she gasped and sucked and waved her fists, and then she wasn't getting any air at all and began taking on a bluish tint.

We both knew next to nothing about babies, but we knew immediately what was wrong.

I grabbed her from Elizabeth, who was in bed, and went running down the hall with Mary Katherine. It felt like football days, the narrow unoccupied hallway a path one needed to travel as quickly as possible, with a dire force in close pursuit, and time the most vanishing, valuable thing.

In the meantime, Elizabeth had called down to the front desk, and an elderly nurse, a tiny little old woman, came hurrying around the corner, and I closed the distance to her quickly and handed Mary Katherine — who was still fighting — to her.

Before I even had time to explain anything, the nurse flipped her over so that she was holding Mary Katherine face-down, cradling her little belly in the palm of one hand, and tapped her on the back, then lifted her upright — and just like that, she was breathing the clean, sweet air of life again.

Back in our room, Elizabeth had gotten disentangled from her bed sheets and was now running down the hall in her robe, barefoot, trailing tubes and towels, as well as blood, and by the time she reached us, she was faint, terrified, and it was hard to believe that, already, everything was all right again. I was already amazed at the astounding miracle of life, and to receive now, scant hours later, a second miracle — salvation — was indescribable. I do remember feeling joyous and terrified both, and wondering how other parents did it: if every hour was to be filled with this intensity of emotion, this aliveness and alertness. I remember consciously wanting to preserve that extreme joy, extreme gratitude, forever, and for the most part, I think I have; I think most parents do. It was like entering a second world, a second kingdom.

I wondered why I had not heard much about it. Or maybe plenty of people had been talking about it and I had just not been listening.

They put her in an incubator thing for the rest of the night, with a little wire strapped to her, some kind of sensor taped to her, so that if she stopped breathing again — for longer than ten seconds, I think — a buzzer would go off. The nurse said it wasn't uncommon for newborns to stop breathing, but that usually they started right back up again. She said she thought Mary Katherine must have had some kind of obstruction, milk or phlegm, and had choked briefly on that.

I hated that she couldn't be with us the rest of her first night in the world, but the nurse assured us she'd be asleep all night anyway and would never even know we weren't there.

Still, I stood there on the other side of the glass and watched her for most of the night. If she opened her eyes, I wanted her to see there was still someone there; and if the monitor failed, I wanted to be there to back it up.

I watched her sleep, and breathe; I counted the seconds between inhalations and exhalations. And once, later in the night, she stopped again, in her sleep — I was counting, with increasing concern, eight, nine, ten, as Mary Katherine stirred in her sleep, increasingly uncomfortable, and by eleven I was rushing back to the nurses' station, though by the time we returned, Mary Katherine was breathing easily again.

The nurse unstrapped the monitor, examined it, recalibrated it, and tested it against the side of the bed; when it had been motionless for ten seconds, it began to beep.

I can't remember what the nurse said, or how she explained it, though she did allow that sometimes the monitors weren't always perfect.

Bleary-eyed, I watched Mary Katherine for the rest of the night. She kept breathing, and the monitor never beeped. The nurses were just across the hallway from her — almost within sight of her — but what was one night, and the first night, at that?

What I think I felt, that next day, was a newness of responsibility that was in a way like a saving of myself: an utter and concrete reminder that I was no longer the most important person in the world — that, in fact, I was now invisible and she was everything.

How such knowledge saves a person I can't quite be sure, but I felt rescued, felt as if I had passed completely through that thin curtain and into some finer land in which the self dissolved and another was born. And I still feel that way, too, anytime I look at either of my daughters, and I know that other parents feel that same way — I have heard them speak of it, had in fact heard such things being stated even before I became a parent, though in those earlier days, such discussions, such statements, had held no meaning for me and had the quality of sound of a radio playing faintly in another room, with the language of the radio's music identifiable but the individual words, and their message, indistinguishable.

When we finally got her home (because of her breathing stoppage, we stayed in town a couple extra days, just to be safe) and walked into our cabin and saw that sun-gold reflected pond light shimmering across the ceiling, and when the geese came gliding in, gliding almost into our laps, Mary Katherine tensed with excitement, and then laughed. She had smiled the moment she was born, and now, listening to the goose music, she tensed and then laughed. For some reason, some doctors will tell you newborn babies can't laugh; but if a flock of wild geese comes sailing into their life in the first moment they enter their new home, they can.

This year, by the marsh, spring (or rather, the first opening in the snow, even if it is only a false opening) is a little later in coming. The marsh is still a mottled slab of snow and ice, but with a few standing puddles, and the sliver-green hues of translucence of more and more patches of thinning ice. The heavier, sturdier birds are returning first — the incredibly powerful ducks and geese, birds flying across the top of the forest each night, returning like rising water levels themselves, hurrying to fill the new spaces created by the snow's departure.

The snow is not yet going away for good: we all know that. But the struggle has begun in earnest, space versus no space — the land rush is on — and as the snow and ice begin to disappear, the ducks and geese are claiming the new water, pothole by pothole, wing splash by wing splash.

By mid-March, they are pouring in like bats, their unseen wing whistling heard always at dusk, so that it seems to me as if with their enthusiastic return they are helping to nudge along the gear works that are leading us all to the advancing equinox, the return of sufficient light, finally, to balance the dark.

It's still cold and snowy, but somewhere — if not yet on the marsh — there's yet another slot of open water just ahead, just opened; and they're anxious, it seems, to be the first, or among the first, to reach it. Perhaps in their power and rush they are not just helping to nudge along the gear works that lead us toward the equinox but are in fact attempting, with their momentum and desire, to speed it along. It's easy to imagine that with their fast, strong flights they are finally pulling back the covers of winter, finally revealing the black bare earth of spring and the coming meadows and marshes that will one day be as brilliantly green as the jeweled feathers on the heads of the mallard drakes that are now reinhabiting them.

You can't see any of this, at night, or into the future. But it's up there, and out there — close enough to hear, if not quite yet see. Whispered promises, now.

The gear works will never break. Easier for our own souls and spirits to fracture and drain away, back down into some rift or fissure, than for those massive, subterranean, and celestial gear works to break.

With the life comes the sound. The marsh is cracking, groaning, speaking to the sun, on the days when the sun returns. The ferocity of life: on the thirteenth of March, I spy the first mosquito. Surely this is no newly hatched wiggle-tail but instead some overwintering veteran, solitary, a good many weeks ahead of the coming invasion of others of his kind. But still, it's an amazing sight, and after so long an absence, almost a welcome one.

I don't mean to sound too fond. And after all, one of the birds is going to get him, anyway. When they return.

Pulling Lowry on her sled across the crust of vanishing marsh ice, skirting around the shallow puddles — each day seems to be the last day, and then the last hour, I can do this.

The trail, the wake, of our fractured ice glints and glitters in the new sun like a path of diamonds, and it seems to me that it is the thunderous, rasping noise of the steel runners themselves, the tympanic rumbling, that will urge the spring along, as much as the whistle of duck wings at night. So much noise: as if these rasps and rumblings, and even her delighted laugh, are what will awaken the sleeping season.

More sun, not just ribbons and tendrils seen through the dense strata of clouds, but entire hour- and two-hour-long stretches of it, the entire sky a blue umbrella, and now the snow seems to be routed, and once again, it doesn't matter to us that it'll be back: the great thing is the return of that sunlight. We feel like laughing, even giggling or snickering foolishly at our great luck, for in no way can we deserve such raw miracle, such raw luck. Hasn't it previously been our lot to know only sodden gray, so much of it that we'd become convinced, inured, that that was all there'd ever be?

More patches of open water, and open earth, appear. Ovals of mud begin to appear on the roads, like the great brown-slabbed flesh of some living thing, gigantic and leechlike, perhaps, rising from beneath the sheets and blankets of the snow.

The exhilarating, joyful sound of puddles splashing beneath our tires as we drive through the slush: a discordant sound, yet as beautiful, in March, as any aria, any birdsong. The blood thinning, in that new light, and quickening again, with joy.

The lichens, wet from yesterday's steady rain, today are already sun-dried and waving in the breeze, not like sodden hair now but like long hair blowing in the wind. The trees with their branches like outstretched arms, the long lichens like hair, the knots and gnarls like eyes, noses, mouths, remind me again how little difference there is between anything — how one plan, one law or rule or desire, seems to govern it all: every rock and tree, every bone and branch and feather and antler, and the path of all things. With the sun having returned after winter's long gray slog, it seems not to matter at all that I have no clue what that path or rule might be.

The scent your skin makes, in intense sunlight, as if it is cooking: I haven't smelled it in six months, not since last September, hiking high up on a rocky ledge. The sun going down, back then, giving up its intensity for half a year. *Hello, welcome back.* At this moment, looking up at the cumulus clouds, the blue sky, the alder branches still bare against that blue sky, but with the birds chittering and chirping and singing and pairing up, and the warm wind pouring now across the thawing marsh, there is only one spider web's strand separating me from euphoria, and in my deepening middle age, forgive me, I'm trying to keep that strand from snapping me and releasing me (like some balloon) into that euphoria. Instead, I'm trying to stay slightly lower and centered, so worn out and frightened have I become — so weary — of the subsequent and necessary and correlative down-swoops of spirit that accompany such euphorias, later on, in the natural law-and-order system of cost and recompense.

I just want to sit here in the mild sun and be happy, peaceful, content. I am no longer always as brave as the small birds around me now, returning to the marsh — birds that are said to, in the springtime, sometimes sing until a vessel in their throat ruptures and bright blood sprays from their mouths.

I aim for these journals to be nothing but a celebration, portraits of joy — this is what I hope to train my eye to look for — and yet to look too closely at one thing while purposely avoiding the other thing sitting right next to it is myopic at best. There is a part of me, hopefully a larger part, that can look at the pattern of the emerging, fledgling springtime and feel the larger spirit of the world — the joy, and awakening — that runs like fast meltwater just beneath the surface of all things, and in the return of southerly breezes, and be swept along, carried along, by this momentum.

But I see the fracturing and disintegration too, the greed and injury — the bizarre geometries of clearcuts, up one mountain and down the other — and as the white world vanishes and the remaining forests slowly release their snowpack to the thawing, hungry, muddy soil, the patchwork of clearcuts hang on to their snow stubbornly and become even more noticeable, and unnatural-seeming, in the springtime.

With no overstory to trap the awakening earth's warmth and respiration, they just sit there, strange little glaciers, hoarding all their water, even though this is the time of year that the soil and vegetation of the surrounding forest most need it, and have evolved to receive it.

Giant unencumbered snowpacks, the old clearcuts insulate and keep chilled an earth that is otherwise seeking to awaken, and they reflect the sun's solar rays back into space.

They sit there and wait, accomplishing nothing, while life — wild, rambunctious, hard-earned, and glorious life — races past all around them. (And when they do finally release, burned by the sun, it is in a useless, calamitous collapsing rather than in the slow, sustainable, nutritious trickling away that occurs farther back in the stability of the old forest. They dump their water load all at once, sometimes several weeks later than what the ecosystem historically was used to receiving — and everything, all movements of nature, are skewed and disrupted, sometimes even scoured away by these clearcut-caused releases of artificial peak flow.)

It does no good to dwell on it, or to allow your one sweet and precious and wild life to be made bitter by such observations, but it's out there, all around you, and you cannot help but see it. Two centuries ago, before the first ax or saw ever dreamed of a place like the Yaak, Gerard Manley Hopkins wrote, "O if we but knew what we do when we delve or hew, hack and rack the growing green!"

Over the years, I've become almost accustomed to the horrific views — not benumbed, by any means, but inured, summoning sufficient residue, I think, to bear up beneath such injurious, daily witnessing — in part, by learning to focus on the wild and soothing beauty of what's still left. But as each new season reveals yet another round of new clearcuts — two hundred or more years of interconnected grace being swept clean — I can't help but wonder what kind of savage and ineffectual people would allow such a thing to be done not just to their own land, or any land, but to the views that flood and fill our senses thereafter in each glimpse of those denuded hills, day after day after day, and ever increasing — such views filling their children's lives too until one day perhaps there is a generation of children that knows nothing else and accepts such a view as due or recompense, with each season's thaw melting new scours and gullies of erosion, the mountains themselves washing away, trading mystery for scab.

Some days I feel we're very near that tipping point — wherein one or two more clearcuts tip the balance of wonder versus rage, joy versus despair, too far the other way, so that we know only the latter, and very little, if any, of the former.

How much is too much?

I love the way the phone calls and e-mail messages spread slowly north, in March. A friend in Trout Creek, more than a hundred miles to the south, and at a lower elevation, saw the first red-winged blackbird nearly two weeks ago.

The rumors drift slowly north.

And here, in my own marsh, two bedraggled but freshly bathed sparrows singing, shaking cold water from their wings and singing, as if completely unaware that up in the mountains, as the earth warms and awakens, the old logging roads are turning into rivers, taking millions of gallons of water straight out of the forest and funneling it, silt-laden, down into the creeks and rivers, and away: the sparrows singing instead as if governed by some mythic, merciful equation in which joy must always somehow exceed, even if only slightly, despair, so that the more there is of the latter, the more there is, or must be, also, of the former.

The willow branches become even more vibrant orange-gold, washed and birthed by come-and-go rains. Where has all this sparrow-song been, all winter? Sleeping, beneath the snow, so that the arriving sparrows have gotten here just in time to intercept it and claim it, as it emerges — or have they carried it with them, sometimes hidden, all this way?

And what of that emerging orange in the willow stems? Is not the sunlight, as it summons that orange-gold, the same thing as song?

The utter excitement — not just pleasure, but excitement — of walking across bare exposed ground, even in boots, rather than crunching through snow, after so long an absence.

Equinox: egg-balancing day. Mary Katherine and I are now officially another year older, she by but a week and me by a couple of weeks, so that each of us is still wearing that new year like a coat tried on in front of a department store mirror, with the wearer not yet sure of or accustomed to the fit.

Every year, after supper, we balance the raw egg vertically on the chopping block in the kitchen and marvel at its equipetal balance, at the magic in the world. And this year there's a perfect full moon high overhead, as well — we're anticipating that the balancing egg might rest, on this one day only, as firm as a concrete pillar.

We've been looking forward to it for days, but come the equinox this year, we forget; schoolwork, or a meeting, or Girl Scouts, or something mundane intrudes, so that the day, the ritual, the tradition, slides past unutilized this year.

We vow to remember it next year. We have in all the years past, and we will in all the years to come. This will be just a little knothole of skip or imperfection in the grain of our lives. All the solar and lunar gear works continue on, as they always have, whether we balance that kitchen egg or not. The absence of it, this year only, known only in our own lives, our own individual little patterns and paths, beneath that greater one rule, one story, one path.

In late March, the southern slopes begin to open up and you can walk around in the woods down low, moving from bare patch to bare patch. It's a pleasure to go looking for the winter-dropped antlers of deer — sheds, people call them. They gleam mahogany in the new spring light, as elegant as candelabras, and indeed, it looks as if they have been dropped, mislaid, forgotten by their owners.

It's a joy to be out walking in the woods, traversing bare ground. I love winter, and snow, but cannot help but think of the bare earth as the "real" world. Some folks go out in early spring, hunting the winter-shed antlers of the deer to sell to curio shops and so forth, but I go simply out of pleasure, and perhaps worship: to see, and touch, the echo of the secret deer that have been passing through our forest. It's hard to describe, and harder to explain, the feeling of richness one gets, spying an antler just emerged from the snow: treasure, discovered.

I think that the deer are our salmon, in the absence of salmon. They serve as the foundation for meat eaters in the valley (ourselves included), and in the transfer of nutrients; they are like fire, or floods, or the ocean tides. And there are people up here who brain tan the hides of our deer, which are prized because there are almost no barbed-wire fences up here to scratch and scour and mar their thin hides beneath the fur.

They feed us, they sustain some of the residents monetarily, and always, when we hunt them, they lead us farther into the forests, farther into the mountains, and in our pursuit of them, and our desire and longing for them, they teach us new things about the landscape. They lead us into corners and crevices where we would never otherwise go, and teach us to notice, with senses inflamed, things we might never otherwise pay attention to — the direction of a stirring of breeze, the phase of the moon, a bent blade of grass, a faint odor, a funny feeling of being observed — and because of deer, we notice these things with an intensity that is both feral and comfortable, as fluid as the passage of the days and the seasons themselves.

Their hoof tracks and droppings are almost everywhere, this other nation of beings, and when we go for a walk in the woods and something unseen thumps away from our approach, it is almost always a deer.

They are our salmon, our currency, and very nearly even our religion; and the dark forests and lush meadows they inhabit, particularly at dawn and dusk, our houses of worship. Their mountains are our cathedrals, and the rivers across which they wade our holy waters.

In March, especially, we are attentive to their emergence from winter's trials. They stand by the side of the road gaunt-ribbed and huge-eyed, too weary to run, and seemingly stunned, sometimes, that they have made it to the other side.

On the drive to school one morning, we watch the difficulty with which one certain deer leaps, sore-backed, over the snowplow's steep-banked icy berm to move away from our approach, this one deer moving like someone's ancient grandmother, and Lowry cries out, "Oh, the poor deer" — learned, already, at evaluating the movement of wild creatures, and possessing, in that glimpse, a wealth of understanding.

March twenty-seventh, a brilliant and warm day, and in a shocking piece of natural history, the kind that makes you want to shout out loud, I spy the first butterfly at marsh's edge, a vigorous orange checkerspot, its wings every bit as dazzling as the branches of the resurrecting willows, so that now there are two pieces of color in this snow-blind world, willows and butterflies: not yet a kaleidoscope, but the earliest beginnings of the carnival, the first tentative brush strokes of pandemonium.

This year, Easter falls on the next-to-last day of the month; and on the last day of the month, a Monday, on the morning drive to school, the girls and I spot a snowshoe hare, still perfectly white, sitting on bare earth, beneath the canopy of a cedar tree. He is so brilliant, the white rabbit against the black earth, and so motionless — like a statue — that it seems, somehow, that he is our Easter, he is the pure and holy unstained thing. The sight is so beautiful that we stop and stare at him; and still he does not move, as if believing himself to be hidden — as if believing his snowy coat still serves him in good stead.

And that same afternoon, out on the snowy marsh, we see his inverse — a black wolf trotting across the frozen hardpan of white — and he too trots along as if believing himself unseen.

We dash out the door with our camera, wanting to document, or somehow capture, the miracle, or what seems a miracle to us but which is really only the way the world used to be — and we skulk through the forest to marsh's edge. But the wolf scents us, or hears us, or otherwise discerns our approach, and whirls and flees; and afterward, when we go out onto the marsh, all that's left are his big tracks and nothing else.

It's proof enough for us, though. A snow white rabbit, and a coal black wolf.

The great world, with all its cast and players, resurrecting: first in black and white, but soon enough in color, and sound. It's starting slowly and powerfully, this birth, the month of my own, and tell me — I want to know — why is it that after forty-two of them, I still feel new to the world, almost as if each one is still my first?

APRIL

....

IT'S NOT A LONG WAIT. The first frog tests his voice against the fading ice and snow on the first day of April. Not until the spotted frogs dare with their bravery to cry out against the season's long tyranny (even if their courage is the bravery of their ancient chilled blood) does winter seem, finally, able to be defeated. A bully melting quickly now at the first hint of the force of a superior heart. It is not really this way at all, but when that first frog begins to call, even while the marsh remains a mix of ice and snow and milky meltwater, that is how it seems.

For all our lives we have been told about, and have accepted, the four seasons and their neat symmetry. I don't know why the fifth season, the space between winter and spring, is never named, but it is certainly as real and seemingly enduring as any or all of the others. If it needs a name beyond the time when all the snow is gone but the ground remains brown and unchanging for weeks on end, I guess we could call it just that — the brown season, or the mud season.

And it is brown. The bare limbs of all the deciduous trees remain as leafless as in the heart of winter. Only on the earnest aspens can you detect even the faintest swelling of darkened buds against winter-pale skin, and even that so insignificant as to seem each day more a swelling of one's imagination than of life stirring within the slender branches.

Stirring it is, though, for even as the ground remains resolutely, stubbornly, recalcitrantly brown, color is returning to the stems of plants, the first new color after winter's incredible abstinence. The shock of gold of the willows, and the crimson of red-osier dogwood, the limbs turning as red as blood. Again, it's hard to imagine that these slender sticks of color will act as fuses for the detonation of color that will soon be our bounty, taken for granted, but in the brown season, these little glowing red and gold sticks are enough — are more than enough.

A single glowing bluebird hurtling across the snow would be too much; we would fall over backwards, smitten. We have to start small, and slow; our bodies must ease back into a world of color, and its specific joys and enthusiasms — emerald, topaz, cobalt, oxblood, winestain, mustard, teal, cerulean, sapphire. Too much too soon and our brains would be bruised by the sudden expansion of color into a place where for so long there has been an absence.

Before the color returns — when the color is moving only slowly at first, in the stems of certain branches, like the quickening river running just beneath the milk-colored ice, or like the sludge of wine-blood deep in the veins of mud-buried reptiles and amphibians, whose blood in winter actually contains shimmerings of ice crystals — the sounds arrive first, as if those subterranean or subspring stirrings of color create, in their first subtle and unseen movements, the phenomenon of music; sound waves traveling across April, just in advance of the subsequent waves of color and light. As if sound is but a preliminary form of color.

And in the beginning, after the brute and lovely length of winter, the sounds are enough. Were the music and color to arrive simultaneously, it would be more than our frail and sensitive systems could handle, and beyond tipping us over backwards with the jetwash of such a powerful dual arrival, such simultaneity might rob some of the individual force of each of the two primal phenomena.

As it is, there is a lovely counterbalance: first one, and then the other, summoned, as if one is leading the other slightly, in some ancient and sophisticated dance.

And what we begin to hear, in April, after that first frog, is the wind-winnowing trill of snipe circling the marshes overhead, making what well might be the eeriest sound in the woods — a quavering, wailing, keening rise-and-fall tremolo that is strangely not borne from their throats, but the beautiful music of their fluttering wings as they pause in midflight and then plummet, letting their quick-beating, drumming wings and the world-specific aerodynamic shape of their perfect bodies create the sound, as might a flute player who utters short and staccato bursts across the opening of the flute: the snipe becoming the flute, with the quickening shapes of their wings opening and closing, and their headlong plummet self-generating the rush of wind that would otherwise be created by the pursed exhalations of the flutist.

What brutal confidence or desperation of heart must such a creature possess to choose such a tack while all the other birds "merely" speak to the world by perching and singing, or by hunkering down and calling with their own equally wonderful but more orthodox melodies?

The owls are calling, mostly the eloquent "Who cooks for you, who cooks for you-all?" of the barred owls, but also the dramatic double-clutch booming of the great horneds, and the much rarer trail-away bellow of the massive great gray owls. The ducks join in too after that first frog summons them — plaintive squeals of wood ducks, and classic duck-muttering gabble of mallards — as does the thunderous, tone-tingling, and soul-stirring resonance of the Canada geese, which nest in the marsh.

These are the big-bodied, hard-hitting cries and calls of the durable and able-bodied — the percussion calls, the tuning-up, that precede the clarity and precision of the waves of songbirds that will be rolling in soon behind them — but after a winter of silence in which the only sounds other than the lonely language of the stay-behind ravens were the howl of the wind and the splitting of frozen trees, these first and newly arriving sounds are all we can possibly stand right now; more than enough.

As it is, it's almost too much. It's like walking into a crowded, noisy party, with loud high-energy music playing — coming in a little late, on a cold dark night, and with the great room so warm and well lit — and there's that surging feeling that is both pleasure and alarm at the stunning and sudden energy of it, the waves of sound felt in your bones, just as later on the waves of color will reach back to the farthest recesses of your throbbing and waiting brain . . .

As if all the rules are changing, as if all boundaries are being restructured, the taut cold-cast iron-skin of the earth is turning to waves of softened, even quivering jelly. Not mud yet, just softened earth, so tremulous that when you step or jump on it heavily in one place you can see a shimmering wave of your energy pass through it, traveling on for some distance. The ground feels springy beneath you — like a trampoline.

It's a devastating time for heavy trucks to drive the backcountry roads — with their mass, they would quickly press and shape the soft and tender roads into some knotted, twisted, rutted impasse — and so there's a weight limit established during these soft days to come by which no commercial traffic can use the roads: no logging trucks, cement mixers, tractor-trailers, backhoes, or bulldozers. And, save for the hollering of the frogs and the birds, and the gusting breath of the south winds, it is a quiet and gentle time, like some kind of vacation, in which homage is paid to the very soil itself during its soft and vulnerable waking-up period.

We're all waking up. We're all cautious and careful and joyful and considerate; and best of all, there are patches of sun appearing again, brief columns and windows of it striking through the heart of gray.

The earth continues to stretch and yawn in the softening metamorphosis, the trembling that precedes the green leap of spring. The stone walls running here and there through the woods sag and sway inch by inch with each warming day, the bottom course canting slightly one way or another as the ground heaves and whispers then belches and yawns, arching its back, arching its belly, stretching and reaching and sending the smaller stones one by one up through the soft brown soil that is still between seasons, and it is another faint night sound, this dull and sporadic clattering, as if in the brown season, just at the edge of spring, even the rocks themselves are striving to be called back to life.

In the subterranean vaults and tombs of their own making, buried beneath the shallow lakes and ponds, the painted turtles, asleep like ancient cosmonauts whose vessels might have been separated from earth centuries ago and which are tumbling adrift through the void now, suspended so precariously between the inanimate and the barely animate, dormant as seeds, find themselves being strangely tilted and canted likewise, like cards in a deck that is being oh-so-slowly shuffled. The earth helps lift them, expelling them, like the upthrust risings of tilted bedrock, the turtles awakening with a dim consciousness at which we can only guess as they ride this slow, slow wave of dull warmth, hauling themselves up from the muck and torpor with the resolve of draft horses.

Salamanders too haul themselves out from beneath the rotting logs and the flat stones under which they have spent the winter, suspended as if in a dream: fire-engine red, with lightning-bolt streaks of cobalt and chartreuse, they crawl across the ice and snow in dogged bravery, as hairless and tender as any organism that ever blinked upon the earth: inching their way delicately across the snow with a force, an endurance, that I hope and believe will surely outlast our interstates and skyscrapers, and even our libraries and churches. As long as there is moisture on the earth, I hope there will always be long-toed salamanders, creeping across the snow in early April, heading from the forests back down into the vernal ponds to arrive just in time for the first opening of the water — getting an early, trudging jump on spring in order to arrive there scant days, or sometimes even hours, ahead of the whirling influx of swooping, swarming predators, snake and hawk, thrush and bear cub . . .

Still the stones in the rock wall lean and list, like the serpentine uncoiling of some new and awkward kind of life being created. Each morning a new section of wall will have collapsed so that the meadow has the look of an unruly graveyard, one with tombstones upended when the sleeping inhabitants below awakened and descended to go for one more stroll, unable even in death to say no to spring, one more springtime, in the northern mountains.

(In less than two months the grass in those fields will be knee-high or taller, wrapping around these stilled-again stones and waving in the wind like the underwater trellises of some mermaid-lover, and the stones will seem content again, as if it was only that short distance that they needed to travel — as if it was they who were on the move, not the buried dead — but that now, with one more year's rotation, all is where it needs to be, adjusted properly.)

To say what day the snow is gone, all gone, really gone, or even mostly gone — that final absence exists as much in the heart's interpretation as out on the land. There are winters when the snow never piles up very high and recedes early but are winters that nonetheless burden the heart as if the pilgrim or endurer had been locked in a lightless igloo for more than half the year; and there are also winters in which the snows pile up high in both the mountains and the

valleys, beginning before October is even halfway done and persist-
ing on into the beginning of June, and are winters that nonetheless
seem as light upon the heart of the sojourner as an easy melody, or a
wonderful piece of unexpected news.

Up in these mountains, you can always find snow if you need
to — any month of any year — but when those first bare patches of
earth begin to appear beneath the heat-trapping limbs and branches
of the trees, and when there is one day in the woods a certain flowing sound that the concertgoer has not yet heard before, all winter
long — well, it doesn't matter to me how much snow remains, as
long as I can see any patch of dampened, darkened earth, a sight so
thrilling and rare as to seem to the winter-snowed eyes and mind,
almost illicit, and as long as I can hear the music of water dripping
from the roof's icicles, and water trickling down the driveway, and
water mumbling beneath the snow.

In my light-starved, bruised-feeling, out-of-shape mind, this
one sound carries all the joy and frenetic energy of children playing
the xylophone; and I am ready, and am finally willing, most winters,
to say that winter is over and that the brown season has begun. I
will still have far to go, beyond this point, emotionally and spiritually, for this declaration to become true — after these many years, I
have learned not to lean too far forward in anticipation of spring, if
at all — but when I begin to hear all that slow, stirring music, and
when I see the first shred, the first gram of dirt, I know that rein-
forcements are on the way, that light will return to the world, and
that my usual cheery good moods, if not my soul, might yet be saved
for one more year, for the world to use in whatever way it might.

So the sound waves precede the waves of color. There is yet another
sleeper besides ourselves for whom much of winter is a mystery.
About these other sleepers, even our learned scientists are mystified; the sleepers are more a mystery than the winter itself. The
bears — both black and grizzly — will have been curled up beneath
domes of snow. The black bears crawl into a hollow log (one of
about ten thousand reasons it's more than okay to have dead trees
in the woods; not every dead tree needs to reach the sawmill to
achieve its highest purpose) or tuck in tight beneath an overhang-

ing rock, content, it seems, to simply let the snow mound up over their stilled and sleeping bodies, as if they have for that period of time taken it into their hearts to imitate the sleeping mountains themselves, with their curved motionless shapes almost identical now to the silhouettes of the mountains in which they have ceased, for now, to prowl.

The grizzlies take this metamorphosis even another step further, tunneling with their hugely powerful forelegs and immense claws into the earth itself — traveling back into the spirit world, according to some beliefs, and in this come-and-go manner are an intermediary between the "real" world and the "spirit" world; though it occurs to me also that in such stories perhaps we have it mixed up and it is that buried, dusty, stony earthen world below, and the time and land of sleep, that is the "real" and durable world, while the brighter noise in the world above is the dream, and the land of wraithy spirits and utmost brevity.

Whichever inversion holds true — sky below, earth above; spirit now or spirit later — I assume that the same thing that awakens and reinvigorates our spirits at winter's end — the bellowing, fluttering, crying, singing, trickling, whispering, shouting, murmuring, cracking, groaning of winter's end — is the same sound that pulls all the bears, like crocus bulbs, back up out of the earth.

It is one of the fundamental lessons of science that like replicates like, and one of the lessons of history is that history too is predisposed to do the same; that only with considerable effort and consciousness can the repetitions of the past possibly be avoided.

In this same manner, sound elicits sound. Sometimes, when going out to my cabin at night to work, walking without a flashlight, carrying my notebook and groping my way through this well-known forest with the other hand, I'll break the silence by cracking through the frozen crust of a shallow puddle — a wintry, surprising percussive sound, which will rouse the sleeping geese into a startled honking uproar, a symphony made all the more dramatic by both the suddenness of the sound and the total darkness in all directions.

So taut-wired is the new-waking world, so attentive to the music or summons of each small sound, that almost anything at all will set off the chorus.

The next day, napping in my wintry cabin, as I am sometimes wont to do around the noon hour, taking a brief break between fiction and nonfiction (curled up on a folding army cot next to the murmuring faint warmth of the wood stove, and covered with deer and elk hides; but after only twenty or thirty minutes I wake back up, shivering), even as faint a sound as my clearing my throat there in the cabin is enough to set off the whole chain of events again: the geese, floating out in the marsh, honking madly, and the frogs answering them with their trills and croaks immediately, as if some electrical voltage has passed through the water. The world feels huge when something like that happens, when even the tiniest gesture sets off, like falling dominoes, a series of grand gestures, the entire marsh roaring with sound simply because you have inadvertently and lightly cleared your throat ...

This tripwire tautness, the spring-world leaning forward with such intensity, attentive suddenly to every possible note of sound, reminds me of how in a previous spring, when the builder was reconstructing and relocating — resurrecting — this old cabin in which I now work marsh-side, each hammer's strike in setting the nails of the window frame, through which I now stare at the frogs' and geese's marsh, would set off a chain reaction in which the frogs began trilling immediately, shrilly, with strident answer-back, and from the frogs' chorus the geese would become engaged, hurling their stentorian rasps into the fray. The lightning-quick immediacy was astounding — as if they had been crouched waiting only for that summons, waiting only to be asked to answer back.

Is this the speed of prayer? Perhaps this simple phenomenon is indeed the easy mechanics of prayer — a one-two seesaw, built on (and fueled by) some amazing bedrock or peat-filled marsh of grace, hundreds of feet of peat, eons of peat and floating bog. Hit the hammer and the frogs and geese will call back instantly. Ask and you will receive. Dream or imagine, and it will be birthed, if in only the right landscape, and the right time.

More and more I am daring to imagine myself as an old person, replete with loving friends and family, a lifetime in the earning. A lake at dusk — or this marsh, which is a lake of sound, a lake of green grass and sedge, changing hues slightly every day of the year — and at the end of the day, lantern light, and a fine meal. An early spring like this one. Forty or fifty more springs like this one. Bats swooping out over the water or the stilled waves of the marsh grass, chasing insects just beneath and then behind the falling curtain of dusk.

When I first moved here, a neighbor, an operator of heavy equipment, helpful in all seasons, offered to dredge the big marsh, to scoop out the millennial funk, the grimy peat, and to smear the new great hollow with enough clay and mud as to allow the new gap, the new vacancy in the earth, to fill with clean, clear water, and around the thin edges of which frogs and minnows might take harbor, and in the depths of which larger fish — edible fish — might dwell.

A dock could extend some certain distance out into those blue waters, and a red or yellow boat — a small sailboat, or a canoe — might be tethered there.

Two white swans, perhaps, drifting, and, at the wilder, farther edge, a pair of loons, yodeling midsummer.

Even if I dared to so alter — reverse, invert, banish, conquer, or eradicate — any landscape, I wouldn't, and couldn't, for the marsh is my lake. I need it in every season, need to witness the slow and powerful hourly changes in sound and scent and texture and tone. I cling to, am buoyed by, the sense its spirit emanates — I am calmed always by even the *idea* of the marsh — and I explained to my neighbor that although I love lakes and their beauty and solace as well, the dredging operation would have been a lot of work and effort for nothing, for I was already content, more than content, with what I had. I knew that even if I had been so bold as to erase a small ecosystem and the communities dependent on it, I would have been bereft immediately of the certain wildness that only a marsh can provide — that excessive, seething clamor of life — and would have been immensely poorer for it.

The marsh is my lake of color, lake of scent, lake of heated and noisy breath. There is a certain mountaintop up here where I hope either my body or ashes will repose one day, but surely whatever part there is beyond body — the part of our spirits, perhaps, to which memory attaches, like a residue — will reside, to some degree, around the perimeters of, and within the heart of, this great peaceful arena of marsh, deep within the old forest. It is the place that absorbs my anxiety day after day, as it absorbs the water and sunlight in April and begins, once again, to exhale the warm and beautiful scent of not just moderate or hesitant, tentative life, but exuberant life, barely restrained, if at all.

Surely I am becoming a pagan; and not through any formal rejection or dubious reexamination of the mystery of my childhood, Christianity, but more through the evolution of some closer, crafted fit between my spirit and this landscape. So glorious does this engagement feel some days that I must confess, in the beginning I wondered if I was not being tempted somehow by the archetypal devil himself — for surely anything this pleasurable had to be sinful, even lustful, and worst of all, placing oneself, rather than any God, at the center of things.

I'm not even sure what a pagan is, exactly — perhaps I'm misusing the word — but yesterday, after I had dropped the girls off to play at a friend's house over on the back side of the valley, just across the state line in Idaho, I encountered a painted turtle crossing the gravel road, traveling from one marsh to another, and my spirits soared, both at the life-affirming tenacity of her journey, her crossing, and at this most physical manifestation that indeed the back of winter was broken; for here, exhumed once again by the warm breath of the awakening earth, was one of the most primitive vertebrates still among us.

It is not a busy road at all, but I stopped anyway and picked the turtle up. Her extraordinarily long front claws, so mindful of a grizzly's, confirmed that she was a female — the longer claws are useful in excavating a nest in which to lay the eggs — and I put her in a cardboard box to show the girls when I returned to get them.

I continued on my way, down across the giant Kootenai River and into Bonners Ferry, to run errands, and then drove back to our friend's, where all the children examined the turtle with appropriate and gratifying fascination. They learned the words *carapace* and *scute* and *plastron,* as well as a bit of the natural history of the painted turtle, but what I suspect lodged deepest in their memory was the mesmerizing hieroglyphics, or cartography, of red and orange swirls on the underside of the shell; and the image that probably went deepest into my girls' consciousness or subconscious, into the matrix of memory and formative identity — or so I hope — was the three of us stopping on the return trip home to release the turtle on the other, safe side of the road, pointed down toward the larger marsh, the direction she had been headed, despite there being still no traffic. Standing watch over her then, as she slithered her way through last autumn's dead grass, and the newly emerging green-up, toward the cattails and chilly dark waters that would receive her, and the future of her kind.

The specific tone of sky at dusk, the call of snipe circling overhead, and the shapes of these specific mountains — *these mountains* — imprint themselves, this one April, as deeply in the minds of my young daughters, along with this leisurely, almost nonchalant yet considered act, as the chemistry of each river is said to imprint itself upon the bodies of young salmon. These are the sights and scents and tastes and sounds and textures, the logic and the reason, that I hope will help form the matrix of their childhood, and their individual characters.

I'm grateful to that one turtle for the opportunity to help show them consideration. I'm grateful to the color of that sky at dusk, and to the unique and specific shape of Haystack Mountain to the north, and to the scent of the pine and fir forests early in the spring for helping form that calming matrix, as sense-filled and tangible as a bough of fir branches spread beneath one's sleeping bag on a camping trip far back into the mountains, the mythic mountains of childhood.

We stood there and watched her clamber on down into the dark waters. We don't have turtles in our marsh. Our marsh is one of several in a chain of wetlands that is perched at the edge of an upthrown fault block that parallels the valley's main river. The closest turtles are but a quarter of a mile away, down in one of the huge wetlands created by the river's high waters each spring; but there are no turtles in any of the marshes on that shelf up above the valley — the shelf on which our marsh, and several others, is perched.

Does that lower wetland not have enough turtles to encourage dispersal and migration — is that the only reason no turtles have ever traveled that four hundred yards up the mountain? (Do aquatic turtles ever wander uphill, or would this be a selective disadvantage? Wouldn't they always find more water downhill?)

Or is it that hundred-foot rise in elevation that's the limiting factor? Our springtime, up here on the shelf instead of down along the bright south-running river, arrives about a week later than on the valley floor, and our winter temperatures can typically run three to seven degrees colder on any given night. Is that the reason these marshes have no turtles while similar marshes, only four hundred yards away, downstream, have turtles?

Wouldn't you think, however, that a coyote might fetch one up here, carrying it in his jaws for a while before tiring of it and then setting it down somewhere in our dark woods? Or that an osprey, or eagle, having seized one for dinner, might accidentally drop it here, like the planting of some wild and fortuitous random seed?

For now — for whatever reason, or reasons — we are a hundred feet too high, it seems, for turtles, an elevation of thirty-three hundred feet, rather than the valley floor of thirty-two hundred. Maybe the warming earth will allow this marsh to receive them, however, in my lifetime. Or it might take a hundred years, or two hundred, beyond that, but no matter; I dare not tinker with so ancient and established a species, trying to coax it into a place it might never have been before. Perhaps this kind of reverence, respect and reverence, more than anything else, defines *pagan;* I don't know. Whatever it is, I know that I feel it strongly.

If this kind of attentiveness to and gratitude for the creation is excessive or unseemly in our species, or, worst of all, ungodly, then I apologize for having been snookered by the dark forces; but know that I will go to damnation for having been an ignorant or mistaken man rather than an evil one.

Some of my neighbors — friends — frown on the zeal, the restless tenor, of my environmentalism. They counsel me that with eternity at stake in the unending afterlife, there is little point or economy in getting so fretted up about clearcuts when our mortal time here is so temporal and the earth is but a proving ground for the far greater and lasting struggle of our souls, our eternal salvation.

And sometimes — when I'm really tired of the struggle — I want to believe them.

But someone — their god, my god, somebody's god — puts the spark and light of peace and joy and worship and awe in my heart when I stand in a cathedral of ancient cedars, or when I am far back in the distant mountains, so close to the sky and a scale of time greater than my own brief stay, and that spark tells me that for me, activism is a form of prayer, a way of paying back some small fraction of the blessing that the wilderness is to me, a way of celebrating and protecting that creation, and a way of giving thanks.

I meant to be writing about April, and somehow I've gotten all religious. I don't mean to suggest that I have any answers. In fact, I'm not even sure I could tell you what the questions are with regard to religion and those kinds of matters.

Maybe I'm being snookered. Maybe I'm not a godly man, for loving the woods so much. But in my defense, if any is needed, it's the only time I feel close to a god, or God. If I made a wrong turn somewhere, well, have pity on me. But there is nothing in this world that could ever convince me that God is to be set against the wild forest and the wilderness. That would be like trying to convince me that God is set also against another of God's creations, humankind itself.

I see no percentage in believing such a dire hypothesis, or any reason for its existence; and it is not the truth in my heart.

The next morning, driving Mary Katherine and Lowry to the two-room log cabin school they attend — one teacher and one aide for but nine students total, ranging from kindergarten through the eighth grade — the school set back in the woods, apple trees ringing the soccer field, deer standing out on the school lawn — we see the usual sights, more deer moving through the foggy forest, back and forth across the gravel road, but also a gaggle of ravens, two bald eagles — one mature, one immature — and a coyote: all within the thirteen-minute drive to school.

This is the daily braid that I want to become part of the tapestry of my daughters' childhood.

I love how the woods open up again, in April, coming back to life. I love how much there is to see and marvel at.

More sounds:
The wild geese.
The chuckling of the spring peepers.
The *beep-beep-beep* of feeding chickadees.
The sigh of south winds bathing all the bare branches, and the enduring limbs of the evergreens. The wind in April, making its quartering turns to come back up from the south and warming the snow and the soil with its return, might be the best sound of all in April, the sound that mixes with your dreams at night and gives you further authority to desire and dream and hope for all things.

Stir, bears, stir. Even with your eyes shut, asleep, see the world resurrecting. This world, the next April twelfth. The first mosquitoes, diaphanous in the fierce sunlight, emerging from the ice-rimmed ponds and puddles: Tourists, beware, go back. There is nothing to see here, only mud and insects and large biting mammals, and an unfriendly human population, astounding unemployment, chronic depression, and poverty, even among the rich, and rain and snow and sleet and wind. This is a place of the spirit, no place for the flesh, and a place of the imagination, but no place for a real life. Believe in this place, and pray for it, but turn back, do not come here . . .

Owls booming, hooting and hollering at high noon, as if even our full light is shadowy compared to the rest of the world. And back in their dark forests, perhaps it is; what does it matter, daylight or nighttime? The sounds, the awakenings, must come first, before the color, joy, and exuberance. It is the fifth season, in April, the one no one talks about. Very few places in the country — particularly in these greenhouse days — are blessed with four distinct seasons, and yet we, in our bounty, have five. The brown season, the sounds-re-turning-to-the-woods season; we do not pass from winter straight into spring any more than a child or even an adolescent enters straight into adulthood.

I want to be clear about this, how intoxicated one is as winter is leaving. Every moment seems both familiar and magical in this re-awakening. Like a wave, a wand stirring over the forest, the hoot of that midday owl rouses the geese into full honk, which bestirs then the great marshy vat of the spring peepers — the wave of life return-ing like a warm tide. You can feel it returning as if it is not many in-terlocking parts but all one vast animal; and sometimes on my walk out to my cabin I have to stop and stare slack-jawed, with a huge gaping grin, at this sheet or rolling wave, so similar to the curl of a wave of sound — invisible, but so deeply felt, stirring the heart again in its furthest places.

I stand there like a madman, or a somnolent, not budging but being swept downstream nonetheless, grinning, tumbling down-stream, vibrant waves passing all around me.

A grouse drums farther back in the old forest, and a butterfly, like a bright-colored spark or ingot midday, flutters past, soundless, with its periwinkle-satyr-blue color searing a trace into my winter-dulled and softened brain. Perhaps it is in the wandering and tiny flight of that single insect that the transition from sound to color occurs — the trace of the butterfly's erratic flight like some elec-tronic wiring, hooking the color switch back on in the deepest sleeping recesses of the mind, and in that moment, deeper nerves being touched, shorting across their synapses, awakening joy, not winter's peacefulness or steady-calmness kind of joy, but a brighter, more leaping kind of joy.

Winter was wonderful, but my God, here comes the other, here comes the *next;* and now I am fully awake and I can barely stand it. What kind of a pig would ask for forty or fifty more springtimes when even one — just one, *this one,* is so perfect, so much more won-derful than anyone could ever possibly deserve?

It is yours. All you have to do is stand at the edge of the woods and look. All you have to do is pause in your steppingstone walk, and linger and look — to wait, in that space between winter and spring. All of it is yours.

As if to produce firm evidence that the old frozen sleeping world is indeed being turned upside down, one morning a flicker chased a raven across the sky: the newly arrived, white-backed, smaller bird harassing the dark prince of winter. It's a sight you don't see every day. I stood there and watched it hungrily, like a sim-

pleton, my mouth open, until it was gone, and then still I stood
there: feeble-minded, and grateful for it, after so long a spell of feeling no-minded.

I don't mean to dress it, April, all up as being nothing but fine,
nothing but ecstasy. April is of course filled with waves of psycho-
logical treachery that will break your heart if you let them.

Sheets of snow roll in from the north, muffling all that emerging sound and blanketing completely the thrilling sights of that bare
black earth. Up, down, up, down, go your hopes and desires, your
moods and your joys. You begin plotting your next winter's vacation
in April. Next year, you tell yourself, you'll be smarter; you won't
travel to sunnier climes in January or February. You will wait all the
way until April, when the alternating pulses of sun and snow are
breaking the backs and spirits of, toying cat-and-mouse with, the
handful of valley residents who are reclusive enough, tender and
fierce and wounded enough, to live here year-round.

The excitement of seeds, in April — all the world held in the palm
of one's hand, the future of a vast forest, like a vast dream — and the
excitement of saplings, apple trees arriving as bare-root stock from
the nursery, to be planted far away from the house in a patch of sunlight, so that years hence it will be a long walk to harvest any of the
apples, and so that the bears and grouse and deer and other wild
creatures of the woods, including the worms, may avail themselves
of the feast, and may do so without having to come near, or become
accustomed to, the haunts of man.

I'll build wire enclosures around the saplings so that they'll be
protected from the hungry deer for the first several years — ten or
more? — until the trees are finally large enough to be free and clear,
and on their own.

April is when I transplant other trees too, wild stock pulled
up from the thawing gravelly terrain of roadbeds — logging roads
that are closed a few years, saplings that would be driven over by
vehicles once the gates are unlocked, as they are almost always unlocked — remaining closed for wildlife security until such point as
the timber companies decide what the wildlife needs is not security
after all but more logging, and open the roads back up . . .

I've got about two hundred acres of trees. It's kind of ridiculous to be planting more, but I can't help tinkering; I want to help return diversity to this grove of woods I'm now responsible for. (It was logged hard around 1970, with almost every tree of any market-able size back then — forty years old or older — being taken, so that most of my forest is between thirty and seventy years old, though there are also a few whoppers that were in too distant a location to fell, or that were spared because the chain saw ran out of gas, or the sawyer took a break that day and then was diverted elsewhere; I cherish those big ones, survivors by mercy . . .)

Cedar, aspen, and ponderosa or yellow pine are the rarities up here. The ponderosa, or p-pine, prefers hot, dry, south-facing slopes, of which I don't have many, but my marshy swamp of a place is well suited for the cedar and aspen.

The explosive deer herds have helped keep the cedar and aspen pruned back, however — more than pruned: there's almost an entire lost generation of aspen and cedar, harking back to the clear-cutting days of the early seventies. The clearcuts promoted the conversion of a dark forest of old growth into big fields of early successional forbs, which benefited (for a while) the deer herds, building them up into unsustainably high populations. (Soon enough, the limiting factor became not summer forbs and browse, but winter range — the shady old-growth forests that had been eradicated, leaving this abnormally high deer population shit out of luck.)

The too-high deer population wandered the valley, chewing down anything and everything — particularly the young aspen and cedar saplings. The deer herd didn't suffer any massive die-off (there weren't enough wolves in the valley to prune them back) until the harsh winter of 1996; and as a result, there's about a twenty-five-to-thirty-year echo, a gap, a missing generation, of aspen and cedar, from the Long Time of the Deer: an indirect echo of all our clear cutting, and the absence of wolves.

So I'm putting wire cages around cedar and aspen saplings, try-ing to bring them back into my forest, at least, if not the whole mil-lion acres, as if blowing on the kindling-spark of a campfire, trying to resurrect flame.

For a while I toyed with the idea of doing something funky and artistic: of designing, in an open area next to an existing grove of mature aspen — remnant survivors of the days before clearcuts, and the days before the too-large deer herds — a corral, a wire enclosure, in the shape of a pack of five or six running wolves.

My theory was that young aspens would safely propagate in this wolfine enclosure, free from the ceaselessly grinding jaws of marauding deer. A dense colony of young aspen shoots would leap up in this enclosure (as they leap up in open fields every year, only to be clipped back by the deer's teeth, every last sucker shoot being clipped back).

In the safety of the wolf-shaped enclosure, however, the aspen would prosper. All they really needed was a three- or four- or five-year head start, to grow tall enough — in leaps and bounds — to be above the height of the deer's teeth, even when the deer stood on their hind legs and endeavored to stretch out their necks like giraffes; four or five years was all the aspen needed to grow tall enough to be safe.

Not coincidentally (there is no machine of man, no intricate feat of engineering nearly so marvelous as even the most basic and simple designs and intricacies of wild nature), the deer herds themselves generally require only three or four years to rebound in numbers adequate to prune sufficiently the aspen suckers that have, in the deer herds' absence, made their break for the sky.

I can't help but be struck how much like a symphony it is. Even when there is no sound issuing forth, there is the rise and fall of measures, sequences of three-four deer time laid over cadences of four-five aspen time. Some trees squeak through that gap, by luck or chance or design, and live to grow beyond the teeth of the hungry deer, given half a chance, given any break at all — leaping for the sunlight, dodging and weaving and hoping each day in that one year of critical overlap to evade the relentless hunger of the recovering deer.

Sixty or eighty years later, the pleasing dry rattle of golden aspen leaves high overhead in a cold October wind beneath incomparable blue sky will be like a tympanic prefatory for the next century, the great score playing itself over and over again with only the subtle variations differentiating one aspen grove from the next — on one hillside in this century, wandering slowly over to the adjacent hillside, in a slightly different pattern, in the next, like a slow-curling wave far out at sea — and with no shore in sight, only curl after curl of gold aspen wandering across the mountains, herded and shaped by the deer: as if the deer, not man, were some kind of god of creation.

But those aspen will also still retain the indomitable refrain from the last score: the echo of color and leaf-rattle again a kind of music that sings of how those sixty- to eighty-year-old towering aspen eluded, if not outwitted, brute fate and hunger — a music, an echo, that speaks to once-upon-a-time hard times, and spindly saplings, and knock-kneed, starving deer wandering the snowy, barren woods, and ferocious, ravening lions stalking silent and big-footed those starving, wandering deer, and overhead no brilliant blue sky amid gold leaf-flutter but instead the purple and gunmetal flat slatiness of January, February, with huge coal black ravens winging through the dense firs and spruce and calling out like sentinels the occasional details of the slow, slow dramatic progression ongoing below . . .

Consider again, please, the notion of sight, odor, taste, and touch as a kind of music: as all lesser complements to this astounding movement of April. It is like nothing if not a symphony out there, certain notes falling in order that others may rise. In the life cycle of the lodgepole pine — a species not much longer-lived than our own — the trees tend to outgrow their shallow root system in their quick race for the sun somewhere between the age of eighty and one hundred twenty years, entire stands of lodgepole being susceptible to insects at that point and blowing over during some fierce windstorm, after which the lodgepole will then rot, re-enriching the soil, or burn, likewise enriching the soil (and in the heat of the fire, the lodgepole cones scattered about the forest floor are mechanically activated to release, in their destruction, the seeds for their renewal; lodgepole cones have evolved to require intense heat to release their tight-gripped seeds).

It is often the supportive nature of the entire forest, and in particular, the other surrounding lodgepoles, that helps keep the individual lodgepole aloft, more than any tenacious root system. More than a hundred feet tall, skinny and limber, in high winds, they sway and bend into nearly U-shaped arcs, these tremendously tall trees bending like nothing more than tall grass in the wind, bending but rarely snapping, each unable to withstand the force of the storm by itself, but resistant and successful as a group, blocking and diffusing the fierce winds, just barely.

Once a lodgepole or two tip over, however, that group dynamic is quickly lost. Sometimes a fast-growing spruce or cedar will leap into the new vacancy and grow tall enough, quickly enough, to help plug sufficiently the gap of that sudden aerodynamic flaw or failing, but more commonly the entire aging stand will begin to fall apart once the initial tunnel of wind and light has found its way into the aging lodgepole forest; and in the next storm, five or six or ten or twelve more lodgepoles might lose their hold on the thin soil, and in the storm after that, twenty or forty, and in the storm beyond that one — the stand falling like dominoes now — seventy or a hundred, or the whole shittaree, the end of one story concurrent now with the beginning of another . . .

Waste, waste, the timber man thinks at night as the windstorm howls and the lodgepoles snap and topple, filling the forest the next sunlit day with the sweet scent of their broken boughs.

But the grid-worked ladder-sticking of those fallen long pines provides, overnight and magically, like dice thrown by God's hand, or, who can say, some other master plan designed and executed, a sudden system of fences, corrals, and walls that will protect the next wave of emerging aspen and cedar that find root within the center of that tangled maw of spilled logs, a chaos, or seeming chaos, too dense and gnarly for even the hungriest deer to travel into, to reach the aspen's and cedar's tender shoots. And in that manner, the collapse of the old lodgepole forest, and the setting of boundaries in its collapse, provide, in that abstinence, the very thing the deer herds need to survive — the protective canopy of mature cedar in winter, when the weakened deer need shelter from the deep snow and bitter cold, and the green leaves of aspen, when the summer's fawns are first learning to be yearlings, and hungry for the world.

By the time the grid of blowdown has crumbled to ferny rot, as happens soon up here in this Pacific Northwest jungle, the aspen and cedar have ascended to a height well beyond the reach of the deer's teeth . . .

Everywhere you look, in April, you see music, and movement;

and after such a long white stillness, even infinitesimal movement is noticeable, and praiseworthy confirmation of life's astounding grand design.

In the midst of such seemingly languorous, extravagant leisure-liness — the glory of spring unfolding, leaf by leaf, with each day edging slowly but steadily back toward a return to the world of color — I must nonetheless confess to a certain edginess, that in the midst of such leisure, there is no leisure; that in the midst of such eternal grace, there is now, both suddenly and cumulatively, a jarring dissonance.

There are days in this narrative when I have to work to keep my head down and believe in, and marvel at, the timelessness of this dream that is my life, and work to block out the creeping suspicion, if not the knowledge, that these days, these seasons, and all days, all seasons, are now changing so rapidly as to render obsolete even the most mundane observations of natural history even before the ink is dry upon the page.

Out of this awareness I'm trying hard to focus on the nonhuman flora and fauna of this relatively unpeopled valley, seeking to chronicle, for the most part, the nonhuman parts of this natural world. Certainly there are fascinating tales to tell — personal histories in the cracks and crevices of this landscape every bit as symphonic and dramatic as the rise and fall by the seasons. But the majority of the handful of residents here (there are perhaps 150 of us living year-round in the half-million acres that compose the upper part of the valley) have not been here for very long; as a resident of twenty years, it's surprising to suddenly realize, one day, that I've been here longer than most in the valley. Almost everyone here, with the exception of three or four families, came here from somewhere else, and even the most ancient of residents have not been here more than the short sum of the days of their lives, and neither their families here for yet a full century, so that again in that regard we are all newcomers, still awkward in this land and seeking our fit, our accommodations and graces within it, whereas the intricately fitted connections of one-day-to-the-next and the sophisticated, sinuous, elegant negotiations that the other resident flora and fauna have struck with the variables of temperature, nutrients, light,

moisture, and each other are a music that frankly I find more interesting, over the long run. Their lessons of patience, endurance, re-
siliency, and tolerance comfort me by observation, if not practice.

It is the landscape, at a single point in time, that I wish to "capture" in this narrative, to celebrate, in so doing, the order and meaning that exist in the turn of every elegant gear and cog.

Yet again, despite my desire for leisure in such observations, it
is too easy now to witness how quickly things are changing, from an
ecological perspective. Often I realize that I want to lay down on
paper, at the very least, for the future, what it is like at this splendid
point in time, tucked away back in one of the last corners of wild
green health, up on the Canadian line, hiding out still beneath the
echo of the last century, before it all quite possibly begins to fall
apart — this blessing, this bounty, to which I and others are so un-
deservedly privy.

The old-timers here say that even twenty and thirty years ago it
was even more wonderful. Some of them damn the Republicans,
who have prevented for thirty-plus years and counting, any of it,
not even one tree, from ever being protected. They say you should
have seen it then. They say . . .

Every morning when I awaken, particularly in the first beginnings of spring, when birdsong starts to fill the day, it is all so new
and wonderful to me, even after twenty years, that I sometimes
have trouble envisioning anything that could possibly be more idyl-
lic than the present moment, despite my foreknowledge of both its
evanescence and imperilment, and the cautions of all old-timers
everywhere who croon their same refrain about the good old days.

Perhaps these observations too, then, are, in addition to a celebration, a way of trying to reassure myself that this patient, resilient, enduring system of fitted green grace will be able to survive almost anything we can throw at it, ranging from mild inattentiveness
to blatant disrespect, all the way to indefatigable governmental fear
and mean-spiritedness.

Only time, of course, will tell, as it always does, as it always has.

It has spoken to the buffalo, the condor, the red wolf, and the
jaguar, in this country. It has admonished the passenger pigeon, the
ivory-billed woodpecker, the prairie chicken, the woodland cari-

bou, and the desert pupfish. It is speaking harshly to the lynx and the wolverine, is summoning with death-rattling whispers the sturgeon and the bull trout, the grizzly and the golden-cheeked warbler, the cave salamander and the desert tortoise, the black-footed ferret and the ocelot . . .

Forgive me, future readers, for my being alive at such a glorious moment. I promise that if I cannot help protect such wild places — though I will try — I will at least try to take full pleasure in the bright-burning, beautiful wick of them . . .

The theory of my little plan, my little idea for an enclosure in the shape of a pack of wolves — or rather, an enclosure in the shape of running wolves, keeping the deer out on one side of the fence — would have resulted in a colony of fluttering aspen out in the middle of the meadow some four to five years after I'd staked the wire out; and to someone flying overhead, or to the eye of a raven, the meadow could have been cause for a second look.

In my theory, the shape of each wolf would have been precise, as sharp-edged as the dream of the artist, with the deer herd's ceaseless gnawings and nibblings all the way up to the edge of the wire trimming perfectly the outline of the thing that was absent; as if the very deprivation of the thing summons first the idea of the thing-not-visible, which then, under some chorophyllous or otherwise miraculous exchange, ignites into the physical, tangible presence of that dreamed thing.

The wire can be removed — rolled up and placed in the garage, or unscrolled elsewhere.

Now — in the theory — there is a mature grove of fluttering aspen, their leaves making a specific and ancient kind of music.

Where there are aspen, there will always be deer.

Perhaps a wolf, or wolves, over in Canada, will hear that distant music, or take in that sweet and specific scent, and put it into their minds, to muse on.

Where there are deer, there can be wolves.

In October the leaves will turn dry and gold, and in the wind they will make a louder rattling, and in their maturing decay, a stronger, and more pleasing, pungent scent; and the adolescent wolves of that spring and summer's pack, seeking to disperse and expand their territory, will remember that first new sound and scent of April and will begin to move in that direction.

By January, perhaps, when the snow is belly-deep on the struggling deer, and the colony of aspen stands leafless and silent, the whitened trunks almost invisible against the new-fallen snow — the outline of the aspen-shaped wolf pack seeming to disappear, in that manner — the final act of the synthesis, the dream's exchange, will occur, as the first traveling wolves, drifting down from Canada, filter into the aspens, passing among the young-standing trees.

Moving silently, searching for what has been promised to them, and the thing — the dream — that has summoned them. Eyes as bright as green aspen leaves.

In the end, I did not have the nerve for the dream, was made uncomfortable by the heavy-handed showmanship, the grand, manipulative, all-knowing arrogance of it. I will roar my opinions in a public meeting to fellow mankind when I feel the wild woods are threatened, but in the face of the forests themselves, and on those windy mountaintops, I am a voiceless, speechless supplicant, a silent novitiate. It was a reluctance not at all unlike that of my unwillingness to transport even a single painted turtle into my beloved marsh.

I love aspen, I love wolves — I love deer. And I have begun making little enclosures to protect the aspen from the deer — to protect the aspen *for* the deer, and the grouse, and the other wild creatures that utilize them. (Even as later in the fall, elsewhere in the forest, I will hunt, and kill, and eat those creatures. Playing God, I know. Does God, in a manner of speaking, eat or consume us — our spirits — and in so doing keep alive some essence of God? Who knows?)

The wolf shape idea was just too disrespectful, too cocky, too knowing and all-sure. It was not appropriately awestruck. The page — art, and storytelling — is the place for such manipulations and hubris, not on the canvas of the landscape itself, which is surely already someone else's creation, of which we are to be the curators and would-be imitators, but not, surely, the Grand Revisers.

I think that little by little we may be inching closer here to a workable and accurate definition of *pagan*.

In the end, of course, my abstention or completion of a dream is of no real consequence to the world — only to the self, and sometimes to a handful of others. Again and again we confuse ourselves as individuals as beings of significance. What I was dreaming, with one roll of hog wire — a mere dream, as vaporous as a single breath of lung smoke in the bright sunlight on a frigid day — nature accomplishes on any given mountain in a single windy evening, with one great stroke of a brush, or in the entire state, the entire intermountain West and Pacific Northwest, in a single season, with a huge winter-kill deer die-off, in which a steadily increasing imbalance (too many deer gorging on an excess of summer browse, but with not enough of the thermal protection they need in winter, the closed canopy of the old-growth forest) finally tips all the way over.

Roughly eighty percent of the deer herd vanishes. "Pruned back" is too delicate a term. It is rank starvation, overkill, decimation, carnage; and of those deer that do not starve but manage somehow to struggle through the long winter, many die anyway, in an especially cruel twist, when, after having endured the magnificently brutal winter, they founder on spring's first green-up: eating too much green vegetation too quickly after having lost the digestive bacteria and enzymes in their stomachs during the winter of starvation, and then gorging on the extraordinarily warm and sudden appearance of green spring.

Their whitened bones, pecked at by hawks and eagles and ravens, with scraps of mummified hide still drawn taut across them, lie scattered in the forest everywhere, like latticed fences knocked askew by some unruly and unreasonable wind. Violets and lady's slipper orchids grow up between the elegantly curved tangle of ribs, safely distanced from the reach of the rabbits, which will find easier plants to nibble elsewhere.

After sixty or more years of oppression, every aspen colony in a five-state region — tens of thousands of square miles, or a forest the size of all of France — is given a second chance at life, another breath.

The young aspen shoots and suckers that have been clipped back year after year, failing relentlessly, are now — as if a wand of grace has been waved over them — free to leap toward the sky unhindered, or at least with a two- to three-year head start, before the deer herds begin to rebuild; and the aspen are free to grow not into the man-dreamed shape of a wolf, or wolves, but into whatever shape is negotiated between the wandering underground nation of their roots and the sunlight and the seasons and the shape and substance of the landscape itself.

When you look at a mountainside of blazing yellow aspen in the autumn, even when it does not appear to be in the outlined shape of a wolf, it is in the shape of a wolf.

How April awakens in us, again and again, the busy hands and hearts of our industrious essence. Spring-cleaning is both metaphor and reality, and though in this valley it is still too early to begin the outdoor garden, the hard-core earth-turners among us are starting their seedlings indoors, in egg-carton dollops of earth perched on windowsills; and those first tiny tendrils, ribbons of green, are nurtured like the true miracles they are while we wait for the soil to warm. Elizabeth is the gardener in our family; my crop tends more to the wild, and in April, as soon as the snow is gone and the black bare earth has reappeared, I will be out in the woods, planting the hawthorn and cedar saplings, and I am not even one fraction of one speck of pigment in the huge brush that sweeps across this landscape in each and every season, but it pleases me to be planting a seed or a sapling here and there, in this swash of light or that one — giving a nudge to the things I love and believe in, here and there. It pleases me too to dream of the future: of my daughters being old women and walking among what will then be an old forest of big trees, and placing their hands on the trunk of a big aspen, or a middle-size cedar, and remembering, or knowing, that in a long-ago April, at dusk in the drizzling rain, I moved through the woods digging and planting, deeply pleased with the rank smell of life returning to the forest.

It pleases me too to think of the pileated woodpeckers, martens, and great gray owls of the future, who will neither know of nor care for me, benefiting from the existence of those certain types of trees, in a few certain places around the marsh; and if that is the size of our paintbrush, or the amount of paint we have with which to work — the sunlight on one day in one season on the fur of a single marten perched on the limb of an eighty-year-old cedar tree, far out into the future, at the edge of the one and only marsh; the marten on that one specific day looking out across the valley to the unchanging curve of Lost Horse Mountain — well, it is an honor to possess even that amount of paint, or even that tiny of a brush, or a dream, and it is with pleasure that I use it.

What fuels a man's or a woman's dreams? Does a paucity of bounty and heartsong summon the dissatisfied dreamer, seeking to make things better, or is it the excess of these things, the unchecked extravagance, that nurtures further the dreams of betterment, if not immensity?

At what point does one release a dream — at what point, if any, *should* one release a dream — and savor, perhaps, more fully the undeserved sweetness of the moment? I am fascinated by the accounts of Thomas Jefferson, who, even as an old man in his eighties, labored lovingly in his gardens at Monticello, seeking (and sometimes, briefly, succeeding) to control with astonishing ferocity (and the help of numerous slaves) the immediate landscape around him — the arrangement of his flower gardens, and the yield of his vegetable gardens, and the geometry of terrace and hedge — but who could not control the growth of trees. He could not make the willows arch and weep across the flagstone walkway down to the family cemetery (the slope was too dry and rocky), and late in life he lamented, "If I had but one wish remaining to me it would be to live long enough to be able to one day see the gigantic girth of those tiny saplings I planted as an old man."

Neither could he grow the vintner's fine grapes from France in that tight red clay, or find permanent or even subsurface water anywhere atop the mountain where he had built, or control the comings and goings of the wild or even semiwild animals within that realm.

He is said to have owned a pet elk, with which he hoped to

impress upon his European visitors the symbol of America as a wild and unfulfilled nation. It was Mr. Jefferson's hope — his longing — that this magnificent bull would remain wraithlike, frequenting that gloomy, dusky band of property just beyond the manicured lawn's edge and the rank woods' beginning, just beneath the crest or knob of the hill, so that in the evenings, the European guests who might be taking an afternoon stroll with Mr. Jefferson, smoking a pipe or cigar and sipping brandy, might have the privilege of glimpsing, from the corner of their eyes, that blue dusky shape of the immense stag, lingering in that quintessentially American no man's land between sophisticated, urbane domesticity and the unfettered dark wilderness.

That was the hope, the plan. Upon this dream too, however, Mr. Jefferson was unable to instill perfect order. The elk seemed on most occasions loath to occupy that strange and perfect place between the two lands, in that suspended blue-tinted pipe-fog dreamspace, and was instead forever galloping wildly off, farther down into the forest, full of wild musk and terror, or was venturing farther up onto the green and manicured lawns, as if lulled by the rampant civilization all around — the orchestra music wafting through the open window, the scented roses by the fountain — grazing his way placidly across the lawn, all the way through the apple orchard, as tame, suddenly, as a child's pet; wandering all the way up to the pulpy, cidery scent of fresh-chewed apples and bedding down for the night there on the flagstone porch, so that the lesson always failed and the European visitors were never quite sure of the message, whether America was a dark and wildly impenetrable, gloaming place, or a sister state, manicured and controllable, even biddable ...

Never, it seemed, could Mr. Jefferson — with the actions of that one elk, in each evening's dimming blue light — capture the ethos of his country.

Now, of course, there is little but croquet lawns and opera music. Or rather, strip malls and highways. Those few rank elk remaining — not the betamed ones but the wild runners, the ones who prefer, time and again, to bail off over the edge and into the darkness, the wildness, beyond, out of sight in a second, two seconds — those wild ones, and the dwindling wild stock they represent, find themselves confined to ever-smaller and smaller gardens of diminishing wilderness.

Wilderness: the last places, the very last shreds of places, where we have not yet put roads, or dams, or mines, or clearcuts. The tiniest, farthest corners of places now, not so much like any wild essence that remains in us — for surely each generation, for better or worse, has been getting successively tamer and softer — but rather like the shadows thrown by the essence of that wildness that was once in us but that now exists in us as more of an echo or a vacancy than the thing itself.

Wilderness. I live in full sight of it, but still a pace or two from it, at the very edge of it, in some green land that, while not in the heart of the wilderness, is nowhere near the heart of any town or village either. Perhaps this is why I identify so closely with Mr. Jefferson's elk: that great antlered creature of the blue gloaming. I think for many of us — for far too many than will ever have the privilege of knowing — there is a deep and instinctual affinity for this place at the edge of things: the edge of the wilderness, and the edge of Montana, the edge of Idaho; the edge of the United States, and the edge of Canada. The edge of the northern Rockies, and the edge of the Pacific Northwest. It is this balance, this high point between two places, that causes us in part to so revere the turn of solstice and equinox.

And I feel like we have more than a world's-full supply of cities, towns, and villages, and far too few cores of deep or true wilderness: the places in the Lower Forty-eight where you can still disappear to the world, even as in your heart you are finding things. The quiet places, reachable only through physical hardship, or perhaps not at all. For the most part, the glorious haunts of the young.

We have plenty of country left in which to be old, too damn much of it already, paved and wired and cable-ready.

We — the old, and the becoming-old — have already taken too much of it, have eaten far more than our fair share.

The Canada geese are the first ones back, preceding by a few to several days the arrival of the ducks. It's about as spiritual a moment as the year possesses, when we hear that first solitary and joyous honking, the first incoming, the first returnee — it is as rare as anything else in and of the year. There can, after all, be but one and only one first wild goose call of each year — and it usually comes at dusk.

Even though we will have been waiting and watching and listening, it always catches us by surprise. I think that the goose (I do not know if it is the same one, year after year) flies first above the tops of the trees, flying silently, flying north toward the river — and whether it is an old familiar traveler, which cries out his or her joy upon first sighting the marsh, or a newcomer, which, intent perhaps on the more northerly and open river, or Canada beyond, happens accidentally upon the marsh, a clearing, a perfect circle, appearing suddenly below him or her in this otherwise dense forest, the goose cries out his or her joy and surprise both at that sudden revelation.

Either way, that first wild call comes from a dusk bird appearing silently and seemingly from out of nowhere, the stentorian bray unleashing itself right over the roof of the house, or the front porch, with no earlier, more distant pronouncements; and by the time we run outside, or to the windows, the goose is circling, seeming to us, after so long an absence, as large as a small plane, banking and wheeling. And perhaps that is when spring begins, when the first goose first splashes down into the thawing marsh, landing so perfectly into the place that lies between the end of winter and the beginning of spring that there are only channels of open water in the marsh; the bulk of it is still milky-colored, aerated chunks of sunlit ice, a frigid soup of discolored ice and glistening open water.

Standing on the front porch, we can hear it all: the splash the goose's outstretched blackened feet make upon landing; the sloshing of the waves from that heavy arrival, lapping over the marsh ice — *wake up, marsh* — and best of all, in the failing light of a dead and dying winter, a winter that is sinking back down into the earth to sleep for another six months or so, the calmer, contented, muted clucks and mutterings of that first-arriving goose, in the vanishing blue light, as he or she returns home yet again; and I believe, parochial bias aside, we are justified in using any animal's northerly range as the definition of home, at least as much as its southerly range.

The Gulf Coast rice fields or even farther south might be where the great creature winters, or vacations; but it is in the north country, and on marshes and bogs such as these, where the animal goes about the serious work of raising its young.

For several days, the goose will paddle the open channels like an ice breaker, laying claim not just to the opening marsh but to the new season itself. Other geese will be drawn in to that bowl of light. The marsh is caught in a delicate balance between frost and thaw. Nights are frigid — the marsh freezes back up with a skim of ice that glints in the moonlight — but each day's sunlight opens it back up, as does the leisurely wandering goose, paddling back and forth, singing.

Other geese arrive, drawn by the first one, and the marsh opens a little more. It is the stretch of the season doing it, far more than the ice-breaking channels made by the swimming geese; but several days later, when the faster, smaller ducks come hurrying in, that is the impression one gets, that the geese have, like snowplows, opened the lanes up sufficiently for those smaller ducks — mallards, mostly, though also goldeneyes and wood ducks — and it is an impression that is heightened by the way the newly arriving ducks often seem to seek out the larger geese and hang out in their company. Whether they do this for protection or companionship, or merely coincidental shared preference for similar microhabitats, I cannot say, though in all my years of marsh watching I have never once seen a single goose or mated pair of geese display even the faintest degree of aggression toward any duck, or ducks, that floated among them.

Perhaps there is some utterly boring and fully explicable scientific reason of selective advantage for this to be so — the geese and ducks existing side by side as matter-of-factly as cattle egrets and cattle — but such a thought generally arises only when considering the mystery as written on paper or in the abstract; for each morning when I walk down to the cabin and first come in sight of the marsh's opening and see the immense and graceful geese sitting serene and gigantic on the open water, and the smaller ducks — tiny in comparison, hunched up next to and amid them — the first and only feeling and impression I get is one of an overwhelming, even holy, calmness. And in those first mornings, I believe my instincts, every time; I believe what the world is telling me — that the geese and ducks *are* calm, and are made calmer by each other's company and, if I may dare say it, each other's beauty, and the beauty of the morning, and the season — and that no other reason is needed.

I stop along the wooded path and stare out at them, mesmerized by the returning of life to the marsh after so long an absence; and they stare back at me, through the forest, and quack quietly and mutter — sometimes one of the geese will announce himself or herself with a single frosty-morning bray, but beyond that, nothing but beauty, and reverence among all of us — I can feel this — for the sacred space of the marsh and the beginning of the season of life.

Everywhere, early in the morning like that, the woods are dense with the humility of living things who have made it through another winter, and who have been vested yet again with the privilege of life.

As soon as the snow is gone, it returns. With maddening duplicity, it comes and goes. The black earth ovals that have been slowly opening up beneath each tree's canopy, encircling each tree's trunk — sometimes you've been waiting six months to see those ovals — disappear again in a single evening, while you sleep; in an hour's time, or less, being covered again by the silence of falling snow.

It's a deception, of course — it is generally but a mild, wet snow that blankets the woods, and whether with an inch or a foot, it is temporal. The earth's skin is warming beneath the increased light of the longer days, and the snow will be shed like an overcoat, the river sound of trickling, gurgling, running water singing all throughout the woods as the soil temps rise; within days, the same patches will reappear, as if their previous sudden disappearance beneath the returning snow was but a tasteless magic trick, a joke or a prank. But even in the full knowledge of this, it's hard to take, for a species as visual as we are. It doesn't matter that some deep and logical part of you knows that this is really no setback whatsoever — the visual part of you thinks, *Ah, fuck, it looks like* January *again.*

Occasionally — about once a day — I think for a few fleeting moments about how the earth is getting warmer, and of the changes that will be wrought by the heaviness of our hands and the astounding hunger of our desires. I think of how the stomata of plant cells might have evolved to open and close, with regard to conservation of cell moisture, in a system with median high temperatures of, say, ninety-five degrees.

But now, in the course of not even one reproductive cycle, the trees are being asked to recalibrate evolutionarily for temperature increases of ten and fifteen percent beyond their accustomed redline max — and I will consider the toll that such stresses will place on all manner of vegetation, year after year, and the cumulative debilitation. The forests growing weaker and weaker, ever less resistant to the necessary cycles of fire and insect epidemics, which will endeavor to purge and cleanse the weak forests.

Only the oldest, most stable and diverse forests, I fear, will have enough buffer to remain intact and healthy and functioning; all else will crumble, I fear, and will one day be overtaken by weeds and other exotic species, with the resilient cant or balance of ecologic grace tipped finally one inch, or one degree, too far one way or another past the point of its forgiving fulcrum.

Sometimes I feel like asking the future to forgive me for seeming — and acting — so cavalier, even when I have before me the full evidence of impending massive change and probably even catastrophe.

There is some animal part far inside me that is made deeply uncomfortable, agitated, by the realization of the present trends, and all the data and variables available to both scientists and laypeople — the world, heavy beneath the weight of our hunger, is tipping over on its side, if not turning upside down — but ever and again, we are almost always primarily a visual species; and mercifully, thankfully, for us, if not the coming generations, we are able to take thin solace in the view of astounding and overwhelming beauty always before us — a green meadow, a child's laugh, the austerity of a glacier, the elegance of a cow moose, or a fawn, or the intricate probing of a red-shafted flicker searching a rotting log for the chattering sawyer beetles within — so that almost always we are able to put away what Wendell Berry has called the grief of foreknowledge and instead concentrate on the matter at hand, which is living.

About once every two or three days, I'll think about the long list of the departed and the even longer list of the quickly departing. As if unable to help myself, I'll consider, as I give thanks for my many blessings (marveling at the sight of a bull moose, or a wood duck, or the emerald head of a mallard duck; and at the taste of the bounty of my meals: aged elk backstrap, duck and dove, wild mushrooms, wild trout, grouse and pheasant and huckleberry syrup), and the tastes I do not know: wild buffalo, for one, with wild salmon on the iffy shortlist. I'll muse on the astounding difference in taste between the domestic and the wild — the domestic replacing insidiously with its blandness the absence of a thing with a specific taste and ferocity many of us will never know, and which no prose can capture, or any other manner of archive, for the taste of the wild ones is not merely a matter of reproducing them in laboratories or stockyards or game farms but rather is surely also a function of the lifelong relationship between that species and its wild landscape — the latter making the individual animal not just taste a certain way but look a certain way.

And my un-remembered litany of the lost is not limited solely to the selfish tastes of the palate, not just the passenger pigeon and heath hen, but the ivory-billed woodpecker and great auk, the Carolina parakeet. Too much of a portion of my life is spent in tense anticipation of what else might soon be lost, with the numbers of so many species down to single- or double-digit populations. We're not only the richest nation but the richest the world has ever known or dreamed of. I often wonder, gazing at the gaudy, glittering shopping avenues of the big cities, if these were not somehow the gilded streets of heaven bespoken in prophecies — we are so blessed, even as we stand side by side with the damned, the evil, the impoverished, and the anguished — and yet we seem unable to keep a Florida panther or black-footed ferret alive in the green world; unable to protect adequately the grizzly bear, the cerulean warbler, the lynx, the wolverine, the golden-cheeked warbler, the bull trout, the woodland caribou, the horned toad, the westslope cutthroat trout, the desert pupfish, the steelhead, the inland redband trout, the spotted owl, the Coeur d'Alene salamander, the leopard frog, the marbled murrelet . . .

I could go on for dozens of pages — ripping out dozens of pages, rather, from the real book of life, which consists not of any momentary assemblages of genomes but rather the interaction between those genomic organisms and the landscapes they inhabit, the rocks and ice and forests and shafts of sunlight and shadow in that regard every bit as living, and organic, as the genome-creatures themselves.

The trouble with noticing loss — was it Leopold who said that "to possess an ecological understanding is to know that we live in a world of wounds"? — is that it can lead to a pattern or habit or trend for such observations: like unfolding upon like, as a sheet of sand or other sediment being deposited over the shape of a sleeping landform can take on the same shape as that of the thing it is burying.

In noticing the yearly encroachment of non-native weeds, useless to the native inhabitants such as elk that have evolved by placing their bets on sweet grass and specific forbs — ceanothus, wild rose, bearberry, and aspen — the eye becomes trained to notice further unraveling of the puzzle: the orange hawkweed displacing the honey-scented fields of royal lupine, and the march of knapweed burning up the meadows in a manner far worse than the most hellacious wildfire . . .

Art and music help, as does poetry and literature — they retrain the eyes in the paths of beauty — as does time spent with children, and good times spent with friends or family. But still, the trained or knowing eye in this day and age cannot help but take notice daily of the diminishment of the crafted or specialized things; and it is difficult, more difficult than it has ever been, I suspect, to sit at a picnic table beneath a bower of alder and listen to the song of a returning Townsend's warbler, and to marvel at the butter-yellow and coal-streak markings of plumage — the astounding, extravagant beauty of such a tiny bird — without wondering, even if only idly or casually, whether such an amazing animal, such a treat for the eyes and the ears, is not somehow scheduled to depart not even over the course of the next century but before the end of one's own days.

You know not to dwell on such thoughts. You know to lean with the wind rather than into it, to hold your winter-pale arms up to the mild, weak sun when it returns, and to close your eyes and turn your face up to that amazing light. You know to remember how tiny you are, and to remember that your own selfish desires — whether we retain the yellow warblers, or not — are really of no more significance than an individual snowflake, a snowflake in mid-April that will be melting before day's end, anyway . . .

But you love them, the warblers, and all else, so fiercely. Your fierceness exceeds your tininess; your passion is in no way commensurate with your overwhelming insignificance in the world.

Is this the way for all things?

I keep trying to figure out how to describe the relief and delight I have when everything that has left for winter returns to the valley. It is better than having a party, and watching as the guests, your friends, come streaming in. It is better than going to someone else's party, and stepping inside to visit with your friends. The feeling has more to do with primal resurrection, and birth, and if you have been fortunate to be in attendance at the actual physical birth of something — a loved one, perhaps — well, it approaches the company of that feeling.

It is not quite as direct as that, but it is in the same neighborhood. Not like the birth of your own children, or even your brother's or sister's, for the blood of the geese and the snipe, and of the bears hauling themselves up out of the earth, is not entirely your blood — it is similar, but it is not quite yours, and neither is yours quite theirs — but rather, it is more like when the young couple down the road a ways has their first child, another addition to the community, and you wander down there at the end of that first week to check in on the new baby — to welcome it, and to be welcomed by it.

Or maybe it is as if you have forgotten, in spring and summer's absence, how much life there is in the world, and are only now reminded, for the forty-second time in your life. Perhaps it is like being a middle-aged or even old person who's been trundling along all his or her life and who suddenly discovers not many new friends, and great ones, late in life, but who reacquaints himself or herself with a good number of those whose full depths of their friendship he or she had never quite understood or realized; but now, with the melting of the snow, he or she can see and know it more clearly.

As if the man or woman had been sleeping for a long time beneath some substantial, even tremendous, amount of snow.

The rock walls along our driveway, and meandering along the edge of the lawn, continue to stir in the night, as well as in the warming light of day, as the jelly-mire soil grows ever warmer, looser, muddier, sloppier. They clack over on one another seemingly apropos of nothing, a sound as if some ghost is piddling with the keys on some crude and gigantic piano; or as if even the rock wall is coming to life, such is life's pull and summons, in April.

The wall is serpentine with the contours of the slope that leads down to the marsh. Grouse scurry alongside it, safe from the aerial strikes of predators, and chipmunks love to scamper its length like acrobats. The wild roses love it, both for the slight extra bit of heat it reflects as well as for the trellis it provides to cling on; but what loves the rock wall most, perhaps, are the long-toed salamanders that live in the cracks and crevices beneath it.

Maroon-colored and delicate, with fluorescent green lightning stripes running the length of their spine, they crave the dampness that pools and lingers beneath the rock wall, and they hibernate beneath the vast sleeping weight of it; and they are safe too beneath those massive stones, from the pursuits of predators.

Sometimes as the rock wall snakes along, following the shape of the land, tracking one single contour, it seems to take on the flexible shape of a salamander, and as the long-toed salamanders emerge from hibernation in April, the rock wall too begins to stretch and yawn. Sometimes I like to imagine that those sporadic piano-key clinkings, as the wall shifts and settles and trembles in places, is the sound of the salamanders themselves awakening, and on the move. As if it is all connected, tighter than a tick, and that you cannot summon one thing, in a blessed place like this, without summoning all.

The glacier lilies, or, as the guidebooks call them, deer fawn's lilies, are among the first color to return that does not crawl or creep or fly; though in a sense too they do that, their bright yellow blossoms flourishing in the unique and specific temporal environment left behind by the daily-diminishing snow line.

As the signature of spring in the high country, the classic black and white script of bare black earth and melting snow, rides ever higher up the mountain until the last of the snow finally disappears, in these low mountains, the cheerful little lilies (each blossom about the size of a wine bottle cork) follow that elegant black and white boundary, drinking thirstily from the steady drip-melt of the vanishing snow and warmed by the solar radiation accepted gratefully by the well-rested new-black earth; and warmed too by the brilliant reflective heat of the snow shield, always just a few to several yards upslope of that day's newest patch of glacier lilies.

As the snow shrinks to a dwindling skullcap over the mountain, the lilies seem to be hurrying and hazing it along, nipping at its heels — nursing the glacier, is what it seems like; and in this manner, the brightest, freshest lilies are always the newest ones closest to the drip line, while below them lie scattered, in successional waves of decreasing intensity, the sun-faded yellowing tatters of yesterday's lilies: yesterday's news, vibrant youth reduced to worn-out prayer-flag-looking remnants in only a week's time, with generation after generation of glacier lilies leapfrogging up the mountain right on the heels of the departing snow, chasing it like a kind of brilliant yellow fire, chasing it up and over that highest ridge, pursuing the last of the snow like silent hounds . . .

It is the same country in which the bears first come out of hibernation, as those sheets of snow pull back like so many blankets being tucked back; and the glacier lilies are edible — they are nutritional and delicious, sweet and crisp, although, truth be told, more than a handful can give you a bit of a stomachache.

The bears, particularly the grizzly bears, which have been sleeping beneath these mini-glaciers, suspended like astronauts in the frozen earth, or like seeds themselves, will prowl these warm sun fields just beneath the snow line, grazing on the delicious lilies, and though insects are the plant's primary pollinators, sometimes the yellow pollen will get caught in the fur and on the snouts of the great golden bears as they go grubbing and pushing through the lily fields, pollinating other lilies in this manner. In that crude fashion, they are farmers of a kind, nurturing and expanding one of the crops that first greet them on resurrection each year; and the lilies follow the snow, and the snow pulls back to reveal the bears, and the bears follow the lilies, and the script of life begins moving with enthusiasm and reckless style once again, a script and a story far more exuberant than any that has been seen so far this year.

And on those same glistening ice shields, growing smaller each day, the grizzly mothers with their cubs slide down the slopes on their backs, riding the ice to the bottom for nothing but the joy of it — cartwheeling into the fields of yellow glacier lilies resting at the bottom of the vanishing glacier, and then climbing right back up to the top — sliding and playing for hours at a time, in the old world, safely distanced from the new and changing world that lies below, along the river bottoms, and in the valley of man, with nothing but joy and new wakefulness running through their blood. And though there are none of us who can tell by a certain murmuring or coursing of our own blood when it is exactly that the bears climb back up out of the earth — out of the spirit world, the natives say, and back into the world of man — I like to think that the other creatures of the forest can feel it, that they can sense it as easily as we might hear and feel the warming south winds moving through the tops of the pines.

I like to think too that that joy is as transferable, as felt and connected among all the inhabitants of the forest, as are the south thawing winds of April upon the land, and upon and among us.

Like any parent, I try to teach the girls moderation, economy, prudence, and forbearance. I want them to know the euphoria of unfettered joy, and the leaps of childhood, and I believe deeply in the ritual and repetition of simple physical models — like a catechism — as a means of helping train them into these patterns and ways of seeing the world. (Each evening before I go back out to work, I let them leap off the porch headlong into my arms — a six-flight leap — and each time I catch them; and midair, their faces are always, always purely radiant . . . I do not want their hearts to be a stranger to the wild flights of joy . . .)

But I want them also to know respect and restraint, discipline and economy. (Knowing that these things are my weakness, and that they are not likely to get it naturally, not through my shared blood, anyway, I suspect at times that I work overly hard at bringing them these lessons.)

Like any children, they love to pick flowers, and because we live amid such a richness and bounty of botanical profusion, in the springtime we always have new-picked bouquets of wildflowers throughout the house. But there are responsibilities and lessons that go with their rights and privileges; they have to learn (and have learned) not to pull the whole plant up by the roots. They have to learn sensitivity and rarity. Although we have numerous trillium, they don't do well in a vase, so we don't pick them. And even though the magnificent and ornate purple and gold fairy slipper — a member of the orchid family — is abundant in this northern forest, they are much diminished elsewhere in the world, and so out of respect for their worldwide distribution, each girl picks only one per year; but I must tell you, we all enjoy the week or so that that little orchid is showcased in our kitchen, and the tradition of it speaks to April almost as much as any other.

(Later in the summer, into the full vegetative roar of the season, they will be able to pick to their hearts' content: double fistfuls of sweet-scented royal blue lupine, huge bouquets of fire-red paintbrush, cerise fireweed, pearly everlasting, and that great and common weed, the only weed for which I can find no lasting enmity, the oxeye daisy . . . We gather the seed heads of yarrow too, to dry and save for use the next winter, in treating the sore throats of February and March, steeped in a hot tea . . .

What to make of such lessons? What hostages all children are to their parents' fears and values! I suspect that rarely there passes an hour of the day that I do not remember this, and think to myself, *What can I do to help them know more joy? What can I say or do to help present to them this lesson, or another?* And again, such fretting or consciousness derives largely, I suspect, from my own clumsiness in the world, my own misdirection and awkwardness. I want them to know the things I do not know; I want them to know grace, and as constant a peace in the world as is possible.

Our tradition with the glacier lilies is this: We try to find some for our evening salads, around Easter time. That Sunday, after the eggs have been hidden and found numerous times over, both in the house and out in the woods, we will take a walk up toward the snow line on one of the south-facing slopes, and there, walking along the snow's edge and listening to the sound of dripping water, we'll forage among the glacier lilies, as if partaking the food of the resurrection, and we'll bring home a handful to place in our salads.

Maybe I'm doing the wrong thing. Maybe I'm being too rigid, too much of an eco-freak. But I try to teach them gratitude and respect. I try to remind them that these flowers are the season's first food for the bears — for the fifteen or twenty grizzlies we have left living in this valley — and I counsel them to take only one or two blossoms from each clump or cluster, as a show of respect; as a reminder, a remembrance, that we are visitors to this mountaintop and that our own needs are usually excessive, rarely as primal anymore as those of the other forest-dwellers.

I can't use that language, of course. I can just tell them to pick one or two from each clump; and to leave far more than they take. To eat some there on the mountaintop and to save some for our evening's dinner of elk steak (sometimes from that same mountain) and garden potatoes.

It's something we try to do every Easter.

I believe firmly in the sanctity of the seasons; in the promised regularity of cycles; in the bedrock foundations of loving ritual, celebrating feasts, and thanksgiving. I don't know why I feel these things so strongly — I know only that I do.

I don't have the words yet to tell or explain these things to them.

Instead, on our hike out, I show them, when I'm fortunate enough to find them, the big footprints of where the bears have been walking, and playing, and sliding in the snow.

Mary, the genius gardener, is coming over today to help Elizabeth design a strategy for this year's garden. Mary doesn't plant her crops in rows and columns but in a wilder mosaic, a little of this and a little of that, certain things flush up against other things, a curlicue of patterns that resembles more than anything, I think, the arrangement of lichens on a rock high in the mountains. Mary says that this "wildness" helps make the garden more resistant to pests and disease, and looking at her garden, a visitor can see that she's right; her garden is but a microcosm for the plan of this landscape itself, which comprises forests mixed with similar mosaics of diversity, and possessing, in that diversity and shared dominance, astounding richness and health.

Just across the state line, over in Idaho, our friend Julie is doing the same thing, planting corn right next to and among her beans, so that the beans will have a natural trellis — the cornstalk — to climb.

After harvest, then, it can all be turned to fallow.

I'm staring out at the garden this morning, continuing to be astounded by the notion of color, mesmerized by the irises and daffodils. Why does color even exist? Isn't it just the differential absorption and reflection of light rays falling on different surfaces? To the sun, isn't everything below just a black-and-white palette of various reflectivities and absorptions — and the pattern and arrangement of all those myriad differences as random and aswirl as the sprawl of lichens creeping across one vast boulder? Why color?

Enough navel-gazing! And yet, upon awakening from winter's grip, it's hard to stop the mind's sluggish, even feeble, stirrings. With appreciation, not petulance, you want to ask *Why?* to everything; and as when a child asks that question, there are no real and final answers, only an unending succession of the same refrain — one *Why?* leading only to the next *Why?*, and then the next.

I'm staring at the bare garden, the black earth receiving the soft morning light (filtered through fog and mist), and watching it strike the garden, and wondering which is better for a garden, morning light or evening. I'm wondering what purpose morning light plays in a garden — if, though soft and seemingly insignificant, it fulfills a function by awakening the plants' cells gradually, gently, perhaps, to some preliminary realignment of stomata that then prepares them to receive more efficiently, later on, the more rigorous photosynthesis obligations of the day, receiving that seemingly useless dull golden glow of weaker morning light as an athlete might perform seemingly menial stretching or warm-up movements before beginning heavier exercise, or as a philosopher might meditate before addressing some long-standing conundrum.

Who will ever fully know the real value, if any even exists, of morning light upon a garden?

Who will ever fully know the real value of anything?

Enough navel-gazing; too much! The green world is rising, beckoning.

And yet I cannot leave the residue of this thought; it clings to my morning mind as does a spider web when one hikes through the woods early in the day. If the sun's soft light "awakens" the garden, do the geese's cries, out in the marsh, at first light, likewise summon other things — including, perhaps, the seeds beneath the soil, and the plant cells within the stalks and leaves, goose music like a kind of sunlight (for that is what it sounds like to me, in April, sunlight) — as we too, listening to the geese's return, first stir beneath our blankets?

I know April is lingering on, but I can't help it, I want to savor every bite and taste of it, every fragment of flavor like the claret of a fine wine, like a communion, like a weeklong drunken wedding party. Sometimes I think that April should be the first month, the portal of the year, leading us first onward into all the other months. The one that starts everything else moving.

I will never be able to decide which is my favorite month, but I know that each year when April arrives it is as if I have been beaten down by a stranger, or a more persistent foe, and am down on my hands and knees, not yet giving up but knocked down yet again, knocked down this time for what feels like maybe for good — I'm down on my hands and knees, head ringing, thinking about, seriously, for the first time, quitting — quitting joy, quitting hope, quitting enthusiasm — but then wait, here comes a sound, a stirring in the branches, and an odor, something carried on a dampening south wind; and here, coming through the forest, is someone, or something, approaching, reaching down to give me a hand up, not because I deserve it, but because this superior force is — in April, anyway — loving, and full of gentleness, with generosity to spare; and thus summoned, and deeply grateful and mystified, I rise to one knee, and then stand.

The mated geese, out in the increasing emerald vibrancy of the marsh, are so elegant: white masks, black helmets; their long black necks craning up from their nests out in the marsh grass, and again those two colors, black and green, seeming to go together so well.

The geese's black necks and the green reef of marsh grass, the blackened char of fire-gutted logs and the brilliant green of the fire's aftermath, the new growth.

The creature of fire itself, the salamander, possessing the lightning bolt jag of green right down the middle of its damp black-and-maroon back. Will we ever fit the world as well as do the other residents who have been here so much longer? What must it feel like to be so graceful in the world, so connected and alive?

Up before daylight, and working this morning, the twenty-fourth of April, not down at the marsh cabin, but in the warm house, working in silence before anyone else awakens. It snowed during the night — again, I felt the temperature of the house rise by a degree or two, as that heavy blanket of insulation was laid over the whole of the sleeping household — and in the dimness of morning's first creeping light, it is an unpleasant sight indeed to see that the world is entirely white once more, and yet again; an extremely unwelcome image to see snow atop the baby lettuce, atop the basil.

The light slides in so slowly, and as it is a slightly warmer breath than that of the night's darkness, the simple breath of it is enough, already, to begin melting the night's snow in patches, here and there. As if — so thin and insubstantial is this latest blanket of snow — the breath of one morning alone will be sufficient to erase it.

That is certainly my hope, as I watch the steam of rising sun continue to melt more and more of the night's snow. Elizabeth, like me, is ready, really ready, for spring, and because I do not want her to have to witness the rude sight of that snow atop the lettuce, I am balancing in my mind, the rate of the dawn's rapid snowmelt, and the number of minutes remaining before she awakens; hoping against hope that the two numbers might balance out so that she will not have to witness this psychologically discouraging sight of even its brief return. How does the old joke go, about how when Mama's not happy, nobody's happy?

There's no way all that snow's going to vanish in the next ten or fifteen minutes. But still, I keep watching it, and listening to that springtime sound of running water, and watching the steam rise, and listening to the morning sound of the varied thrush.

Not for another two or three hours will all the new snow be

gone again — not until the sun crests the tops of the trees will it burn off and the grass and new garden will glisten with life and new growth again. But still, so fatigued are our spirits by winter, and such is our eagerness for spring, that any little additional amount of snow that manages to vanish between now and the time Elizabeth awakens will be only to the good for not just Elizabeth but all of us. We're really, really stretched tight on this, worn down to a nub from the gauntlet of cloudy, snowy days. As lovely as snow can be, we've had enough.

What is life? April is surely when the pulse of it returns with the first truly noticeable leap; the month when the blanket is finally pulled back from the sleeping, or the sleepy, world.

The fresh-cut daffodils sitting in the vase on the table before me have continued to drink water, even after being cut. They drank a cup of water yesterday, and a cup the day before: thirsty, even into death. Maybe that is what April is most like, those daffodils, and that thirst — only it is an inversion of that force, so that it is a thirst into life rather than death.

The older I get, the more I love April, snow and all.

Wood ducks squealing at dusk. The geese, seeming as big as airplanes, circling the marsh twice before coming in for the splash-landing; coming down as if in slow motion. Once they drop beneath the canopy level of the dark old forest that forms the ring, the amphitheater of the forest, their calls echo wilder, more loudly — amplified in that closed arena, even though it is only just the two of them, these greathearted creatures sounding, once they are down below the treetops, as if there are dozens of them. Always, upon hearing that miraculous and sudden amplification, the dramatic moment when after all that circling they choose and commit to this marsh — *this* one — and set their wings and feet and drop in from the treetops so that the marsh captures and magnifies seemingly tenfold their sound, as well as the wild joy of its tone, always, the heart lifts and swells, is summoned: wonderfully confused, in a strange way — are we a wild species, or are we a tame species? — and always, exhilarated.

This too is what April is like: lifting you, dashing you, lifting you, dropping you. Stretching the awakening heart to amplitudes one would not normally reach on one's own.

Spring's so close that it could be nudged in with a feather. I'm waiting now only for the trill of the first red-winged blackbird, and the return of the felted nubs of the deer's antlers.

Again, the snow is pulled back farther. A hike with Lowry to a nearby grove reveals a carpet of deer bones, the mass boneyard of a mountain lion's winter cache: a dozen whitened legs strewn atop one another, beneath the boughs of a big cedar. Old stories from the winter gone by being revealed, even as the onrush of new ones comes muscling in, honking in, flapping in, surging.

I tell Lowry the usual nature rap — the oldest story of all. The bones will dissolve, and the cedar will absorb their nutrients. The deer will be lifted into the sky. The cedar will grow even taller and thicker, even shadier. Deer will wait out heavy snowstorms beneath the protective spread of its boughs. The old deer legs will be caught up within the sweet grain of the wood, between the growth rings of one year and the next — the deer traveling vertically now, in the xylem and phloem, as they once picked their way gingerly and horizontally through the old forest in winter, pausing sometimes to paw at the snow with shiny black hoofs and nibble at an exposed frond of cedar seedling.

I often wonder what will constitute the moral fabric of a child raised in such a setting as this time and place, this wild green valley. I am aware of the excessive blessings, aware of the shortcomings. But what does it mean, if anything, to a child who can take for granted the most wondrous sights — and for whom bulldozers, strip malls, cell phones, and the like, are not the steady background?

I'm not saying these other things are good or bad. I'm just saying that I wonder daily what it will mean to the girls, as adults, to have had one certain fabric — the senses and images and lessons — form the matrix, the background, of their lives, instead of another.

I'll go ahead and say it right out loud: I like to imagine that when they are grown and I am old, they will say "Thank you."

What's wonderful and frightening now is, I suppose, what's

wonderful and frightening about any childhood, and any parent-
age: it is all accepted as normal and taken gloriously for granted.
And that, I think, is the great blessing of childhood. We can find
the track of a grizzly and they do not have to lament that there are
but perhaps fifteen of them left in the whole valley. We can find an
exquisite salamander beneath one of the frost-heaved rocks in the
rock wall and they do not have to consider that the entire species
may become absent from the earth within the span of their life-
times, as so many of the species that frequented my childhood in
Texas have vanished entirely, in only half a lifetime.

None of that. Only the slow, sweet normalcy, the constancy, of
the days; and from that, the braid of the seasons, as stable as a parent's love.

It's a nice thing to be so welcoming of spring, for there's certainly no force on earth that could slow its arrival. This morning the
south wind is swirling, gusting, rowdy, the sky breath sending huffs
of smoke back down the chimney of my wood stove and back into
my cabin, with sudden drops of air pressure all around the cabin as
the wind reverses, twirls, counterspins, dances: exhalations, bursts,
as if some great animal is running across the sky, breathing hard.

Another first: this morning, as I am writing by candlelight, the season's first moth shows itself, drawn by the flame. I'm too busy staring with delight at this tangible proof of winter's end to think far
enough ahead to snuff the candle; instead, I watch with a thing very
close to gratitude as the moth dances around and around the candle's breath, but then it tips a wing in too close and crashes into the
pooling wax, and sizzles quick and sputtering malodorous pyro-
technics.

From now on — now that the moths have reawakened, or are
hatching — I'll be on alert. I'll catch them with my hands, one at a
time, and toss them outside, into the cool breath of the marsh,
where they came from, and where they belong.

They can pool outside at my windows of light, and bat muffled
wingbeats against the glass; as if I am in the cocoon, warm and dry,
while outside, the living world of the marsh at night seethes.

The laughing, drawn-out trill of the sora rails. The geese, the
frogs, the ducks; the gulping, hollow-gourd sound of the bittern.

The wind huffing and chuffing, the owls, and the sound of running water. The symphony, no longer just warming up in the pit but beginning, finally, to play.

In April, it all comes down to this: the astounding return of both sound and color. There is life in winter too, and often it is keenly felt, with the senses sometimes poised and heightened in their deprivation. But April is like sitting in a dark theater thirty minutes before the show, or an hour before the show — arriving early, and waiting, and waiting, and then finally seeing the light come on, on the screen before you, and hearing the reel-to-reel tape begin to flicker. The restlessness, the delicious anticipation, among the audience — or in your own heart, whether the theater is full or whether you are the only one in attendance. Your full attention is directed to the screen; with those first words, that first scene, you are galvanized, transported away from wherever else you were just a short time earlier.

It seems that I can't stand how happy I am that winter is finally vanquished. The sparkling effervescence that returns to my blood in April. Sometimes I'm so overwhelmed by it that I have to get up from my desk and step outside and walk out into the marsh a short distance and just stand there, in the night amid the moths just beyond the throw of window light from the candle still burning in the empty cabin, or, if it is daytime, with my face uplifted to the sun and my arms spread wide, pale skin open and absorbing the dull but strengthening return of light, and just stand there, resting, so glad to be alive, nothing but alive. No ambition, no envy, no angst, no nothing. Only life.

Against all my better efforts, I'm slowing down, growing older — becoming, despite my wishes, though perhaps also in full step and pace with my wishes — an old man.

It was not so long ago that I would never have dreamed of slowing down enough to do such a thing — to wander tired like an old hound, or warhorse, out into the marsh in April, and just stand there, face tilted back and arms widespread: to do nothing but stand in the sunlight, like a scarecrow, for the longest time.

Back at the house, bopping around on the front porch, or inside, my daughters — my modern daughters, modern despite our remove from the central fuss of the world — lifting their heads from their CD Walkmans to greet me when I come back inside from a day's work, still love me.

But the next day, in April, and the next, and the next, there I am again, out almost up to my knees in the marsh, sinking deeper and deeper into the marsh, it seems, and moving slower and slower.

Listening.

MAY

....

MAY IS THE MONTH of disorderly conduct.

In the uproar of spring, the shouted vibrancy of life re-creating itself, you expect for order to be woven from all the matted strands of the long, hard winter; and you expect, from all the long waiting, an exuberant and elegant, considered grace to finally occur.

And in the end — far into the heart of May — that's what will come. But at the dawn of May, it's not that way at all. It's all rush and indecision, with everything scrambling to be first, then changing its mind and hurrying to the back of the line, or ducking for cover. Jostling, shuffling, swelling.

I might as well jump right in and be honest and inform the reader that sometimes in May — most Mays — I get pretty low at one point or another. I used to be ashamed of it, when it would come — mortified at this fantastic personal lethargy, with the world before me so fine, and especially so, in May — but I've gotten better about accommodating or accepting it. (Fighting it, I've found, does no good, and often only worsens it. The sadness is not a character flaw, not a question of reaching deeper or trying harder, but rather some sluggishness of blood that is of the larger world's doing, not my heart's — do the bent winter brown mats of marsh grass yearn for green brilliance? — and where I've come to lay the blame, if any blame is to be placed, lies in what I suspect is a supreme imbalance between the accelerated pace of the enthusiastic year — a pace that all of wild nature, graceful and well practiced, leaps into at full tilt, each May — and my own stiff and clumsy inability to find or assume that same pace.)

I'm not sure how to describe the feeling, beyond a heaviness of spirit, a leadenness of both body and mind. I'd liken it to a strange mix of terror and numbness, if such things can be said to coexist, or to even battle for the same territory. There is heaviness, or sadness, or confusion — I hate calling it a depression, for I do not want it to be that; I want only to be uplifted by the world — sometimes, in early May, as sharp and alarming as the edge of a newly honed pocketknife held tight against the arc of one's thumb. The world rushes on, fussing and squawking and preening, while this confused and hesitant heart of mine waits, indecisive and motionless — waiting for what? — until finally, mercifully, some inner signal is given, some adjustment is made (surely it is biochemical), and I can enter fully the joy of the month.

I don't mean to prattle on about a thing that should be of no more importance to the reader than the depth of my bellybutton. And it seems slightly dirty to even mention it, that occasional heaviness, in the midst of so much of the world's beauty — almost as if, in some sad way, that excess beauty is somehow, strangely, one of the precipitating factors, in a way no one could explain or understand — and yet it seems dishonest also not to mention it.

Consider it mentioned. By the time the grass is green later in the month, and by the time the last of the partygoers have arrived — the Wilson's snipe, up from South America, and the trilling red-winged blackbirds, from the Gulf Coast, and the first wild violets, from their earthen chambers below — the matter will be behind me, sloughed off like the dead scaly skin of the garter snakes as they emerge from hibernation.

What grace and calibration of every tiny gear exists in the forest, and in the wilderness, and still even upon the echoes of wilderness — upon any place that has not yet been overcut, or dammed, or paved, mined, overplowed or overwrought. Those same scaly, fluttery snakeskins, for instance, are shed just in time for the returning birds to line and weave their nests with that opaque material. (And, weeks later, as those nests have produced and nurtured the writhing, chirping fledglings, many of those same snakes, lithesome and clean-skinned, will slide up the branches now to investigate those tiny birds; the giving and the taking never ends, the world in that manner perhaps nothing more than a continuum of desire . . .)

I'd like to believe that my late-spring funk helps serve at least some tiny purpose in the larger, wilder good of the world — that as the scaly residue of it finally flakes away from me, some use might in some faint manner be made of that flaking detritus of tired soul and wasted time.

Nothing in nature is ever wasted. Perhaps this is part of the guilt I feel, in my early-May near paralysis. I'm forty-two years old and still haven't learned to accept that strange heaviness as a necessary time-out, a resting period, in which to prepare for the year's coming exuberance.

I am a slow learner. But my heart is willing. I'll keep trying. There has to be a reason.

The green wave of May moves so fast, and with so much power, that it only seems disorderly and rambunctious to you. What is really occurring is that May's leap is laying the foundation for all the coming intricacies of the growing year — the foundation itself a complex and elegant assembly of preparations, but moving so boisterously and in so many directions at once as to seem random, reckless and unconsidered, to our eyes. We are too used, I think, to gauging the final constructed edifice rather than the glorious biological roilings and writhings of the work in progress, the living thing being created. I suspect that too often, to the detriment of our imaginations, we prefer result and destination over process and journey.

Even for a free or willing spirit, however, the challenge of following May's lead can be daunting and disorienting. As if rushing pell-mell over April's long list of firsts, here comes May now with its own frantic, surging, savage list of firsts. First hard rain, first scent of cottonwood. First fringed bud of aspen leaf, the tapered green swollen bud-flame opening slightly to reveal the unfolding miracle of true leaf rather than engorged bud: and a thing of beauty in its own right, that sight of the first pair of unfolded leaves, as well as the foundation for all of the summer and then autumnal music of clattering leaves, quaking and rattling in the wind, each aspen grove its own sighing symphony, and each symphony's first score and movement harking all the way back to those silent first days of May, when the first bud swelled in the earth's new warmth until it could finally swell no further, and spread apart to make the first two leaves of spring — silent, and yet part of the music.

In addition to the disorder and youthful, exuberant, greedy rush, alternating with the last adolescent moments of indecision — rain, or sun? Neither mood lasts for long; they wash across the landscape in alternating tiger-striped bands of darkness and light — there is intense sogginess, mirthful muck and jelly-swamp, as the last of the snow and ice departs, and as the sweet-scented rains drum down on the thaw-softened, sodden, buckling thin soil.

The last bridges and cornices of ice cave in alongside the river, floating downstream like rafts or leisure boats, sometimes stacking up at the bend in the river or against a logjam: piling up quickly into a hastily constructed but impressive piece of jumbled architecture. The little rushing river piles up higher behind that ice jam, swelling and rising and broadening across the floodplain until the river appears, over the course of only a couple of days, to be as wide and brown and ambitious as the Missouri or the Mississippi, a giant sprawling through our little valley; and in those shallow, spreading floodwaters there is a shimmering glitter of silt and all kinds of other organic matter — bear dung and rotting log mulch and deer pellets and dead trout and winter-killed elk and everything else within the river's hungry reach — sparkling suspended, distributed far and wide into the forest and across the brown and sullen flood-plain.

The river will keep rising, choosing at first those myriad paths of lesser resistance and carrying the richness of its spreading breadth into all the places that are so hungry for that distribution of wealth.

But beneath the easygoing demeanor — beneath the gentle, sleepy, wandering flood — a desire is quivering, and an anxiousness. The river is running late now, on its path to the great curve of the Kootenai, which receives this straight-running river (notched with the many feathery fletchings of side tributaries) as the arc of a bow receives and cradles an arrow drawn. The Kootenai flows into the greatest American river of the Pacific, the Columbia, which follows, as much as the dams will allow it, its mandate to the ocean, and the salmon, and the sturgeon and the cedars . . .

For a while, then, before its release, the be-jammed river meanders, seemingly confused, and spreads nutrients and richness into the most unlikely places, or so it seems; appearing to ignore — even avoid — the pressure that continues to build and strain against that thickened bridge of milk-colored ice.

The river wanders chocolate-covered off into the woods, seeming lost, moving away from the ice bridge — just wandering, and even in a fashion seeming to retreat or draw away from the ice bridge.

One day, though, the ice begins to tremble. Not noticeably, at first, but faintly. Trembling, then stilling itself, trembling, then stilling. It might be only one's imagination. Perhaps nothing of consequence is occurring.

A few days later, however, the trembling is more pronounced, and noticeable — audible all the time, as a shuddering. And at night, as the day's surge of high-mountain meltwater only now, twelve hours later, makes it all the way down to the ice bridge on the valley floor below, all the way down from the tops of the mountains that had been bathed in May sun a dozen hours earlier, the first melodies of cracking or straining ice can be heard, sounding at first like the perfunctory stroke of a fiddler's bow drawn but once or twice across the quivering taut strings of the instrument: the warming-up, the preparation for the real thing.

It will sometimes take a full week beyond that first draw of the bowstring before the entire opera is engaged; before the gates of ice crash open and the river is born or resurrected again and goes hurtling down its old waiting stone canyons, carrying along in its roar a winter's worth of driftwood, entire forests bobbing and surging along in significant — for now — disarray.

The sun returns and dries out the coat of mud slime that was deposited in the floodplain, these rich gardens of river dirt speaking in a mosaic to where the ice bridge, or bridges, were that year; and in subsequent years, rich willow and meadow encroach upon, and are nourished by, those flood gardens; and in late May, and on into the calm of summer, moose and deer and elk wander out into those wild and seemingly random gardens to graze and browse on the fruits leaping up out of the legacy of that random richness, with the same story told over and over again, the same story in only slightly different places, up and down the length of the wild river, each year ...

There are other kinds of gardens too. And what is grown is not easily if at all replaceable, and cannot be measured by any scale other than that which acknowledges depthlessness, timelessness.

From such gardens a harvest is possible, though not in the traditional sense of any of the hard commodities of the world — oil, gas, timber, hay, livestock, electricity, gold, copper, silver: the detritus of industry — but rather, a harvest of spirit, though perhaps it is not even a harvest, for perhaps no more is taken from the mountains or the forest than that with which the traveler already arrives. Perhaps the mountain, the forest, is only the catalyst, so that these wild gardens merely summon or elicit the reverence, or potential for reverence, or joy, or potential for joy, that already exists within the traveler.

In our valley, we have but fifteen such gardens of any significant size left. They require a minimum size of one thousand acres to be classified as potential candidates for wilderness designation — formal, permanent protection by Congress — and in order to qualify must not ever have had any roads built into them.

Such has been the frenzy of extraction on this forest, the subsidized liquidation of the biggest and best of the timber — well over a million loaded logging trucks have rolled out of this forest, out of this valley, and out of this impoverished county (Where did all the money go? Was there ever any money, or was it all simply given or traded away?) — that in the million or so acres lying between the Canadian border and the curve, the bow, of the Kootenai River, east of Idaho and west of Lake Koocanusa, these fifteen gardens are now scattered in a gasping strand of one wild archipelago, and are refuge not only to the last threatened and endangered species such as wolves and grizzlies and caribou and wolverines but also to those reservoirs of spirit.

Fifteen gardens: and worse yet, not a single one of them has any form of permanent protection whatsoever. Despite the living, pulsing, breathtaking wildness of this landscape (a biological wildness, rather than a recreational wildness — perhaps the wildest valley in the Lower Forty-eight, in that regard), there's still not a single acre of designated wilderness protected on the public wildlands of this valley.

It's a big injustice. I hate the flavor, the taste, of that injustice.

I love the scent, the taste, the feeling — and certainly, the ecological justice — back in the farthest hearts of those fifteen gardens.

I've said it before: This isn't a place to come to. It's a place to dream of. It's a biological wilderness, full of frog roar and swamp muck and tangled blowdown and mosquitoes and deeply angry, suspicious people, none of whom would be pleased to see your happy, vacationing face.

This is a place of mud and muck, a celebration of the rank and the fecund, the cold and the uncomfortable, the frayed and the wild. This is a place whose last wild gardens should be protected for its own sake, not yours or mine.

They are gardens. While much or most of the world in May is puttering about in the warming black earth, coaxing carrot seeds and lettuce sprouts into the bright new world, the gardens I am most interested in have not been planted by the hand of man or woman but are instead bulging, swelling, shifting, on the verge of delivering kicking spotted elk calves back into the world, and are delivering bears back into the world, tumbling once more to the surface from their earthen burrows like astronauts returning from the strangest of journeys; mountains delivering torrents of rushing water, recharging the buried aquifers between immense slabs of tilted stone. The fossils of ancient sea creatures tumbling with the season's new talus down into the bed of bright glacier lilies below: trilobites, fenestellids, cephalopods, and ostracods on the prowl once more, and the earth itself stretching and yawning like a wildcat, supple and hungry, awakened, youthful, vibrant.

A garden of dragonflies rising from the waving marsh fronds like sunlit jewels summoned by no gardener we will ever meet in this life, and one whose careful and calculated, fitted and meaningful work, closely studied, can bring, I am convinced, immeasurable blessings of peacefulness to the student of that work, the careful student who observes and ponders the goals of that precise gardener . . .

A garden of loosened fur, a garden of fire, a garden of recovered earrings, or the dream of recovered earrings. One May our friend Tracy, while roughhousing with Lowry, particularly around the slide and swing set, lost her earrings, and searched for them to no avail. It was late May, almost into June, so that the grass and clover were high enough already (and the earrings were small ones) that we were unable to locate them, though we looked until dusk.

"Don't worry," Tracy said. "They'll show up."

Except they haven't. Every year, in early May, before the green-up — once the old dirty snow has pulled away and the earth has warmed to sodden mud, dappled with glinting puddles and the shortened silvery stubble of the winter-dead grass — we go out and search, again and again, for those earrings, combing the yard in all directions, though never to any avail.

How can they just disappear? Year in and year out we search, confident that there will be some accrual of luck, some cumulative tally or summation that will eventually transcend failure, and that no matter how secretively they might be slipped into the ground — two little silver leaves hidden beneath a flake of bark, or a bent matting of grass — our diligence will be rewarded and we will find them; that each early May spent searching is not a new beginning, isolate and unconnected to all the other years, but is rather an extension, a continuum of all that has come before, and if our efforts and luck in previous years have not been quite sufficient, well, never fear: all those years' labor plus one more, *this* one added to all the others, will surely turn the tide.

But nothing. Each year, nothing.

We'll find them. There's plenty of time. If not this year, then next, or the next. Sometimes I feel a wonderful urgency, while down on my hands and knees searching, in knowing that the green grass is onrushing, growing higher each day, like tongues of green flame rising higher and higher, diminishing my chances of finding the earrings with each passing day, though most days the green fire doesn't bother me.

Instead, I put in my hours — the days, then the years. If not this year, then next. The earrings will be found — they cannot have traveled anywhere — when they are meant to be found, and it will be like a little miracle when they are. The important thing in the meantime is to keep showing up, to keep putting in the hours.

All through the winter, the deer have traveled the same paths over and over, packing the deep snow, their sharp hoofs cutting down to form lanes, and then nearly tunnels, through the soft hills of snow. They keep these trails so packed down that the snow in them gets compressed to some kind of superdense cobalt- or galena-colored substance, more slippery than mercury, denser than lead — and, paradoxically, or so it seems at first, these trails, which once marked where the snow had been worn down to its thinnest margins, is now the last to leave, the last remaining thread of winter: fifteen feet of snow supercompressed to a height of only a few inches so that even in the returning warmth of May, these luminous dense ice trails linger long after all the other, fluffier snow has long since melted; and having no need to use these trails now, which are slippery, the deer avoid them.

Instead, the deer step carefully across the spongy dark duff — surely they must feel sprightly, unencumbered, at long last — and in this yin-and-yang inversion, old snow to black earth, they shed their winter coats, leaving their hollow hair in tufts and clumps all over the woods, the braided, winding rivers of it running now at cross angles to the old paths of hoof-matted ice.

The hair glints in the newer, sharper light of springtime, looking like spilled straw, or silver needles — trails of it leading all through the woods — and this shift in the riverine sentences that echo the deer's passages, a shift even more pronounced than the reversal of a tide, are for me, as with the coming of the first trillium, one of the most visual markers of the season, the true and irreconcilable end of winter. Though the mud and forest puddles will dry out, and the winds will soon enough scatter those tufts and concentrated rivers of hair to a more democratic and widespread distribution, in May it is still all clumps and patches, the deer shedding great wads of hair against any rough surface: the bark of a hemlock, the stub of branch on a fallen lodgepole, the branches of a wind-tipped fir tree. Appearing all throughout the forest too are the whitened, ribby spars of winter-killed deer, appearing like so many ships stranded by the white tide's great withdrawal, and in caves and hollows too, beneath the fronds of great cedar trees, entire mattress-nests of deer hair can be found, in places where a mountain lion has fed all winter long: dragging one deer after another to his or her favorite cache and gnawing on it, almost always in the same place, until the bones stack up on one another like a little corral and the disintegrating hides shed their fur. After the end of winter, in such places, the ground may be half a foot deep in white belly hair, belly hair as white as snow — the tide pulling back, retreating horizontally, with new life, *springtime*, poised now at the leaping edge of vertical green roar . . .

May is a wonderful time to see the eagles, both bald and golden, the former returning with the opening of the river ice, and during this period they feast gluttonously on the moraine of an entire winter's worth of road-killed deer. Nearly every morning on the drive to school in early May, Mary Katherine and Lowry and I will pass at least one such eagle banquet, with two or three bald eagles — both the mature adults and the adolescents, which are just as large but don't yet have the white head — accompanied often by a golden eagle or two; and when the eagles see a car or truck approaching, they leap up from their roadside feast and on great wide wings flap wheeling in all directions to their various sentinel perches, eagles swirling in all directions, like children who have been roughhousing while their teacher steps away from the classroom for a moment scrambling back to their seats upon whispered news of the teacher's return.

Fur from the deer carcasses swirls in the air, glinting like pins and needles, loosened from the eagles' talons, deer hair stirred on the currents of the eagles' departure and by the truck's passage.

Time and time again I am astounded by the regularity and repetition of form in this valley, and elsewhere in wild nature: basic patterns, sculpted by time and the land, appearing anywhere I look, everywhere I look. The twisted branches back in the forest that look so much like the forked tines and antlers of the deer and elk. The way the glacier-polished hillside boulders look like the muscular, rounded bodies of the animals — deer, bear — that pass among those boulders like living ghosts.

The way the swirling deer hair is the exact shape and size of the larch and pine needles the deer hair rests on, once it is torn loose from the carcass and comes to rest again on the forest floor.

As if everything up here, everything, is leaning in the same direction, shaped by the same hands, or the same mind; not always agreeing or in harmony, but attentive always to the same rules of logic, and in the playing out, again and again, of the infinite variations of specificity arising from that one shaping system of logic, an incredible sense of connection and attachment developing: a kind of unconscious community, rarely noticed, if at all, but deeply felt.

Felt at night when you stand beneath the stars and see the shapes and designs of bears and hunters in the sky; felt deep in the cathedral of an old forest when you stare up at the tops of the swaying giants; felt when you take off your boots and socks and wade across the river, feeling each polished, mossy river stone with your cold bare feet.

Felt when you stand at the edge of the marsh and listen to the choral uproar of the frogs, and surrender to their shouting, and allow yourself too, like those pine needles and that deer hair, and like those branches and those elk antlers, to be remade and refashioned into both the shape and the pattern and the rhythm of the land.

You feel surrounded, and then embraced, by a logic so much more powerful and overarching than anything that man or woman could create or even imagine, that all you can do is marvel and laugh at it, and feel compelled to give, in one form or another, thanks and celebration for it, without even really knowing why . . .

In this manner, I feast hungrily each morning in May on the sight of the eagles pulling loose with their beaks and talons the tufts of fur from the winter-killed deer. The trees and bushes then growing up out of that deer-enriched soil to sprout the branches that are the same shape the antlers had been. One story. Many parts, but only one story, and the rhythm of each month carrying us along beneath or within that one chorus.

It seems to me to be extraordinarily wonderful to see such a sight on the way to school nearly every morning, in the awakening days of May, and I like to consider how such images, in both the singular beauty of each, as well as in the braided rhythm that is created by their regularity, help to comprise the fabric of the girls' childhood, days of wild green regularity so incomparable to and unquestioned by any other experience that such sights seem "normal" to them. Though even in the dailiness of it, the wonder of May, and of all the months here, I try to explain to the girls to not take such things for granted, saying this even as I am fully aware that there is a part of me that most *wants* them to take such sights for granted; to accept such bounty as their unquestioned due.

In a way that I haven't yet figured out how to fully articulate, I believe that children growing up who get to see bald eagles, coyotes, deer, moose, grouse, and other similar sights each morning will have some certain kind of matrix or fabric or foundation of childhood, the nature and quality of which will be increasingly rare and valuable as time goes on, and even cherished into adulthood, as well as — and this is a leap of faith, by me — a source of strength and knowledge to them, somehow.

I believe that the quality of such an experience, though intangible and immeasurable, will be, and already is, priceless; and I am grateful to this landscape for still being able to provide such daily sights to all young people: to children still so naive that they do not even yet realize such wonders are now rare elsewhere.

For as long as possible, I want them to keep believing that beauty, though not quite commonplace, and never to pass unobserved or unappreciated, is nonetheless easily witnessed on any day, in any given moment, around any forthcoming bend. Around the next bend. And that the wild world still has a lovely order and pattern and logic, even in the shouting, disorderly chaos of breaking-apart May, and reassembling May.

Is it too strong a statement to say that I want them to someday know that they were married at birth, even before birth, to this landscape — to serve it and be served by it, shaped and supported — the power of it in them like the charging ice-melt release of the cold mountain rivers in May?

Perhaps that notion, as much as any, speaks to that idea, that belief I have that in the daily witnessing of the natural wonders a strength and a base form in them, a kind of education of logic and assurance that cannot be duplicated by any other means, or in other places: unique, and significant, and, by God, still somehow relevant to the blood's and heart's call, even now, in the twenty-first century.

Why am I so comforted by ritual and tradition and the regular unfolding of knowable patterns? Why do I love so much to hunt, search, discover, and gather?

Every May, after the snow is finally gone but before the world burns green, I go back out again and search for those lost earrings of Tracy's, even knowing somehow that I will probably never find them, that with each passing year, the odds grow longer, as the earrings sink and sift deeper into the forest duff, and into the detritus of each passing year's bent brown grass, the chaff of time. Perhaps the earrings are resting flat on the ground, far beneath such matted hay, covered each year with another annum of silt and dust, or perhaps they are turned on their side, slender as a paper clip, and invisible, unknowable, except to the blindest of lucks or the most certain of destinies.

Each year, however, as a practice both in hope and in the hunt, under the pretense of searching for the earrings, under the pretense of believing, I set the dry brown sheaves of grass-hair on fire in the vicinity of where Tracy lost her earrings. Part of it is for the purpose of remaining, each year, brazen enough to believe in the possibility of a miracle, and part of it is, again, because I love to search and hunt — but part of it too is because I love to paint the field orange with flame and then black and green, with but a single struck match as a brush.

Sometimes a major mistake that you make reveals itself to you slowly, unfolding through all the various stages of dubiousness, inching inexorably toward certainty — the faint prickle in the scalp, the fear that one feels fairly confident is paranoia and yet which can't be dismissed and in fact continues growing, until finally the fear, and the mistake, blossoms into reality.

Other times, the mistake is revealed immediately, arrived at with a kind of *Oh, shit!* alacrity.

This grass fire that I set in my front yard this year was of the former variety.

Seen from a distance, it would have seemed laughable. Why was that man getting so carried away with his task, swabbing the great square field of dried yellow-brown grass with one match after another? And why was he running as if along a strand line as he set them, so that the little fires could join together like falling dominoes, moving quickly, as if with desire, one wave leaping quickly over itself to grow into the next one, rather than setting methodical backfires and letting the desire, the yearning, for the dry grass work against itself in a kind of trap?

Why wasn't the man taking his time, and stomping out the little fires after a while, before they got too big, instead of just standing back and watching them run? And why, for God's sake, didn't he have buckets of water lined around the perimeter of the area he wanted to burn, and garden hoses at the ready?

Why hadn't he checked the wind? Why hadn't he waited longer, for the last pregnant purple moments right before, and even in the face of, one of May's many spring thunderstorms? Why did he instead need to be so god-awfully impulsive and impetuous, so reckless and disorganized?

The glutton, *Gulo gulo*. I wanted to see the field paint itself from yellow-brown to leaping orange to smoking coal black aftermath, and I wanted to see it immediately.

Even as I stood back from time to time and watched the athletic beauty of the fires skipping and stuttering across the field, then roaring across the field — even as I felt those first pricklings of doubt — I was still bending down with that box of matches and lighting new ones. It was just so incredibly beautiful. I remember thinking, *It'll all turn out all right, won't it? It always does, right?*

For my own edification, I want to see if I can explain clearly how the change occurred; how it came over me slowly but steadily, like a great tide, this conversion or metamorphosis from calm confidence, even joy, at watching the flames leap and run (watching them with the same pleasure that a farmer might gaze at a field of growing corn), to a subtle and then increasingly a not-so-subtle feeling of uneasiness, then concern, and then flat, out-and-out worry.

The mind and the body are such a strange set of wirings. Even as I was hurrying across the field, still lighting matches, still goading the fire on, that other wave, the opposite wave, was coming in from the other direction, merging with the gleeful or joyful waters; and yet even in the moment when those two emotions were equally balanced in me, the joy fading and the worry rising, I continued to race about the field, still touching match to dry grass, a prisoner or puppet of my own momentum.

How unlike the wild animals we are, in this regard; how loose and relaxed, how unwary, how unable or at least unwilling to change direction quickly, to dart and dip and reverse, to whirl or sprint or flee or leap, but preferring instead to almost always continue on, as if trudging, in the same habits, same directions.

Finally, through some awkward titration, I became aware of the imbalance of the situation and ceased lighting matches, and instead began trying — belatedly — to control and corral the fire, moving out in front of the quick-running flames and stepping on them with my hiking boots, trying to snuff them out.

It wasn't working. There were too many of the fires and they had grown too tall, too exuberant, and were moving too fast. In the time it took to snuff out one boot-size lick of flame, two others would race past me, one on either side; and then when I lifted my boot to go chase after those other two forward-leaping flame licks, the one I was just stomping out would gust back to life.

Soon I was standing ankle-deep in yellow flame, like some heretic; the cuffs of my overalls caught fire, and with a bolt of adrenaline, I slapped them out and danced away from the heat. As if sensing my retreat, the flames surged and skittered forward a good ten feet, rushing on up the hill toward the house.

I remembered idly that the nature lover Thoreau once accidentally set fire to the forest, burning nearly ten thousand acres, and wondered if there is not something strange in all of us, some critical paradox that helps keep us poised and balanced, upright in the world, working at times against even our own hopes and convictions.

Already, I was longing for the luxury of prickling doubt I had harbored scant moments earlier, and was instead in full-fledged panic, running back and forth from one corner of the fire to the next and panting, barely able to catch my breath in the thick gray smoke. Waxy green juniper bushes were exploding into biblical plumes with crackling whooshes each time a flame reached them, and the juniper threatened to send the fire from the yard on into the forest, and into the tops of the trees, with a great fire that would then swing this way and that, swallowing the house.

The junipers burned with far too much energy and enthusiasm;

more boot stomps and slaps of my sweatshirt-like-a-blanket were in no way able to subdue them, and I whirled and ran into the house to grab a five-gallon plastic bucket before beginning to fill it at an outside faucet.

It was a helpless feeling to be urging the bucket to fill faster, even as I sat there watching and listening to more junipers as they plumed into flame.

Finally the bucket was filled, and I dashed down the hill and doused what I gauged to be the most strategically dangerous burning bush — the one that was scant seconds away from transferring its fire to the next, and the next, and the next (the flames were sawing and shifting their way quickly toward an old barn, in which old lumber was stored, lumber so dry it might as well have been dynamite; the fire was only three or four feet from that structure) — and then I raced back up the hill and crouched again by the faucets, panting, waiting for the bucket to fill once more. After it did, I hurled myself back down the hill, stumbling and sloshing, jittery-legged and fatigued already from the heat and smoke, to the next bush, and splashed the five gallons of water onto it like a slurry bomber unloading its cargo from far above; instantly that bush was extinguished, but little matter, for in its place, along the other perimeters, two or three new ones lit up to replace each one that went out.

It was a losing battle, and worst of all, the fire's heat was creating a breath, a wind, that was helping drive it up the hill toward the house; and seeing this, there was no way to not believe that the fire was desiring the house.

I was just about beaten down, already. I like to believe that I'm a hard worker and, when need be, a ceaseless worker, but there must have been some combination of the smoke and the panic — surely not age, not yet — that got me so whipped. I kept trudging up the hill, gasping and filling the bucket as quickly as I could, but the fire had gotten the better of me, and really, I was just going through the motions. It seemed like it was all over; there wouldn't be time to call the VFD, and neither could I tear myself away from the scene, abandoning the flames to make that call.

I kept looking up the driveway, hoping to see Elizabeth come driving down at any moment — perhaps with a second bucket, and a second person; it would make a difference — but she did not appear. My wishes were not enough to summon her, and I imagined that she was still a half-hour distant, crossing the summit only then, and that she would return to nothing but ash and rubble, with a disconsolate husband sitting at the edge of the smoking char, trying to formulate an answer for the question that he knows will be coming: *What happened?*

It wasn't exactly as if I was praying, in my desperation. I fucked up — that's all there was to it — and it seemed silly to ask some greater force for mercy and help in a situation that was completely of my own making, and when I had not been particularly diligent heretofore about staying in close communication with that greater force, grateful for all my many blessings, it's true, and for the spirit and mystery of the woods, and life; but *praying,* well, no, not really. But I have to say, the thought did cross my mind, and it did occur to me to wonder, *Oh, if there is a spirit of the woods out there, the forest, that bears any kinship and mercy toward me, how wonderful it would be, what a miracle it would be, to get a little help with this damned wind right now.*

I want to be very careful not to misrepresent what happened next. I want to be extra certain that I am not suggesting my desire for the wind to cease had any bearing on what happened next, which is that the wind, indeed, ceased.

It lay down like an animal going to sleep, lay down at the last possible second, just before its own impulse carried it up the slight rise and into the house; and in that lying down, that breath of stillness, I was able to begin fighting the fire back. Each bucket I hurled onto the trouble spots now was effective — no other flames rushed left or right around my efforts — and like a pool shark running the table, I was able to begin knocking the fires out, anchoring the corners and front first, and then the flanks, making a stand.

Darkness moved in from out of the woods — dusk was coming in as if made curious by the spectacle of all the smoke and steam — and with each new bucket tossed onto the perimeter, the fire grew quickly tamer until there was almost nothing of it left at all. I was strolling through the blackened field now like a man watering his garden, *sauntering* from one fire to the next; and by the time true evening had arrived, the wind still had not returned, and neither would it, that night. The last little embers and candle flames were snuffed out, and the spring peepers were calling as they did every evening from their floating marsh swamp below, and the snipe were performing their eerie wing-whistling aerobatics above; and there was time enough for me to go back into the house and scrub up all the telltale boot prints of ash and mud and charcoal from where I had earlier thundered through the house, searching for a bucket when the fire had first raged out of control.

And by the time Elizabeth's headlights came sweeping down the driveway accompanied by the crunching of gravel under her tires, I was sitting out on the front porch listening to the night songs and sipping a glass of wine and looking out at the dark patch of field like some successful farmer for whom everything had gone entirely as planned.

It was too dark for her or the girls to see or notice anything, and even then, the next day, they did not at first notice the great swath of black until I drew it to their attention; and even so, the burn looked planned and calculated, geometric and safe. The girls were chagrined by the blackness of the field — I had to explain to them that it was like painting, that that deep black was but like a primer for the most incandescent sort of green, which would be arriving now in only a couple of weeks — but Elizabeth was completely nonplused by it, assuming that the fire had behaved precisely as I had intended it to, accustomed, even this far into our marriage, to the myths of men, and competency, and lovely predictability.

I went out each day, for the following week, before the grass greened up, and searched the barren field for Tracy's earrings, but found nothing; and I shall not look for them in that manner again.

Rain, sun; rain, sun; rain, sun. The tresses of old-man's-beard are sodden, and the entire forest is draped with such dripping, tangled strands, and when the sun comes back out, those tresses begin to steam, and the forest steams too; after a while, this baked-out increase in humidity makes it rain again, warm thundershowers, and it's easy to imagine the plants and trees sucking up the moisture with the straws of their winter-thirsty roots, as my skin and the sleeping chambers of my mind are thirsty also for some true sun, high-angle, long-lasting quality sunlight, and each hour that I have of it, I feel better, that much closer to joy, and then, beyond joy, euphoria.

The fawns are just before being born. It's the last week of May and it seems that in the swollen bellies of the does you can see the bony knees and elbows of the fawns-to-come, and you wonder why the wait, why don't they come on out right now?

It's almost painful to watch the distended does leaping over fallen logs and easing their bulky selves through the narrow hallways and brambly tunnels of alder and hawthorn, and yet you know that it's these last few days that count the most, as the fawns continue to grow, even in their mothers' wombs, gaining every bit of advantage they can — and which they need, in spades, once they hit the ground, birthed into a land with perhaps more predators than any valley in the Lower Forty-eight — bobcats, lions, lynx, wolverines, black bears, grizzly bears, wolves, coyotes.

As the green landscape explodes into emerald life, so too do those leaping nutrients — burgeoning wildly, each day — pass from the forest into the does, and from the does into the fawns. The forest's reckless growth — particularly that last week of May — is evident and palpable, but it is somehow a reassurance to know that the things beneath the surface, the unseen things, such as those fawns within their wombs, are also growing at the same wild and exuberant pace and pattern; that everything, despite running at full roar, is still in perfect step-and-rhythm synchrony. Some think of Handel's shouted *Messiah* as being a Christmas song, but sometimes when I hear it it makes me think of May — complex, exuberant, shouted May.

Like the larch needles themselves, or the fawns-in-their-mothers'-bellies, so too are the deer's antlers expanding quickly now, leaping, accelerating toward some pull of light with a force and reckoning that I suspect is at least as powerful as that of the moon upon the tides. And just as each beach possesses a set of lows and highs, neap tide and spring tide, specific to its unique landscape, so too does each valley, and each ridge and mountain range, possess its own unique angle and rhythm of light's return, with each valley's in-dividual variances as subtle yet distinct as would be the musical compositions of a thousand different composers: each feeling the same raw emotion in May, *joy*, but each composition as different as the composers themselves.

The sunlight flooding down, bathing the land in longer light, is the music, but each unique landscape is the composer; and in May, after the goose-honking cacophony of the music warming up in the pits, the fuller piece, in all its true complexity, begins to rise above the chaos, and to emerge, each year, with brilliance and elegance.

In a harsh climate like this one, a northern climate, snugged in tight against Canada as we are, spring usually comes a week to ten days later than it does down in the towns where we do our shop-ping, Troy or Libby, which are forty miles farther south, and at a slightly lower elevation.

But this difference between landscapes, this other-ness be-tween nearby but different valleys, is not always measurable in lin-ear miles or vertical feet, is not quantifiable just by run-of-the-mill Cartesian advancement and regression of the sun. Once the sun-light, the spring-light, does make it over that northern stone wall and into the Yaak, crossing that invisible divide explained in part by Bergmann's rule — it comes rushing on, I think, even faster and more forcefully than Bergmann himself could have proposed, be-cause we too are in a low-elevation landscape, anomalously so for the northern Rockies. So it is like there's one weird cant, some an-gle, some mathematical torque, involved in the equation.

There's extra force too that's easy to understand, and you sense it, see it, in the robustness of all the plants and animals in the Yaak. Simply put, they have only about fourteen weeks to put on their growth, whereas the same species forty miles south might have an extra four weeks — two weeks on either end of the growing sea-son — to do the same. In the Yaak, then, that compression of growth could surely be assigned some straight-line mathematical number, some coefficient of growth, or coefficient of spring, that relates di-rectly to the explosiveness of spring upon that landscape — just as some tides on a steep pitch will rise with calamitous speed and ac-celeration. If springtime in northern Utah comes on with a whump-force of, say, 7.8, and in the Pleasant Valley, near Libby, with an 8.3, then by the time the green wave of life crests the icy summit and rolls down into the northern Yaak, perhaps it carries a sledge power of, say. 9.3.

And that extra force, that extra power (again, different for every landscape, every valley up here), could be measured in the explosiveness, the recoil from winter, of the larch needles sprouting, and the speed of growth in the antlers of deer, elk, and moose — and can be felt keenly in the blood of all the region's inhabitants, as distinct and unnameably unique to them all, to us all, as the springtime tune of a bird whose name we do not know but whose song is long familiar to us.

Thank goodness the Yaak is merely called the Yaak, rather than "9.3," or "10.0." The name of the place is all we need to know for those of us who live here to be aware of the nature, of its power, and of course, even if we did not know its name, we could feel it — that 9.3-ishness — simply upon first entering its realm and its spell.

Because I am not a mathematician, I can fool and play with math. In addition to our valley high-ending the scale of life, due to the compression and brevity of sunlit days, the so short growing season — residing at the very northern end and range of things, in one of the last few wedges before one goes to the glaciers and total snow, and total sleep, of the farther north — I think there is some cant or twist or torque to our already substantial coefficient of force.

And then upon that cant — call it 15 or 20 degrees plumb of normal, deliciously cockeyed from "normal" — there is yet another torque, so that ours is a strong, strange land upon a strange land upon a strange land, factored thrice away from anywhere else, at least.

The cant — what makes our 9.3 already unique, even more so, not a straight north-south 9.3, but a uniquely tilted 9.3 — comes from a number of other factors, including the scrambled topography, the many J-hooked twists and turns of our ravines and creeks and canyons, so that when spring's forceful green breath and gold light finally do crest the summit and come crashing in, they do so in a crooked, tilted fashion that is once again unique to only our hills, only our mountains.

No artist, no man or woman, or even any committee of the

gods, could have dreamed up such a place. Perhaps one God dreamed and then crafted this one place, or perhaps this valley, kicking and fussing, or sly and secretive, seized and carved its own unique fit in an otherwise seething and occupied world — but for certain, something is going on here, something powerful that should by all rights make scientists fall down in quivering, awe-struck supplication; and that should make us take care of this land-scape, preserve and revere it and its remaining healthy wildness. This power is felt at least as strongly in May as in any other month, if not more so. And for my purposes, as a poet and a resident, we don't need to know the coefficient, or the angle of cant. Simple reverence will suffice.

Perhaps only when we are dead and buried in the valley's rich soils will we understand more clearly the shapes and natures of its many forces.

Perhaps the shapes of those forces — visible to us only now on the outer limits of our understanding, and our vague hypothe-ses — will become firmer then, in the manner of the shapes of shad-ows at firelight's edge stepping closer to reveal their truer and fuller forms, their infinite specificity, revealing the shape of black-backed woodpeckers, long-toed salamanders, grizzly bears, woodland cari-bou. Maybe then.

For now, however — with us not yet immersed in the soil — it is enough to run unknowing into, and through, the quick green light.

And beyond our 9.3-ishness, and beyond our 15-degree cant, there is still another mystery at work — a torque, a wiggle, upon the force of those other two combined forces, yielding even more specificity, more uniqueness, and even more strength. Torque — also referred to as "natural force" — is measured in foot-pounds, or Newton me-ters. Let's just say, for argument's sake, that the torque upon the cant of the force of Yaak is somewhere between seventy-five and eighty-five Newton meters. (Perhaps this last coefficient, unlike the others — the brute power of the place, and the ellipsis of that force — is variable, relaxing and then contracting again, like a clenching fist, or a pumping heart, or a striding, upright animal, squeezing tighter on breezy, gusty, swirly days, and releasing, becoming softer, on balmy calm ones. What handheld computer, or what mainframe, could ever chase down these daily, hourly variances? Surely, only the receptive human spirit — in May, or any other month.)

Anyone who's resided here for any time at all — not even four full seasons, but for even a month's cycle of days — can feel this tightening and loosening of things, out in the woods. Hunters, I suspect, can feel it most intensely — moments when the woods begin to stir, and moments too when all goes slack and still, when the inhabitants of the forest seem not to be thinking anything (there's a distinct sag in the forest's energy) and neither do they seem to even be breathing, but instead resting, almost catatonically, in the manner of a fish that rests for long minutes, motionless, in the seam between currents, or the backwater of an eddy formed behind a boulder.

As to what might help determine this specific and unique degree of torque within the Yaak, I cannot say. I sense that, more than the physical, formula-like character of the previous two forces, cant and topography, this one is more organic, perhaps even a living entity.

Some of the factors that might have a hand in the care and feeding of this organism could be the fact that not only do we lie so severely north — so inflamed to the max with Bergmann's rule (and the rule of his associate, Allen, who noted that the farther north one went, the larger the animals became, as a means of retaining more efficiently their valuable body heat during the long winters) — but also that we lie so severely west: more westerly, and in some regards wetter (because we're snugged in low against the wet side of the Continental Divide) than many other valleys deeper into the Pacific Northwest.

Another aspect of this torque, then, would have to do with the double richness of our incredible sampling of biodiversity. Not only do we possess much of the representative flora and fauna of the Pacific Northwest, coexisting in often unique assemblages and relationships with Rocky Mountain species, but many of our species also are represented from a third ecosystem, the far north of Canada's northern Rockies — the massive Purcell range — and are the southernmost extent in the world where those icebound denizens are found: woodland caribou, and snowy owls.

Even if such numbers do exist, in the end they are no more than metaphors or abstractions for understanding the stories of this place, which sometimes go hurtling past our sleepy eyes, and other times seem to progress at an infinitesimal creep. But if the picture or model of what I'm proposing has any authenticity or integrity to it, then the pattern of it should hold true in the glance of a moment, as well as be expressed across a season, or a year, or a century — just as the principles of the life of a cell should hold true, in logic and pattern, for the principles of an entire organism, and beyond that, a population.

And I believe that this is the case. I believe that there are certain days when the leaning arc of a single hour's worth of sunlight contains in each moment, all of the physical aspects, and the structural patterns, of the entire canted power of the entire season, and the complete year; and in those perfect and distillate moments, those perfect hours, you can taste and feel and know and sense in a single moment the essence of a place's nature and character, a place's voice. Such recognitions carry in them the echo of a time back when such awareness and fluency in the natural world was more common — was in fact perhaps one of our birthrights, as it is that still of the wild animals, for whom a single glance into the woods, or a single wisp of odor, or a single sound detected, might carry to them a better understanding of the identity of that one place than you or I might be able to accomplish or know in a year or even a decade of traipsing methodically and studying those same hills.

In those kinds of moments, however, in which the patterns of a place are to be glimpsed or known in that single hour, what the nature of that light, that hour's revelation, might be like late in November, with the cant leaning down more precipitously than ever, and the days shortening frightfully — an entire day's worth of sun appearing, rising, and then falling between the hours of two and three p.m. — is the quality of fireworks. That one hour's worth of sun, in November, might rise straight up over the ridge, like a sputtering Roman candle, but then descending too within the same space of that very hour. In May, however, the light contained within that same hour's passage, rather than possessing the quality of a lone, fizzling firework, might be more like the taper of some long and wavering blossom, or the fire on some distant August ridge, growing brighter even into the dusk, and on into the night: a flame, a light, that it seems not even night itself can extinguish.

In May, such is the richness and length of the newly arriving light that the languorousness and confidence of it, the *fullness* of it, carry over into our blood, and our spirits, and our own patterns of the heart, and rhythms — just as winter's strangely compressed light (and absence of light) can carry in it a density that can at times be a bit too much to handle, sludging up the blood of those older folks whose blood no longer burns or boils bright enough to keep the sludge at bay.

(Increasingly, I think that one experiences the lightless winters up here as one might a series of concussions, in which, although each individual blow is not too bad, a kind of cumulative effect begins to exert itself — a toll with a price and a cost not apparent sometimes for many years. And when we are young and our blood is joyous and tumultuous, May-like in its own unique and powerful uproar, we do not hear or heed or otherwise notice the arc or cant of those patterns of light and rhythm and mood; but when we are older, and more settled into and accustomed to the world, our moods and rhythms will more closely track those of the sun's and the season's arc across the skies.)

In May, when the sun returns — and not just any old sun, but the delicious, exciting, lengthening sun — then there is for me a feeling of gratitude toward the very earth itself, as you might feel gratitude to some Samaritan who helped you back to your feet after you'd just been knocked down.

And herein, in May, is perhaps one of the definitions of grace in the world: You don't even have to reach out a hand for help. You can crouch or even lie there whipped and beaten finally by the density of winter's lightless weight, disheartened or even defeated into a stupor by the great mass and length of darkness, and yet without your even lifting a hand, the world will find you out in May, will find and reach each and every citizen — both the human and the nonhuman animals, and each and every plant — and will pick you back up and deliver the long slant of that green light into your heart, will pick you up and breathe a warm breath back into your soul, no matter how cold and stiff and dormant it might have become in the winter, and in the absence of green, and the absence of chaos.

You cannot escape this long shaft of light, in May — no more than the warming black soil and flame-tapered green buds of aspen and cottonwood can escape it.

Nothing can hold the light back when it is unleashed into May. We all receive it — the animate as well as the inanimate — as if being lifted onto, and riding, a great green surging wave.

You may not understand or know any new patterns, staring at the cant and cycle, the rise and fall of light, in any of those one-hour windows in May — but you will remember, enthusiastically if you have forgotten it in the long lightless winter, that up here, you are still connected to and fully a part of all those cycles that appear and play themselves out, effervescing, within that one hour of light, for you can feel the same shapes and twists and movements of light going on in your own blood.

A part of you is riding along with each hour of the new light; a part of you is feeling the big river-surge toward its high-water marks; a part of you is feeling those deer's antlers leap from their skulls, restless in the extra-long having-waited. The earth itself seems to shake under your feet, quivering like an animal tensed. It might be what it's like to be a king or queen, except that you rule no one other than yourself, but when a part of you is to be found connected to every other thing in the landscape, riding that green wave, it is quite enough to be a sovereign ruler of yourself; it is an honor.

There is a roaring in your ears, and a joy in your blood, as you ride on that building wave of light.

It's different, here. The wave has its own shape and characteristics. I'm foolish, I know, to even propose that math can capture it. Let the snipe calls capture it, and the density and frequency of the spring peepers, and the black *Bryoria* back in the old forests. Let the scent of spruce sap mixing with ice-snapped fir boughs capture it, and our ten thousand other living things, our ten thousand other living measurements. Our only chore, our only task, is to ride that green wave when the light comes back, flooding around our ankles, and now up to our waists, lifting us.

The weaving continues, accelerating according to that secret cant — all the spilled sprawl and disorder from the beginning of the month lining up now into firming braids of strength, like many creeks and brooks conjoining at the base of the mountains to hurtle us toward June, as if June's warm breath is already looking back at us and blowing its breezes back across green living May, the wild green garden.

Staring out my window one rainy morning, mesmerized by nothing, and thinking nothing, simply entranced by the world, I notice that pulses of green are emanating from various places in the marsh. Stripes and bands of the lengthening marsh grass are illuminated as if slashes of sunlight are falling across them, but there is no sunlight coming down through that steady rain. And gradually, and with some astonishment, I come to understand that the glow, the green light, is coming up in waves from out of the marsh, up from out of the earth itself — subtle variations in soil or peat-richness, perhaps, imbuing one stretch of marsh with extraordinary nutrition, so that the shifting, wavering beams of green light I'm witnessing, rising and moving across the marsh like some immense yet dimly visible creature walking, are nothing less than the sight of life being created, the marsh grass sucking in the rain and warmth and blossoming, leaping, into life. Gray-coated deer, their fur drenched and matted from the steady rain, are emerging from the curtain of the alders on the far side of the marsh and passing now through those waves of pulsing green light.

The deer are wading knee-deep in the marsh, veering from one green place to the next, chewing almost savagely at those living, glowing places of green life — the marsh grass surely so vibrant and alive to the deer, this one day, and so rich in protein, that it is as if the deer might as well be grazing on living fish, or frogs — and now the rain is roaring against the tin roof of my writing cabin, and is beating the deer's already flattened fur tighter against their bony haunches and ribs and shoulders, winter's signature still written sharp upon them, even the swollen-bellied pregnant does.

But they don't seem to care at all, seem in fact to be luxuriating in the rain and the warmth and the richness — and across the far distance of the marsh, they seem to be swimming in the marsh, the grass up to their chests already, so that they might well be swimming in the green light itself, riding its waves . . .

How the simple sight of this severe marsh heals my sadness, and hones my euphoria! It's fine to observe and learn from as many of the infinite patterns and rhythms and cycles as possible, almost all of which are visible out this one small window, beside which I sit butt-anchored for several hours each day — but more than that, it's the great and calm and simple sight of the marsh's beauty, and of the forest's beyond, which soothes my heart the most: the witnessing, more than the understanding.

It's true that any understanding I'm able to glean from the comings and goings of the marsh serves also to deepen and enrich my love for the place, but as far as the great calm hand that touches my heart each time I look out at the marsh, I do not need to know or understand the workings of the bones and muscles and internal organs of this one small landscape, but instead need only to sit quietly beside it and watch, and listen, and smell, and sometimes touch.

The phrase *vast amphitheater* is often a cliché when used in writing about landscape, but it's true nonetheless: in May, that's what this marsh is, as the chaos of disorder continues to swell into shimmering order. Around and around the sounds go, out in the perfect circle of the marsh, rising and falling at all their different scales and notes and levels, and stirring tired hearts back up into joy, and joyful hearts up into euphoria. The tag-team baton-relay music of sora rails: one rail calling to the next, who calls to the next, who calls to the next. The near silent winging of a raven, high above, followed by a shouted cawing that fairly alarms the listener, even though the listener knows the raven is up there. The earnest but still joyful workmanlike trill of blackbirds. The flutes of Townsend's warblers and wood thrushes, and the wet-tennis-shoe-squeaking-on-linoleum cries of the spring peepers. And in the midst of it all, the dull hum of sun-glinting, armored dragonflies, and the silent music of moths, rising by the thousands from the tall grass of the marsh, like marionettes worked jerkily by the strings of the sun's warmth.

Sometimes I wonder if this journal might stand in the near future as some naive treatise of nearly overwhelming innocence, as do the older texts from the last century appear to us now; and whether or not this journal might possess a tone someday like that of the sweetly halcyon chronicles of the ancient travelers who encountered the landscapes and cultures of this country for the first white man's time. There is a part of me that wants to believe fiercely that all these wonders will still be present in the world, even as another part of me knows they will not.

June is coming again, with its ellipses of sun, its ellipses of force. The bear grass, with its wild abundance of every seven years, will be returning. It's looking like an unusually good year out on the marsh for the large crane flies, and for beetles, and white moths. A good year — here on the marsh, anyway, if not so many other places in the world — for yellow-cheeked warblers.

People who know about the deeply specific things of the world — yellow-cheeked warblers, and grizzly bears — say that those things, and hundreds of others of fine-tuned species like them, are not long for this world. I'm committed to becoming more involved and relentless of an activist than ever, which I think is nothing less than the obligation of each of us, in the face of such a terror, and such a theft — such a waste. And yet I'm increasingly aware too as I get older of another obligation I have to the future, in the face of such terror — a world without warblers, or wolverines! — which is to inhabit the present fully, forcefully, joyfully, as would those coming inhabitants of the world themselves, given the opportunity: inhabiting it with a spirit of greenness, a spirit of leaping and reckless, flamboyant life.

I squint my eyes almost to closing, staring out at the sunlit marsh. The ancient buzzing, clattering dragonflies could be pterodactyls far in the distance, doing battle. Already these pages, and this place and time, are but an echo, as are any of our lives when measured against the mountains or against anything other than the abstraction of a calendar.

Still, the marsh grass waves in the wind like a woman's wild hair — no less beautiful than it was a hundred years ago, or a thousand. As it may still be a thousand hence, or for as long as there is sun and rain and snow, and heat and cold, and the color green, and the movement of wind, bathing these things.

I sit hypnotized before my one bright window again, listening to the laughlike trilling of a lone sora rail, and to the faint and distant sound in that wind of last winter's dead alder branches clacking together like bones.

Which matters most, the serenader, or the serenaded?

The grass out in front of the house is a richer and deeper green now than even I, with the paintbrushes of the matches, could have imagined. "Remember how terrible it looked just a couple of weeks ago?" I tell the girls. "Remember how it was nothing but char and scorch?"

They nod, impressed but not overly amazed, and again I have to marvel at, and be grateful for, a life so filled with miracles, visible miracles, which, while such miracles are not quite taken for granted, are not viewed as anything too far beyond the extraordinary, or beyond one's due.

I take off one afternoon to run up on one of the mountains above my home to look for the false morels that sometimes grow in the burned forests up there. It's one of the mountains that feed my family, one of the mountains on which we are fortunate enough some years to take a deer or an elk, and this one day, strolling through the maze of standing fire-gutted black spars, and also among the living trees that survived the fire, I'm fortunate enough to find a patch of morels, which will be delicious when cooked in the same skillet as the elk itself, which also came from this mountain: the decomposing rock, the soil itself, bringing to springing life both the elk and the morel, as well as me, so that if we are not mountains ourselves, moving and gifted briefly with life, we are always a part of those mountains, the arms and legs of those mountains, wandering here and there though returning always to the base of these mountains, which feed our bodies and our imaginations . . .

There is a certain recipe for preparing an elk, when one is fortunate enough to take not just an elk in autumn, but later, in May, morels. You lay the slice of elk meat in the heated iron skillet, with some melted butter and a little salt and pepper, and slice in those morels, sautéing them with the elk meat; and after only a short while, you shut the flame off and let the elk's muscle, warmed in that skillet as if back into life, continue cooking on its own.

Because there's no fat in the meat, the elk-meat muscle conducts heat quickly, as copper wire conducts the galvanic twitchings and shudderings and pulsings of electricity; and the flavor of the morels is absorbed into that warming meat, as the elk in life once browsed on the same terrain, the same soil, upon which those morels were growing, yesterday. And in that manner, once again the meat is suffused with the flavor of the mountain, so that you are eating the mountain, eating the mountain straight from the black skillet, so delicious is it; and timing this last wave of skillet heat, knowing when to turn the flame off and simply let the heat of the meat cook itself, is like catching a wave, a surge, and riding it on in to shore; and the deliciousness of such a meal is no less a miracle than a blackened field turning to green life almost overnight.

The elk roaming through our chests and arms, the elk galloping in our legs, the mountain sleeping in our hearts, present always, whether we are waking or sleeping: rhythms within rhythms within rhythms, which we will never know but can always honor.

The thought occurs to me again how strange and perhaps hopeless this chronicle is, destined to disappear like melting snow, with regard to its calendrical observations, beneath the rude and quick-charging climatic alterations that a warming earth is fast bringing: the tilting of the lovely cant, the wobbling of that fine-tuned cant. That these days will never again have compare; that not only is time rushing past, but so too is the four-seasoned, temperate nature of this place. As if it is all finally, after so many centuries, becoming only as if but a dream.

But my God, what beauty.

JUNE

....

IF I MAY BEGIN with one of the most ancient of clichés, *it's been a long winter,* you will hopefully forgive me. I live on a million-acre island in northern Montana. A cold, wide, deep mountain river bounds me to the south, as do Idaho's castles of mountains to the west and Canada's clearcuts to the north. I am bounded on the east by a vast lake, like a moat. My valley is an island, and within the cold and snowy year, here in Canada's shadow, June is its own island within the island. It's not quite as if you've been sleeping in all the previous months — neither after June passes so quickly, like a flame, will you immediately close down your year and begin preparing for hibernation — but it is not until June arrives that you realize, without having understood it earlier, that this is what some relatively huge part of the winter-ravaged husk of your body and soul has been waiting for: the long reach of days, the barefootedness, and the extravagance of warmth in the north country. Every cell in your body drinks in, absorbs, that new long light, clamors for it, as if you are sipping champagne from some tall fluted glass.

Each year it is as if you have never felt warmth before.

There have been cycles going on all along, an infinitude of cycles — sheets and braids and overlays and intertwinings of cycles: rise and fall, birth and death, motion and stasis — but in June, so illuminated and heightened are the dramas of these cycles that they are visible even to our often benumbed senses.

They are more than noticeable. In June, they are dominant.

Beyond the new warmth, and the tongues of gold light, tongues of green flame, the thing that most announces itself in the drama of these heightened cycles is the deer. At first they too are as luxuriant as any of us; like us, they too pass through the new light with seeming wonderment. Hugely pregnant, the does wander through the standing water in the marsh, pausing to browse the newly emergent subaquatic vegetation that might carry four hundred times as much calcium as do the dry-land plants.

So rich is their diet at this time of year — the first of June — that
the deer will be shitting a stream of clearish fluid into the marsh
even as they are feeding on that new growth there, so that you realize it is as if the slack-water marsh has been given a current by the
sun's energy and is flowing now like a stream, passing straight
through the deer as if through an empty vessel, though at least that
calcium is transferred to the deer, calcium deposited as if scorched
into the deer, while all else rushes past. Calcium is the one thing the
deer most need at this one time of year, this one week — and it is
not the marsh that is moving like a current, but rather, the deer
moving through the marsh that is the current.

I think that deer are to this valley as salmon are to the Northwest: they have their own lives and passages, but they are also immensely, dramatically, a key part of the larger picture, the larger
pulse, of this place. Just as the salmon gather nutrients from far out
at sea, packing those nutrients into the slabs of their flesh in the
form of rich, dense protein and then ferrying that protein inland,
upriver during the spawn, where the bears and eagles and ravens
and lions and every other carnivore capture and eat that protein
and then carry it in their bodies farther inland, up into the mountains, depositing in that manner, in their spoor, deep-sea salmon
atop an inland mountaintop — so too are this valley's white-tailed
deer the bearers of dense protein, slabs of nutrients moving muscu-
larly from one improbable place to the next, in ribbons of grace:
from a marsh plant drunk on sunlight, to a deep cedar forest, to a
lion's belly, to a sunny ridge in the mountains — a passage, a narrative, for which there is never any end, only new beginnings, always
all over again, for as long as there is sunlight in June, and deer.

Early into June, hiking down the trail to the waterfall — flailing at
the mosquitoes that form their own sheath around this north country — I am trailed by the season's first hummingbird, following my
red shirt through the old forest, down by the rushing creek.

Around this same time — it can happen as early as the first or second day of June — the green cottonwood buds, swollen and turgid
with the quick rush of chlorophyll, will begin shedding their heavy,

sugar, resinous husks as the leaves emerge, looking like nothing else so much as the green tips of candle flame. Entire trees are alight in this manner, like candelabras, and if you are standing beneath one of these trees late in the afternoon, you can hear the sound all around you of the heavy, sticky bud husks falling to the forest floor, pattering like rain onto the forest's carpet of last autumn's dried yellow-brown leaves. And as you listen, beneath the blue sky, to that rainlike sound of the leaves being born — sticky husks landing on you, bouncing off you like hail — you can scent the exquisite odor of their emergence, and there is no other smell like it in the northern Rockies, no other smell like it in the world, when the cottonwoods begin to breathe and to exhale their sweet green breath into the valley.

(Later into June, not too much later, on an even warmer and windier day, you will be walking along a rushing creek and will stop with amazement as the sky before you fills with swirling white feathers and flakes. The temperature might be eighty degrees, the wind warm and from the south. The cottonwoods have just released their seeds, their cotton — you know this, you remember it from this time last year, and the year before, and the year before, but so ass-whipped are you still from winter's brute and sun-cheap passage that you physically flinch at the sight of what appears to be more damn snow, snow in June, even on a hot, windy afternoon . . .)

Shortly into June — usually within those first couple of days, as the sticky green pods of cottonwood resin are oozing and pattering to the ground, and as the cries of warblers, vireos, and red-winged blackbirds return (the snipe have been here a long time already, wind winnowing) — the deer disappear, as if they have left the country. They simply vanish, like guests leaving a party much too early — and you know that they have gone off into the most remote places, the safest, shadiest, most hidden places, to begin preparing to give birth to the fawns, which, having been conceived back during the falling snows of November, were then carried across the long perils of the sleeping winter, crossing all the way across the warming spring, finally, safely, into the tumultuous country of June.

The world knows the fawns are born before you do. Sometimes you'll be fortunate enough to see one newly emerged, knock-legged

and groggy, limbs still unfolding from that long sleeping passage — but usually it is not until a day or two later that you know
the fawns are being born. You generally don't yet see the fawns
themselves but see instead their little button-size hoofs, still black
and shiny, undigested in the piles of scat left behind by the bears
and wolves and lions and coyotes that have been feasting on them.

(Soon enough, the predators will stop catching so many fawns;
soon enough, the fawns will be big enough and strong enough to
escape. It is only in those first few days, when most of the fawns are
born all at once, that they are so vulnerable. Prey swamping, it's
called, an evolutionary mechanism that ensures some fawns will
survive by sheer mathematical probability — the lions and coyotes
are too busy eating this sudden bounty to catch them all.)

The world tells you of the fawns' arrival too with the sound
of the ravens. The sky is much more active with them, their black
shapes flying through the dense forests of spruce and fir with greater
agitation and purpose, and their raucous cawing, particularly in the
heat of the day, when normally they are silent, tells you of the ravens' excitement, and you understand that they are traveling to and
from the many kills, hoping to feed on a scrap or two; though rarely
is anything left, only the sound of the ravens flying overhead, circling and swarming the lion, or wolf, or bear, or coyote, that is eating that fawn.

You can tell too when the fawns are being born, I think, because
the same legions of mosquitoes that have been swarming you for
the last couple of weeks are one day suddenly bloated. They've
been feasting on the defenseless fawns for the last few days, and
now when you swat them there's usually a splash of red on your
arm — blood from their last meal, deer blood.

(Later that night, on the grill outside, I'll find myself cooking
a venison steak taken from a deer the previous autumn. How we
struggle to continue to try to believe in the myth that not everything in the world revolves around the consumption of another
thing, even as time itself gnaws at the world equally, the animate
and the inanimate, the living and the dead. How we labor to believe
that, for a moment, or a few moments — as during the high pendu-
lum of solstice or equinox — things can and do exist outside the

embattled realm of the utilitarian and the manipulated. How we treasure and cherish the peaceful occasions, too few in number, when we gaze upon something without evaluating its cost or its usefulness, without evaluating it at all, only gazing upon it.)

Sometimes in the mountains I will come upon a bear or an elk from behind and will observe it looking off a ridge through the trees at the valley far below and beyond, and it will seem to me for the moment in which I watch the animal unobserved that it is considering nothing, only watching the view of the valley below.

And then a shift in the breeze or some other sense or impulse will seize them and they will know that even as they are watching, they are also being watched — the bear or elk will whirl, will discover me, and in wild alarm will then gallop down off the ridge and into the timber, crashing through dry sticks and breaking branches, as the world resumes again its unfathomable but lovely forward motion . . .

Landscape can be a kind of body, and the rains and snows, the streams of sunlight, the creeks and rivers and marshes, and the wild lives of the animals that filter through these forests can be like a kind of blood, drawing a community together as close as if by blood, with all its attendant fidelities and frustrations, the inexplicable, passionate loves and fights. As the red blood that passes through a family connects one member to the other, so too does the integrity of this landscape, with its many complex workings, pass through and around us all, binding us.

You can see this while standing by the side of a lake, watching the mosquitoes swarm; watching the fish in that lake cruising the surface, sucking down those dancing sunlit clouds, water splashing. You might cast out into those fish, might catch one and take it home and clean it and eat it. If you did, you would be eating the flesh of the fish that had eaten the mosquitoes that had been living on the blood of deer and ourselves, ourselves who had been living on the blood of the deer from last autumn's harvest.

It's enough to make you dizzy. It's enough to make you fall down in the high green grass and call out in some sort of surrender, as if all your life you have been struggling to hold up some false idea of how you fit into the world.

It's like waking up to realize someone, or something, loves you.

The tender fury of June! Nearly every little thing, every tiny thing, is born in June. Even as the world is swelling to its full and busy drama, the tiny world-to-come is murmuring beneath the grass, wandering and creeping and plotting and planning for the world-to-come, for the next wave, and the next. Little yellow grouse chicks the size of Ping-Pong balls scuttle through the forest, following their mothers. Salamanders the size of fingernail clippings wriggle beneath damp leaves, barely larger than mosquito larvae.

The needles on the larch trees, those ancient, primitive trees that are both one thing and yet another — the world's only deciduous conifer — are just now beginning to grow, surging on the sudden leap of June sunlight, even though in ten to twelve weeks they will be done growing, will be dying already, gold by August, September at the latest. The larch attack the summer, with their vigor and beauty, like a man and a woman who have been told they have only one day left to live, and all the rest of the forest, in June (and every other month), acknowledges their strength and beauty and bravery.

By the second week of June, as the soil begins to warm, on a hot day when all else is momentarily still and silent, you can hear beneath the new heat a rasping, grinding sound coming from the fields and the forests — coming from the soil, is what it sounds like — and you can spend hours down on your hands and knees searching for its provenance without ever finding it.

It sounds like croaking frogs, or a strange kind of cricket, and yet it's strangely disembodied; it's all around you. Whatever it is, there must be thousands of them, and sometimes even as you are down on your hands and knees, parting the grass to search for the rasping sound — lifting rocks and peering under them, and stalking the sound — the tenor and directional flow of the sound will change so that now it seems to be coming from above you, from up in the trees. It's as if the forest is shouting, or at least grinding its teeth, and it's extremely unsettling.

It's sawyer beetles, doing their best to eat the world.

In his book *The World of Northern Evergreens,* E. C. Prelou describes the mechanics of the sound.

You are most likely to hear it if you go into recently cut-over conifer forests while the logs are still on the ground. If the logs have been there for any length of time, they will almost certainly contain immature sawyer beetles, voracious grubs with no legs but strong jaws. The steady, rhythmical sawing sound of their chewing is easily heard from as far as ten meters. On a hot, windless summer afternoon, when the birds are silent and (except to a naturalist) the cut-over land seems lifeless, the only evidence of active life may be the sawing sound of the sawyer grubs, steadily chewing wood with the relentless regularity of metronomes.

And what of our lives? Are there always subterranean disintegrations, reverse currents of disassembly, moving beneath us, even in green June? Even as one thing is being built, is another being torn down?

Can such sound be detected? Or in June — green, wet June — do such gnawings cease in our own scattered and confused lives, bringing us the momentary peace that early summer is so adept at delivering?

I think it is the latter. In June, when I lie in bed at night, in the cool evening, and muse upon, and look forward to, the rest of the summer, and the rest of my life, I can hear no subterranean gnawings. I can hear only the chorus of the frogs down in the marsh, and the snipe up in the stars, and the owls booming down in the old forest. I can hear only the here and now.

By the fourteenth of June, the scent of the wild roses is in full roar — perhaps my second-favorite fragrance of summer, next to the green cottonwoods — and around this time the days are often filled with alternating thundershowers followed by intense sunlight, so that the effect on the roses is that of being in a greenhouse; each new thunderstorm waters the roses, summoning brighter colors and denser odors, and then each new appearance of the sun lifts the petals of the blossoms slightly farther apart, releasing a new wave of scent, and the sun-warmed air currents carry the odor in that clean-washed air just a little farther, until by the end of a day of such intermittent rainstorms and sun passages, the scent of the wild roses is so strong as to be intoxicating, as fulsome as a large meal.

What I like best, with regard to the roses, is the way some of them smell when they are next to a cliff, a talus slope, or a rock wall. I love rocks and stones, and because the roses prosper in rocky, fast-draining places, I'll often find a tangle of scented roses nestled amid a tangle of rocks, and my happiness will be doubled.

As well, the rocks act as a reservoir for extra heat, so that with that refracted heat they help elicit even more odor from the roses in their vicinity: a rose growing out of a rock wall is always going to smell stronger, more wonderful, on a sunny day, than a rose growing anywhere else — and again, it's a cliché, but sometimes passing by such places I'll pause, feeling intoxicated, and might even lean in against that rock cliff or rock wall for a moment, dizzy — leaning in against it as if for support, or to worship it.

And if it is this intense for our dull senses, what must it be like for the animals?

Often the rose blossoms, still studded and sparkling with rain from the day's earlier shower, will be humming, shaking, as round bumblebees burrow into the heart of the rose, and the sun will be warm against the back of your neck, so that you understand clearly the one basic gospel of all this activity, all this music and noise: that the gospel is heat, heat is the driving force of change — the thing that has been missing for so long but is finally here, once more, and right on time.

Other things you can count on, in June: the rich scent of lupine, blazing so royal blue beneath the old larch that you understand, perhaps for the first time, that blue *does* have a scent, or at least that particular deep shade of blue, in this particular forest. It is a sweet smell, yet so dense that that night as you undress you can still smell it in your clothes.

Heat and rain, heat and rain, are what lift June, in this forest, from the wreck of winter. No month passes quicker up here, despite the absurd lengthening of June's days. June growing like a crop, like those green fields leaping into grassy flame; June leaping past us like the bucks' antlers, which, still sheathed in velvet, can grow as much as an inch a day as the deer feed on the richness of those newly emerging plants.

If you do not hold on to your reason, you might for a moment become confused, watching the deer browsing the fast-growing bush, the shape of which is almost identical to the fast-growing branching of antlers — the bush shaking as the deer browses among it, and the antlers shaking, as the deer nibbles and chews — and for a loosened moment, off-balance by the drama of gentle June, you might feel again that you are falling, even as the curtain of grass leaps quickly up and past you. Up in the north country, the first time you encounter this feeling you're a little bereft, initially, feeling fooled as the old belief in which the world has instructed you — the belief that you, we, all of us, are huge and important, significant and dramatic and creative and daring — falls away like a small brown coin dropped into the middle of that field of rising grass . . .

In subsequent years, if you survive and accept the shock of that initial surprise, you will still be thrown off-balance by it — June's whooshing, singing, scented, bright-colored arrival — but you'll take pleasure in the reminder of your invisibility; you'll be comforted by the graves of grass, the graves of shouting, stretching life leaping up all around you, with your own life so small and sedate and safe by comparison that the world is entirely as it should be, that you are like a mouse down at the bottom of that cool green waving grass, hopelessly lost, hopelessly safe beneath the huge mystery and motion and uproar of the world above and beyond . . .

You can smell the grass growing, in June. You can smell the shafts of sunlight piercing the translucent blades of grass.

You can smell all the forests' different odors as they cool and settle in pools and eddies, later in the day, as the light grows soft. Cooling lupine, cooling chlorophyll, cooling cottonwood. Spruce, fir, tamarack. Cooling yarrow, cooling sedges. Owls hollering, down by the marsh, and back in the old forest, beyond. Snipe.

Sometime around the seventeenth of June, the first wisps of panic are able to be scented. In the beginning, it's not even so much actual panic as much as the idea of panic: a dawning awareness of how truly fast June is moving.

Oh my God, you think, one morning around the seventeenth or eighteenth of June, waking up to it like a middle-aged life, or a middle-aged marriage; or a feeling like sleeping late, awakening at nine or ten to find the morning half gone and the day itself considerably reduced.

You can't keep pace with June. No one can keep pace with June. It's this realization, of the distance between reality and desire, that conspires in you one morning to cause you to sit bolt upright and exclaim, *My God, where is it going?* or *My God, it's going so fast.*

Relax. Later into June — almost into July — you will begin to take naps. After the initial panic, you realize how truly long the days hang this month. It's true, by the third week of June, nearing the solstice, there are only nine weeks of summer left. But more than half a year's worth of light will be crammed into that sleepy, dense richness in the nine weeks to come. There's no hurry. You can slow down. You can pretend that there's no hurry, can pretend it until you will it into becoming the truth, and it's true, there *is* no hurry. You can make it be so simply by wishing — in June, at least.

Rain, heat, rain, heat — the two elements alternating like the twin hoofs of some prancing animal, drumming on the land, then summoning the grass, raising it higher each time. On a walk down an old abandoned logging road, you stop beside a puddle and notice the dozens of baby salamanders, barely larger than these commas, resting in the sun-warmed water. You lift one out of the water on the tip of your finger and hold it up close to your face so that you can see it. Even embryonic, almost humanly so, its sleek body is muscular and appears to be tensed, as if ready to spring back into its puddle, as if ready to leap back into the forest. You stare at it, and it stares back at you, unblinking. Its gold eye looks back at you, beholds you steadily, as if looking through the lens of the millennia, or as if watching you from the moon. You're a little spooked by the hint of sentience in a creature you can barely even see. You set it down carefully back into its puddle and walk on, huge-footed.

The solstice comes and goes. It's an absurdly long day. You think of those sawyer beetles, chewing, gnawing, breaking those logs down, crumbling from within.

My daughters and I go for a hike through the old forest, the ancient forest, along a rushing creek not far from our home. We walk for a long time, passing through shafts of late-afternoon summer light filtering in beams and columns down through the latticework branches of old cedars, light falling softly through the feathers of the old larch, and later in the day, on the walk back, Lowry asks, seemingly from out of nowhere, *Where is God?*

The question catches me for half a step, maybe longer.

Everywhere, I answer.

Lowry considers this, looks around, then points to a huge cedar. *Is that tree him?*

Yes.

Where's his ear?

Well — he really doesn't have ears. I can see her considering an earless visage, and so I change tack and fall back on the familiar: *Everywhere.*

She peruses the woods more closely. A tree has fallen across the trail and been sawed into pieces by the trail crew and shoved to one side.

Is that cut-down tree him?

Yes.

On the drive home, once we get to the gravel drive, I let Low sit in my lap and steer. As she does so this time, I notice that she keeps looking out her window and flashing her pretty smile, and holding it for several seconds. When I ask her what she's doing, she says, *Smiling at the trees.*

It's very late into the month now. I'm sitting in my cabin, working on an essay in the broad daylight, looking out the window occasionally at the green marsh, and beyond that, at the dark blue of the old forest. The day is shining — no deer are out in the marsh, midday as it is, and the marsh grasses are stirring in the breeze only slightly, moving like the gentle swells of the ocean, far out at sea, as if something immense is passing by, just under the surface, and the climbing heat of the day is lifting the metal roof of my cabin as the metal expands ever so slightly.

The metal is beginning to creak beneath the sun, making a steady ticking sound as if trying to register or quantify the sun's warmth, and so accustomed am I to inhabiting this place — this chair, this desk, this cabin — that I soon find myself lulled, as if by hypnosis, into comfortable rhythm with the ticking roof, so that my heart is beating in slow and steady resonance with it, even pausing or skipping, sometimes, as my heart lingers for half a moment, waiting for that next tick; as if waiting for or seeking permission from something — the sun — for each next beat.

For just a moment, an image comes to me of me stepping outside myself; for just a moment, I can imagine a person, a man, like myself, sitting in that cabin, his heart beating in unison with the midsummer sun — sitting in that dark, cool cabin, beneath that green metal roof, which is swathed in shady green glowing alder light — and in that image, the man is imagining, dreaming, writing, dreaming with his heart lifting, ticking to the pulse of the sun.

With great difficulty — again, as if hypnotized — I pull back from the image and willfully turn my back on the man, and the scene of him at his desk, writing. I must hurry outside and into that rare light and warmth. There are scant hours left.

JULY
....

JULY ON THIS ISLAND is, I think, the strangest month for a writer. The euphoria of June's wild courtship has settled into you, has integrated youthfully into the powerful rhythms and patterns of the place, as well as the season, high summer — and likewise, the girls are in full vacation frenzy. There are hikes I want to take, explorations into the backcountry, and always, activist tracts and op-eds and letters of comment to address, meetings to attend; and there are outings to take with Elizabeth, both in the city and in the country — a raft trip in Canada, an art exhibit opening in Washington, D.C., a concert in Seattle — and, theoretically, there are stories to write too, hunkered down in the little log cabin at marsh's edge.

But first and foremost, these tender few years that they are young, there are the girls, and their summer needs and desires. It doesn't take a rocket scientist to observe that the girls are their own seasons, perhaps compressed into several years of girlhood rather than into a single year, though again, who can say that they are not also the year into themselves, for no one year is the same with them; they are changing daily and nightly, and unlike the seasons, which rotate annually with precise and reassuring sameness and repetition, affording a careless or inattentive or distracted observer opportunity again and again to examine the marvelous construct of each day and each season, there exists no such return opportunity for the girls, and my parenting of them. I must notice it now or miss it forever.

So they take precedence, particularly in the summer. Still, I cannot afford to abandon my trade completely — there is the so-called living to be made, and there is also that even more restless stirring or gnawing of craft. Always, you want to try something you haven't tried before — to discern some new story, to visit some new territory, to meet some new characters, and to reach a place also where your sentences are drawn tightly, or if not tightly, then elegantly.

All of that takes a strange and unreplicable mixture of happiness and despair and dreaminess and urgency. And summer — particularly July — is an ideal time for the luxury of possessing, and maintaining, all those writerly emotions, keeping them separate for a while, then mixing them together for a while, as if in a recipe — except for the beckoning, lovely call of childhood summer.

So I still wander out to my cabin each morning and stay there until the afternoon. But too many days, especially in July, I don't dive as deep as I could, or should, to get where I really want to go. Even before I settle in and prepare to descend, I'm already thinking about pulling out. And that's all right: I am not complaining. In fact, it's wonderful. If I can just manage to stay close to the dreaming, in July — not quite reaching it but neither letting it slip away — then hopefully, the ability and energy and desire to dream will be accessible and available in August, or September, or even October.

So this summer, particularly July, seems to summon the dream-time, and makes a space and a way for it — but I can only try to keep that dream-garden, that mental place, briefly weeded and watered, and can occasionally cut some herbs from it, for drying; I can't harvest it, or prepare any elaborate meals. I can instead only glance out the window at it from time to time and know that it's a good growing season for such things.

Likewise, in my cabin, the pen just doesn't want to move across the paper, even though it seems that it should. I'm thinking about the chance all that extra daylight gives me to do chores — piling brush, stacking rock, changing the oil in the generator, cleaning the trucks, or any of ten thousand other non-writerly things — and I find myself working slower and slower, if at all, staring out the window at the green marsh for long minutes at a time. Fifteen, twenty, even thirty minutes will pass without my thinking a single worthwhile thought.

Instead, I'll just watch the color green, and listen to the birds, and the wind, pitching and swooping and rushing around, the wind as active in July as I'd like my mind to be — racing, wondering, exploring — and finally I'll lower my eyes back to the page and scratch out a paragraph or two, telling myself that tomorrow will be the day I'll really get into the good stuff, tomorrow, tomorrow. Having finished my thermos of coffee, I'll close my notebook and wander on back up to the house — where has the morning gone? It always seems as if I've done nothing but sit there and feast on the color green, or green and gold, as if on a meal, and nothing else, as if I have only taken, and have given nothing. And when I walk into the cool house, with its high downstairs ceilings, the girls will hear me enter and will begin calling out the plans for the day, incorporating me into whatever play of the moment is transpiring, whether it's Barbies, or watering their garden, or playing in the wading pool, or dressing the cat up, or swinging on the swing set, or packing for a picnic, or a trip to this or that lake, or this or that waterfall: incorporating me, in that fashion, into their day, their days, as July itself incorporates us all into the middle of the braid of summer. And in July, things feel calmer, less rushed, as if, for once, you truly can say, if you want to, *Tomorrow, tomorrow* . . .

Every month has its flavor, as would any certain spice — tarragon, marjoram, fennel, cumin. I am not sure what the taste of July is, but I think it is something sweet, like a dessert that you might eat slowly, after the full and complex and dramatic onrushing meal of June, and before the next-days of August. I think that July is also like one of the very best fieldstones we find occasionally for use in the rock walls we like to build (rock walls that serve no purpose but instead travel only as if of their own accord off into woods, tracing some line of contour that is pleasing to the eye). The long, flat, thin rocks are my favorites — "Sweet!" I'll cry while driving down the road when I see such a specimen, talus-slid and winter-tumbled to road's edge, and the girls will groan, knowing it means I'm going to stop and try to grunt-wrestle it into the back of the battered old truck. It is these rocks, so level and balanced and sturdy and durable, so *fixed,* and perfect for linking one run of joints to the next, that remind me of July — or rather, vice versa — with the dense, unchanging slab of July laid as a bridge between June and August, seeming somehow twice as long as either of those other two months, as befits our orthodox concepts of the classical, elegant shape of beginning, middle, and end. The animal- or muscle-shaped lens, with the middle twice as long as either the beginning or the end.

My life, I realize suddenly, is July. Childhood is June, and old

age is August, but here it is, July, and my life, this year, is July inside of July.

The girls love to go on picnics, even to the point that they'll hike
for an hour or more to a favorite spot — a little tumbling waterfall
or a certain lake. (Both girls, when each was younger, for many years,
pronounced the word *pig-net;* they loved them before they knew the
name for them.) They love to pack their straw hampers with chips
and apples and grapes and bread, and they love to cook hamburgers
over the fire. When we go to the lake, I'll carry the canoe, portag-
ing it ridiculously far into the woods, along with life vests and such,
and we'll take turns, two or three at a time, when paddling around
out on one of those round lakes; and for the life of me, I can't tell
if I'm helping to teach them leisure or industriousness. We walk a
long way, sometimes, with the girls carrying their baskets, and yet
once to our spot, wherever it is, we'll lounge in the green grass or on
some huge and perfectly tilted slab of rock. We'll wade in the clean
creek, or swim, with our life vests on, in the clean lake.

Perhaps I am confusing the word *leisure* with *luxury.*

Is *privilege* the right word for this life — and for being able to
show the girls such places, such things? We're conditioned to believe this, I think, and while I bear great gratitude to the world for
all of its beauty and richness and bounty, I also sometimes grow
angry with myself, and even defensive, when I find myself falling
too much into that trap of thinking in those terms. The girls — and
Elizabeth and I — are lucky to know such a vital landscape, with its
pieces still intact; we're even *fortunate,* and yes, it's true, we're even
privileged.

And yet there's a part of me too that knows, even if dimly and
far beneath the surface, that such natural treasures were once everyone's birthright, that landscape was inseparable from being, and
that one no more had to ponder the issues of clean air, clean water,
and the presence of grizzly bears and bald eagles and old forests
than one did one's own name, or identity. There was gratitude and
wonder, even awe, and yes, a feeling of privilege, I'm sure, even before these things became rare. But somewhere across the generations, I think our vision of landscape has been worn down in this

culture, so that gradually we have ceded an understanding that our public lands and parks are owned by us to a vision instead in which they are a commodity, so rare have they become, and that they are to be managed by industry, even as we understand that industry will not be kind to them.

I don't know. I'm angry and joyful both. It's an incredible privilege — I guess that's the right word, after all. But still, I want to argue that it's more luck or good fortune than privilege. *Privilege* seems to possess a faint air of special entitlement — entitlement beyond the norm, available only to the elite, and that, of course, is precisely how the industrial elite would like it.

There's not an hour of my life that passes up here, I don't think, without my being aware, sometimes acutely, of my good luck, my good fortune. But still, I balk at that word *privilege,* for once such a world belonged to all of us, or at least the option or possibility of such a world before it was taken from us, before we failed to protect sufficient quantities of it from our own appetites, for the future.

I do believe that clean air, clean water, and wild mountains and old forests are our birthrights; that a wild and healthy landscape is, or should be, a constitutional right, a freedom, to be protected and celebrated. And as with any right, there is an attendant responsibility.

I want the foundation of it — this luck — to be set within the foundations, like stone, of who they are. And July will still be July, if not for another ten thousand years, then for a while longer anyway, with or without the perceived rights and responsibilities of one species, human beings, and with or without those emotions of awe and gratitude, as well as fear and anger and love. I will try hard only to paint with the green and gold brush of the month — to celebrate, not lament, and to not question tomorrow — but the reader needs to know of this confusion. (As, I suspect, the girls are already aware, to some extent, even if as a current running just beneath the surface — a hidden creek, trickling beneath a talus pile of jumbled lichen-clad boulders.)

There are times when I forget my fear for the future of this landscape, and when I exist only in the green moment. And maybe that's what this narrative is about: trying to isolate those moments from the periods of nearly daunting fear, and even outrage.

They do still exist, those utterly green moments. And I find them more often within the girls' company than not.

By July, the garden is up, even in such a northern landscape as this one. The girls have their own little fenced-in patch, and they wander it in the evenings, snapping peas off the bush and dropping about every third one into the pan for dinner while eating the first two, and then, on the walk back up the hill, they'll browse on those that managed to get into the pan in the first place, so that we'll be lucky if even three for four make it to the dinner table.

Am I being too soft on them? Should I be sterner and insist on a firmer demarcation between the harvest and the consumption? Am I serving them poorly to take pleasure in this lax and vaguely feral method of seeing that they eat a balanced diet?

Somehow, it seems a part of July.

The days are getting shorter, though we will have not yet really noticed it. If anything — as we become more and more accustomed to, and comfortable with, the rhythms of summer — it will even seem to us that they are still lengthening.

A bath, brush your teeth, and then story time, alternating between Mary Katherine's room and Lowry's. *Old Yeller, Savage Sam, The Hobbit, Harry Potter and the Chamber of Secrets, Treasure Island.*

Day after day there is a sameness, a suspension, that comes in July.

I was wrong about saying those rock walls we're building — rock walls leading nowhere, neither containing nor restricting anything — serve no purpose. And likewise, I think the July summer days have purpose, even if in untraditional or unquantifiable ways. Even if their purpose is to have no purpose.

Beauty, and rest, alone.

The irony is that it's not entirely restful, for Elizabeth and me. Mentally, its reinvigorating, but physically, under a northern summer's heightened and ambitious pace, it can become exhausting. Cook late, after getting in from the lake, clean dishes, get the girls to bed, read for a few minutes — suddenly it's midnight. Up early, then, with the world growing light again so soon (the girls sleep on, until nine, sometimes ten o'clock in the morning), and do it all over again.

The course of the invisible rock walls of childhood continues to extend itself, on through the seasons — and the seasons in the landscape itself act as the mason at least as much as do our hopes and dreams.

What is the name for this unspoken, elegant fittedness, possessing not the invisible joints of the stone wall or any noticeable mesh of cog to gear but instead an utter seamlessness? In July, as the fields and meadows begin to bloom with the white blossoms of yarrow, and clusters of pearly everlasting, and even oxeye daisies, the deer fawns, similarly spotted, lie in these fields, camouflaged within the season, calibrated almost to the day, even to the hour.

To cant our entire world, our weather and our seasons, by ten or fifteen degrees, as if striving to tip the world over on its side, leveraging it with some huge pry bar — how will that listing, that destruction, affect all the invisible angles and hard-gotten, beautiful negotiations of the world?

This astounding unity that we live in and amid, this community of order and elegance so blatant, so powerful and just beneath our nose that often we do not even see it — will we notice it only as it begins to fall apart, the running joints finally beginning to present themselves, widening and wobbling?

And again, there must be some word for it: the fittedness, and this overarching sameness of pattern and even desire. In July, the orange checkerspot butterflies whirl around the orange poppy coalbright blazes of orange hawkweed, while the yellow sulfurs, also like sparks, dance and skitter across the fields from one butter yellow dandelion to the next, or from the similarly yellow blossoms of one heartleaf arnica to the next. The blue sulfurs, of course, pass from one bellflower to the next — watching them stir, you think at first the bellflower blossom itself has suddenly unfolded and taken flight, and it all seems like a kind of inaudible music, their movements and fitted order like the score and composition for some beautiful sheet music that in life we cannot hear, can instead only see; though sometimes I wonder, were any observer to watch and listen long enough, and deeply enough, if some faint and distant orchestral stirring might somehow be heard, like the preliminary warming-up noises underlying preparations for some even vaster symphony playing always, and always just beyond our notice, no matter how careful the listener, or the observer.

(I think that hawks, red-tails and peregrines, kestrels and sharp-shinned hawks and harriers, with their high drifts selected, can hear better this music, and all the sounds between that music; and that wolves and bears following almost constantly the shifting, dissolving, unraveling scent trails of their prey can also smell such orchestral fullness. Where we as our own lately arrived species fit into this orchestra, I'm not sure, unless as I suspect it is in the audience: that we came here last and latest, or were put here last and latest, to observe, and celebrate, and perhaps be the caretakers . . .)

This fine-tuned sameness, this tendency, predisposition, even yearning, for one thing to follow the lead of another, like the wheeling of an entire flock of birds that gives itself over surely to no considered forethought but that instead pivots on some invisible point in the sky with not even whisper or rustling of wings, deflecting the flight of a hundred individuals as one being for no apparent reason, like water flowing around a boulder placed midstream . . . What is the name for it, the way the deer and elk and antlers, designed for battle, look nonetheless exactly like the limbs and branches of the same forest thicket in which they take refuge? Or for the way you can walk far up a mountain, here in the Yaak, and find a little hand-dug pit where a miner picked at a quartz vein a hundred years ago, and then, traveling only another few yards upslope, but nearly a hundred years in time, you can notice the freshly overturned slabs of rock (perhaps thrust there by the miner himself) where a grizzly has been hunting for ants and digging for *Eriogonium* bulbs in that mountain soil, and chewing on blossoms of glacier lilies, bright as gold itself, two miners digging in the same place, only a century apart?

We do not have a name for it, in our language; perhaps we need to make up a name for it, to help draw more attention to it, in order that we might be more respectful of it — this fittedness, this elegance in which we rarely participate, but with which we have been entrusted to notice, and safeguard.

What would the word be? Would it be different, in different

seasons, different weather, different landscapes? Would an adult have a different word for it than a child, and a man a different term than a woman?

Certainly, the birders of the world are not shy about making up a new language to help fill all the cracks and joints of our own brute and limited existing vocabulary. Gradually, I've come to learn the names of many of the plants of this valley, though infinitely more elusive have been the names of the tiny birds flitting through the high forest, and their calls. The task is not made easier by my red-green colorblindness, but slowly, I'm learning a few, the easiest ones first; and if I live long enough and learn even one or two a year, then at some point in the distant future I'll have a much better grasp of those cheeps and trills and chirps that are always rustling above me, and farther into the thickets, in the summer. (I've tried listening to one of those birding tapes but have had difficulty pretending I'm in the woods — no matter how accurately the calls are recorded, I have trouble making myself believe it's a real bird making that call when there is no other accompanying stimuli of the natural world: no odor of marsh or spruce, no slant of sunlight or dimming of dusk; no breeze, no grass rustle, no sky, no earth, and I have to confess also to becoming frustrated with the pace of the narrative on those tapes. I'm a glacially slow learner, cautious to a fault about accepting or processing almost anything that anyone says, and when the brisk narrators on those birding tapes barge right in over the top of the last bird's call and inform me, "As you can so clearly hear, the call of a blanky-blank nut-dobbler is characterized by its reedy timber . . ." Well, it's too much too soon for me; the truth is, it seems to me that nearly all of them have some kind of reedy timber, or a throaty buzz, if you listen deeply enough.)

My durable old *Audubon Society Field Guide to North American Birds* pleases me, however, in a way the tapes don't; and I am delighted by the phonetic spelling of the birdcalls, which so far in my limited experience I have found to be unerringly accurate.

The evening grosbeak "calls incessantly to maintain contact with the flock. In flight, *tchew tchew tchew* or a shrill *p-teer.* Also a cleared, downslurred *tew.*" Clearly, this description is the inspired labor of love of an obsessive, for up until this point, surely, there has never been in our language either the word *tchew* or *p-teer*. Even *tew* I find remarkable, although I think the guide might be coauthored, for some of the birdcalls — too many of them, in my frustrated beginner's opinion — are described merely as a "chip" or sometimes "a soft chip," or even, if that second coauthor is feeling particularly descriptive, "a rapid series of chips." (The yellow-rumped warbler, on the other hand, when wintering in the desert Southwest, sometimes utters a sharp *chep*.)

The bobolink's alarm call is a deep *wenk,* and the Townsend's warbler — such as the one that summers in the big alder tree just outside my cabin window, and which is accustomed to the sight of me (How long do they live? Is it the same one that returns to this same branch, every year?) — gives a "distinctive *weazy weazy weazy weazy twee,* or *dee dee dee-de de.*" I don't know about the *dee dee dee* part, but the *weazy weazy* part is dead on, and not on my most ambitious day as a writer could I ever have hoped to capture the sound, and the dialect, with that linguistic accuracy, and I am indebted to Author Number One.

(The olive-sided flycatcher is another easy one, and hence a favorite. Found in the mountains, it is often encountered by me while I'm hiking late in the afternoon, hot and tired, and its inarguable call of *Quick! Three beers!* was, I feel certain, described also by the first author, rather than the chipping author.)

There's so much to know, and so many ways of knowing; and again, while I prefer to find things out the slow way — across the years, if necessary, and at close range — by touch, by sight, by scent, by sound, by dreams, if possible, and by the constancy or reassurance of repetition, as with the seasons' cyclings themselves, I also love getting information from the miracle of the printed page.

I'm forty-two years old — suddenly, looking back, that seems like a lot of years, a lot of seasons, a lot of opportunities — and yet I think there's a pretty fair chance that even if I lived to be five hundred and forty-two, I might never know or discover that based on analyses of the stomachs of olive-sided flycatchers (from the family *Tyrannidae* — the tyrant flycatchers), it has been revealed that everything *Nutallornis borealis* eats is winged, that it eats no caterpillars, spiders, or other larvae.

Perhaps an engineer would see it differently, or perhaps not, but it seems, from a poetic perspective, that such specialization — such fit — speaks at least as much to a notion of gentle cooperation and gracefulness in nature as it does to the old hammer-and-tong model of scrabbling competition. This is not to suggest that nature is anything less than fiercely clamant, with every individual scrambling hourly for tooth-and-claw survival, and for the sustenance and continuance of each individual's genes and genomes, but upon closer examination, it might seem that there are always two worlds, like one overlaid on the other — two worlds at right angles to each other, perhaps — the savage, competitive world, and the gentle, co-operative world, and that it is not just God's, or the gods', desire to fill the world with beauty and order, with a full elegance of fit, so that every niche is miraculously and intricately occupied, but that it is wild nature's gentle and cooperative desire also.

What else are we to make of the knowledge, for instance, that as the olive-sided flycatcher perches high in the branches of conifers, waiting to catch the wind-stirred vertical tide of winged summer insects, the insects' lacy wings glittering and whirling diaphanous as the day's warming currents carry those insects in plumes up toward the waiting flycatcher (as a stream carries tumbling nymphs and caddis flies to a trout waiting in the eddy behind a boulder), the water pipits hop along on the ground just below those *three-beer* whistling flycatchers, gleaning from snowmelt puddles and patches of ice the next day's leavings of those insects that perished overnight in the alpine chill — those insects which, having evaded the acrobatic swoops and pursuits of the olive-sided flycatcher, found themselves stranded nonetheless, and stippling the ice the next morning in dark flecks and nuggets on the snow?

There's no need for the flycatchers to hog the ice; there's no need for the pipits to try to compete, up in the stronger, loftier currents of wind. An agreement has been struck — if not between the pipits and the flycatchers, then by someone, or something.

Is there something wrong with me for finding landscape, more than mankind, such a marvelous invention, such a marvelous palette for whatever force, or forces, created this world, and set it into motion, halved in hemispheres and quartered into seasons, as neat and tidy and efficient and complex and unknowable as a single cell, or a single melting second in time?

Bounty. I can do both, in July: can wander out to the cabin in the cool morning and sit there for a few hours, writing or not writing but instead simply watching the sunlight walk across the marsh, and with the deer slipping back into the forest as the sunlight warms the green grassy sea of the marsh, and with the insects and, simultaneously, the birds, beginning to stir and rise like smoke, as the marsh temperature begins to warm — and not long after that, the wind, too, begins to move — and yet I can still have the second part of the day to hang out with the girls. The four of us can go down to the river, or out to the swing set, or on a hike or a bike ride. Or if Elizabeth wants some time alone, the three of us can go. The panic of summer's rushing-past quality has faded, and if anything, there is sometimes a midsummer lull, almost a weariness, that sets in, for there will have been a tendency in the previous month to fill the long days of light with as many fun things as possible, so that the revelers now want, and need, to take a breath, and rest.

I sit in my cool, dark cabin at the edge of the marsh, staring out at all the green light, and feel sometimes like a hunter in a blind, just waiting.

Some days nothing comes; but in all of the many thousands of hours I've been seated in this chair, at the edge of one of the most productive ecosystems in the world, it seems there is little I haven't seen, at one time or another, across the years. Black bears wandering through the marsh, bull moose walking past the window, golden eagles striking Canada geese, ruffed grouse drumming on my picnic table beneath the shade of the big alder, a mountain lion running through the woods with a dappled deer fawn in its jaws, a herd of elk passing single file through the deep snow, and on, and on: all seen through either of these two main windows, each like a periscope into the wilder, fuller world that I hold at bay the first half of each day so that I can submerge vertically into the dreamland of writing, but a wilder, fuller world that I can then reenter in the second half of each day and can wander horizontally and laterally.

It is a strange dynamic, to sit and wait and look at such a beautiful image, and to be eager to get back out into it — to taste and feel and smell it, to hike across it, and camp in it, and explore — and yet, for the first half of each day, to be merely sitting there at its edge, looking up from time to time and watching it and trying to resubmerge into a place of dreams, not entirely like the landscape or terrain or moods of the night before's sleep . . .

July, more than any month, is rich enough, and long enough, to accommodate this duality. In every way, it is a bridge between two worlds, and two seasons, and two rhythms or paces: and again, this quality of surging bounty, surging excess, is even more exaggerated here at the marsh's rich edge.

Day after day I sit in this same chair, often ignoring my work and instead literally just watching the grass grow. I *listen* to the grass grow, and watch the shade deepen as the leaves and needles of all the trees around me continue to grow, spreading wider and wider, making more and more shade for my little cabin, even as the bowl of green light that is the marsh, the basin, grows ever warmer and brighter.

The winds that pick up in July are like nothing but the breath of a large animal moving or laboring: bellows of noisy, heated wind building in strength all through the course of each day, bending branches and limbs and needles, causing them to grow stronger, I think, forcing them to hold on if they are to survive.

As the short growing seasons and shady old-forest conditions up here help create a tighter-grained wood, with its growth rings closer together than in other places — a higher-quality, stronger wood — so too perhaps are even our leaves, our needles, stronger, denser, different: for how can the story of an organism be different from the story of its cells, and vice versa?

The new leaves dip and dance and flutter in these ferocious July winds, but they hold on. The branches shake in July, but filled with sap, they are limber and do not snap. The alder leaves, particularly, shading my eastern window, blow wildly, out on the little point, and shudder a crazy, flashing, dancing green light across the inside of my cabin — across my face and arms — and that flashing lulls me, almost hypnotizes me. Unlike the leaves, I'm able to relax, and let go, and sink a little deeper, releasing myself from the branch of the day and any damning awareness of time, and for a little while, as that green July dancing light bathes me, I sink down into a place where I can rework both time and space, or at least where it feels as if that's the case.

Early in the morning, and then on through the middle of the morning, all the birds will be singing from around the marsh's perimeter, and chirping and trilling and chipping from back in the forest. The Townsend's warbler, a vivid yellow-breasted, yellow-hooded, black-masked male, is my sentinel, year after year, July after July, perched on the same branch, surveying this one marsh and singing that same song, day after day and year after year — *weazy weazy weazy weazy twee* — a sound that for me announces and unlocks the middle of summer, the heart of summer, as surely as if a key has unlocked a door that has then swung open to reveal a vast and unexplored chamber, a great room; for even as every July is always the same, so too is there always something newly seen or discovered or experienced in each one, always. And even as the other birds begin to fall silent under the oppression of rising heat, the Townsend's warbler, way out there on the point, just keeps on singing, as if he cannot help it, as if he cannot stop — and in that rising heat, the winds continue to increase accordingly, proportionately, bending the marsh grass flat, as if sweeping across the fur of an animal, ruffling it this way and that, with swirls of ever-changing text scrolling across the tops of the tall green marsh grass so that it appears as if a giant hand is scribing quickly, then erasing almost immediately, some hidden text out on the living canvas or tablet of the marsh —

And these sounds, the lone Townsend's warbler and the rushing of the wind, also allow me to sink deeper, to ignore time and to turn my back on my beloved physical world, and to travel down once again into the other land of pretend and make-believe and what if...

Sometimes, in July, I don't make it all the way down into that netherworld of story and imagination and instead, like a fish in a blue lake, descend only halfway, just beneath the reach of the sun, and hang there suspended, in that perfect interface between darkness and light, so that someone looking down from above would not even notice that fish, which would seem to be part of the depths itself.

On those days, it will seem to me that I could will myself just a little lower, and I would be there, in story-land — but so beautiful and engaging is that upper world, particularly in July, that I just don't want to let go. And so I'll hang there, finning, in the interface between the two, able to ease down a little deeper if need be, but able also to begin rising slowly back to the surface if need be: if opportunity arises.

Anything can lift me back into the green world, in July. The sandal-flopping sound of the girls hurrying down the path to my cabin, wanting me to come out and play. The barking of my dogs. The snort of a doe out in the marsh, or the cawing of the ravens.

Other sounds, though, send me deeper, down where I need to be — or rather, where I need to be if I am to get any writing done. The heat itself, its steady increase buffered by the cool and shade of my cabin but rising nonetheless, is like a blanket being laid over me, urging me downward; and beyond my cabin, as the day progresses, the heat is such that the birds fall silent, even the Townsend's warbler, for a while.

Though as with my own sleepy, suspended ambiguity — the landscape and me in synchrony, in this rhythm or pace — the darkness tries to rise back into the overpowering light, and the cool shade tries to ease back out into the heat: for as the day's winds stir across the tall marsh grass, gusting and combing the tall grass in those indecipherable directions, the wind lifts from the roots of the grass the scented, secret coolness that has been lingering there, beneath all the light above. The wind searches out, finds, and lifts up the last of those cool green shadows and scents from deep within the marsh grass and swirls them across the marsh and through my open windows, even as I gaze out at a paradoxical vision of dazzling heat and brilliance; and in the going away, the giving up, for that day anyway, of the marsh's last coolness — the dying of the last of that day's coolness, not to be resurrected until dark — I'm able to descend that last remaining short distance into the lull of writing-land, and pretend-land. And in that new silence, the absence of birdsong, there is now only the rush and roar of that summer wind, a wind so strong it seems to be generated from the bowl of the marsh itself, this strange prairie landscape deep in the dark north woods — and that steady, roaring sound allows me to sink still deeper.

And again, for all its roaring, the wind itself pauses, as if wanting to be two things, to do two things: to make its lovely rushing, roaring, sweeping sound, and yet to also admire and observe silence. Often through the course of a July day, the winds will stop for a while — as if the weight of the heat that has spawned them finally oppresses them too for a bit — and in that lull, and despite the heat, the Townsend's warbler will begin to sing again, as if calling out to the heat, or as if frantic to fill the space of that lovely midday silence. As if he cannot help himself.

And though he will be perched right by my open window, and though his call is sharp and strident and clear and urgent, I am usually too far gone, by that point, too lulled and waterlogged, sunk to the bottom of the sea like some ancient wreck; and the sound of his call will sound much more muffled and distant than it did only a few hours earlier, when I first sat down at my desk and began staring out at the brilliance beyond.

First baby robins on the porch, where they fledge each year, first Pacific tree frog in the garden, seeking each day now the watering can's moisture. First bellflower blooms, first twinflower, first monkshood, a brighter purple than any king's robe. First wild strawberries — so much color! — and, unfortunately, but inescapably, the first blossoms of hawkweed, a noxious invasive weed that is infinitely more aggressive than even the scourge of knapweed and thistle. Knapweed's bad, invading dry sites and displacing native grass directly — nothing eats knapweed, and as it spreads, it chokes out the grasses that the elk herds rely on — but the hawkweed grows everywhere, dry or wet, shade or sun, and seems to know no limits. It displaces all of the complex and crafted native flowering plants — lupine, bellflower, kinnikkinnick, paintbrush, yarrow, Oregon grape, wild strawberry — and while it's bad enough, from a biological perspective, the colonization seems also to taunt a lover of wildness and diversity from an aesthetic standpoint, for the blossoms of the hawkweed, by itself, are beautiful: a brilliant, almost hallucinogenic orange, the roadsides and old logging roads now ablaze in July like fields of poppies.

(Though in those monochromatic sweeps of such rich, even luscious orange, I think that even someone unfamiliar with the ecology of the region might sense the ominous danger beneath that beauty, might notice the mosaic of diversity throughout the forest and notice the homogenous and wide blazes of orange as the anomaly, and the dis-uniter, and not possessing the cohesive cooperating, fitted spirit of the place, no matter how beautiful the orange might seem, in and of itself.)

So there is a sleepiness in July, a summer leisure — an in-betweenness — though there is also the beginning, already, even in the midst of summer vacation, of a rising responsibility; for those weeds must be picked, if not sprayed. And for as long as we can combat them by hand, we will, for it seems that to bring spray and poison into our lives, and near the marsh, with its tender amphibians, and into our watershed, and our lives, would be to admit defeat — what good are the natives, if they possess poison in their veins? And even if we did decide to try to poison the hawkweed and knapweed and dandelion and thistle, and this year, increasingly, the St. John's wort, the same poison that kills these broadleaf weeds would also kill the natives.

Instead, we pick. We get down on our hands and knees in the tall waving grasses of July, and pull up, by the matted, tuberous roots, the insidious runners of moisture-robbing hawkweed. Like hunters, we know where the weeds are likely to recur each year, and we keep pulling them, hoping to weaken and stress them so that the natives can outcompete them. We remain vigilant for new outcrops too. Our battle is just one tiny battle in the wilderness here at marsh's edge — we will change nothing, will at best only buy a little more time — but we have not yet reached a level of acceptance at which doing nothing is tolerable, and so we pick, and pick, in July: kneeling in the mixture of tall grass and weeds, surrounded by mosquitoes, sweating, pulling, stuffing trash bags full of weeds. It is such a break-even battle — some years, our progress is visible, though each year, we have to pull harder, and again, from the entire landscape's perspective, two million acres of national forest, so ultimately futile, that we realize early on our efforts are really like nothing else so much as prayer and penance to that landscape: a sort of Zen exercise, or tithing to the land, and to the marsh. Though I can't help but wonder too, some years, if the truly Zen or prayerful thing to do would be to stop fighting loss and change and to simply let the weeds of the world come rolling in.

Each year, however — each July — I pick each weed, every weed, that I see, on our property at least, as well as on my hikes through the woods; and I suspect that even when I am old, I will still be picking them, out of some deep and stubborn allegiance to my own perhaps arbitrary and singular concepts of integrity. And I think that it is not that I hate weeds so much as it is that I love this landscape, this incredible ecosystem, so deeply, just as it is — in the fullness of its incredibly unique diversity, ten thousand years in the making.

What I mean to say is, even the weed pulling in July is one of the ways I relate to this landscape now, is an aspect, a component, of that relationship, so that it is not even so much a matter of whether I "win" or "lose" (I'll lose, for sure; no one can defeat time) but rather that I continue on in that relationship, according to my beliefs and values, for as long as I am able — which, I like to imagine, is for as long as I am alive.

July is its own month too, in addition to being a bridge between others — July is the hammock, July is a crowded West, happy people on vacation, crowded gas pumps in town, crowded gas stations, crowded trailheads — and yet July, perhaps more than any other month, seems to me also to be connected, almost like a twin, to the month that will succeed it. Or July is that way with regard to fire, at any rate. Sometimes, in a dry year, July is the month of the first fires, but usually up here it is the last month before the fires — and while it would be concise and neat to partition the twelve months into equal wedges of pie, it's hard to do that because of the incredibly primal, elemental, and dramatic force of fire (the destroyer and creator both). The coming fires are always somewhat on our minds, upon this landscape, in any month, just as those who live in farming country are almost always aware, even if calmly, of the year's running total of precipitation, and in this regard too we are farmers of a sort, though we seek not so much to grow any certain crop as to simply receive the merciful precipitation for its own sake: the snows of winter and the rains of spring sculpting this Pacific Northwest forest, and in that lushness, that excess and rank bounty and splendor, shaping our moods, our culture, our days.

But because we lie in a seam, a borderland — the landform of our twisted geology, glaciated and slip-faulted, is more that of the northern Rockies — we are shaped and sculpted too by the breath of fire, the animal of fire. Ice birthed this country, at the end of the last ice age, but it is fire as much as rain that brings the pulse of life to it, helping select our biggest, healthiest trees, and in particular the thick-barked larch, with its unique beauty and strange and ancient duality — a deciduous conifer! — and while we love the look and fit of what the fires have achieved across the many centuries, we fear them some years, and respect them always.

Usually we get a good rain on or around the Fourth of July. And always we get a good rain on Labor Day, without fail — like clockwork. But of the sixty days between those two holidays, we might some years get only one or two thunderstorms; and the trouble with thunderstorms, particularly in parched and heated years, is that they fill the sky with lightning.

It's thrilling, invigorating, terrifying, intoxicating. In a hot year, as the forests begin to dry up and grow snappy-crisp, oven-baked beneath greenhouse temperatures that the vegetation on this landscape never evolved to deal with — fields and forests both dying from the heat as much as the drought — we watch the skies, and the weather reports, in an anxious kind of emotional dance, in July: wanting rain, but not wanting a thunderstorm. Or if wanting a thunderstorm, then a big, violent drenching one, so that the downpour extinguishes the simultaneous lightning strikes from the selfsame storm.

As if our wishing has any bearing on any of it. Wishing it with the fervor of farmers, or sports fans. Totally lacking in control. Learning, year by year, humility.

The specific anguish, in a drought year — watching the tender green vegetation wilt, and then die, across an entire landscape, a beloved landscape, and looking at the seven-day forecast and seeing not even a thunderstorm. The forest, and people's moods and tempers, growing as brittle as thin glass. The specific outpouring of gratitude and relief, and the feeling of incomparable richness, if or when cooler temperatures ease in, as well as a soaking rain, in the second or third week of July, cutting that long run to Labor Day almost in half.

The irony is that anyone who's lived up here for any amount of time, and who's been through some fire seasons, knows firsthand how incredibly beneficial the fires are: how they thin and prune the weedy overstock of tangled saplings that the timber industry could never afford to take. The larger trees survive the fires, far more often than not, and benefit from the reduced competition and increased nutrients. (Industry, and indeed, even people within the Forest Service itself, continue to try to sell us the emperor's myth that clearcuts imitate wildfires, and as such, are healthy, but clearcuts don't leave behind the forest's nutrients, and don't leave behind standing spars and snags for hiding cover and cavity nests for birds and small mammals. Saying a clearcut is like a wildfire is like saying a bank robbery is the same thing as a savings withdrawal.)

So we love what the fires — all fires — do to a big and dramatic landscape, over time, we love how the wild morel mushrooms pop up in their aftermath the next year, and love how the deer and elk and moose rush in the following year, to graze and browse on the rich new feed. And we even love the pretty sight of them, I think, mesmerizing as a campfire, orange and black, Halloween colors, flames twinkling on a hillside in the distance.

But we also know how utterly wild and uncontrollable they can be, possessing certain predictable desires, such as a yearning to run uphill, and to travel on the breath, the convective currents of their own making, as they consume and sometimes devour great helpings of this forest's bounty — twigs, branches, grasses, leaves, limbs, weeds, needles — and as long as they are not moving toward anyone's home or property, and as long as the firefighters are safe, and as long as the political powers are fairly balanced so that industry will not be able to swoop in on the burned landscape following a fire, "salvaging" the landscape in too overzealous and unregulated a fashion, well, then, the fires can be glorious: again, as long as no one is living underneath, or in the path of, that volcano.

But here I am, talking about what is essentially an August event while still in the month of July. It's really only in our minds, I think, that such forbearance and brooding exist. Out upon the landscape, it's just July: some years green, some years not.

What is fire? In a drought year such as this one, even on the eighth of July — five days since the last rain — the stupendous heat has returned, and today I catch the first scent of truly dry heat, oven-baked dryness: the odor of baking pine needles, as sharp and distinct as if they were laid upon a cookie sheet and placed in the oven. There's been no ignition yet, no spark or flame, but smelling that scent — it's so strong that it seems almost as if they're already burning or at least smoldering, even in the absence of an open flame — you have to wonder, really, how is the readying different from the finishing, and at what point does the one become the other?

The further along the summer moves, with us riding in its midst, the more the hidden nature of the world, which is surely fire, reveals itself, as if rising with confidence from some reservoir not even at the world's core but at some lesser depth: just beneath us, at first, but then to the surface itself, warming the bottoms of our feet, and then up around our ankles, and then higher, until everywhere we look, it seems, we see fire — or if not the flames themselves yet, then the paths the flames will follow, and the material they will consume, the fiber that will be converted to their breath. The animal of fire being born.

It's all fire. There is a point at which even the lush green meadows, their grass tops blowing in the wind, become no longer like ocean waves but tongues of sawing green flame. And rising slowly from those grasses, over the course of the summer, are the weeds; and it takes no special vision, no leap of metaphor or understanding, to see that even more than the waving grasses, or the swaying, branch-clacking forest itself, the weeds are fire: that they are the first flames, hot cinders dropped already lit among the tinder, and that even if they do not ignite this year, or even the next, or the next, they are already burning, consuming the terrain across which they sweep, and that they are a different kind of fire, one from which there is no subsequent rush of rejuvenation the following year. Instead, the fire of the weeds is geological, as ongoing and close to eternal as anything in this world.

Often, late into dusk, in July — not having finished my other chores and lists but unwilling to let the day end without having addressed the weeds — I will be out among the tall green grasses, feeling the cooling, scented breath of the fields' exhalations: the grasses stirring, inflating with life again, now that the frying-pan force of the sun is shielded from them, for a while, by the shadows of the mountains' wall, and the desiccating, swirling winds of the day have likewise settled down to rest for the night. And finding myself surrounded by the seemingly endless and impossible task of plucking each weed, all weeds, and with darkness settling in fast, I'll feel a kind of panic rise within me. The fiery nature of the weeds all around me will be revealed as if their essence too has come more clearly and fully into life, in that subdued light, and I'll find myself plucking them quicker and quicker, pulling the tallest ones first — the ones capable of spreading their fiery seed drift farthest, leapfrogging like skittering sparks across the waving canopy of the cool green grasses.

In that panic, it will feel that I have to move quickly — that each orange-blossomed hawkweed is a burning coal — and while a firefighter might attempt to attack a fire upslope, seeking to cut off the fire's ascent, I attack this other orange fire downslope, trying to contain its perimeter in that direction, which is where the hawkweed spreads quickest and easiest, following the sloping contours of watercourses.

Orange blossoms or not, it is nothing but fire, for after the hawkweed has displaced the native grasses and wildflowers, it then withers, in August, to tinder-fluff. Nothing can eat it, and it sits there like a fuse waiting for a spark, entire fields waiting for the inferno; though the irony is that by that time, whether the ignition occurs or not, the inferno has already passed, and with our inability to act, our inability to stop the weeds, we did not even notice that first fire until after it had already passed through.

What scale of time is appropriate for us to use — in our own lives, as well as in our management and perception of the public lands? Four weeks? Ten years? Threescore and ten? A hundred, or a thousand?

In the blink of an eye, in day's failing light, the field of orange weeds wavers, at the corner of my vision. It's a drought year, and in less than three weeks the valley will be filled with smoke and flame. It seems to me often that the shadow of a thing can precede the thing itself, even though our present understanding of time indicates this is an impossibility, that time cannot run backwards.

Perhaps it is more that there are simply predisposed patterns and pathways, like contours, carved as if by ancient glaciers (time, like some immense chunk of glacier formed long ago, slowly decomposing, and creeping, as it dissolves), and that those earliest-made paths and patterns help influence the shape and direction of all that falls into their provenance — like the wind-borne and water-drifting seeds of the hawkweed itself, creeping ever lower, following every runnel and swale in the landscape, seeking and colonizing, spreading and pooling like glowing lava spitting down a slope.

Perhaps this is the nature of that word, the one for which I do not know the name, describing how the shape of the elk's antlers is the shape of the branches in the forest in which he lives: a thing that might be seen to be as simple as the style or voice of one single artist, one original creator, whose imprint is as recognizable in any work as the voice of one's mother or father.

I want to be very clear that as I marvel at all this sameness, it is not nature, or life itself, or individual species and their complex and intricate adaptations in which I see that sameness; in those things, I see incredible diversity and infinite mystery: rampant and beautiful un-sameness.

Rather, it is in the patterns and even contours of all this virtuoso diversity that I catch glimpses of what I suspect might be an overarching sameness just beyond our sight, just behind the scenes: a sameness that goes much further back, it seems, than the Adam and Eve bloodlines of any living creation. A sameness, or echo or shadow of sameness, that again is evident, in those glimpses, in both the animate and inanimate. The rocks and mountains that are shaped like muscles — like quadriceps and breast, like recumbent man and woman, like sleeping animals, like waking animals striding the earth . . .

What I see in those glimpses of the sameness of pattern is not just metaphor, or "simple" cold, hard scientific life, but instead life upon metaphor upon life upon metaphor: a dense, rhythmic layering of substance and meaning, the substance of a thing *creating* its meaning, and then that meaning creating another, similar substance.

Camping last week in an intensively metamorphosed wilderness basin in the Cabinet Mountains, just across the river from here, Elizabeth and I reached a windy ridge in darkness, set up our tent, and slept. In the morning, the vision from our tent of the canyons just below us was so twisted and fantastic as to be almost unbelievable, and I found myself glancing at the topo map from time to time, as if comforted by reducing and compressing all those contours to the size of the map.

Hiking farther up the mountain, we noticed individual rocks, severely eroded quartzites, the surfaces of which seemed more than once to replicate perfectly, ridge for ridge and canyon for canyon, the same landscape magnified almost infinitely beyond. And climbing farther, I paused for breath and placed my hand on the smoothness of one timeworn rock, the flexion and indentation of which was exactly that of a bare kneecap, with part of the shin below, and part of the upper leg above. Every tendon, and every smooth run of muscle, was reflected perfectly in that gray stone, Cambrian-era quartzite that was formed perhaps a billion years before the first bacteria even existed.

My own mortal knee was aching, and after resting a while longer, we climbed higher, scrambling over that exploded boulder field of seemingly random talus and erratic rubble, and on past more of those same map rocks, each one of which afforded us, I think, a brief glimpse behind the curtain.

Sometimes I wonder if it is not as if some timeless master artist — God, or gods, surely — bored perhaps by a lack of challenge with canvas and palette, decided to limit the next project to but one or two patterns or themes, and yet strove — and strives — to see how complex and miraculous a thing could be made from even the limitations of those one or two rules or laws or patterns. And that we the living are the beneficiaries of that magnificent force, magnificent creation. And are perhaps at least partially central, or perhaps not.

Did we come last in the story, in the metaphor, because we're special, and the shining one-law world was made for us? Or was there simply — barely — room and fit for one more thing, us, after all the other cracks and corners were filled with their various treasures of lives and minerals and flowing waters and crackling fires?

Were we added in at the end, again as if in some kind of bored test — or challenge — to see if, or for how long, we could sustain and preserve and protect the glory of that incredible creation, that pulsing palace, into which we have wandered?

Frightful questions, and I suspect that our answers might be guided as accurately by ancient instinct as by science; that sometimes a rock in the shape of a knee, a billion years before life, has as much to instruct us as any fossil, fern, or snail, or anything that once, briefly, possessed life.

Orange hawkweed in July, prefacing the color of the coming fire; orange and black checkerspot butterflies pollinating the hawkweed, sparks of fire now flying through the air, swirling in the breezes just over our heads. Orange and black ladybugs, in July, flocking to my picnic table to reconnoiter in the dappled shade of the alder, in a light so rich and subaqueous green, subaqueous gold, that it seems conceivable that the ladybugs are drinking in that light as they would a nectar. Orange and black visible, that one July day, in at least a few peeks and glimpses, orange flames skipping over the blackened char of the already burned, Halloween colors, orange and black, story and metaphor from substance once again; and once more, there is a part of me that catches the scent and sight of a greater, occasional sameness, and I have to wonder if sometimes, as with the elegant orange and black, the message isn't perhaps being simplified, so that even we, with our own crude senses, can "get it," as if in a beginner's paint-by-numbers kit.

Or if we do not "get it," at least we can take notice of it.

And why, then? Does it matter whether we take notice of these things? Why is our one eye for beauty so ill balanced with our other eye, the one that would seem to focus on the ability, the desires, to preserve and protect: to utilize the best of our hoarding, hunter-gatherer instincts? *This is beautiful, this is desirable. Protect this,* and *this,* and *this.*

What is our purpose, our fit in this world — to preserve and protect, or to destroy and consume and lay level? Does the plan, the force, that designed us know which we are — creators and protectors, or destroyers? Does it — that force — want us to be one way or the other?

And what is the purpose of such war within us? Is something forged and fitted by such strugglings — something graceful, and worthy of the world — or lost, in each of us as individuals, and as communities, and as a culture?

If so — and how could that thing not be called *spirit* — then why isn't it bright orange and black, brightly visible to even the most inattentive gaze or ponderer?

And yet it, that spirit, whether growing and developing within an individual or being worn down and disintegrating, does glow orange and black, at certain times and in certain seasons. It burns white hot; it glows cold blue. It shimmers and skips with green and gold light; it sleeps or rests in the hazy color of autumn-cut wheat stubble. It idles within us, possessing no more color than the fog breathed from our lungs, our mouths and nostrils, on a cold day, silver plumes trailing away in whichever direction the wind is blowing.

And these days that we have of living — not enough, but in such a wide world as this one, ample — are the only opportunity we have, the only chance, to strike the sparks that will ignite those colors and build that spirit.

I'm not saying I think we're central to the turnings of the world, or that it was created expressly as a proving ground — a tool chest, of sorts — for our spirits.

I am certain, however, of the sparkings, the ignition within that occurs, for instance, when I stare at a vase of sunflowers, or at an uncut field of them, staring as if mesmerized — and of the peace and ease that remains within me for some time afterward, for nearly as long as I will allow it to stay, burning quietly, slowly, comfortably. Traveling.

I'm fairly certain that these days in the living, walking around upright, noticing sunflowers, noticing children, noticing elk, noticing rain, are our best and probably only chance to light those fires within us, again and again. And that, as with a healthy forest fire, they can prune away the clutter and debris, the buildup of tangled twigs and branches, leaving the new forest, the old forest, cleaner and stronger.

And that's one of the wonderful things about a fire too, after it's swept past and cleaned up all the litter. There's a new start, a clean surface, and you can see so much farther. Things stand out more starkly; it's easier to notice.

Against a briefly blackened backdrop, every bit of returning color is noticeable, bit by bit, piece by piece. One yellow blossom, one blue bird. One emerald fern, one orange blossom, like a spark uncovered, a spark that never quite burned out. It all comes back. Life comes flowing back into a burned forest like water flowing downhill, summoned as if by a force as dense and specific and enduring as gravity itself.

So July is two things: its own sleeping summertime, suspended and whole, as round and complete and balanced as a full moon, and yet it is the second thing too, the steppingstone to the fire. There's still a little time left to be lazy, to be slow, though soon enough the mind, and one's actions, will need to quicken, and be more alert, less leisurely.

July's a time for lounging, when you can, if you can — for pausing to watch a young goldfinch wrestle with a buzzing dragonfly nearly its size, clipping with its beak the dragonfly's glittering lacy wings, and then like a savage eating the prehistoric insect one piece at a time, head, thorax, and abdomen, before flying quickly away, that little bit much more strengthened and fattened for the coming migration, leaving behind on the picnic table outside my window nothing but that twin pair of sequined dragonfly wings, the only clue to that sixty-second war.

But it's a time for beginning, already, to prepare for what's coming: to continue pulling those damn weeds, and to be picking up twigs and branches around the house — the fine fuels — and to be moving any flammable materials away from the house — lumber, fiberglass canoes, and so on — to be sweeping last fall's larch needles from the roof, and to be watching the weather reports. To keep the hoses rolled up and ready, attached to all the outside hydrants, and to be knocking back that summer-tall grass all around the house, with either a lawn mower or a swing.

Although it takes more time, I greatly prefer the latter. I love the sweeping scythelike motion, love the rhythm of it, and love the whispering, cutting sounds too, particularly in contrast to the two-cycle smoky roar of a lawn mower. The rhythmic murmur of the swing disturbs the birds down in the marsh, I like to imagine, no more than the wind itself, while the roar of a lawn mower would surely be displeasing to them.

Who am I kidding? Would surely be displeasing to me.

There's really nothing quite like it, swinging the blade through tall grass. When the blade is nice and sharp, you can feel it intimately, can feel in your arm and shoulder and all the way into the rest of your body the way the energy of the meadow changes, over the course of even a day, let alone a season.

With the same swing, day after day, you can tell the difference between high overhead sun and cooling green evening, just by the way the grass falls. It cuts easiest, falls softer, in the evening — lying down quietly in bundles and sheaves — whereas the midday cuts are ragged and resisting, and the grass scatters wildly in all directions. I would have guessed differently — the opposite. Is the grass still growing midday, so that you're disrupting that force? Is it resting in the evening? Where does the water go? What balance or relationship exists between the roots underground and the waving blades of grass above, and how does that change with the weather? Right after a rain, the grass is heavy, and harder to cut. If you can afford to wait, it's nicest to cut it right in that first cooling of evening, when

it's dry — though by mid-July, or the third week of July, you're definitely starting to ease into that quickening of the current where it
might be best not to wait but to go ahead and cut the tall grass
around the house, whether raggedly or gracefully. Where the most
ragged thing of all might be not to acknowledge that current.

There is rarely a set day for any of these whirrings, or any of these
relationships, much less the relationships within the relationships,
but this year, on the twenty-fifth of July, I look out my window for
the first time that morning and notice, as if with the focus one gives
a ringing alarm clock, or some shouted beckon, that there is complete leaf interlock between the alders, just outside my window.

Each day, the light coming through my window has become
greener and shadier, more dappled and cooler; and my correspond-
ing view of the brighter, wind-waving marsh beyond, a softer green
(against the dark blue of the old spruce forest beyond), has grown
smaller and more kaleidoscoped each day, until finally, this day, the
twenty-fifth, some last growth has fanned the alder leaves into the
last available light, and the mesh and interbranching of them has
clicked fully into position.

And enveloped deliciously by them, it seems to me that they
have achieved a moment of earned rest; that though the solstice,
the balance of light, was almost five weeks ago, only now has some
balance or peak of growth — of heat, perhaps, and the exhalation of
nutrients from this rich site — been reached.

And as with mountain climbers who have ascended some daunting and glorious summit (and who will be descending not along the
same route but rather a back side familiar from all the previous de-
scents, yet also daunting despite that intimacy), the alders, on the
twenty-fifth of this year, seem to me to be spending a brief window
of time paused at that summit, taking in the balanced view.

Very soon — tomorrow, perhaps — they will need to start down
the mountain, but this one day, they seem to be hanging poised;
and the world, this world, seems inflated, as saturated with life and
growth as it possibly can be.

Is it this way for every living thing residing in the bowl of this
landscape? Are the larch likewise holding their breath, having also
reached the summit, and are now gathering their thoughts and

preparing to loosen their energies and begin the same slow descent, their vivid green needles, previously almost fluorescent, starting to dull toward the ultimate lovely gold and bronze and orange of the fall? Has the landscape itself taken one last long, full breath and is now preparing — the next day, or the next — to exhale?

Such a model or pattern is pleasing to consider, and yet the thought itself possesses a life no longer than a moment's rest, a held breath, for I remember almost immediately that it is not this way for the bears, who will later be entering hyperphagia, gorging on berries in order to put on as much fat as possible prior to winter's hibernation; and that the antlers of the deer, elk, and moose are still wrapped in the blood-filled nourishing tissue of velvet, still growing.

But for the vegetative world — the underpinning of life — perhaps it is this held-breath way, for the huckleberries are fruiting and beginning to fill with sugar and color; their leaves too have stopped growing as they now pour their energy into seed production, wrapping their seeds in luscious, desirable packages for greater dissemination into the great wide world, and the coming years . . .

And it makes me wonder, if there is indeed a summit or held-breath moment for the vegetation in a landscape — a specific construct of invisible formula and cant, like some vast unseen complexity of hidden wires and planes and arcs and angles and movements and countermovements, both subtle and large — then could there likewise be such a moment for even the underpinning of the vegetation: an earlier, similar moment for the sun-warmed soil, and even the ancient shield of rock itself? The stony mountains loosening slightly, stretching and expanding in the heat, and weathering in the summer thunderstorms: releasing their ironclad nutrients grain by grain. Heat waves rising in shimmers from the slick-rock domes and crests of glacier-scalped mountaintops, as if, in that moment, they are burning, coming back to life after only a billion years of rest: as if it all has been but as a nap.

I can't see the marsh grass through this day's final interlock of alder leaf, but with the window open, I can hear it rustling in the wind; and even the grass sounds a little different, as those spirited, swirling winds pass through it.

I rise and walk over to the other window so that I can see out into the marsh. I watch the patterns of the dry west wind spreading and fanning and parting the high, luxuriant sheaves of marsh as if searching idly for something misplaced, if not hiding — something left behind, is what it seems like.

The graceful rhythm of the wind, a thousand rivers of wind sweeping across and braiding and unbraiding and rebraiding the marsh, caressing the grass, sounds only slightly different this morning — a little drier, a little more rattly — but otherwise the visual patterns of those rivers of wind seem little changed: as if I am mistaken and that today they do not hold somehow in their essence the coming secret, if not quite a betrayal, of their departure.

Or betraying July while shifting allegiance to August.

It is no betrayal. It is only a fullness: a thing being completed. You can hear it out there in the marsh, for the first time, on this one day.

It's still early enough in the summer that you can turn away from it. You can tune it out if you want to. You can go back and lie in the hammock a while longer. But it's out there, rustling beneath the drying grass and among the reed nests of the rails and blackbirds, like tiny mice scampering through the drying husks of the grass itself.

And what of our own seasons, both external and internal, physical and emotional, or spiritual? In this too are we obstinate, resolutely individual, with some of us reaching full breath early, others midlife, and still others, on the last day, in the first darkness of the last evening, in the last breath, the last thought?

How we must seem to the rest of the natural world like random scattered leaves blowing across the landscape, in all seasons: not like matrix or foundation or centerpiece, but like filler, like dust, seeking to rest and finally fit between the cracks of all the other existing systems of grace. Perhaps this identity, more than any other, explains our restlessness, our almost ceaseless motion.

Perhaps this identity — our whirlingness — helps explain also our deep affinity for stone, and tradition, and regularity, and enduring-ness — the things we have not yet earned — though how we might ever earn them, other than by letting go and releasing ourselves as if into some current, I could not say; neither could I guess as to where such a current might be found, either within us or without.

How else to consider the slight components of both comfort and loneliness that attend to our watching of the movements of a flowing river, or a wavering fire, or even the movements of the gusting summer wind passing through tall grass?

After twenty years of listening and watching and hiking around and hunting — twenty youthful years, no less — we're starting to learn some things about this valley. We'll never know enough, or even a fraction of what we'd like to; but we know, for instance, or believe that we know, where the wild strawberries are sweetest, in the tiny little lanes and clearings no larger than a house, where little patches of soft, filtered, damp light fall down from the midst of the old-growth larch forests, little clearings where the snowshoe hares come out (despite the protestations of timber company biologists who say the rabbits, and their primary predators, lynx, don't live in the old forests) to nibble on those new sweet berries, in July.

Late in July, we like to try to get into some of those patches just before the legions of rabbits do, and pick a little basket of berries. The girls have a tiny doll's basket (the berries are no larger than the nub of a pencil eraser, but contain more sweetness within them, concentrated, than an entire bushel of the supermarket mega-irradiated jumbo giants), and because I'm red-green colorblind, I can't find the tiny strawberries and have to rely on the girls to do the harvest.

They're delighted by my weakness, and by their sharp-eyed superiority, and delighted also, as junior hunter-gatherers, to be providing for me. We all three have little baskets — in the dimming blue light of dusk, I absolutely can't find a single one — and from time to time the girls take pity, and come over to where I'm searching, down on my hands and knees, and drop a few into my basket.

And as is their habit, they eat far more than they pick, not even really hunter-gatherers but more like wild animals, feasting in the moment, letting their bodies do the hoarding rather than jars or cabinets — the girls more a part of the forest, in that manner, in that moment — and by the time it is too dark to see well and we

walk back toward our truck, our baskets have barely enough strawberries to drop into our pancake batter the next morning. But they
will be memorable pancakes, and it will be enough.

Just as we reach the truck some friends come driving by, and
they stop to visit for a while in the dusk, with the old sentinel
larches so immense all around us. Their children are grown now,
and they reminisce about picking wild strawberries with their children, when their children were Mary Katherine's and Lowry's ages.

They keep telling me what everyone has been saying since each
of the girls was born, and what I have found to be true: about
how fast it goes — and I agree, and thank them for their counsel.
My friends keep looking at the girls' little baskets of berries and
smiling, and saying that same thing again and again, throughout the
course of the lazy-dusk conversation — about how fast it goes — and
yet I don't know what to do about that truth, that inescapable
flight, other than to go out into the patches of light scattered here
and there along the edges of the old forest and pick strawberries
with them in the evening, just as we're doing. And while I'm very
grateful for the advice, any advice, I also wonder often if it, the time
of childhood, doesn't pass faster for the parent sometimes by considering, and noticing, the speed of its passage as opposed perhaps
to a sleepier, less attentive, less fretful awareness of that passage
and its nearly relentless pace.

Either way, it's going to go fast. I know I'm doing what I can to
slow it down. Reading to them in the evenings, cooking with them,
taking them on hikes, and swimming in the mountain lakes . . .

Any activity I do with them could be done faster and more efficiently, but only recently have I come to understand that the slower
and more inefficiently we do these things, the greater is my gain,
our gain; the less quickly that galloping stretch of time passes. Taking three hours to fix a single, simple meal is a victory. Coming back
from two hours in the woods with only a dozen strawberries left
over is a triumph. Chaos and disorderliness can be allies in my goals
of spending as much time as possible with them. If I'll only watch
and listen, they'll show me — for a while — how to slow time down:
instructing me in a way that I could never otherwise learn from the
caring counsel of my friends, and their experiences.

Still, it's good to hear it, even if bittersweet. I know not to argue with them, or deny it. I know, or think I know, the sound of the truth, and it's wonderful to have their support in the matter.

We say our leisurely goodbyes and part company in the hanging dusk turning quickly now to darkness so that we need to turn our lights on, traveling down the road on our way through the old forest. On the way home, the girls would eat every single one of the last of the berries if I let them — would run right through the last of our supplies in only a minute or two — and so I put the little straw baskets in the cab of the truck, out of reach.

A couple of days later, after an afternoon spent at the falls, we're walking along a gravel road, again at dusk, and again the girls are finding the tiny wild strawberries. The twenty-seventh of July: hot days, cold nights. It's a couple of miles back to the truck, and the girls alternate between running and walking slowly; and again I try to relax and release, and give myself over to what seems to me to be the irregular, even inscrutable logic of their pace, their seemingly erratic stops and starts. Stretching their freedom, then coming back.

They run pell-mell for a while down the road, then slow to a saunter. Lowry stops at one point and looks up at the sky for long moments.

"What are you doing?" I ask.

"Listening to the leaves," she says. And she's right; just above the louder sound of the rushing creek, the drying leaves of the riverside cottonwoods are rattling slightly, and sounding different, drier: autumnal already.

She's four! It pleases me deeply, so much so that I don't even say anything other than offering some mild concurrence.

Farther down the road she stops again, and announces, "It smells good here." It's the creekside bog orchids, intensely fragrant — almost overpoweringly so, like cheap perfume — and both girls walk out into the orchids to smell them better, and Lowry tells us that they "smell better than the shampoo with the silver cap."

They run for a short distance, with me trailing right behind them, for safety — giving them their freedom, yet guarding them in lion country — and they stop yet again. And when I ask what they're doing this time, Low says quietly, as if from dreamland, "Listening to water."

They're both just standing there, staring at a glade below, in the dimming light: mesmerized, it seems, by the very fabric of the landscape, the interlocking of all those different species and sizes of trees; and I realize with a wonderful bittersweetness that I really don't have a clue as to what either of them is thinking or feeling, only that they are fully suspended in the business of being children — that they are in a place I want them to be, and yet where I cannot go; though even as I am thinking this, and thinking about how totally oblivious they are, in the moment, to my adult presence, Low turns her gaze from the mountains and tells me she thinks I'm standing too close to the edge of the road and the steep slope leading down to the river.

"Don't slide down there," she says, taking my hand. "I don't want to lose you." Like something dropped in tall grass.

We resume our journey. Not too far from where we've parked, we encounter a dead garter snake in the road, tire struck, but intact. They're fascinated, of course, both by their instinctual, archetypal fear of snakes and by the archetype of death; and they examine the snake, the specimen, like little scientists, stirring it gently with a stick — it still looks alive — and Lowry sprinkles a little dust on its head, as if in some pagan ritual.

We pass on, then, though she's quiet all the way to the truck, and when I ask her what's the matter some fifteen minutes later, she says, "It makes me sad when things die."

What do I know about girls, or anything? Would not a little boy — a boy such as myself, perhaps, have wound the dead snake around his wrist to wear as a bracelet, an amulet, or tossed it on his sister?

All I can do, often, is watch, and listen. So often it feels as if I'm treading behind them, observing, listening, and learning other rhythms, rather than being out in front, as if breaking trail for them, the way I had always assumed it would be, being a parent.

This is supposed to be a book about the months of the year, and about this one singular landscape. But again and again, watching the girls watch the landscape helps me see it more fully, and in new ways, whether down on my hands and knees at ground level, or staring off at the horizon.

There's still time for me to learn some of what they see and know and feel. It's not too late. I can still learn, or relearn, some if not all of what they seem to know intuitively about, among other things, an engagement with time. When to walk, when to run, when to rest, when to dream. When to be tender — more often than not — and, by extension, when to be all other things, as well.

I want to believe that my bitterness and cynicism, and my fears for the environment, fade when in their company; that such worries leach away, as if back into the soil of the landscape itself, where they might even be absorbed by the rattling cottonwoods and the scented orchids. It probably is not that way at all, but some days, after a good day spent in the woods with the girls, that is how it feels; and I rarely come away from such days without feeling that I have learned something, even if I'm not sure what it is, and that although time certainly has not ceased or even paused, at least it has not accelerated in that awful way it can do sometimes, slipping out from beneath and away from you, as if you've lost your footing on ice or some other slick surface.

I guess it's better to be aware of the briskness of its passage than not, after all. It's going to go fast either way. But if you're aware of its brevity, then at least you'll be aware too of the eddies and slow stretches.

But my friends who stopped and visited the other evening when we were picking berries were right as rain. It's going to go real fast either way. The best I can do is try to keep up.

More guests, guests pouring into the homes of all Montana family and friends, in the summer, pouring in like water through a breach in the earthen wall of the other nine months, friends and family flooding a year or more's absence, compressing it to the point, vacation, where we can only joke about it among ourselves, the intensity and busyness of summer: entertaining, cooking, taking hikes, doing so at a recreational pace that we would probably never otherwise attain, left unchallenged by summer visitage . . .

Elizabeth and I have it pretty easy: most of our guests are low-key and self-entertaining, particularly useful traits when one batch is leaving on a Sunday morning and another arriving on a Sunday evening.

Ferocious games of badminton out on the grass-clad rocky drain field, like some crude parody of Victorian England. The shuttlecock fluttering upward while just beyond the stone wall, and in the dark forest, lions and grizzlies wander, their footprints squishing in the mud along the little creek bank. A great gray owl, with its four-foot wingspan, cruises through the yard at dusk, made curious by the shuttlecock perhaps, and alights in a tree at the edge of the woods and watches for a while, its head seeming as large as a man's.

The girls manage to capture a tiger swallowtail, one that has already been wounded in a previous engagement, and decide to keep it for a pet for a few days. They bring it into the house and put her — they have named her Zoey, so we know she's a female — on the cut flowers in a vase. For the rest of the evening, and much of the next day, she flies around the house, looking so festive and exuberant that it makes some of the adults wonder, *Well, why not have a butterfly for a pet, and let it have the run of the house?* What's a little occasional yellow dusting against the kitchen window? The tiny little sound of butterfly wings fluttering, at night, just before going to roost.

Some accident befalls Zoey, however. We're not sure what. Some excess of kindness or attention from the girls is my guess — perhaps they tried to fashion a dress for her, or even a leash, to take her out to their clubhouse — and only the next day Zoey breathes her last: languishing and then expiring, with a sad and disturbing shudder reminiscent of a Hollywood heroine, and the first and easiest lesson is learned well: *wild things don't belong in captivity.* And I can't help but believe that there are all sorts of other lessons, or at least the foundations for other lessons, laid deeper, as well, in a manner that stopping roadside to examine some grille-stuck moth or butterfly could never have accomplished.

With a garden hand shovel, we dig a grave on a sunny patch of hill, amid a blossoming of the yarrow on which she liked to feed.

The girls have spent the last couple of hours making a little box for her, lining its cardboard walls with scraps of velvet ribbon and pictures from nature magazines, and when it is time to lower her into that spot, we place a few flowers around her, and Mary Katherine officiates solemnly but succinctly, informing us, "She was a good butterfly, and we will miss her."

There are half a dozen of us standing around the graveside. I quote the epigraph from Jim Harrison's novel *Dalva* attributed to an old saying — "We loved the earth but could not stay" — and then we fill the hole back in with its three shovelfuls of loose, sun-grayed dirt, and tamp in the headstone, a piece of broken clay tile, upon which the girls have scrawled, in black Magic Marker, "Here lies Zoey. She was a good butterfly. May she rest in peace. She filled our days with beauty."

We stand around a few moments longer, each of us thinking our quiet thoughts, and then wander on back up to the house, to begin preparing the evening's feast.

They see me out the window, picking those weeds: stooping to pluck up a daisy, to unroot a thistle, to grub a sprout of hawkweed, to assail the gentle dandelions. Sometimes, when they are with me, they stoop to do the same. It's a dilemma. How much do I teach my children to fear the weeds of the world? Do I want their happiness to be even slightly or infinitesimally diminished, or rather, prevented — by an occurrence as common as the pressure of weeds, an occurrence that will be made only more common in the future? Who would wish such a thing upon his or her children?

And yet, how else to define beauty, and how to define values and standards? It seems easy on paper to parse out an equilibrium of moderation, but less easy out in the real world.

I want them to know of unrestrained love — not just mine for them, but even for lesser things, such as a meadow of green grass. I want fiercely for them to know of uncompromised things, both large and small. Of the lessons of compromise, I believe there will be plenty of opportunity later, and always, to learn those.

Can one know compromise and unrestrained joy or love or any other passion both? Like a landscape perhaps that is sometimes one

thing and other times another; or like an animal, some certain species, that has two dwellings.

More wind, rivers of wind further into July — brushing against the
end of it — so that not only the tall marsh grass itself is bent flat,
shuddering, but even the more slender of the lodgepoles are bent
over like taut fishing poles that have hooked their tight lines to
some invisible underground force, one they might or might not
have been seeking in the first place. Bright orange sparks of hawkweed rest in the trash can in my cabin, as if the fires have already
arrived. The wind gusts through my open windows, knocks pictures
from the wall, and heat lightning flashes and rolls to the west, but
still no rain, nearing four weeks now without rain, only an ever-increasing heat. The faint scent of smoke somewhere, and the slight-
est haze. *Change.* I pick the pictures up, hang them back in their
places. The heart quickens.

The next morning, a goldfinch is perched on the alder branch closest to my window. Though it's early, already the dry wind is blowing again. Out along the marsh's edges, Bohemian waxwing chase
moths, stalling and swooping, but that one bird, the greenish-
yellow goldfinch, sits there next to my window with its head cocked,
looking in. Its eye is dark and wet and fixed, and as I stand motionless so as not to frighten it, looking back, it seems certain to me
that across that short distance — three, four feet — I can feel deeply
the first summonings, already, of migration. As if only this morning,
for the first time all summer, has that biological imperative sur-
faced. As if today, only today, finally today, it is time to begin to begin. As if there is somehow an immeasurable but profound difference between yesterday and today.

Even in July, perhaps the surest and most stable of months — the
safest and most reassuring — there is almost always, in every moment, and in every moment between a moment, the steady march
forward, or downward, and some aspect of leave-taking, whether
seen or unseen, like an underground river that flows just beneath
the surface of a fixed slab of sun-warmed rock.

AUGUST

....

FIRST BELLFLOWER BLOOM, first twinflower, first monkshood, a brighter purple than any king's robe. Wild strawberries too, red as fire, and hawkweed, colonies and colonies of it spreading through the forests and meadows, displacing native plants, eaten by nothing, its blossoms brilliant orange, like glowing sparks. Butterflies congregate in huge swarms near any cliff-side seep or spring as water dwindles, with the swarms, the butterfly colonies, becoming larger as the heat expands. To our north woods shade-loving selves, it feels as it does when you stoke a stove too full of dry wood, too much too fast — as if someone is throwing such wood on the sun itself — and though doubtless one of the reasons the butterflies gather in such immense numbers around the drying-out damp patches is to feed on the saturated mineral residue left behind as the puddles and ponds evaporate, they are after the pure water too, I think; and to happen upon such a colony while on a walk through the heated woods (trying to stay in the shade of the trees), the impression one receives at first — just before they all spring into the vortex of flight in a random chaos swirl, disrupting all those thousands of fruit vendors' stands over in India, Morocco, and Hong Kong — is that the butterflies have been gathered at those seeps and springs, hunched over them with fluttering wings in an attempt to fan some faint coolness onto those waters, or even to provide, with the stained-glass church windows of their wings, some glimmering protection, as if even trying, with the filter of their wings, to disguise or camouflage that water from the consuming gaze of the sun.

Almost every year it is this way, in August — hot and dry, with the guessing game that really began back in the heart of winter, as we watched the snow fall, or not fall, coming right down to the whittled point of *now*. Will the fires come today, tonight, tomorrow? Later this week, or the middle of next week?

As the woods become ever more still and hot, as the last

ghosts of moisture oven-bake dry from the last twig, and the last pine needle — as the green and living trees themselves begin to dry out, with some of them dying even while still standing up, their needles browning as if the fire has already passed through — the question that back in January or February might have been an *if* seems inescapably now a *when*.

Weather reports shift by the hour and take on the immediacy of war briefings: wind directions and velocities, temperature, humidity, and storm forecasts. As the heated rock shell of the mountains grows hotter each day, like so many bricks baking in the oven, the convective updraft from those violent heatings takes on the force of coal-fired bellows, or even the exhalations of a lung-heated living thing, sending invisible towering plumes of heat, pistons of unlit fire, straight up, where — thirty and forty thousand feet later — they finally cool, condensing and spreading into apocalyptic-looking mushroom clouds.

They are not yet done, in their cooling. The fire is still in them. It seeks to return to the rocks from which it was birthed — or if not yet birthed, conceived, in that August heat.

The weather reports tell us who is getting what and where, all around the state: lightning with rain, or lightning without rain. Worst of all — or rather, most frightening of all, if one is frightened of these things — lightning with no rain, accompanied and driven by high winds.

It comes slowly, in August, the awareness that the lush bounty of spring and green summer, the rampant growth, has now become like a sort of trap or prison, if one allows oneself to be frightened by such things — the cell walls of every living plant, every grass and forb, twig and branch and limb, leaching paper dry, kindling dry, gunpowder dry — all this botanical exuberance, all that *life,* surrounding you now, surrounding everything, with its husks — husks everywhere — and even if you love fire and love the pulse of life it brings back to a landscape in its aftermath, you cannot help but be a little frightened, standing before the immensity of such a power, and waiting.

The sun seems almost always to be overhead, beating down. Ten o'clock seems as hot as two o'clock, barely tolerable, and beneath such an unchanging zenith, the already weak human sense of direction becomes further challenged so that only the silhouettes of familiar mountains can guide you to north or south, east or west, rather than the traditional cant and tilt and rise and fall of the sun.

Except for the force of the life shriveling from the forest, the woods are extraordinarily silent. Sometimes a lone raven will glide past, high overhead — how can they fly in this heat, and them black as obsidian; are their wings as hot with absorbed heat, perhaps, as fire itself? — and you will see its shadow on the ground as it passes in front of that directionless sun. And spinning, looking backwards, trying to see where the bird that cast that shadow is, or was, you can rarely find it, for by the time you have turned and looked up at the sun and then quickly away, trying to figure out which way the bird was traveling, it's already gone, and it is as if someone again has tossed another stick onto the fire of the sun.

In this, the hottest month — just as with the coldest — there are long days in which nothing happens, or in which nothing seems to happen. A journal no longer even bothers reporting the weather, which is always the same — windless, clear, hot — and there doesn't seem to be any significant or dramatic animal activity. Even the trees and forbs and grasses are dormant in their drying out, beginning to seem as lifeless as if already in the true leached-out heart of winter. The birds are silent in the heat, as are the fledglings on their nests, tiny, fuzzy, bulge-eyed, crooked-limbed scrabbling things that are due somehow, miraculously, in Costa Rica and points farther south in only three or four months.

This is the key to peace, I think, or at least one of the major keys that will allow one inside one or more of the gates that might surround the kingdom of peace: a learned ability to observe and catalogue, perhaps even if only intuitively and emotionally, as many of the different paces of life, and its changes — order into disorder, and vice versa — as possible; and to become comfortable, even fluent, in the recognition of these cycles: whether the one-day's arc of light across an equinox sky, or a month's tracking of the moon, or a deer or elk herd's annual migration from mountaintop to valley bottom, or the thousand-year cycle of a cedar forest growing old, or even the tectonic creep of continents, the imperceptible slip and thrusts of glaciers.

To not automatically apply a human-centered or individual-centered scale of time and its perceptions on a subject other than oneself surely allows one entrance through at least one of the many gates of the high walls surrounding that kingdom of peace.

It's hard enough to learn our own cycles, and even those are not so intimate and always with us, completely in our control; how can we possibly expect to control those of the world, at the fringes and in the margins of which we stand briefly, for our eighty-eight years, or whatever strange and ultimately small number we are allotted?

I would like to think this is what spirit is like, what dying is like — and what waiting to be born is like too: looking down on the green earth, the gold and red earth, the white earth, the black and brown bare earth, and watching all the changes drift across it, again and again — deserts becoming old forests becoming ice-capped mountains becoming oceans becoming deserts again, the changes drifting across the calmly scrutinized terrain below with the gently inexorable power and assurance of cloud drift, or even the shadows cast by cloud drift.

From such grander scale, more beauty, not less, would be able to be seen and understood. The brief lives of humans, and humans' histories, would appear like tiny flashbulb poppings of light in the darkness — the synapses of a moment. The blossoming of an individual flower on one hillside on one mountain range, another flash of light.

What scale should we use when we look at a thing? Different scales for different things, right?

I'm old fashioned, I know, but I'm convinced that in almost all regards, the slower and longer and more moderate a scale, the better, with regard to our own plans and machinations, and particularly with regard to our relationship with nature. There's certainly nothing new in such a thought — isn't this but a windy attempt to define the words *patience* or *humility,* or even *forbearance?* But for someone as impulsive and scatter-minded as I am, this is a task, even upon so substantial and assured a landscape as this one: a task that still, twenty years later, I seek to learn hungrily, in almost every moment of every season, on every hill and along every creek bend, in every consuming glance, every quick, ravenous memory, each one like the spark of light made by a single match on that dark mountain in the night.

Even these pages however are but a compression of the events and images I've gathered in my drift across this landscape, and in the seasons' cloud drift across me, anchored or moored here at the marsh: a gathering of the sparks, or the things that have appeared in my mind as sparks.

And again, in the spaces between those sparks (not spaces in which no sparks were occurring, surely, but merely spaces in which I failed to perceive or observe the background cyclic sparking), there are long spaces of landscape and long spaces of time in which nothing seems to happen: as if such space, such nighttime, is the matrix for those sparks. From a distant enough perspective, then, even amid that vast night, there would be light anywhere you care to look, perhaps; light everywhere, a sky and firmament of light, perhaps, even where we might perceive darkness.

Or maybe these pages, with their compression of the days forming a filter through which to look at this landscape, are not even so much like match strikes in my mind (though even now, in the re-membering of them, that is still how they seem to me: ignitions of yellow light flaring up in an otherwise black and sleeping void in which nothing is perceived). It's not even as if I'm sleeping, but as if I'm simply resting again, waiting to be born, or having already lived.

Perhaps in these pages, as I remember the hours and the days even as they are vanishing behind me, these observations and notes and memories become for me like the mineralized residue, the con-centric rings of salt rime left behind in each vanishing August seep and puddle of moisture, thin shining layers of glittering salt dust being fed on briefly by butterflies before being scrubbed entirely clean again then by the rains that return later in the autumn.

Even as the world seems to become beaten down by the heat — browning, wilting, entering dormancy, even dying and pre-paring to burn, or to be tested by the burning — the marsh itself re-mains, as ever, a thing of beauty, as astounding in its senescence as in its spring and summer vibrancy, or its winter serenity. Neither words nor paint can capture the sepia tone of the marsh grasses as they dry out, for their color, or vanishing-of-color, is somehow more than compensated for by the mysterious rustling and clattering sound that accompanies the grasses and sedges in any rare bit of breeze; and the loss of color, the indescribable nature of it, is somehow also accompanied — compensated — by the increasingly metallic reflectivity of the August sun glinting across those bronzed blades, like ten thousand or ten hundred thousand drawn swords.

Dragonflies rise from those dying tangles of swords, seemingly as infinite as the grass blades and sedges themselves, and they alone are the only movement out over the great plain of the marsh, swirling in no ordered migration but merely each to his or her whirling and clattering own, stirred by the heat, and filling the air with the sunlit prism-glitter of their lace wings, each dragonfly illuminated in this manner as if lit from within, as if burning, and as if fueled by that beautiful jewel-fire.

Even from a distance of four or five hundred yards, clear across to the other side of the marsh, your eye can fall on, and watch, the flight of any one individual dragonfly, filled as it is with its own corona, and with the cool, dark blue-green of the old spruce forest standing as backdrop.

The sight of all those dragonflies is calming, as the marsh always is, and it occurs to me that often it is the two poles of the extreme that becalm us; that we can be led to serenity by austerity, and yet we can also be comforted by extreme bounty: the fruit stand with its bushels full of vibrant color and rich odor and supple textures, the full smokehouse with its hanging array of meats, the full woodpile, the immense and diverse green-leafed garden . . .

As if we are trying to find a way — a confidence — to live in the more complicated space between these two larger, more visible, more nameable primary poles or places, the black and the white. As if — still so relatively new to the world — we are not yet fully accustomed to the middle ground and its mosaics of subtlety and paradox.

How can we love a kind of animal such as a deer or an elk and yet love to eat it too — and worse yet, or so it seems, love to hunt it, even to kill it? How can we love the deep wilderness, the places

where there will never be roads, and yet love the museums and concert music halls, the fine restaurants?

These vast distances, these extraordinary poles — these dramas
of boom and bust, of rank wilderness solitude and exploration, and
of seething humanity, are the easy things to love, the things that
clamor for our attention. I suspect that one of our more unobserved
challenges as humans — as a species — lies not so much in the noisy
explorations of those occasional and highly visible dramas, but in
how well we pass through the middle ground, the quiet days: the
drift between the rapids, and the lovely distances between flood
and forest fire and blizzard.

This is the last place there will be water. Even when the creeks
and rivers themselves are but dry racks of bones, shining cobbled
and white beneath the eye of the drought, and beneath the pro-
longed accumulating weight of climatic change, the peaty depths
of the marsh will almost always retain some moisture, deep in its
earthen breast of the centuries.

Yet even the marsh will not be here forever. As it slowly dries,
the trees standing at its edges — nurtured by the marsh's center — will fall into the center, sinking and rotting, and feeding the
marsh grasses; feeding, in their decomposition, the sun-struck, waterlogged soup that helps support, like a puff of warm breath, all
those beautiful clattering dragonflies, and so much more: geese and
moose and wolves and deer, warblers and vireos. But eventually, if a
drying spell continues for a long enough time, the rate of rot will
slow and the tree carcasses will begin forming soil.

Seedlings will take root in the nurse-log carcasses of the fallen,
and will rise, living long enough to provide some shade, which will
be the beginning of the end for the marsh. The process is called eu-
trophication, and is one of the slowest nongeologic organic processes I can think of. It might take thousands of years, until one
day — was it really only the blink of an eye? — the marsh will be a
buried lens of coal, a lake of brittle carbon beneath ten thousand
feet of time.

We want stability, we want reassurance, we want knowledge. And
yet how frail we are, really, how wonderfully we quake and trem-

ble beneath the fullness of emotions (or knowledge), purely felt or deeply known — wavering beneath such weight like windswept grass, or as if in ecstasy. This is part of what it is like to be human, so new to the world, and all in all, I do not think I would trade it for the quiet confidence of the other animals, so much more assured in the world and in the seasons; though I have to say, there are times when I envy them the majesty of that assurance, and that instinctual knowledge: those whose reservoirs are so much deeper and older than our own still developing wells.

I think that to look down on the larger passage of time — beyond a day, beyond a season or a year or a lifetime, or even the quick shudder of human existence — and to see not only all the geese drifting south in their annual migrations and all the elk winding down single file off the mountain, through the deep snow, but to see simultaneously the larger drifts of geologic and meteorological change, and of speciation, to see even the slight and gradual canting wobble of the planet itself, would be both sublime and terrifying, and too magnificent — for now — to even imagine.

By August, the weeds, their own kind of fire, have been mostly pulled. Left untended, they are like a kind of double fire, or eternal dead fire, rather than the rhythmic, living pulse of true fire. They displace the native plants and grasses and give nothing in return — nothing eats them, and often the August-brittle clot of them, explosive with seed heads, acts as a kind of fuse, making a thick mat of extremely flammable fine fuel buildup that can carry a fire quickly in places where it would not otherwise creep or travel. The weeds are the sign of an injured landscape, a harbinger of loss, and a great compromise: of trading the specific for the general, the acutely crafted for the abstract. Fecund plenitude for sterile paucity.

Grant me the serenity to differentiate between the things I can and cannot change, goes one famous prayer; and the encroachment of weeds lies somewhere in the nebulous middle, sometimes on one side of the line and other times on the other. I don't know if I can keep the weeds out of the land I perceive myself to be most responsible for — the relative postage stamp of land that I own, which is to say, live on, and pay taxes on — but I can try, and each year as I fight that battle, pulling the weeds — knapweed, hawkweed, this- tle, St. John's wort, and dandelions — I do not so much delude my- self into thinking I can hold back the tide, the drift, of their own movements, but instead look at that annual work, the dozens of hours spent on hands and knees in ultra-close proximity to the ground, grubbing and pulling, as a kind of sacrament, or insignifi- cant tithing, or even a modest kind of prayer.

There are those who will say that change is inevitable, and that weeds are nature too, but I am not sure I would agree. For me, there is already plenty of change just in the normal cycles of the seasons, and in the infinite and specific time-crafted cycles within each day of those seasons. It's my observation that the weeds fragment and isolate and disconnect those other, more supple and intercon- nected changes, and that it can be said then that not only are the weeds enemies of life beyond themselves (they prepare the land for nothing other than more of themselves) but enemies of change as well.

Even a glacier, with its frozen cap of hundreds of feet of blue ice, would be more loving and life-giving than the weeds, as the gla- cier growled slowly over the stony world below, grinding and carv- ing out great buried hanging valleys and magnificent cirques and rivers and mountain ranges, all to be revealed tens of thousands of years later, once the glacier retreated, like the lifting of a sheet; like the unveiling of a work of art a hundred thousand years or more in the making.

Eventually, however, the weeds are vanquished. Perhaps, like some foolish machine, you have traded the hours of your life for the lives of weeds — or rather, the lives of weeds in the one small patch of ground for which you've decided to assume responsibility. One morning or afternoon, they are finally all gone, you've got them all pulled, and, as if your prayers have been answered — all those hours spent on bended knees — you are rewarded once again with the beauty of what was once a simple and even unquestioned thing, the sight of a field of grass, for as far as you can see, unblemished by either weed or toxin, and a forest likewise with its full complement of native ground cover, a place still quintessentially native, quintessentially local, quintessentially unique — as unique and fitted as if it were handmade by someone long ago, for the occasion of a gift.

Maybe I'm just easily entertained, but I can sit and stare at a forest or field free of weeds for the longest time, and be filled with a pleasure and a calmness, beholding that beauty, so deep that surely it transcends any conscious thoughts of phrases like *biological integrity* or *native diversity*. Instead, there's a spiritual component to the depth — like staring at a painting by a master, transfixed for long moments on end.

I feel the same emotions, the strange combination of joy and peace and calm and assurance, when I stare at a rock wall crafted by ancient yeomen to fit the contours of the land — the rocks, the sweat of the yeomen, and the stones fitted so tight as to seem, even from a slight distance, seamless — and too, it is not unlike the same feeling of joy, peace, relief, and wonder one gets while watching a herd of elk or deer moving through the forest, or a flock of geese passing overhead. Everything is still working. All the gears in the fine watch are still fitted and functioning. And you — tiny you, within all those gears — are therefore likewise.

It seems to me there are two vital ways of looking at the world, beliefs that have contributed to the various wars and religions throughout our history — all the various *isms* and experiments in commerce, all the centuries of yearnings and muddled strivings.

Mankind, as typified by the individual, is either but a tiny cog within a magnificent, majestic, unknowable larger whole or is the very reason for the world's existence, the fulcrum for all other turnings of fate and the seasons, and divinely empowered, made as we are in the image — the exclusive image, mind you — of God.

For my own part, and like a glutton, I believe both. My own life seems like that of a yellow upturned leaf that has landed on a stream, a river, and has been carried along on the larger current. Sometimes the bright leaf is in the center of the river, riding elegantly and with such verve that it seems to be the center of all else around it, and imbued with meaning and direction, even fate; other times, as with a drawing back of scale or perspective, it is just one yellow leaf on one small river in one small valley in one small mountain range, on one vast continent moving very quickly through the even vaster mass of time — mountains and glaciers of time, wildfires of time, oceans and deserts and prairies of time.

What I mean to be saying is that it is not the labor of my hands pulling all those weeds, pulling them like prayer or beseeching, that causes the berries to arise, in August, after the weeds are gone. But there is a story-making part in us, an eye for flow or narrative, and an attempt to discern order and pattern and rhythm and perhaps even meaning, which lures us again and again into wanting to believe in such connections.

To believe that not only are we included, fully participatory, in the seasons, but that our own desires help drive them. That our desires supersede those of the herds of elk desiring fields of green grass, or the desires and yearnings that cause millions of wild geese to rise from their autumn fields in the north and travel thousands of miles each year and thousands of miles back again. That our brief desires, the sparks of our lives, should power all such miraculous turnings — that we hold the world stable and aloft through power and cunning and divine blessing, and that these other desires, the millions of such other desires of all the other species, and all more deeply seated, time-tested, and enduring, do not even exist, or are entirely secondary...

Still, it's a lovely temptation, to feel in rhythm, to feel fitted to the place where you live — the place you have chosen, the place that has chosen you. As you hike up into the mountains, empty plastic water bottle in hand, and begin plunking the plump sweet huckleberries into that bucket, one by one by one, a bounty as full and seemingly interminable as the day is long, you cannot help but be reminded that this is the exact same movement, the reaching and pulling, with which you addressed the weeds only weeks earlier. As if all that work, or prayer, was but preparation for receiving this bounty that now appears for the taking, and that therefore it might somehow be your reward, your due.

I suppose what I think about all this is that sometimes for brief, shining moments the gaze of the world falls and rests on us, with favor and even undivided attention — though most other times, that gaze lands on the mountains themselves, or on the rivers, drifting downstream then, awash in and amid so much beauty: our own, and all else.

The roar of the ceaseless winds, high in the mountains, turning the world — not us. We are just leaves. Beautiful leaves, but leaves.

This is the beginning of yet another change, then. It seems to me that this valley almost always has something to give — but in August, the turning of the gears is such that even in our occasional inattentiveness, we cannot help but take notice of the gifts.

The bears are entering the huckleberry fields, just as we are, and with far greater earnestness — desire — than any human pickers. They're beginning the stages of hyperphagia, in which they eat almost nonstop, particularly the sugar-rich sweet berries, in an attempt to put on as much weight, as much fat, as possible with which to journey though winter's long sleep. The bears are almost like funnels as they pluck the berries from the branches with their teeth, stripping the ripe berries with their jaws: as if the earth itself has shifted to begin pouring its autumn bounty into the bodies, the lives, of grizzly bears, in order that they might make it through winter. As if the world, or the force that created the world, desires grizzly bears to be in these mountains.

The trance of the hunter-gatherer: it is a joy to remember that there are many kinds of peace, including that of doing contentedly without — the clean and spartan lines of abstinence, or even puritanical moderation — but it is a human joy also to sit quietly on a hillside on a cool sunny morning, before the heat of the day is up, or in the late afternoon as shadows are beginning to return to the land, and to pick steadily, sometimes daydreaming though other times possessing no thoughts at all, only the moment, and the repeated and nurturing image of purple berries all around you, and leafy cool green foliage. You will be sitting, perhaps on bent knees, and looking about, though no farther, usually, than arm's reach; and there will be berries everywhere, more berries than you could ever use or eat, and there's no rush, you're simply sitting there in the silence, alone or with your wife and daughters, picking.

Occasionally you'll pause and refocus — will lift your head and look out at the view of the green valley beyond — but for the most part, you're just focused on the here and now, and on the very close: arm's reach, or a little farther, but beyond that, no more. And there is plenty, and you are gathering more than plenty, laying in for winter — huckleberry jam, and pancakes, and pies — and even though the earth is pivoting strongly now, it is lulling. It seems that river of time has stopped, or at least paused — that August is an eddy — and no matter that it is a fulcrum for change, considerable change, and the resumption of movement; sitting there in the berry fields, gleaning bounty, you are in the valley's eddy, and every part of you knows it, every part of you feels fitted to all else in the valley, with a clarity, even an elegance, that seems almost as if it could only have been achieved by preconceived design.

I think that the realization of such fittedness, or the possibility of fittedness — the full and once ordinary connectedness of things — can inspire in us one of two primary responses: awe and reverence at the mysteries of a world sometimes just beyond our consciousness, wherein myriad such puzzle pieces are constantly interlocking and shifting and rebalancing, or, perhaps foolishly, or perhaps smitten with hubris or some degree of both, we are tempted to believe that, like little gods, we can impose similar order on the events of our lives — the human world, set apart from the rest of the world. That our desires need no balance, and that further, we are clever enough to come up with similar elegance of fit within our random human world, our comings and goings, and that within that design, we can control things; that with sufficient desire, we can control the very turning of the world, and can improve upon and, where desired, destroy the blueprints for any existing master plan.

Living in this valley — among its fires and blizzards, and the floods of spring, and the inexplicable, unstoppable bounties of autumn — tends, I think, to lead one more to the former idea than the latter — the awe-and-reverence response rather than the control, destroy, and redesign camp.

The truth is, the best horticulturists in the world haven't even been able to grow huckleberries domestically. What appears to be a nonchalant afterthought, up on the mountain — fields of purple berries extending for as far as the eye can see — is in fact largely ir-reproducible in the laboratory, or the garden; the roots simply will not propagate, requiring instead some mysterious combination of fire and soil and sunlight and chemicals, and, I suspect, some lock-and-key combination of a rhythm and pace that can be delivered only by the wild, only by the mountains themselves. And even in the mountains there are years when the berries do not appear — lean years, with the berries' absence seemingly unconnected to any factors able to be observed by us — irrespective of basic patterns of temperature or rainfall.

It is the same way with the grouse — the ruffed, spruce, and blue grouse that inhabit these mountains. Although they exist some years in great numbers — early in the autumn, hikers might encoun-ter coveys of up to a dozen birds — biologists have been unable to raise grouse in captivity. We can probe the furthering perimeters of outer space and can map the genetic outline of almost any liv-ing creature, but we cannot do something as seemingly simple as breed grouse in captivity — something these mountains do cease-lessly, year after year, and in humbling, sometimes breathtaking abundance.

Again and again, I am reminded that the wild cannot be managed or reproduced; it can only be recognized, protected, and honored.

The woods are drying out, and the mountains' stones and cliffs — particularly, I think, the igneous ones — are crying out for fire. The drying grass that rubs together in any faint breeze gener-ated by the pulse of the rising heat itself is like a friction that calls for fire, and the rich, waxy oils of the pine needles from last year, and all the years before, call out for the cleansing fire too, and be-fore it is too late — before there is such a buildup of twigs and branches and needles that it prevents most moisture from soaking into the ground, so that the trees die from heat and drought stress far more surely than if they were to burn in all but the most severe of fires.

And as the accumulation of dead needles and branches builds each year around the trunks of the trees, unburned, it creates a kind of self-made sarcophagus, one that will finally cook the trees if — when — the fire finally does come, so that we understand now even the trees themselves are crying out for fire — frequent fire, sweeping here and there, like a man or woman with a broom or a rake.

No amount of industrial derring-do, or even public works initiatives, could keep the forest, year after year, from drowning in the breath of its own living and dying — its own lovely detritus. Only the breath of fire can accomplish this. To cut off fire from the forest would be to take away the forest's lungs, the forest's breath. The history and identity, the character, of every tree in the forest has been shaped and sculpted by fire; some trees have developed thick bark to summon and withstand the fire, and others have chosen to run from it, seeking out the wetter places; but fire has helped create and birth them all, and it sustains them all. The forest cannot continue to survive without fire's breath.

In the Yaak, from a human-social perspective, we're fortunate in that we have a pretty high rate of rot — its own brand of fire, with many of those twigs and branches and fallen tree carcasses turning quickly into delicious orange mulch rather than even-quicker gray ash and black char.

It's one thing, however, to think these thoughts early in the year — in the safety of winter, perhaps, with snow up to your waist, or in the lovely, rainy autumn, after the fires have safely passed — and quite another to think them while the heat waves are rising from the cliff faces like the vapors of smoke already, or when the scent of smoke itself is in the air, and the creeks are dry, and the forecast calls for dry lightning and wind, and everywhere you look there is fuel — fine fuels, as combustible as hay.

The spark from a single cigarette could awaken the forest to fire, much less the galvanic birth of some million-volt lightning bolt. The best you can do with your objectivity in August, in the heat and the wind, is to keep the brush cleared away from your house, as well as the plastic ABS canoe (which would flame like a marshmallow), and hope that the animal of the fire, when it comes, passes near but not too near.

You can pick up twigs and needles on an acre or two, or even

three or four, with effort. For the million acres that form this ecosystem, however — and for the ecosystems to the north and south,
and east and west — you can only wait and watch to see where the
animal of the fire will walk, and hope that no one gets hurt. For this
scale of change, this pace of breathing and being, it's harder to find a
rhythm; though with the passage of enough years, I want to believe
that even the fires can be accommodated, and even appreciated.

Once you come to understand certain of the most basic facts
of fires — that they tend to run uphill, driven by the heated breath
of their own combustion; that they skip and jump, moving slower
through wet and shady areas and faster through the fields and openings, and that ultimately, it's all up to the wind, that the tongues of
flame and showers of sparks will follow wherever the wind swirls,
sparks traveling on the wind like leaves riding on a river current — then you begin, even if somewhat uncomfortably, to accept
the rhythms of fires.

And tell me again — what other option is there?

To me, they're like a disruption, a breaking point, in the grace
of the year. So incomprehensibly powerful and erratic, as if the sun
itself — lovely, at a distance — has come down to earth; they disrupt and scatter and disintegrate, wreaking chaos, or what to us, at
ground level, appears as chaos.

Only after they are gone are we able again to observe — usually
more clearly than ever — the return of the slower and more supple
graces, and rhythms and patterns of less dramatic amplitude.

Even in dormant August, this valley is dense in the world of things,
vibrant upon the senses. Even in this driest of months, when all
damp molecules of scent should have vanished, there is still a richness of odors — fainter in the day, but with a long finish that begins
again at dusk and continues through the next morning. The scent
of sun-baked pine needles, as they await the fire. The odor of shiny-
leafed, snowy-blossomed ceanothus as the oils and turpenes of
that plant become superheated on the south slopes (growing usually where a fire has already passed through): their own sweet, peculiar odor that tells me better than any thermometer that the ground
temperature is higher than ninety degrees and climbing toward one
hundred.

Such a richness of things. Surely I am the richest person in the world, to love a place, and a life, so deeply — to have been accepted readily into this place of things.

On one of our huckleberry outings, we find a surprise, a bonus — a wild blackberry bush, spectacularly loaded, rich black fruit bending and sometimes even snapping the slender thorny branches: the bush itself a remnant of a previous fire not so long ago. And for the rest of that week we have blackberry pie with vanilla ice cream, blackberry cobbler, blackberry cheesecake; and the little latticework of faint scratches on our arms fades quickly to ghostly pale scars, and then nothing, as we move on further into the season, encountering bounty now almost everywhere we turn, and even still further ahead, all the way to the horizon, and beyond.

Here is another tiny element that is one of the innumerable parts of the cant, the tilt and angle and rhythm and movement that is specific to this one place on earth, only this place: the differential, in August, between the hottest days and the coldest nights, with the amplitude regularly reaching fifty degrees, doubling, and then halving, all within the space of twelve hours, a neap tide of temperature, of heat.

We get to where we can set our clocks by the wind, as the days grow hotter and begin creating their own wind: the first subtle movements in the grass around ten-thirty; the first sigh, twelve-thirty; the first movement in the treetops, one p.m.; the marsh grasses bending halfway back by one-forty, or two or three at the latest. The awakening, the yawning, the stirring, the stretching. The world — or this one place in the world — waiting only for that one spark of ignition. And it seems that between pulses now you can even hear it calling, asking, summoning that spark, those sparks. *Praying* might not be quite the proper word — but definitely, there is a fervent, confident, necessary asking. The forest wants, needs, fire.

Even as we are watching the middles of the days, calibrating our biological clocks to the various stirrings of the wind, the days are wobbling, melting, burning at either end, with the solstice halfway behind us and the equinox halfway before us. Look away for a day, an evening, and you lose only three minutes of light. The sun still sets around ten. Look away for three evenings in a row, however — a short trip elsewhere, or simple preoccupation, around that time each evening — and suddenly you've lost, misplaced, ten minutes, and then twenty.

I love the children this valley produces, the children these parents produce, the children this community produces; the children this landscape shapes and instructs. Our friends' twelve-year-old daughter, Wendy, joins me and Mary Katherine, eight, for a hike into the backcountry, to a hill, call it Huckleberry Hill, where we are finding — this year, at least — more huckleberries than I have ever seen anywhere: enough huckleberries, it would seem, to feed the world for a few days.

We pass through an old stand of cedar, the trees' odor fragrant in the cool shade, and then back out into the broad sunlight of an old burn. Blackened sentinel snags, riddled with the excavations of woodpeckers, tower over the hillside, with jigsaw- or Rorschach-shaped openings burned through the husks of their still-standing carcasses, through which we can view the portals of bright blue sky beyond. Bluebirds flit and swoop through the blackened poles, disappearing briefly when they pass in front of those portals of blue sky.

To get to the berry field, we have to pass through a mind-boggling array of blown-down, blackened cedar and lodgepole spars, a matrix, the interstices of which are filled with new-sprouting alder and cottonwood, and more cedar and lodgepole, a boisterous, shouting vegetative exclamation of the world to come.

The girls cross through this tangle as if it is a game, not a task. They tightrope-walk along the fallen trees, and hop from one to the next. Wendy, not knowing we would be going into the backcountry, is wearing only her summer sandals, but she has insisted she'll be fine; and though the branches and bark are scratching the tops of her bare feet as we bushwhack upward, she pays no mind, is instead only aflame with the pleasure of the day, stopping to admire and point out the beauty of a sublime layering of afternoon clouds to the south: gigantic heat-spawned cumulus clouds, vibrant with distant electricity.

The girls sing going up the mountain — traditional childhood songs that I can't remember now, and songs too of their own making. Soon Wendy's feet are crisscrossed with blood scratches, as well as charcoal, and our arms and faces are smudged from where we've slipped off logs and fallen into the maw below — but eventually we gain the bald hill above, the berry fields, and begin picking, rewarded with a bounty that was previously simply unimaginable.

We settle in comfortably, quietly, each nestling down into our own spot on the hill, between bushes, each folding our own specific body into the one curve of earth that best accommodates it — eventually finding a fit so comfortable that it seems it was made for us, and that we have journeyed all this way to arrive here, only here — and again we fall quickly, comfortably, into that somnolent, satisfied trance of the autumn hunter-gatherer, even though autumn still lies just over the next hill. Eating, picking, eating, picking: *lulled.*

After our buckets are filled, we still have some light left — the slowly setting sun is beginning to paint those faraway, towering clouds with streaks of pink and rose and purple, and even tinges of copper-green — and we climb higher on the hill, toward the crest, where we begin to encounter the fresh berry-filled scats of bears — big scats — and it is an honor, an excitement, and strangely comforting, to be so near to the presence of so wild and powerful a creature and to understand at some level deeper than that to which we're usually accustomed how alike we are to this animal, how much we have in common — not just landscape, but tastes, cravings, pleasures.

Looking down on our distant valley and the mountains beyond, and feeling the release of peace spreading through us, it's easy to understand that perhaps this is how it is for the bear too, as he or she wanders these same hills, fitting these hills, and comforted too, doubtless, by both the sweetness and abundance of the berries, the rich purple sugar fuel that will carry him or her, like an underground cosmonaut, tumbling safely through the long, silent dreams of the coming winter.

I like to believe that those dreams, and those sleeping memories, will be all the richer for having a little extra berry fat to draw on, and that in this richness it's even possible to imagine some crude biological accounting: that *this* bush, loaded to groaning, will ensure a safe and good sleep for the fifteenth of January, and *this* bush, the sixteenth, and *this* bush, the seventeenth — and so on, and so on, even as I know it is not that way at all, that there is nothing linear or definable about the birth or manufacture of dreams, any more than one can plot or direct the shape and direction of a childhood.

It's hard to imagine snow, or hibernation, as we wander heat-struck across the mountain, gulping water and sweating: salt-rimed, berry-stained, charcoal-smudged, blood-scratched.

A little higher on the mountain, we encounter some overturned quartz boulders, summer residue of where the bear — probably a grizzly — had been digging for ants, as they do often in July, after the vegetation begins drying out but the berries have not yet appeared. And then a short distance above that, thirty or forty feet higher on the hill, we find an old hand-dug mineshaft — little deeper than a grave, really — where some gold-crazed wanderer of a hundred years ago picked apart this same little seam of outcropping yellowed quartz, scratching and scraping, trying to reach deeper but evidently not finding anything, for no mine was ever developed. The hammer-broke detritus of his efforts, the quartz rubble being slowly covered with lichens, looks like the treasure itself, not the gold: as if some master jeweler had carried a huge bag of jewels all the way up near the top of this mountain and then spilled them out in an immense pile, for no other reason than as an offering — to his God, or the mountain — or even as if offering them to some grizzly bear, or even the idea of a grizzly bear, a hundred years hence, which would paw and sift and scratch through those same boulders, feeding on the ants that lived beneath them: mining those ants, year after year, turning the larger quartz rocks over and over, first one way, one year, and then the next, the subsequent year; and in that manner, moving some of the quartz boulders slowly down the hill over the years, like the workings of one small glacier or one lone miner . . .

I love the children this valley, this landscape, makes. I love how the berry-stained girls, with their buckets of ripe fruit and uncomplaining of heat or thirst or scratches, are continuing to notice and marvel at the beautiful sunset clouds, as the storm builds. I love how they examine the old miner's rubble with interest and gather a few of the crystals to take home for their windowsills, as careful with and pleased by their selections as any window-front jewelry shopper on Madison Avenue. I love their values, their choice of sunsets over silver or gold.

I love how, when hiking back down off the mountain — half galloping, really, in the long blue dusk — we surprise a bear bedded down in a lodgepole thicket, how we hear the bear's *chuff* of alarm, his or her call to let us know of his or her location, and the noisy thrashing of saplings, then not a sound of either escape or advance, but merely a noise-making, a standing-of-one's ground, designed to let us know where the bear is; and a sound designed, we understand immediately, to encourage us to detour to another route down the mountain, which we do carefully, quietly, speaking calmly to the bear, or in the bear's direction, as we do so.

I love how the girls are a little jittery — I've got them tucked in behind me — but how also, by my continued enthusiasm and expressions of amazement at our good fortune to have just had such an experience, I'm able to help them understand how lucky we are to be having such an experience — how rare it is, and how rare these bears are in this day and age.

I love how when they get home, they will have a story to tell, several stories. And this might sound a little abstract and ethereal, but I love too how I think the lessons of place and fit must come together for them here, eventually, as naturally as puzzle pieces that assemble by themselves: the observation that this rich, wild land can include them in its giving; the observation that other beings are included in this giving, this bounty, the great bear napping there at the foot of his berry hill; the observation of beauty in the clouds, beauty stacked on top of beauty, which is, after all (how easily we forget this, sometimes!) the essence and identity of the world.

I love too how all these little puzzle pieces go uncommented on in their lives, for the most part, but instead only form the braid, the fabric of their lives, day after day, as we travel into the future, in the manner of a mason laying down stones for some course, some wall or structure of the mason's making, the final design of which even the builder does not yet know, concentrating instead only on that day's work, and the next, and only occasionally pausing to look back at that which has already been laid.

In the gathering dusk, nearer to the bottom of the hill, we find yet another lone blackberry bush, once again so burdened with fruit that its thorny branches are splitting, and so we sit there even into the darkness, plucking and eating — what are a few more scratches, among so many? — while the stars begin to appear above us and, or so we imagine, as the disgruntled bear we so rudely interrupted moves slowly up the hill in the night's returning coolness, browsing and grazing, storing up fat for the coming winter.

It's hard to imagine ice and snow and hibernation as even being on the agenda in the midst of the broiling days, but it's merely another of the valley's lessons, that nothing stands alone or unconnected to anything else; everything is still attached, even if sometimes only tenuously now, to something else, to almost everything else. And whether I am spoiling them with a worldview that may not mesh well with either the future or the world beyond this place, I cannot say. I know only that this valley and its rhythms offer them riches — not just physical richness, but of the spirit — and for this I am grateful, and astounded. The richness of landscape upon the richness of childhood.

On the way home, we talk about pies, debate the merits of cobblers and tartlets; discuss milk shakes, berries with cream, berries in muffins and pancakes and waffles, berries in yogurt: worshiping them, and the force that crafted their wonderful specificity, just as up on the mountain, the bear moves through the bushes, down on all fours, worshiping too — giving thanks, no doubt, and praying his or her way toward winter, even though there are still the flames of summer to pass through first.

When the fires finally come, we are up in Canada, having driven up there with Elizabeth's mother, who has always wanted to see Banff and Lake Louise. It's pretty country, I suppose, although I'm reminded, as I am so often, of how much we tend to look at the notion of wilderness from a human recreational viewpoint rather than through the lens of biological wilderness — species richness, diversity, and biotic productivity — so that as a result, our swamps and lowlands and other less visually glamorous places get short shrift during the discussions of whether to protect a place or not protect it.

I'm made more than a little antsy by all the roadside miniature golf venues, nearing Banff, and the bide-a-wee cottages (such as the one where we'll be staying), and am reminded again how very much this country, this continent, needs to protect the last of its big wild — the last of its rank and unruly and often impenetrable places, which still contain in their core that essence of spirit that, as Wallace Stegner and others have pointed out, has had such a vital hand in shaping and influencing the very American culture that we profess to cherish: the strong, the free, the wild, the individualistic.

I'm made antsy too, on our little vacation journey, by the ferocity of the lightning storm we've driven through — a truly spectacular, even phantasmagoric display of electricity bouncing around in the tops of the craggy Canadian mountains, the sky crackling and booming with wind and lightning but no rain.

It's probably not doing this at home, I tell myself. *This storm probably went north of us.*

We put in our two days at the resort swimming pool, the water slide, the games of horseshoes and volleyball, yadda yadda — *Forgive my wolverine-ishness,* I beseech my family, and myself, silently, and focus on being in the moment and participating in the midst of the world rather than its outer fringes, which I so love to haunt. And finally, though not soon enough, we're ready to journey back home, and it is only on checking out and paying for our room that the desk clerk hands us a message, a note, that they received the day before, which says, in essence, that there is a forest fire in our yard.

"We tried calling your room yesterday afternoon," the clerk notes, "but nobody answered."

We make a quick call to Wendy's mother, Sue, who tells us that things are under control — that the FedEx driver, Darrell, was delivering a package and noticed the smoke and reported the fire, and that a Forest Service crew composed of local high school students was able to get in and scratch a ring around the fire to contain it before it got out of hand. The fire was back in an old-growth stand of cedar and larch and spruce, protected from the wind, and the soil was moister there than if the fire had been out in the open, exposed to the drying of the sun — but still, they caught it just in time, felling brush and ringing the fire with bare earth as if hastily building a corral around some unruly wild animal before dashing off to other fires.

In the last twenty-four hours, Sue tells us, there were tens of thousands of lightning strikes on the Kootenai, and hundreds of fires sprang up overnight. In fact, after the fire crew left our fire, another, larger one was discovered several hundred yards farther south — downwind — and Sue's husband, Bill, and other neighbors went in with their saws and shovels and attacked it, felling the flaming trees and fighting the advancing walls of flame, and they were barely able to get that one under control. Even so, they needed the help of helicopters airlifting thousand-gallon buckets of water.

Things have stabilized for now, Sue says — there's no real need to rush home, but we might want to start thinking about it, she says, because the forecast is for more wind and dry lightning.

The drive seems to take forever, and we have not traveled even an hour before we see that, in addition to the Yaak, southern Canada is on fire too. Huge plumes of gray smoke rise from various mountains like the activity from vast and scattered encampments. The sight of it is primal, deeply affecting, and not altogether unpleasant. Part of your body responds with instinctive fear, understanding that the landscape you call home is being changed dramatically, not by the pace of glaciers but by an acceleration of time that rivals almost the proverbial blink of an eye.

There is a part of you too, however, that is mesmerized by the beauty of it, the spectacle and magnitude of nature's fuller force revealing itself — of the sleeping or latent energy of the forest combusting to manifest itself all at once, so that anyone can understand, suddenly, how powerful nature is, and how ultimately our illusions of control are but fragile myths. And even though we're traveling in a twentieth-century automobile, on a paved road, it feels to me at least as if we're getting a glimpse back in time: that this is how these hills and mountains looked in late summer a hundred years ago, and two hundred years ago — even five hundred years ago — and that the columns of smoke could be the signs of various Indian camps gathering for trade.

The morning sun is obscured by smoke and haze, casting a sepia-bronze light over the landscape, and the closer we get to home, the more smoke we encounter, until finally, crossing the bridge at Lake Koocanusa, it is as if we are driving through fog: and above us, military helicopters swirl, journeying to and from the lake, dipping their giant buckets like dragonflies dabbing eggs, and they ferry their loads into the mountains, and then back out again, empty — each thousand gallons little more than a single launch of spit against the mountains' fires.

Forest Service trucks, military green and with headlights blazing through the smoke, are everywhere, as are the yellow-slicker-suited fire crews, their bright gear already dirtied by charcoal and ash: the hardest, dirtiest work there is.

There are fires everywhere, and wisps and plumes of *Bryoria* lichen, old-man's-beard, are drifting through the sky, as are entire branches. I can feel the whole earth stirring, rising and then lifting up as surely as if it is some immense animal on whose back we have been sleeping, each of us smaller than a flea: and now the animal is standing, and now the animal is beginning to stride forward, going about its own eager business, and we must scramble to even simply hold on; and whether the animal is even aware that we are on its back or not seems irrelevant, for now the world has other needs and desires, in August, which is to burn, to seek the burning, and to move toward and into the burning, so that old things may be cleaned and groomed or otherwise retired or refreshed, and the new things born.

Is there one massive fire making all that smoke? Or are there hundreds of smaller ones seeking to conjoin? (After all is said and done, only four percent of the forest will have burned — but four percent of a couple million acres is a lot, and even a small fire yields a lot of smoke, so that to our thumping, frightened hearts, it seems as if everything is burning, and as if there is no chance, none, that anything cherished — such as a home, or a favorite grove — will be spared. As if it has all been but a bright dream, and that now the rug is being pulled out from beneath our feet, the very earth itself being pulled out from beneath our feet, and some other, perhaps truer version of the world, some abyss of loss, revealed. Such is the nature of panic, and weakness . . .)

I don't know what we're expecting, when we finally drive up: the sight of flames, perhaps, advancing like the tide; trees burning like candlesticks, perhaps, and swirling sparks. We're veterans of past fires in the valley, but always before they have been in the mountains, never down low, where people live.

The crew has already come and gone — has moved on to other fires, other defense. In the dry bent grass, it's easy to follow their path into the forest; less easy, then, to track them, and I can't discern any one towering column of smoke, as if from a single chimney, like I'd imagined; instead, there is smoke everywhere, smoke low to the ground like fog, smoke in the trees, smoke in the sky, smoke lost inside of smoke.

It seems different, however, from past fires — in a way I can't quite describe in words, it smells closer, and living, somehow, and it even seems to me that I can discern the odor of green, living trees burning as well as dead and dry logs, and twigs, and branches, taking in the scent of it as one might the nuances of an aged wine in the first sip.

It's odd not to be able to pinpoint the fire at first, for it to be so close. As I draw nearer, I can smell it — the charcoal odor of burned-black wood denser than the living smoke — this burned-tree odor anchored rather than drifting, and then, even before I see the flames, I can hear them crackling, and it's a most unsettling sound.

I ascend a little rise and look down into a swale where the fire is still burning, and the sight of it is both beautiful and awful, exhilarating and terrifying, and I stop for a moment, spellbound by this sudden change. All the hundreds of times I have been through these woods, in all seasons, they have always been more or less the same, and unsurprising — comforting in their regularity, reassuring in the predictability of the face they present to me and the world, in step and on time with the meter and rhythm of the seasons.

Now, however, it is as if the woods have changed identity entirely, as if having abandoned that old logic and accepted a more reckless and less calculated course, or even as if the woods have thrown off some mask, one that had led me to believe I knew these old woods — patient, steady, and enduring — and that some deeper and more volatile and completely contrary way of being has sprung flaming into the world, rising from so far beneath the surface that there had never even been any clue to its prior existence; or none that I had recognized, at any rate.

My first impression is that the fire is still totally out of control and is still consuming whatever it wants, eating anything and everything it can reach. Breaking out of my frightened reverie, however, I walk closer, down into the ravine where it is located — the fire is about an acre in size, circular in shape, like a glowing, burning eye — and now I can see the human presence that was here yesterday, the new-sawn brush cut and piled away from the fire, and the foot-wide scratching of bare dust, a tiny barrier across which the fire, in theory at least, will be loath to creep, if indeed no wind arises; or rather, if indeed the old forest remains windless, even as the rest of the valley, and particularly the mountains, receive their winds.

In technical terms, this fire is only contained, not controlled, and certainly not extinguished. In theory, it's burning in on itself, wandering, gnawing at tree trunks and pine needles and branches and limbs, and eating its way underground too, when it can, consuming even the buried roots of trees: traveling anywhere there is a sufficient combination of fuel and oxygen.

With my heart pounding — even the heat from this small fire is intense, and the wild energy it's throwing out, the unpredictability and forcefulness of it, is considerable: far more than any one person's, or indeed, even any small group of people — I turn and hurry back to the house, where I begin filling gallon jugs of water and loading them into my backpack.

For the next twenty-four hours, I will haul water nonstop, ten gallons at a time, and will water the fire as if tending a garden, or an antigarden, in which I want a thing to stop growing. Later, in my exhaustion, it will come to seem like a form of prayer, a sacrament and offering both, breathing in the smoke, and making an offering with each labored step, one after the other after the other, back and forth: offering the water to the burning soil and hissing coals and ashes, and to the flames themselves, and understanding, with each additional trip, that there can never be too much water, can never be enough water, and continuing on anyway.

Fallen tree trunks gleam in a beautiful latticework of glowing red coals that reveal the gridlike structure of the cell walls once the mask or skin of the trees' bark has been burned away. And it is sobering, each time I think I have extinguished even a single burning log, or the roots of a single burning tree — thinking, finally, that I have at least put out that part of the fire — to find, upon my return a half-hour later, with another ten gallons of water, that the stubborn log has burst back into flame again, is sucking air with every bit the vigor of some newborn, strident creature.

It's amazing to me how much heat has been produced in only forty-eight hours of burning. It's amazing to me how much fuel, how much *biomass,* can be contained in one acre — how much history — and no amount of water is going to put it out. I'm only fighting hot spots within that acre, and dampening the edges. *Puny.*

It quickly becomes an exercise, a lesson, in the giving up of control. The fire might appear one way to me upon leaving — upon emptying my paltry ten water jugs — subdued, even, in that one certain hot spot I might have targeted, only to appear completely another way when I return an hour later: as if I had never been there, and with wild new orange flames blossoming elsewhere, as if in some beautiful, savage garden.

And even within this one simple lesson, observed each time between the back-and-forth of my trudging, the lesson expresses itself in even smaller, similar patterns, the same rule and law written now in miniature, within that acre. I can be pouring water on one end of a flaming, cracking log, for instance, and the flames will be extinguished for a moment, but then the other end of the log will begin to flame, spontaneously, it seems, or as if on some sort of seesaw in which some perfect balance must always be struck: where some certain amount of fire *must* exist, and displacing it from one area only sends it elsewhere. That it is a meteorological phenomenon, as impossible to control as rain or drought, or a hurricane; or a living, biological organism, as impossible to control as life. Or that it is its own thing, a hybrid that is partly meteorological, and yet almost alive too — as time itself sometimes seems to have almost a biological, physical component. In these moments, the fire seems to be almost an organic, living thing, with all of life's various stages — birth, youth, middle age, old age, senescence, death, decomposition. Birth.

Clearly, the fire is feeding on something at the surface — the various fuels, particularly the decades' buildup of needles and twigs and branches — the dust and detritus, the shed skins, of life — but it seems to be feeding on something in the air, too — temperature and humidity, I suppose — for it is more becalmed early in the morning but then increases in energy throughout the day, each day, as the temperatures increase, no matter how much water I tote, so that it soon seems to me that the fire is exactly like a restless, living thing, corralled only tenuously by that hastily scratched fire ring; and that the animal of it sleeps or at least rests at night but then gets up and wanders again in the daytime, looking for a place to feed.

(Even as up in the mountains, similar but larger animals of fire — indeed, entire galloping herds — are running, accelerating in the daytime, on the rising convective winds of their own consumption, up the slopes of the mountains, driving themselves up into higher, rockier, drier country, where they will eventually run out of fuel, or food.)

It seems to me too that the fire is feeding on a third thing, not just wood at the surface or the heat and aridity of the day's air, but on some secret set of instructions or code below — almost like a yearning or desire, perhaps: some conspiracy or partnership between geology and time (if indeed the two are dissimilar enough to even deserve separate names) that calls out for *this* type of forest to grow in this one place, at this certain point in time, and for *this* tilt of mountain to receive *this* much sunlight, and to drain away *this* much moisture, and to generate, and receive, *these* certain winds, until one day finally the fire must come as if beckoned.

And to the land, at the confluence of that hard-rock essence of geology and the wandering animal of time, the fire might feel as pleasurable, as necessary, as the scratching of an itch, as complete and satisfying a fulfillment of fate, perhaps, as when the natural histories of our own lives conspire to assemble with such fitted grace that we are compelled to use words like *destiny* and *preordained*.

After the first twenty-four hours, by which point I've come to understand that though still dangerous and unpredictable, the fire is — for the moment — contained, I'm able to sleep, weary and sore, having learned already to adjust myself somewhat to the rhythms of the fire: resting when it rests, and awakening when it awakens.

And as I learn the terrain of that burning one acre, I become more confident, walking out through the ashes to douse a burning stump or to rake soil and ash together with water to make a slurry, a paste, helping to cool down or even extinguish the various hot spots within that acre.

The woods around me are filled with the militaristic sound of helicopters that I cannot see through all the smoke, the airships coming and going, fighting other fires, many of them hundreds or even thousands of times larger than this one, and I can hear also the deeper, steadier drone of the B-52s and C-130s, giant carriers loaded with thousands of pounds of fire retardant. The air is tense with the electricity of engagement, of battle, and the news of each day's developments passes quickly from neighbor to neighbor, through phone calls and visits.

Fire meetings, briefings, are held regularly at the community center, and there are firefighters and people in uniforms everywhere, coming and going, responding and reacting. People in the valley — residents — begin making checklists, in case a few days of strong dry winds should sweep through. Family photos, heirlooms, that sort of thing.

Sometimes when I wade out through the ash to get to a burning log with one of my jugs of water, I will encounter a deeper well of ash, as if plunging into a snowdrift, and I'll stumble, momentarily off-balance, and I will have to remind myself to be more careful, to go slower. What if I were to pitch forward into some bed of glowing coals just beneath that blanket of cooler gray ash? How quickly we become accustomed to almost any situation; how readily we learn to assume that as a thing becomes familiar it can no longer be dangerous.

The smoldering roots are the hardest to extinguish — impossible, really, so that only the snows, when they come, will accomplish that — and there are instances in which root systems smoldered all winter long, venting through the husks of the fire-blackened spars like chimneys. The roots take the heat far underground, as if that is where the fire came from in the first place rather than from the sky, and as if the fire is seeking to return to its secret lair. Sometimes you can feel the roots burning below, even though the patch of ground above is unburned, and that is one of my main concerns — that even though the fire line might hold up all right at the surface, little fingers of fire will burrow beneath the containment ring, like escaping prisoners tunneling to freedom, following the paths and fuel of the underground roots, traveling slowly but undetected, before finally popping back up to the surface on the other side of the line.

And indeed, I find evidence where such a phenomenon, such a yearning, is occurring — places over on the "safe" side of the line where the ground cover, kinnikkinnick, wild strawberries, and pipsissewa, are drying out and curling, scorching and browning, for no apparent reason; and when I touch those places with my bare hand, the ground is uncomfortably warm, so that I know the fire is just below. When I dribble some of the precious water onto those spots, steam rises from the ground and I can hear the muted, underground gurglings and hissings and belches of the smoldering fire protesting, pausing, and perhaps — for a while — retreating; and my sleep is troubled, and in the afternoons, the dry winds continue to blow.

This is where we live, however, and because I want the girls to learn it all, to know it all, and to respect rather than fear the power of this place, I recruit them to help me work on the containment, so that by the third day, they are walking through the woods with me, carrying their little garden can sprinklers and splattering the flames and coals and ashes with me, and scratching at the hot spots, turning the older, cooler ashes up to reveal the warmer ashes below, doing this again and again, ventilating the fire, trying to get some of the heat out of it, turning the ashes over and over as if working autumn tillage into a garden, or as if furrowing the soil already for a spring planting.

It's a new world for them, this burning forest, and their eyes are sharp; they quickly spy a singularly beautiful sight that I have over-looked, a lone bead lily plant growing unharmed, untouched, near the fire's epicenter, its bright blue egg-shaped fruit glowing like a jewel in that coppery, hazy sunlight.

The fire crew has been coming through at dawn some days, checking on the fire, stirring the ashes themselves, and Lowry and Mary Katherine have baked a plate of cookies for me to leave for them on a stump there at fire's edge, as if the crew's comings and goings are as mysterious, and appreciated, as those of Santa Claus. When we return the next day, most of the cookies are gone, with only a couple of fragments remaining, with human bites taken out of them, to show us that it was indeed the fire crew and not bears or squirrels or deer or wolves who nibbled at them.

One of the larger cedar trees still has a steady fire burning in its gut — the heartwood has been hollowed out, so that it's like a chim-ney — and it seems that no amount of water I can pour down into its roots will faze that fire. Every time I return it is burning again, as ceaseless as an Olympic torch — and when I tap on the tree with the end of my shovel, it makes a wonderful tympanic drumming sound; and again, I'm disoriented and nearly mesmerized by the speed with which the landscape, or this portion of it, has changed. I used to be a geologist, and am more accustomed to the pace and rhythms of glaciers, to the scribings of ice and stone rather than this breathless work of fire.

Many people, when they are in love with a landscape, will speak wistfully of their desire to have seen that landscape in an earlier time, before the fragmentation and reduction — before its dimin-ishment to what is indisputably a more human scale. I share that useless wistfulness often, and sometimes find myself trumping it, wondering what the country, this valley, would have looked like when the sheets of glaciers last melted away and retreated: when this most recent reincarnation was completed and the new land lay glistening and just born, sharp-edged and brilliant, awaiting its eco-logical destiny, or ecological opportunity, as the colonists first be-gan to explore it with fingers and roots and waves and pulses, wind and water and fire and crumbling stone mixing together across the centuries, reassembling as if clay thrown by a potter, and that re-mixed assemblage blooming, blossoming, with specific life; and from that life, spirit, and from those accumulated layerings, a certain density of spirit.

I would have liked to see that being born. (Of the time, and the land, before the glaciers came and did their carving, I cannot even imagine: easier, perhaps, to imagine the deserts of Mars, or the ice rings of Saturn.)

It occurs to me, however, that this might be as close as we can come to such a witnessing — to being present at such a birth. To someone who has not lived through a season of fire, it might seem like an odd comparison — speaking of the life that fire brings rather than that which it ushers out — but that is how I perceive it. I like to believe that after the fire has retreated, sinking back beneath the surface to rest for a few more seasons, the newness and cleanliness upon the land — the fields of cooling gray ash, still smoking, and the new architecture of bent and fallen spars, charred and hollow — possesses a new openness, a raw new readiness of spirit, a *tabula rasa,* that is as close to how it was when the glaciers finally retreated as we will ever see; and that the speed with which new life comes rushing back in is how it had first been, ten thousand years ago, when this valley — or rather, the latest reincarnation of this valley — was first born.

I find myself standing for long moments, heel-deep in the cooling coals and ashes, shovel and bucket in hand, delighted by the realization of how infinitesimal I am, how microscopic against both the scale of time and the land itself; and delighted too by my realization that time is not the only thing moving, as organic and alive as a river, or a horse, or a herd of elk, but that even the land beneath us is moving slowly, in similar fashion. That when we were created from the dust, perhaps the rib of man, the image of God, was plucked from a mountainside; that that selfsame image comes originally, initially, from the sleeping-body humped-animal shapes of the new-carved mountains, and that the voice of God is in the wind that once swept, and still sweeps, across those mountains, across these forests.

So the forest is burning: little cells and pockets of it, one acre here and a thousand acres there, the weave and fabric of this valley's million acres as punctuated by these fires as are the demographics of any human population complemented by daily births and daily deaths. The presence of the fire is normal; the absence of it would be abnormal.

And as with a birth — those final contractions, and the expulsion, then, of the living, breathing, bespirited thing into the world — the matter of timing is one of primal, archetypal fascination. At what hour, what moment, will the new life arrive?

And in a reverse sort of conception, which of last winter's snows, which extra bit of moisture, was it that has caused the fires to first be delivered to us on this one date rather than yesterday, or the day before, or the week before?

Was it that extra foot and a half that fell on New Year's Eve? Was it the last big wet snow of April that helped to shape and foretell the timing of this fire's arrival in this one time, this one place, with me standing deep in the ashes, as if once more amid snow?

History; cause and effect, connectedness. Which impressions of childhood, I wonder, act similarly as anchors, as foundations, for the subsequent timed release of awe for the natural world — precursors for the birth of conscious reverence for the grace of our last remaining truly wild places?

Which slant of light, which odor of fir boughs, which cry of wild geese laid itself into the subconscious mind and then grew slowly, like character forming?

How does landscape braid itself into, and form and reinforce, our memories, our character, and our reactions and responses to things — our compassions, our understandings, our patience or impatience? Surely there can be no formula for this question, or any answer, but what does it mean for a child, or a population, to be bereft or unknowing of any significant or unique landscape? What emptiness, what gap or hollowness, loneliness or impoverishment, might exist within that place of absence?

Day by day, I become increasingly familiar, and then comfortable with, the wildfire that continues to pace and gallop in its dirt corral just beyond my home. Night is one of the calmest times to visit the fire, with only the hottest spots burning actively, and all else either a dull glow of orange or complete darkness. It's beautiful, moving through the woods at night toward the fire, and even the burning mountain walls beyond are beautiful in the distance, on the cooler nights when the smoke grows heavier and damper and sinks and the mountains are visible.

On those mountain walls, the flickers and flares look like the glimmerings of countless jack-o'-lanterns, or even as if the night sky has been lowered and filled with more stars; and no one is being injured, nothing is being hurt, the mountains are merely breathing.

It's like the rest between rounds for a boxer, late in a fight. In the daytime, when the temperatures rise again and the humidities drop and the animal of the wind begins to stir and yawn once more, things will become dangerous again and fire commanders will worry incessantly and justifiably about the vagaries and unpredictabilities of fire and weather and fuel, and about luck, and chance; about new or inexperienced firefighters, particularly, and about the dangers of getting upslope of a fire, or upwind; about violent shifts in wind direction, about falling trees, about helicopter malfunctions, about water supplies and fuel logistics and food and shelter and medicine for the firefighters, about communications between squadron leaders, about the homes and property of people living in the valley — but at night, when the fires are calmer, the fires are beautiful, and I cannot help but stare at them and feel that deep-seated lure and attachment one gets while staring at a campfire, or even a lone and wavering candle.

And as the fires wander through the forest, August visitors, like some vast herd of migratory animals — caribou, perhaps, down from the north, braiding their way through the forest, unraveling one thing and yet weaving another — people in the valley will sometimes drive up into the mountains at night to look down upon the bowl of distant winking, glimmering light that is the valley afire, while those whose homes seem to be more directly in the path of one of those wandering herds of fire will stay at home packing, to be ready, should the time for leaving approach. They cut the grass around their houses extra short, and sweep the larch needles from the roofs of all structures, and water the ground around their houses.

The sheriff's department visits each house, tells them that

things look fine now, but to always be prepared, in August, for a quick evacuation. Each house is assigned a number, so that the fire teams can locate it on their maps and respond if the need arises. And in every pulse and breath of our waking moments as well as our dreams, there is the remembrance of a thing that many of us had forgotten long ago: *we are not in control, we exist as if only because of some strange and wonderful mercy, we are not all powerful, we are not in control . . .*

By the eighth day, my fire is as common to me as a hound or a horse that might need feeding and watering each day, and my usual schedule of work and play is but little disrupted by the tending to it. One morning there are deer tracks in the still warm ashes, as if indeed the fire is a hoofed thing and has passed through and gone on its way; and some of the needles from the hemlock trees that were scorched are already falling, sometimes landing on the cooler ashes and resting there like a fabric of gauze bandages laid across a wound, though other times landing on a hot spot and igniting, flaring up one by one in quick, tiny winkings of fire that burn cleanly, purely, leaving no trace, not even smoke.

This fire, at least, is running out of things to eat, but I keep pouring water down those root chambers and listening to that underground, gurgling music of hiss and belch — as if some great stable of circus animals, or wild animals, still resides uncertainly below, animals that might finally be considering moving on — gathering to migrate, perhaps, or to sleep, to hibernate, beneath their blanket of cooling ashes.

Other times, the fading fire seems to me to be now like a drowning or sinking swimmer, trying to rise for one more breath, looking for air and looking for fuel but finding neither, and sinking lower and lower under the weight, finally, of the residue, the ash, made by its own exuberant burning.

You think you know the world; you think you have seen it all. Then you wake up one night and look out your window and see that smoke lies dense over the marsh, again like a blanket of fog — and that the moon is shining on that silvery smoke, as luminous as metal, and that there is a rainbow in the night sky, that the intense light of the moon is filtering through smoke particles in the air and making a prism of colored light, even in the middle of the night, right out over the center of the marsh.

The smoke shifts and the rainbow dissipates, like prisms of colored glass disassembling themselves — but it was there for a few moments, and, who knows, might yet one day be again.

During the days, as the August sun and the summer wind and the fire itself dries the forest out even further — how much drier than dry can we get? — it's possible sometimes to notice the odor of the smoke that stacks up over the valley, and even the smoke coming from the fire nearest the house, changing with the subtlety of a different kind of wine: creeping its way through kinnikkinnick, then ground cedar, then into an old decadent forest, then back into a flashy young green stand of lodgepole. The odors of burning alder are significantly different from those of cedar, or spruce, or larch. The intense sappy scent of Doug fir is its own thing.

In the mix like that — the whole forest burning — you can rarely be quite sure of any one scent, but they keep swirling, mixing throughout the course of the day, as the fire creeps and crawls, runs and leaps, stretches and gallops, reaching for some things and avoiding others, pushed by the wind, and sometimes rendering the essence of a thing all the way back down to dusty ash.

In the heat of the days too, there is the odor of life as well. Not new-beginning life, coming in after the fires — not that, quite yet — but the old regular hanging-on life, sweeter than ever. The hotter the days get, the more intense the odor of the shiny-leafed ceanothus becomes, until it seems you can almost see the oils dripping from their waxy green holly-like leaves; and the browner and more desiccated the other vegetation becomes, the greener the ceanothus shines, and the more forcefully it exudes its almost overpoweringly sweet scent, which, like the fires themselves, all but shouts the word *August.*

My old writing cabin, and the newer house, creak, in August, in the extra degrees of heat that they are experiencing — that the world is experiencing — since they were built: creaking in this drying, windy weather as they never have before. One can imagine in that sound that the house is turning on its foundation to look in the direction of the fire.

August is supreme leisureliness — it's often too hot to get out and hike in the middle of the day. Instead, the days drift, like haze. And yet it can be a time of supreme focus too, of supreme waiting, not unlike that of the hunting season, in which, while deep in the woods, you strain to hear the sound of one deer's approach, stepping through the snow.

Yellow butterflies drift through the yard, buffeted wildly by the roaring afternoon wind that continues to feed and drive the fires, and for a moment, in that waiting, and in that focus, they look like the sparks flung by an advancing fire.

My little fire is almost nothing now, just a few fallen logs burning like the remnants from a party's bonfire, and ash, so much ash, and those simmering root fires, which I am still watering twice daily, again as if tending to some garden. And while contemplating my other garden, the domestic one, four hundred yards distant, it occurs to me that it will be nice, once the ash cools further, to take a few buckets to work into the soil like compost. This entire landscape was once buried with a thin sheet of ash from the Mount St. Helens–like explosion of a volcano known as Mazama, seventy-five hundred years ago — the gray sheet of the ash lies several inches below the ground now, and still serves as a source of nutrients for the trees, the roots of which still suck at that ash, back in the wild forest. And in this manner, while enriching our garden, it will be somewhat as if we are eating the fire itself, distanced only a few months in time — just as the deer themselves, browsing the new forbs next spring and summer, will be eating the fire, just as later in the fall, we the garden fire-eaters will be eating the deer that ate the fire.

What lasts? Not even the mountains. But it is all here, right now, in our bellies and in our eyes, in our hearts and in our legs, and in our wakefulness and in our dreams, for a little while. Today, and maybe even tomorrow.

Fires or not, we're cresting and now passing berry season; timeless leisure or not, the year's berries must still be gathered if we are to have huckleberry jam in the coming year, and pancakes and muffins and milk shakes, if we are to have huckleberries on our ice cream, if we are to prepare huckleberry glazes for the grilled breasts of wild duck and grouse.

Late one afternoon I head back up by myself to the mountain where Wendy and Mary Katherine and I surprised the bear. The blackberries are gone, but there is still an ocean of huckleberries, though not for much longer: a few of them are beginning to wither and wrinkle already beneath the astounding heat.

Will they have the slight scent of wood smoke in them, this year? I try to taste it as I sample them, but can't; they still taste like huckleberries. Or perhaps everything is so saturated with the scent of smoke that I no longer notice any difference.

It feels a little silly, up there on the mountain, to be so pleased, so *assured,* at having finally put my little fire to rest after eight days. It feels silly to believe that everything's tidy and in order, just because that one acre is controlled — even as tens of thousands of others are burning untouched. Nonetheless, I can't help it. Even as I recognize the intellectual folly of such a feeling, the physical pleasure of it is as real and present as when one completes any long and arduous project, and never mind that the world may never see it, or that the project will almost assuredly never have any bearing whatsoever on the larger world.

The energy has been expended, the job has been finished, and, tired but satisfied, you feel good and whole and complete, fulfilled. It can be as simple a task as digging a hole or cutting and splitting a load of wood. It is a feeling of deep satisfaction, the resonance of which, I think, dates back to the not-so-distant echoes of hunting and gathering.

The valley remains filled with smoke and heat. Nothing has changed. The valley is filling even fuller with smoke and heat, as if it is but a vessel for these things to be poured into it; but my little one acre is extinguished, or rather, rendered to contained smoldering, and I feel fine. I sit in the middle of a rich huckleberry patch and pluck berries contentedly, falling quickly into that daydreaming lull, the satisfied trance that seems to fill me, with its deeper echoes of older times, as if I am the vessel. And having wandered, luck filled, into a place of bounty, I will do well to just sit here for a while, pleasantly satisfied, daydreaming and harvesting, daydreaming and gathering; and no matter, really, that the valley might be burning down around me, for what can I do, really, even if it is?

I pick for about an hour, suspended in this lovely August grace, before I discern the change coming. I can feel the drop in barometric pressure almost as violently as when a plane in flight bumps and sags suddenly, pitching silverware and playing cards to the floor in a clatter. The wind of a coming storm is not yet here, but I can see it, dark in the distance. I can see the wall of dust and smoke it is pushing ahead of it, like a piston; and up on my berry mountain, in that compressing dead-air space caught between the approaching storm and the mountain, I can feel the vacuum that is being created, and it is as unsettling a feeling, physically and emotionally and even spiritually, as was the berry picking of only a few minutes ago fulfilling.

Next, then, I can hear the wind as the advancing plume of it slides in over the air sandwiched below, the air in which I am still sitting, trying to pick huckleberries, trying to gather up the last of the summer's harvest — sensing or suspecting somehow that this might be my last leisure day in the woods for a while, my last leisure hour — and as that approaching upper tongue of wind slides in across the mountain, just above the mountain, it passes through the upper reaches of the Swiss cheese excavations from all the many woodpeckers that have riddled the blackened, towering spars left over from the last fire, six years ago, and through the fire-gnawed Rorschach shapes, the strange gaps and apertures left in the husks of those old tree trunks.

The result is a kind of music like none I have ever heard before, somehow both somber and joyous, and intensely powerful, fueled by more wind than all the human lungs in the world could ever provide, and it is singing right here, right now, on this mountain, and I am in the center of it, and part of me is frightened and confused. Part of me is not frightened; and I keep picking berries, though now in the distance I can see tremendous bolts of lightning and can hear the cannonade of thunder.

There is no rain. The air is as void of moisture as a laundered sheet taken crisp and hot from the dryer.

The wind is still above me, the lower waves have not quite yet come sweeping up the mountain, and above, as the wind moans through those hollow burned-tree keyholes and pipe flutes, it bangs and rattles also against the taut hides of the larger hollow snags and spars, creating a deep drumming resonance to accompany all the strange organ-pipe howling, which from a distance sounds like a thousand calliopes playing for some demented, wonderful, terrifying circus — though right here where I am, beneath and amid the drumming and the howling, it sounds like tremendously amplified symphony music, a thousand of the world's largest chamber orchestras vying to play either their own version of Mozart's Requiem, or perhaps (can it be?) "Three Blind Mice." And now the wind beneath the wind is reaching me, splashing in over me like dry waves at the ocean, the wind coming so strong that when I stand up I can lean downhill into it without falling down, suspended like a hawk, or a heavy kite — and this lower wind is carrying pine needles and grit, which stings my face and arms and bare legs, and I have to turn my face to shield my eyes against it, and I know more than I have ever known that there is no hand of mankind, no technology or science or knowledge, that can influence in the least this expression of power, this breath of a living, restless earth. And again I feel tiny, puny, even invisible, and it is exhilarating, and I am reminded intensely of what an astounding privilege it is to be alive, of how rare the circumstances are that conspire to bring life.

I can see the lightning walking up the valley from the south, striding toward me, and I hurry down the mountain, through the stinging needles and grit, with entire tree limbs torn loose from the canopy and floating feathery, lichen laden, through the sky. Now entire treetops are snapping off occasionally, and being launched into the air a short distance, like failed rockets.

Farther down the mountain, I can hear still more tree trunks snapping, a sound like cannons. It seems to me that the earth beneath my feet is buzzing or trembling, and the sky is plum-colored now, but still there is no rain, only wind and fire, and boiling clouds of dust.

I hurry through the tangle of old blowdown, old fire char and new berry bush, new green saplings, running as a deer might run, into the wind, hoping to weave my way unscathed through that maze of falling branches — and once I'm back at the truck, and driving down the logging road (hoping that no trees fall across the road: I have a little emergency bow saw in the back, but it would take a long time to cut through a tree with that), I'm disoriented by the way the entire forest around me seems to be waving like nothing more substantial than the undersea fronds of kelp or reedgrass, or like the thick hair on an animal's back, pressing flat and then swirling in the wind.

What a revelation it is, to have one's perceptions — one's universe — so startlingly reordered, so corrected or amplified. Yes, the forests of immense trees are powerful and awe inspiring, but yes, even they are tiny beneath these gusts of breath from a living, sometimes restless world.

Once I'm home, we all four go out onto the porch and watch the lichens and limbs continue to sail through the sky, and to gaze at the strangely glowing sky, a greenish hurricane sky, and to watch the streaks of lightning, and to count, with thumping hearts, the number of seconds before we hear each crack of thunder. And still there is no rain, not even a little spit of it, and like a beggar or a miser or even a rich man gone broke, I find myself remembering again that wonderful big silent snow of New Year's Day, and those heavy, wet surprises of the late snows in April. I'm hoping that that moisture has been retained to hold back some of the fire, even as I understand more clearly than ever that the fire must come, that it is no different from the wind or the snow itself — that it has shaped and continues to shape, this landscape: that it is its own kind of season, and that the time for it has arrived.

The informal, unofficial volunteer fire brigade, led by my neighbor Phil, comes by the next day to see if I might be able to help them fight a larger fire that's started across the road, about a mile to the south. There's also an official Yaak volunteer fire department, but they're stretched too thin already, and their specialty isn't forest or rangeland fires anyway. It's Phil's hope that if enough neighbors jump quickly enough on these new fires that have sprung up all around the residences down on the valley floor, those fires can be stopped a lot easier than if we wait the extra day or even half-day for a fire crew that may or may not be able to attack each low-elevation fire.

About the fires burning up in the mountains Phil is unconcerned, even adulatory, having spent enough time in the woods — sixty-two years, thus far — to know that in those upper, wilder reaches, the fires are exactly what the mountains need most.

For that matter, they're pretty darn healthy down here in the flatlands too — we just don't want them burning up anybody's house, or property, much less risking any lives.

Increasingly, fire managers and postfire analyses are indicating that the best thing you can do to protect a structure is to create a "defensible space" around your home — that land management activities beyond a certain distance from your home have no significant bearing on whether the breath of fire, as well as the breath of wind, travels one way or another, but that if you clear or reduce flammable materials within two hundred feet of your house, the home can be defended, even if a fire does pass through.

Still, this fire that Phil wants to jump on is headed toward a small group of cabins of the four or five families that live just to the south of us. If the fire continues on its present course and tries to travel upslope, it might pass right through their midst.

I have deep respect for Phil — he's a staunch and brave conservationist, an environmentalist who practices what he preaches, walking instead of driving whenever he can, and living a life almost completely unencumbered by possessions. A seasonal laborer in Washington's apple fields, and a carpenter, he lives close to the land. He engages actively, regularly, in dialogue with the local Forest Service, isn't afraid to call *bullshit* when he finds yet another high-grade clearcut masquerading as something else.

Even in the best of times, Phil's a little ragged, and at this time of year, already a couple of weeks into the fire season, he's real ragged, having been on his own free-ranging unofficial duty almost nonstop, sleeping only a couple of hours every other night or so. He loves to fight fires, and strangely, despite his own lack of material belongings — he lives in a tiny little hut of a cabin — he wants desperately to help keep anyone else from losing theirs; and so every fire season, he's out there roaming the hills with shovel and hoe, running through the woods from one fire to the next, scratching and grubbing and sawing and digging, David dueling Goliath, David dueling Medusa's serpentine hair, each strand a snake of flame. And by the time he shows up at my door asking if I want to go help, he's as haggard and blackened as a fire-charred snag — as if the fires have already passed through and left him behind and he is now hurrying to catch up with them.

In typical Phil fashion, he's grabbed anybody he can find on his way over to the fire, and isn't going to waste or spend time on the phone when he could be in the woods, in the flames, grubbing. He's put in a request for a water truck — the fire is up behind a gated road — but in the meantime Phil and his neighbors, Chuck and Chuck's teenage son, Cedar, and another teen, Chad, are going in to do what they can.

I grab a couple of my old bicycles from the garage, for us to ride behind the gate, and some old shovels and axes, and we drive over to the gate and start up the old logging road, some of us walking and some of us riding, carrying our bristling assemblage of odds-and-ends makeshift firefighting tools.

Nearly all of us are wearing duct-taped overalls, and it seems inconceivable to me that our ragtag militia is going to be capable of defending anything against so powerful a force as fire and wind; but the fire is too close to our neighbors' homes not to try. To not make the attempt would require a fatalistic acceptance of an inherent rightness in the universe that is deeper than any of us — even Phil — currently possesses.

Phil hasn't even seen the fire yet — I get the impression that he overheard some of the bomber pilots discussing it while he was monitoring their reports to the dispatcher — and as we walk and ride our bikes up the road, through the lovely green forest on a warm summer morning, it seems a bit surreal to imagine that around the next bend, or the next, there is going to be a forest fire: but there it is, finally — a blackened landscape appears before us, on the right side of the road — and from the looks of things, it has already been busy for quite a while, has already burned itself out in places, it appears.

It seems so strange to me, the way we assess it immediately, instinctively, as hunters likewise assess, in that first glance, an animal that might be their quarry.

Even as we are marveling at the visual astonishment of it — so much smoke and ash, so much fire-scorched black, and the flames themselves, still dancing and leaping — we are also evaluating the shape and size of it, the general vigor, and the direction it is heading, as well as possible escape routes, and possible angles of attack. It amazes me sometimes, what's in us — old memories, the old loves and fears and cravings and shunnings of nearly all of our ancestors — and among us, Phil seems the most transformed, the most alive, and he is staring at the flames with a rapt and unguarded appreciation for their beauty, power, mystery.

He deploys us to the four corners of the fire. It is about the size already of a large airplane hangar, and has angled steeply uphill, where it seems to have burrowed into some rocks and then disappeared. It would have been a sight to see, in its full glory — last night, perhaps — but other than one rushing finger of flame down low, it appears to be burning itself out already, like a dog that has chased its tail into exhaustion. From time to time a juniper bush explodes into noisy flame, as the waxy oils sizzle and crackle — the teenagers, with their limitless energy, rush right over to those and begin beating at them, chopping at them, rather than waiting the ten or twenty seconds it takes for the junipers to flame out anyway, while Chuck and I work a little more methodically, trying to dig up some bare earth in advance of that one wandering finger of fire, which is moving now through a stand of cedar and lodgepole, leapfrogging its way across the ground at about the speed of a man or woman walking briskly.

The fire seems to be carrying some secret message that it wishes to pass on to the country in front of it, passing it forward as if handing off some unseen baton; and it seems too as we approach with our shovels, grubbing and scratching at the matted duff, that the fire is seeking to evade us: that it dodges and wanders laterally, that it feints and backs up, and even lies down for a while, as if waiting for us to turn our backs or relax a bit, before making another charge.

The heat is intense, making the work, which would be tiring even under normal circumstances, grueling, and it's hard to breathe amid such smoke. As we work in the still warm ashes, our boots are hot, but finally, or so it seems, we have a little line scratched around that one groping, troublesome corner of the fire. And although there are still trees and logs and old sawn stumps burning in the center, the fire has already passed through there, and in our exhaustion, and our short-handedness, we are content to let them continue burning, isolated and not menacing.

"Some water would be nice," Phil says, meaning a few bomber runs to cool things down, to take the edge off this vast bed of hissing, glowing coals, but there are too many other fires elsewhere, larger and wilder fires, and too few planes, and too few pilots — we're truly on our own — and we stand there coal blackened and sweat begrimed, smoke scented, and consider yet again such things as mercy and luck and chance. And once more, we are reminded deeply of how tiny we are, and how incidental our own hopes often are, compared to the flow of the larger world.

Even Phil, with his intense love of firefighting, is beginning to look slightly sated. He looks up at the sky as if hoping for a miracle — if not a cloudburst, then even a single plane, or a single helicopter, with one big bucket of water — and says that when the bombers do fly over, you have to hurry over and hug in tight against a big tree for shelter to keep from being walloped with that four-ton water drop.

Little glimpses of the world tilted onto its strange and burning end — different visions, different perspectives, that week:

The fact that the ash looks so much like snow falling from the sky — the two things so different, and yet so linked, so similar, so connected;

The sight of a boy named Cedar fighting a fire in a cedar grove, battling a burning cedar tree with his ax;

The curse-out-loud irony of my burning a forgotten grilled cheese sandwich to a smoking crisp in the iron skillet one day, smoke rising from the black skillet even as just outside the kitchen window smoke still rises from the woods and helicopters pass over the marsh like gigantic dragonflies. As if there are really only a very few set patterns to choose from, in the world — though within those few grooves or patterns, infinite variety.

All of the fire we have seen up until now — nearby flaming gardens of it, as well as distant billowing mountainsides, Popocatépetl-like — has been as nothing, compared to that which builds, which blows up, one certain windy day, a windy day with forces that surpass even those of the winds that spawned this second wave of lightning strikes. Phil and I and the others were puny, battling our little fires bush by bush, and gnatlike too are the bombers, tiny flecks in the sky with little faucet drips of water, against these larger fires that are now merging and running like a pack of wolves, like a river of salmon, like a herd of buffalo. (The Plains tribes referred to wildfire as "the red buffalo" for the way it moved across the grass, rejuvenating it with its quicksilver passage.)

Some of the fires, in their rushing and braiding together, can now be measured in the tens of thousands of acres — still but a fraction of the two-million-acre forest, but more than was here a week ago, a month ago — though within each fire, there are different degrees of burn intensity, ranging from untouched to crispy. (After the fires, one of the strangest things will be to walk through burned stands, forests in which some of the trees have vaporized like marshmallows, and to then encounter islands of green within those charred areas: as if here, the fire paused to take another breath before moving on, or turned its attention, for a moment or two, elsewhere. Or as if the fire just got moving too fast to burn anything — skipping over certain places like a scrap of paper tumbling down the road in a high wind.)

The fire on the hill above our house — the one that Phil and Chuck and Cedar and Chad and I went up and fooled with — has resurrected in this new, more powerful wind, and has sent sparks and flames skittering downwind, and is now threatening those homes directly in its path. The bombers and helicopters are fighting it, as well as another thousand-acre fire that is trying to creep strangely downhill, into the bogs along the South Fork; and all that afternoon, towering mushroom clouds of smoke build and build, until they're visible more than a hundred miles away, looking precisely like the violent mushrooms of Hiroshima.

The winds beneath those mushrooms — the winds in our yard — are flattening small trees, are swirling counterclockwise, and bits of ember are floating down on the neighbors' tin roofs less than a mile away.

By fiery coincidence, Darrell, the FedEx driver, happens to be making another delivery — another manuscript to read, which strikes me, under the current conditions, as quite possibly shoveling coal into the furnace — and as it's his last delivery of the day, his truck is empty. Elizabeth has an old antique sofa, a great dense crypt of a thing, as uncomfortable as an old Greyhound station bench, and though I'd be only too glad to see the thing return to dust and ash, Darrell offers to load it into his truck and take it, as well as the boxes of photo albums, down to town to put in a storage unit for safekeeping.

For my part, I've got a box of favorite books, and a shotgun, which can fit easily in the back of my truck — the evacuation is beginning — and Mary Katherine brings down some stuffed animals, while Lowry, strangely, or so it seems to me, brings her bedside lamp.

It all goes into the back of the FedEx truck. We thank Darrell, wave goodbye to him as he drives off into that wind-bending forest of smoke, and I feel like telling him, *I'll see you when the war is over.* As the ash continues to swirl, and the mushroom cloud continues to build, rising now to unimaginable heights, higher than any cloud we've ever seen, and glowing with a beautiful rose and mustard color, we put out the call to other friends, who arrive quickly in their old pickups, and we load the second tier of possessions — extra changes of clothes, a china hutch, a favorite painting, the children's artwork, a dining room table, four chairs, sleeping bags — and the mood is both festive and alarming, though not quite frantic. As we ferry boxes and furniture out of the house, Elizabeth prepares a blender of margaritas, to fight the heat, and we stop and sip them briefly.

The boom box is playing the Live Wire Choir's rendition of "Shady Grove," and from the hurried chaos of evacuation, those are the four things I remember most sharply, woven together in a strange way to form one new and denser memory: the towering mushroom cloud, and the heat and wind outside; the goodwill and industry of neighbors; the luminous green of the frozen margarita — just a sip, just a swallow, as we'd be driving — and the music of that one song, "Shady Grove," with the evacuation in full swing.

Todd and Mollie, who live farther upvalley and who, for now, are out of harm's way, have several jugs of an experimental new gel goop that you can spray over your house to protect it from the flames. I'm dubious at first, but Todd tells me he's seen the video and that it works, that it's phenomenal: that the goo protects against even a direct flame of something like fifteen hundred degrees. It's what the firefighters use, when they have time to deploy it.

There are two limitations: it's expensive, and it's effective only for about eight hours — you basically have to wait to spray it on until you see the flames advancing, and then run like hell — but I'm touched by their generosity, by their insistence that I hold on to this product that they've gone to the trouble to purchase from the fire department, and which they've had on hand for their own needs.

The plan is for Elizabeth and the girls to go stay with our friends Bill and Sue, along the river — on the other, nonburning side of the river (we'll store the furniture in their barn, which, while not fireproof, is at least out of the present path of the running fires) — while I'll stay here at the house, truck pointed out and ready to run, if need be, with chain saw and gas in the back. I'll be keeping the new-mown grass good and wet, and will nap out on the porch in that high wind, listening and watching for the flames — ready to begin applying that pink or purple goo before turning and running like Bambi.

I have no illusions about my frailty before such a force. I think I have a complete understanding of how important I am to my family — particularly to my young daughters. I am not going to be foolish, am not going to attempt to be a hero over a *thing,* or things. I am going to be careful, cautious, conservative.

And sitting there that evening, watching the marsh grass bend and blow after everyone has driven off — sitting there with the house so much emptier than it was before, and waiting, watching the treetops bend into almost perfect horseshoe shapes, each one a fly rod battling some giant fish just beneath the ground — there is a lonely feeling, but also one that's more than a little liberating: like exploring an entirely new country after having traveled on a long journey to get there.

The roof and lawn are watered, the fire-retardant gel is at the ready, the photo albums are safe. There's nothing else to be done, really, but to sit on the porch and wait, and ponder the beauty before me, and to contemplate — having finally reached the nature of acceptance.

And later that night, stretched out on my sleeping bag, with the trees still swaying and the night so warm around me, I awaken with a start to see the stars flashing between the waving boughs of the trees above, and am disoriented, thinking at first that they're sparks swirling on that wind, that they've finally arrived, and that I've almost overslept and it's time to leap up and begin spraying the house.

But they're only stars, and little different from how they were last night, and the night before, geared to ride as ever in their slow, methodical creep across the sky, like the pulleys and cables and cogs and guy-wires for all that transpires below.

Still, for a moment, I thought the windy treetops were full of sparks. My heart's still thumping hard, racing nearly as fast as the fires themselves, perhaps, as they're driven by each day's dry and heated winds; but as I lie there on my back and stare up at the stars, my pulse eventually begins to settle, slowing perhaps in much the same manner as the fires at night, beneath night's calmer, cooler blanket.

The next day brings news that the forest will be closing at the end of the day, that the public lands will not be available for hiking, or berry picking, or fishing, or firewood cutting, or anything else, until further notice — until the rains return, which usually happens on or around Labor Day.

The forest closure is a real hardship on fishing guides (as well as bird-hunting guides, whose season begins on the first of September); and on people who gather firewood for their own use, as well as to sell. The closure is hard on berry pickers too, and the lesson learned is a hard one: in a dry year, don't assume there's going to be a tomorrow for getting your chores done, in August. The stars' march around the sky might be pretty much the same, decade after decade and century after century, but down below, some Augusts might be leisurely and long-reaching, like an old man nearing the end of a full and considered life, and others might be compressed dramatically — as if whittled down to a single remaining day.

Huckleberries are like firewood: it's almost impossible to have too much, too many. They can keep almost forever, preserved as jam, and will last several years in the freezer too. I *think* I've gathered enough already to last the coming year, but I'm not quite sure. Another half-gallon, or even a quart, would sure let me rest easier through the winter.

That morning, I call over to Bill and Sue's to check in on Elizabeth and the girls, and then, because the fire seems to be moving northward — it looks as if its momentum might carry it past our house and up the ridge, half a mile away — I hurry over to one of my favorite berry-picking mountains to gather extra berries as well as to get in one last hike.

And again, even in the accepting, I find that my heart begins racing once more as I climb higher on the mountain and watch all the various other mountains smoking and smoldering, as if, despite whatever my intentions, I am so much a part of this valley, even at a subconscious level, that as the duff burns, as the twigs and limbs and piled-up branches from all the years past burn, so too does something within me — though what that accumulated detritus within me might be, I cannot say, only that I can feel it and that I am agitated by it, and restless, though cleaner-feeling too, and lighter. Perhaps it is only the sense of refreshment and understanding that often comes whenever the scales are lifted from one's eyes and one is able to look at an old thing in a new way.

On the distant road below, I can see a few trucks traveling, pulling horse trailers behind them — some filled with household items,

I suspect, while others have the real item, horses, being transferred to other, safer pastures.

It seems strange to me, to be trying to carry on in my same old routine — berry picking in August — even as so much unraveling and reordering is taking place below, and in the woods beyond.

By late afternoon I've filled two empty water bottles full of berries — I'd like to have a few more, but if the season has to end today, which it appears it must, I think we'll have enough to last us — and in the dimming light, I hike the rest of the way up the mountain, thinking about freedom, considering the presence of it, this day, and its impending absence, in the coming days, as well as looking over the other side of the mountain and the great forests beyond, stretching all the way over and into Idaho and Canada.

Once up top, I sit there on the knife-edge blade of the divide and look over at the two sides of the valley, the burning side and the nonburning side, and even as I am watching one of the unburned stands, a forest that seems to have no fire in it, a single tree silhouetted on the next ridgeline over bursts into sudden light, shrouded by a tall and tapered yellow flame. Nothing else around it seems to be burning, just that one tree among so many others, up on the skyline, and as blue dusk comes sliding in over the day, and then true night, the distant candle of it keeps burning, mysterious and isolate, and I continue watching it until finally the flame grows subdued, is no larger than the glimmering beacon of a faraway lighthouse; and then it extinguishes altogether, with no others springing up around it. And in the darkness, with my pack full of berries, I start down the mountain, with the forest closing itself off to me and the slopes before me shimmering with all their little fires, looking strangely festive.

By the eighteenth of August, the big fire has climbed on up out of the valley floor, up into the safety of the farther, stonier mountains, and my family has moved back in with me, though the devil couch and china hutch and chairs remain stored in Bill and Sue's barn for safety. The mornings are much colder, and it seems that the fires are settling down, are being worn down, with each day's run becoming a little less vigorous, as if they are being sapped by the vitality of each cold morning.

I'm in my cabin, trying to close out the novel I've been working on for years — trying to keep, or find again, its rhythm — and am staring out at the sunlight on the bent grass of the marsh, the sunlight filtering through the smoke, with that blue haze not just pressing against the dusty windowpanes of my cabin but seeping in even through the chinks between the logs, blue haze floating in small clouds between my eyes and the page.

Helicopters are still coming and going, trying to snuff out the fires in the mountains above town, and I can hear the sawyers buzzing away on the steep slopes of the twin humps of Roderick Buttes, cutting fire lines designed to stop that fire's slow, damp downhill creep.

I'm staring at my blank page through the blue smoke, trying to dive deeper into the novel: trying to find a silence, and another reality, within. Trying to hear other music as beautiful as this is, and as the sights are, in the land above.

We grow antsy, impatient, irritable, for all the various reasons: the steady presence of helicopters, the ever-present smoke, the astonishing heat, and the slight feeling of imprisonment — of not being able to wander off into the forest. We consider, with perhaps some degree of paranoia, a changed and warmer earth in which many months of the year are like this one, decades hence, rather than these few weeks.

Summer itself seems to be burning like a chunk of coal, or a fire laid of dry sticks, and autumn seems to be on the other side of a high mountain wall, on the other side of a divide that despite our endurance grows no closer. And at night, as the stars continue their march, it seems as if we are being left behind, even betrayed.

We are awakened one morning at dawn to a sky the color of smoke, or fog — at first I think there is another, newer fire nearby — and to the sound of our dogs barking the way they do when a stranger comes down the driveway.

I go to the window and look out to see who might be here at this hour of the morning and realize that the dogs are looking straight up at the sky, their heads tilted back, and are barking at the rain itself, which they have not seen in so long, and which has disturbed their sleep. And it seems to me that I feel another clicking of the gears, of cogs entwined and intermeshed, rotating the valley, and our lives, back into a pace and pattern with which we are more familiar — as if the stars have paused just long enough for us to catch back up — and I go over to the other window and look down at the garden, which is glistening, and at the water dripping from the eaves of the roof, and there are no helicopters flying this morning, only my hounds barking their fool heads off, and I am filled with the strangest sensation, the strangest image of domesticity: I am like a commuter waiting outside of a subway, about to step on a subway to travel to work — call it the 6:45 — and once again the world is filled with predictability and punctuality, and all of the quick uproar of the past few weeks was as if but a dream, no more real than smoke or fog.

It's a nice, steady, gentle rain that lasts for two days. It bathes our hearts.

I think we enjoy fires, are drawn to and even mesmerized by fires — that our lives, and our spirits, can often possess the characteristics of wildfires — but it feels right too for this settling rain to be falling, as if it came just in time; as if everything is working exactly the way it is supposed to — in step, and on time.

SEPTEMBER

....

THE RAINS COME every Labor Day, as if reading a calendar, as if they have an engagement, an appointment, not with the gear works of effect and recompense but with the more arbitrary, even frivolous ideas of man: as if we have succeeded in our petitions for rains to fall by the first Monday of September, as if we have negotiated with some deity, saying, *All right, bring the fire in late July and August, if you must, but we demand rain by the first or second of September. Or by the third or fourth, at the very latest. Otherwise* . . .

Otherwise, what?

Regardless, the rains always return. Perhaps the heat and smoke seed the clouds sufficiently that once the cooler, longer nights of September return, rain cannot be avoided — just as in a long, hot, dry summer, fire cannot be avoided. Whatever the reason — a negotiated settlement with God, or the unavoidable mechanical clockwork of a tilted, cooling earth, with the days foreshortening in an ever-steeper plunge now — the rain comes.

It extinguishes the fires and finally begins to mute the politicians' brayings, and their patrons, the multinational millionaire or billionaire CEOs, who have been assuring the American public that, despite half a century of clear cutting, if only we would allow them to clear cut it all, there would be no more fires . . .

Peace. Always, I am stalking peace. Some days it gallops away from me, other days I seem to be very close to its presence, and still other days it almost seems to be searching for me, as I am for it; and occasionally peace and I will find ourselves in each other's company. And with the heat and haze and smoke beginning to be vanquished, September is as likely a month to find it as any, and perhaps even more likely.

You can never have enough firewood; you can never have enough berries. In September we'll begin gathering a little bit of firewood (not until the autumn breath of October, however, will we really kick up into production gear), and in the first few days of September, there are still, amazingly, sometimes a few more huckleberries to be found up in the high country, where summer is only just now arriving, as if squeezing in through a barely open window, where it will then visit for but a few days, or a week or two at most, before departing again, sliding back through that window crack and on down the mountain, with autumn coming in over the mountaintop, then, like a blanket drawn.

Another pint, another quart, sometimes another half-gallon. Each day could be the last, the berries shriveling in the sun or withering finally from a fierce frost; and as we sit there in the huckleberry fields (the bushes lower to the ground, up at that wind-scoured elevation), our fingers and faces stained purple, while it would seem that our thoughts would be on the coming months and all the different ways we'll use these berries throughout the year — jams, jellies, syrups, pies, cobblers, cheesecakes, in pancakes, on ice cream, in smoothies — what's really on our minds is nothing, only the somnolent peace of the moment.

We sit there in the high mountain wind and the thin sun, lost in the hunter-gatherer trance of provision, connecting and reconnecting to a deeper, older place with each berry chosen, each berry plucked, so that already, it is as if the mountain is feeding us, and the berries are nurturing us, even before we have eaten the first serving.

The haze of the sun-heated mountains, haze seeming to rise in shimmers from the rocks themselves, will waver before us, and the unending blue waves of mountain ridges will likewise span before us to the horizon, and beyond.

Is there a gene within me that so fills me with love for this wild landscape and makes me so willing to fight for its defense, and to guard so fiercely against the going-away of any of this landscape's other inhabitants, be they grizzly or wolf or sturgeon or rare water lily?

Butterflies drift past us, colorful wings paper thin, sometimes translucent, rallying for their autumn migrations: sucking down the last of the blossoms' nectar, drying yarrow, still pristine white, and blazing blue aster, and the incredible other-planet-seeming magenta of the last of the summer's fireweed.

The ravens have been fairly silent for much of the summer (with the exception of early June, when they feed so lustily on the scraps of lion- and coyote- and wolf- and bear-killed fawns) — but in September they begin to grow more vocal again, often audible as only a single taut-screw croak, like the winding up of the last of summer: a one-syllable, one-note guttural sound of cinching up and battening down.

And whether that one note is saying *summer* (*is over*) or *autumn* (*is here*), I can never tell. Perhaps the perfect one-note sound is made as the raven flies over the perfect cleft or crevice between these two seasons — as visible to the raven's bright eyes as would be a literal niche or crevice in the cliffs in the physical landscape below, formed only a few hundred million years ago.

And sometimes, if we're up in the berry fields early enough in the morning, or late enough in the day, into the cooling blue light of dusk, we'll be lucky enough to hear the utterly wild, hair-raising flute-and-grunt call of a bull elk, bugling to announce to the world, and the season, his presence on the landscape, and his position, as powerful and focused.

I have crept in on the big bulls when they've been announcing themselves in this manner — have peered through the brush and watched, from a distance of only several yards, as the giants thrash their shining antlers against the trunk of a young sapling, scraping the bark from it in joy or fury or something else before lifting their head (their eyes wide, bulging with life) and bugling again, a sound that resonates in my own chest, so close, and causes tremors of vibrations similar to those experienced when you stand too close to the railroad tracks and a locomotive passes by, roaring its wail-whistle and shaking the ground, causing a tingling in your jaw and your arms and legs, even all the way into your hands and feet.

Sometimes, from the tops of mountains, the girls like to roll big rocks down the mountainside — not down toward any trail or road but down some steep slope, to see how far the rock will go before reaching its angle of repose. This is totally opposite of how I like to be in the world, and particularly in the woods, and yet occasionally I let them roll the thunder-rocks, not so much for the joy and power the act gives them (and I have to say, the sight of a rock cartwheeling down the slope, sometimes bolting twenty feet into the air, is hypnotic, awe provoking) but rather so that they will at least have a fighting chance of not becoming exactly like me. Not that that's good, bad, or indifferent, but rather, what matters to me is that they at least have a chance, now and again, of taking a different path.

I let them roll these rocks, and then we move on. "This is the bears' home," I say, unable to resist. "We have to remember they live here too, and they probably don't like too much noise."

Still, I tried to let them choose their own way. For about thirty seconds. How unchanging, it seems, are any paths, and instead as foreordained as the runoff of snowmelt down the grooves carved in mountaintops from the claws of the glaciers that scratched their way down these same mountains ten thousand years ago.

Hiking down, we spy a pale, curved stick, a branch, that is the exact size and shape of a deer's rib — so much so that we have to pick it up and examine it more closely to be sure that it is not — and this reminds us, again, of how nearly identical are the shapes of deer and elk antlers, and the branches of the trees and bushes behind which they take shelter, so that without a doubt, as in Genesis, the one thing — the forests, arriving on, say, the third day — has shaped the next thing, the beasts and fowl, arriving on, say, the fourth.

We lie on our backs for a while and watch the astounding clouds, with their animal shapes. Indeed, just this moment, one of the larger ones, drifting up from the south, looks almost precisely like an enormous bull elk — so much so that even the cloud's shadow, projected on the mountain across from us, looks like that same elk.

It's gliding like a schooner, nearly galloping, as graceful in its traverse of that mile or two of distance traveled as would be a real elk, and it calms and soothes us, lying there watching it: not as if it is being presented to us for any message or instruction, but merely beauty, only beauty, and the tight order of a day among the living.

The girls want to roll one more rock down a slope of bear grass far below. It's the seventh year of the bear grass's cycle — a year of outrageous blossoms — and so I let them, promising, *Only one.*

It's the best roll ever. The small, round boulder gallops straight down the hill, as if fleeing us, then inexplicably veers, as if consciously choosing another path, and then veers back again, choosing the same old route. It hurtles through the field of late-season, high-elevation bear grass, snapping the drying stalks and sending up puffs and plumes of pollen, which rise and drift slowly downslope — long after the boulder has disappeared into the woods — with the rising yellow pollen tracing an arc that briefly mimics the twisting shape of a deer's rib.

And yet, surely such formality, such stricture and allegiance to oneness does not exist everywhere, and at all times. There is a life, a pulse, and respiration — a fuel, or a force — governing the reaching toward these shapes, formulas, patterns. The bear grass, for instance, with its wild seven-year blooms, the giant sweet-scented pompom stalks rising so high above the other flowering plants: surely it is in these seven-year runs that it attempts to expand its range, not merely resting and conserving the nutrients in the thin soil where it is found, but timing its next run in order to achieve maximum colonization.

In this regard — the six years of inhalation, and the one bright year of powerful exhalation — the bear grass might be seen to possess a cunning, if limited, singularity of purpose. And yet to back away and look at the entire mountain from a distance (from the other mountain across the way, perhaps), you would note that there are so many other puzzle pieces, each with its own path and pattern of inhale and exhale, that the mind spins and you understand that it is all always moving, even if just beneath the surface — moving with the alacrity of an elk galloping laterally across a mountain, or even a boulder cartwheeling directly down the mountain.

We rise and continue down the mountain ourselves. At one point, still high on the mountain, we startle a pair of large spotted frogs, which spring away from us in spirited, terrified leaps, heading directly upslope. They're a long away from any water — the nearest seasonal pond is still a good quarter-mile away, and several hundred feet higher on the mountain, up near the crest — and it occurs to me that these frogs know that rain is imminent, and that despite the summer heat, they are migrating, expanding their own range, traveling beneath the shade of the silvery hummocks of bear grass; and that they are gambling their lives, their territorial explorations, on the belief or perhaps knowledge — the faith — that it will rain soon, before they dry out, so far from home.

The seasonal ponds will not hold water again until later in the month — it will take days of September's or even October's rains to fill them back up — but perhaps if these frogs find these ponds in time (perhaps it is where they were born; perhaps they are returning to them, after a summer of exploration, and egg-laying, downslope), they can somehow burrow down between the wide fissures of the mud cracks, squeezing down through those frog's-width crevices between the polygon tiles of the parched mudflat, and can be lubricated and nourished by the brief rain they seem convinced is coming.

We continue on our own way, astounded by what we have seen — spotted frogs, a mile or more from the nearest permanent water — a veritable herd of migrating frogs, perhaps, literally leap-frogging their way across the mountain, up the mountain, even as we are hurrying down it, and by the time we reach our truck, jagged bolts of lightning are flickering to the south, hurled from clouds no longer the shape of elk but immense purple mushrooms, and the first drops of rain are beginning to ding and speckle our dusty truck.

August's fires linger, even after their death. For the most part, they're out like a light, but a few still smoke and smolder, even if no flames can be seen. There's still a faint, sweet odor of smoke in the air, the sharper scent of burned twigs and needles and forest duff and downed logs different somehow from the more mellow, pervasive scent of morning fires in people's wood stoves; but where this other, wilder scent might be coming from would be hard to say, because everywhere I go on my walks, the coals are extinguished, and in many places the ash is sodden. Sometimes the last of the fires will go underground, taking bitter refuge in the roots of trees, smoldering among those roots or even crawling up into one of the drummy hollows that the fire itself might have carved and hiding there amid the punk and charcoal, holding out and hanging on, not unlike the last surviving grizzly bears in this region: stubborn survivors, waiting for a break that may be a long time in coming.

Mostly, though, by September — after those great rains of Labor Day — the fires exist now only in our memories. And as they remain a shadow or a wave, we still dream of them, in dreams that are hauntingly specific. So deeply lodged is the tension and engagement of the previous month in me that, even though I'm moving around free in the beautiful new clarity of September, in my dreams I am still back in the time of fire and am helping other people fight their fires: counseling angles of attack and plans of defense, watering hot spots, setting backfires, evaluating wind direction and possible ignition fuels, and scratching fire lines in the dirt. I awake from such dreams the next morning exhausted, as if I have physically been doing those things; and the scent of the old fire, particularly in the mornings, is dense and everywhere.

Still, nothing can be held on to beyond its time. September must flow out of August, pushing eagerly on with its own life, through the eddies of time and heat and dreams, and one cool morning not long after Labor Day, two black bears come striding through the center of the marsh in single file, noses pointed into the cool north breeze, just out wandering in the middle of the day, and like the actors in a school play who usher in a new scene, they might as well have been pulling behind them a banner that said AUTUMN.

I do not mean to complain about the imbalance or loneliness that resides somewhat in all of us, I think — sometimes deep-rooted or all-aflame, though other times merely hidden, like dull coals hunkered warm in the trunk, the cavity, of a hollow tree — but I mean instead to accept and marvel at it: this slight (though other times significant) clumsiness that almost always sets us some distance apart from the rest of nature, and the calling of the seasons.

There is a different calendar, internal and pulsing, alive, like the creature of time, that is slightly tilted from the mechanical overlay of our own precise but lifeless calendars. This other calendar is not metered by the precision of solstice and equinox, but is fluid, maybe even cunning or stealthy, and our separation from that hidden river, whether below us or farther above, may be to some degree the measure of that strange loneliness, the scent of which we all catch, from time to time, unbidden and inexplicable.

Certainly, the changes in our own self-imposed or self-described seasons crest well before true solstice or equinox. The panic seems usually to crest in us a couple of weeks earlier than in the rest of nature. Impulsively, we rush, we roar. Hence summer arrives in our hearts on June seventh, say, rather than the twenty-first; and autumn, with that bittersweet mingling of pleasure and confusion — a feeling very much like, come to think of it, first love — comes in the first week of September rather than matching the balanced grace of equal dark, equal light, on the true equinox in the third week.

What is the reason for this cant, this tilt, and will we ever earn our way into the larger flow? Did we once exist in it, and fall from it? Or is it — this distance, this wobble or separation — the fuel that inspirits us, that gives us life and moves us across the landscape of the centuries; this distance, or slight loneliness, at first glance seemingly regrettable, all the difference, just as the antlers of a deer or elk are different from the branches in the forest through which that deer or elk moves?

The larch are starting to glow at their tips — the needles on the uppermost branches turn yellow first, with the wave of gold progressing steadily downward through each tree, each forest, then, as autumn progresses, an amazing thing to witness in any one tree, the color *gold* washing through the entire tree, gilding it, much less to witness that slow, beautiful fire happening to an entire mountainside.

The straight and simple truth of it is that September becomes so beautiful so quickly that you can scarcely bear it. The berries are finally all shriveled up by the frosts in the high country, the leaves of those low bushes burnt as red as garnets and the leaves of aspens are turning yellow, and the rain-washed sky is bluer, and the soil, moist again, is softer when you walk on it.

The bears are eating the kinnikkinnick berries — their scat is everywhere, through the forest — and the sophisticated, complex matrix of odors specific to the enormously complicated, enormously diverse vegetative mix in this valley is returning, strengthened by the new moisture and cooler temperatures.

The tall dead-yellow grass of summer still obscures the gray stone walls — the umber grass one of the last visual clues of a summer gone by so quickly — and then one day there is frost not just up in the mountains but in the marsh, each saw blade of grass glistening with its crust of ice — the morning-world sheeted with silver and gold — and the elk are bugling even more loudly, high in the last remote untouched backcountry. And even though you always knew it was coming, that first hard frost on the valley floor, it still hits with the same surprise as when at the beach, as you try to walk along the strand line, an onrushing wave nonetheless comes skating in and surges past you, suddenly up to your ankles.

And then another, and another. And more elk bugling, as if they are not simply announcing it but creating it with each breath, each grunted exhalation.

The larch look exactly like candles or matches just struck: as if this fire-loving species is so determined to burn — and in that burning, to have its world made newer, and grander — that it will manufacture its own flame, in September; as if August was not enough. It's the grizzly bears — the last tiny population of them — that many people think of when they consider the Yaak, and they are an amazing and powerful and unique story. But I think that it is the paths and patterns of the larch that might be most fitted to this land of fire and ice, of intense wakefulness and then deep sleep. And in September, the forest, and the burning larch, are nothing if not awake.

The antlers of the deer are free of their summer velvet now, are unsheathed and fully hardened and polished, ready for fighting. The deer bound through the woods, their antlers the color and texture of rich mahogany wood, glinting and flashing in the patches of sunlight, reminding you they are not ornaments but weapons.

The ravens have been still in summer's heat, but grow more active. They've never been away, but now you see and hear them more often. *Awake.*

Driving to school some early frosty mornings, we'll see them sitting on the side of the road, jet black in a slant of crisp September sun, steam rising from their bodies, as if they are but one step away, one wingbeat from vaporizing into pure spirit. But they are not pure spirit; they are as alive and physical as anything on this earth, and as beautiful, and they edge farther to the side of the road, still steaming, as if newly born, and watch us pass, as if waving or ushering us on through the woods — as if we've passed some check-point.

On the fourteenth of September, the girls capture the most amazing spiny green caterpillar, a huge thing with garish yellow eyes. We watch it crawl around, as fat as a sausage and as green as a lime, for fifteen minutes before doing the childhood thing of putting it in an empty mayonnaise jar for closer examination.

We take it to school the next day — "It's so cute," Lowry says — but when we enter the room with it before school, this caged, horned dragon, the little boys scream and scatter from the computer.

That afternoon, we release the caterpillar into the alder grove at the edge of the marsh. I know that we stand at the verge of creating life in a test tube — that indeed, we might already have passed that threshold — but before we get too arrogant or boastful or even confident, tell me who, please, could have dreamed such a thing as this caterpillar?

Every September, when the marsh is still fully dry from the heat and drought of summer, and before it begins to rehydrate under autumn's rains, the girls and I go out into it some afternoons to play a game we call Tiger in the Grass. The marsh grass is over their heads — a maze of fecund, vegetative uproar — and we play hide-and-seek in the labyrinths we've created below, forming warrens and burrows with our crawling around beneath that high, dense canopy of grass.

The rich, cool, sweet scents of the marsh down at the roots' level are like those of a candy store, of ginger and chamomile, and while the September light glints off the bent tops of the grass, reflecting as if off a curved shield, the world-below is not bronze like above, but instead, deep, cool, dense green.

We call to one another, delighting in our hidden-ness, our invisibility, and track the new-made paths of each other, crawling down those hollow tunnels. Shafts of light occasionally filter through the tall grasses with pencil beams of light. One person is the tiger and the others hide, and try to run to home base — popping up somewhere in the marsh, up from the green, cool, subaqueous light into the bright, shimmering bronze haze, often emerging fifty yards or farther from where we thought we were, or from where the tiger thought we were; wonderfully lost, wonderfully disoriented, in even so short a time as the span of one game.

Running for home, then, shrieking and laughing. The tiger bounding after them, after us. The grass shaking, rattling. A thousand sweet marsh scents stirring in our passage. The girls' laughter reminding me, somehow, of that shimmering light rising, reflected from the tops of the grass.

The world is full: as one thing is taken away, another fills its place. Surely this is but a myth that is convenient for us to believe, and the closer you look at any cycle, pattern, or process, the more you see that it might be more than a myth; that it is also an observable article of science.

The earth tips and turns farther in its angle from the sun and the days grow shorter, but the quality of the available light becomes finer, so that even though the weight and contact of things is shifting, a kind of balance is being maintained. It is neither a physical nor an emotional balance, but some other kind.

How few words we have, really, in our language, and at our ultimate disposal. I suppose the best that can be said is that it is a kind of spiritual balance, and it is somewhat a source of comfort to consider that it must exist in the hearts and center of all things — in ocean tempests and typhoons, in the eye of the hurricane, in the wobble of an elk calf, in the leaf chewings of any one species of caterpillar — everywhere, always balanced, or seeking balance, even when our own eyes or minds cannot discern it: even when we cannot feel it in ourselves.

It has to be there. If it is everywhere else, how can it not also be in us?

The fading light just keeps getting richer and richer as it shortens. Even the candle glow of aspen and larch seems to conspire to gently fill the heart — even a heart previously believed to be full — and the blood's strange autumn chemicals themselves seem to be filling with light as the days grow shorter and we are

weaned — gradually at first, but then quickly — from that summer
bounty of light, that summer bounty of yellow and gold.

The twenty-ninth of September, and I feel further buoyed, life
swept, by this autumn light, so rich now as to seem almost tangible,
like the rattle of parchment paper or the sound and sight of a crisp
pear being bitten into.

The girls and I spy another black bear on our way home from
school — a big fat one sitting out in a meadow, beneath a lone hawthorn tree. He's sitting there like a man at the beach, is pulling the
branches down with both front paws and eating the ripe hawthorn
berries, and just watching the world go by. The field he's in is the
color of bright yellow straw; his rippling coat is deep black, almost
iridescent. His white teeth flash as he chews the berries, his com-
posure is utterly relaxed, and surely the September sun is filling his
blood as well as mine, and he is soaking it in.

On some of the frostier mornings, I've had to start making a small
fire in my wood stove again to keep warm enough to work. It took
me a long time to get comfortable calling it work. The issue is not
whether you enjoy it or not. The issue is, does it make the blood
leave your head, do your cells feel afterward as if you've physically
traveled to the places encountered in your mind, are you pleased
with but weary from those travels, those creations?

It fulfills a need in you, this creation — a fit you have bartered
with the world — but wouldn't you rather be out on a mountaintop more often, or canoeing an autumn river? Aren't you making
a trade, a morning or an afternoon at the desk instead of on the
mountain? Is one more real than the other?

September raises these questions more intensely — awakens
them more sharply, if they have been slumbering below, perhaps
more than any other month.

The woodshed in my cabin is filled with split wood for the coming winter, but I don't want to dip into that stockpile yet. Instead, I
keep a loose pile of unsplit wood by my cabin door, and it becomes
for me part of the process, the transition from the physical world
into the dreaming world, to split each morning's supply there by my

cabin door before going inside to light that small warming fire by which I will work until the day itself grows warmer.

An adult lifetime of splitting wood, and yet it never fails to amaze me — the beauty, the astonishing brightness of a newly split piece of dry lodgepole, the shock of white flesh, the fiber opening before the maul's blade, like the bright and perfectly paired pages of a book opened in that brilliant morning sun. The vertical lines on the growth rings land open in cross-section, reading like the lines of text.

One of the loveliest things about sitting perched at the edge of the marsh, day in and day out, across the span of each year, is how once you're deeply enough immersed in the year, you find yourself more often than not totally forgetting not only what day of the week it is but even the months — the names of them — and instead see the days, the patterns of them, in mosaics of color and temperature, as thick-bodied and animate as a living creature. Their passage seems a flow rather than any named or bounded thing. Or if boundaries exist, it is as if only for the purpose of showing, pointing, the way to freedom; and with the scents and colors of the passing months, and the seasons, rolling along like a path or a map and with no real need for the names of months or any other things. A clacking grasshopper does not have to be August; a yellow leaf does not have to be September, and neither does the first hard frost.

So sharply felt are the senses at this time of year for me however that the names of the things fall away and in my heightened and marveling awareness, it seems I can forget once again the names of the things and instead live only more fully in the presence and taste and odor of the things themselves: as pungent as they surely once were to me before they had names, and as they will still be after the names are forgotten. At least as much as any others, September is the month of touch and scent and taste and sight and sound, with language and other filters somehow being partially removed, in this new and foreshortening light. The world is — dare I say this? — more real, it seems.

As September's intense senses travel more deeply into you — being transmitted in their new richness and sharpness faster, and more completely, I think, than the time it takes to stop and name them — it seems that time, conversely, and perhaps paradoxically, slows.

I know intuitively as well as intellectually that the physical world is every bit as real in every month — that there is just as much wonder to be prized out of the world in any one month as another. Perhaps then it is simply me who feels more real, in September — less bounded by the tradition and trajectory and momentum of old paths and habits.

The frost hangs longer now, clinging to the coarse marsh grass and sedges with glimmering blades of ice and hoarfrost until noon. By this time of day the children will have already said their pledge of allegiance, will already have completed a couple of lessons, will already have laughed, and sung, and might at this very moment be out on the playground, their school day half done, while this long, slow, lazy light seems to hang forever.

I continue staring out the window, adjusting yet again to the world's changing gear works. I watch as those blades of frost finally release, steaming slightly, as the cold sun slowly warms them, and in that gentle sliding down, the tumbling of those intricate frost plates into the deep grass below, the dry grass stirs slightly, briefly — all else is still, the day is perfectly poised — as if unseen animals are moving around in it, just beneath the surface.

Still later in the day, the grass is entirely dry again, ready for play — and I'm ready for the girls to be home from school.

Did I get much work done today — any labor of world-changing substance, any acts of merit or consequence on the global stage? No. Elizabeth and I baked a huckleberry pie, which rests, cooling by the open screen window, completely uncut, awaiting the girls' return.

If you can't reexamine and reprioritize your life in September, then I feel pity that you may not be able to do so at all. If you cannot remember what it is about the world you love most, and which matters most to you in this slowing-down time, as the days return to a more equitable balance of darkness and light, then when, if I dare ask, do you think you can?

In September, writing is not the real work. In September, taking the girls to school, then staring out the window and thinking about them, and waiting for them to get home, is the real work.

Any year now, they will be hurtling past you, with their dreams and desires and ambitions. If you are smart, or lucky, you will slow down your own and turn away — will turn and go back to meet them in their territory, while it is still so slow and leisurely and timeless, so poised between then and now.

OCTOBER

....

CATCH ME ON ANY ONE fine certain day, any month of the year, when things are going well and I am out in the natural world, and I'm likely to say that *this* day, *this* week, is the best of the year, superior to all others. Eventually, then, after enough of those kinds of pronouncements, such statements would lose all currency; but I have to say, the case can be made, yet again, for the first week of October being far and away the finest. Sure, October is suddenly cold as hell, or seems that way, with lows in the twenties each morning, a sheet of frost spangling the bent and submitting tops of the marsh grass — diamonds everywhere, once the lazy sun finally struggles above the trees — and with your skin, and your mindset, not yet thickened to winter's demands. And the days are so unbelievably short now, with the downhill slide of the equinox still a surprise, still a shock.

In that first week of October, you understand that it's not any kind of laziness with which the world is slowing, but a heroic fatigue; and that from that fatigue, even as all manner of vegetative matter are dying, crumbling and disintegrating, there is an elegant new thing blossoming, the crafting of a plan and pattern every bit as sophisticated and complex as spring-and-summer's roar of clamant growth.

It is an invisible blossom, this new plan, and as such, it rises before you like a ghost, so that it takes a different sort of seeing to know it. The increasingly leafless frames of the deciduous trees and shrubs are not that flower's absence but its new presence.

The newer silence of birdsong (save for the going-away clamor of ducks and geese, and the shouting of the ravens) is likewise simply the inverse of the complicated thing rather than its utter absence.

If only we could learn this same lesson of brief senescence and strategic withdrawal when weary; to push hard and strong, living fully for as long as possible, but then to back off in graceful taper, and to descend, almost seamlessly, into the lower levels, when it's time to rest.

It's simply a different kind of living, a different pace. The sleeping dream-world beneath the snow can be every bit as rich and colorful as the bright world of stone and antler and feather above; and for a little while, anyway, if parsed out sparingly enough, and wisely, the memory of the bones and antlers and stones and feathers can be as real as the bones and antlers and stones and feathers themselves.

And if the exodus, the descent to sleep and rest is graceful enough, even the disintegration and disorder will not matter, for in these elegant dreams and memories, desire will still be maintained and nurtured: a desire sufficient, when the time becomes right again, to reassemble those loosened pieces and raise them all back up again, in resurrection and ascent.

The bears and larch, it seems to me, help orchestrate this descent to rest. Even their coloring — the golden bears, and the blaze gold needles of the larch — seems designed to draw our attention to them as they remain active on a landscape where all else is going away. (And then, in only a few more weeks — if that long — they too will leave, descending. But they are the last to go.)

Like conductors, they are more active than ever in early October — the berry-fat bears, their winter coats thickening in the cold weather, able to prowl the hills even in broad daylight now, so pleasant are the temperatures; and the needles of the larch turning their strange gold color, as if determined to experience, one way or another, the fires they evaded in August — the very fires that birthed and now sustain them.

And in their beauty, entire uncut mountainsides of beauty, the eye is drawn toward them — and in that engagement, the mind begins to dream.

You have to adjust. It's not September anymore, or August, or, certainly, July. You've got to begin considering a slowing down: and again, the beauty of the season tries to help us with this attempt. All the clues are there, illuminated and ablaze in their once-a-year rotting beauty.

Still, being human, we cannot help but be tempted by the flesh.

We dream of dreaming — of hunkering down in the shortening days in front of the wood stove and just watching, witnessing, this graceful descent, this softening of October light and fading away — but there is a part of us too that wants to be conductors, a part that loves the surface, and loves being noticed; and so we struggle and clamor between the two choices.

The fading light inspires in us one last surge of energy, one last boost of output. Like the great bears prowling the hills in broad daylight, or the larch needles hurrying through the sky like tiny arrows loosened from thousands of quivers, we hurry on, inspired by our last chance to touch the world before it is covered with snow.

The berries are long gone, and have been made into jam or stored in freezers, but the grouse are still plentiful, if not wilder, by this point of the hunting season, and once or twice a week the dogs and I are fortunate enough to hunt them.

The grouse too are things of beauty, even after I've shot them and brought them home, where they hang on the side porch in that gold light, drawn and aging toward full flavor and tenderness. And after they've hung there in the steady chill for a few days, it is an evening ritual for the girls and I to sit on the front porch, just before dark, and pluck the grouse. (I pay the girls seventy-five cents a bird — the equivalent of about three dollars an hour — and as such, it seems to me sometimes that they've taken a perhaps overly keen interest in the success of my hunts, inquiring about them with full attention when I came in from the field some evenings.)

(They are also paid for being able to memorize and recite lengthy poems by Mary Oliver — "The Summer Day," for example, fetches a whopping five dollars.)

Beauty thrice, or four times or more, then; the dog pointing the bird in the autumn colors, and the bird flushing, and me sometimes making the shot, and the dog retrieving the bird; the bird hanging on the porch in that soft cold light for days afterward, hung high as if in a position of respect and celebration; and the beauty of a job done well, then, in the plucking. And beauty a fourth time, in the preparation and dining, whether the grouse is brushed with flour and cooked in the iron skillet, in melted butter, or brushed with kosher salt and coarse pepper and stuffed with jalapeños, garlic, and onion, basted with balsamic vinegar, and cooked low on the grill over mesquite coals, or in any of a number of other recipes, involving wild blackberry or huckleberry reductions, or wild cherry and chipotle pepper barbecue sauce, or apples and brown sugar . . .

We know we should be shutting down, in the autumn, slowing ourselves down in preparation for the time of the dream-world; but the world is too beautiful, our appetites are drawn ever upward and outward, and heedless of any depletion of reserves within, heedless of any basic need to conserve our energies, our passions. "I may not survive my affections," Terry Tempest Williams has written.

So we sit there, early in the evenings, listening to the geese and feeling the crisp bite of cold air, silent and focused on our tasks, our hands working like weavers in reverse — weavers unbraiding the lovely feathers. (We save the barred tail feathers of the grouse as keepsakes; they line our bookshelves and mirrors, our cabinets and dressers, and bookmark the favorite passages of favorite books; they continue to frame our lives long after we've cooked and eaten the birds and made stock of the carcasses.)

By all rights, this time of year should be a stepping down, but we keep reaching out, seeing more and wanting more. Perhaps we were made for nothing but the surface, like the delicate water striders one sees skating across the glassine surfaces of small ponds and lakes in the glinting heat of summer.

Firewood, too: we enjoy laying in a good supply of it, going after it with a zeal that makes it seem almost as if the wood is fuel for our very bodies rather than our stoves. And again, at a time of year when it might seem the senses should be reining in and turning back for home, heading back to the stables for the long sleep, we instead find ourselves feeling the world even more sharply than ever: as if, after these first nine months of practice, we are now finally, in the tenth month, just starting to work ourselves into shape, with regard to being able to experience the world more deeply.

Maybe it's the beauty of the October light, or the cold nights and cold days, or the kaleidoscope of colors — red-osier dogwood, crimson bunchberry, blood-frosted vaccinium, blue sky, gold larch and aspen and cottonwood. For some reason, the wood is more beautiful to us in October: not just the forest itself, but the forest that gives itself to us, the forest that we take. The gleam of new-cut dead lodgepole, as bright yellow as butter, with the vertical fracture of it dry-checking already visible, indicating to us the precise place where the maul should strike to split it into halves, and then again to quarters, and even eighths — the round length of firewood diminishing, it seems, in rhythm with the startling reduction of days, so that here, perhaps, in the physical labor, if not in the spirit and the mind, you have begun to find the rhythm of the season.

Even the scent of the toothy, heavy chain saw, and of the gas smoke on your clothes, smells good, in October — it smells like October, in this valley, as does the sawdust — and from a distance, even the sound of other sawyers' chain saws, burbling on and off at all times of the shortening days, sounds good, a faint kind of October music, with a cadence somehow different from the steady gnawing of clearcuts in progress.

It might take a few hours for a firewood-getter to work a single downed log — limbing it, cutting it into lengths, splitting it, and then stacking it into the back of his or her truck. (In that same time, a crew of sawyers, working often against their will or with no other choices for an out-of-state company that, by virtue of weaker workmen's compensatory requirements, has successfully bid on a national forest timber sale at a fraction of the resource's true cost or value, might have leveled to ruin ten acres or more of mature green forest instead of a single dead tree, and with the day still young.)

On a trip to town, then, late in the day, or a trip into the woods with the dogs to go look for grouse, you'll see your neighbors, at any hour of the afternoon, heading back into the woods with their trucks filled with wood, old groaning schooners packed tight with that gleaming bounty, hard earned, and with the battered old chain saw stuck vertically, like a sword, into the top of that mound of firewood.

(Another dusk ritual: You unload that wood, piece by piece — the dry tinkle and clatter of it as you toss it from the back of your truck into an errant pile, the mountain in the back of your truck slowly diminishing — and then, with a weary back, you climb down and begin to stack it again, neatly, in the woodpile, order reassembling of disorder, and you finish right at dark, or sometimes even after dark, in these diminishing days, and then head on in to the yellow square light of the house, for supper — grouse, perhaps — and a shower. And again there is the double-rich, doubly alive engagement with the world — the pleasure of crafting something fitted, even if so simple a fit as that of firewood in a shed, and the human imperative of the hunter-gatherer, now gratified.)

Almost everything else in the forest is descending, or winding down into dormancy, or leaving, heading south — though it occurs to me now that perhaps on those night journeys south, the travelers feel as rich and alive, in their leaving or their descending, as we do still above, and still pushing on, deeper and more richly into the senses.

Autumn is when the native people here, the Kootenai, used to travel east, across the Continental Divide, for a quick buffalo hunt (while hoping to avoid the savage Blackfeet, who guarded the Front Range country, and those distant grasslands, and the buffalo) — and in October, we'll sometimes make a quick run east with the dogs to hunt the grasslands' native sharp-tailed grouse, so different from our own forest grouse (blue, ruffed, spruce, or Franklin's), and to hunt the grasslands' ring-necked pheasants and Hungarian partridges too: introduced species that weren't even present a hundred and thirty years ago, when the last of the buffalo were being killed off.

We'll hunt antelope also, and in fortunate years might return with all kinds of wonderful and exotic meat, and memories of wide-open golden grasslands, and horizon-to-horizon blue skies, and ceaseless dry wind, and all but abandoned trailer courts, cottages where we can stay, dogs included, for less than thirty dollars, with clean beds and hot running water. It's a landscape of tangled thickets of chokecherry and wild roses, of rattlesnakes and porcupines, and with grasshoppers clattering in front of us with every step we take, and the wide Missouri hauling its muddy load through an empty landscape, writing sentences in the very geology of the earth.

It's lovely country, but lonely, and after even only a couple of days we find ourselves homesick for the dense green intimacy of our forested valley, lonely for the music of our creeks and waterfalls, and the richness of the specific scents of our forest, and the sight of our own plants and birds and mammals; and so we head back home, across the wide state that belongs to us, and to which we belong, even though it's easy to forget such things, living holed up like recluses in the dark, shady, inaccessible corner. We forget that there is another world beyond ours — a world of Conoco one-stop stations and big chain stores and interstates and commerce, a world beyond our world, which is itself but one step beyond the dream-world.

Sometimes it feels as if, in going east, we have gotten too far from that dream-world — have removed ourselves one step too many from a thing that breathes into us the vital elements of our existence: not just food and air and water, but the very spirit that animates us.

As if, out here on the grasslands, we become someone else — the people we might have become, perhaps, had we not found our lush green valley — and it is a frightening, lonely feeling, and soon enough, we hurry home.

Our own deer and elk are going to be calling to us, before too long. You can lay in all the berries you want, can catch the little trout from high mountain lakes, can gather sacks and sacks of mushrooms from the previous year's wildfires, can harvest your potatoes, can make jams and jellies: but none of it compares with the thrill of going out into your forest — your forest, in the woods where you live — hiking for five or ten miles, or farther, and finding the animal you want to take, that year. The staggering bounty of hunting fairly, passionately, intensely, and then — suddenly, after many days of pursuit — finding yourself with several hundred pounds of meat to pack out and butcher and wrap . . . It's an entirely different process from the day-to-day procurement most folks have become accustomed to, an entirely different rhythm — a tour de force of boom and bust — and when it happens, we are deeply grateful: aware, I think, that such mercy is tolerating, even catering to, our grasping and reaching-out, even in a time when we perhaps should be slowing down, hunkering down.

More, more, more, beats the metronome within our own hearts, set somehow to a slightly different meter, it seems to me, from much of the rest of the world.

It is not time yet to go into the forest looking for deer and elk — looking for meat, for so much meat. It is not yet time to follow their tracks, and their scent, wherever they will lead you. But soon: a couple or three more weeks. This is the last quiet, mellow, fruitlike time of hanging out at home, battening down hatches, before the dream-time of the hunt arrives, and, usually a short time after that, when the first snow arrives.

So in many ways, it's the sweetest time of year, as can often be the case with any going-away thing. We know the thing — the "real" world, in this instance — will be coming back, though not for a long time. And despite our hungers and desires, the great wheel of the world *does* begin to work its way upon us, even if our own cant is slightly off-balance by a few degrees, and a few weeks.

Belatedly, and almost against our wishes or impulses, we do finally find ourselves beginning to move more slowly: lingering, on those bird-plucking evenings on the porch, to smell the scent of wood smoke in the air, as people begin once more to build fires in their wood stoves in the mornings and evenings.

And in the daytime, the sunlight seems to become both denser and softer, so that sometimes it is almost as if we are becoming trapped, even entombed in it, as if preserved in amber, preserved in beauty.

We move slowly around in the yard, picking up loose things — a child's toy, a hoe, a stray piece of firewood, an empty dog bowl — in the last days before the snow comes.

It could come as early as mid-October, or as late as mid-November. But it will be coming, and in October, there is only the thinnest, last little window of possibility, and the freedom of the old world, before the cleansing new white world returns, with that world's own new set of dreams and possibilities.

The larch and aspen and cottonwood hang golden for as long as they can, as do the drying brown leaves of the alder, and the blood red leaves of the red-osier dogwood. They're able to hold steady, even in their own dying, though as the winds of autumn increase, more and more of them swirl through the woods, in patterns like smoke, gold whirling spirals and dervishes that for a moment or two seem to take on the shape of a man, or a deer, before the leaves settle down randomly into the autumn-dead grass, like gold coins spilled from someone's pocket.

When will the gold leaves run out? They all seem to be on their branches still — the trees are still ablaze with color — and yet the ground is decorated with the gold coins of the aspen, and the elegant tapered yellow leaves of the cottonwoods.

The alder are shedding their noisy leaves too. Not as tall as the other trees, usually only as tall as a man or a woman or at the most, twice as tall, the summer screen they once provided — the bowers and corridors and hallways through the woods — are becoming bare and open, allowing a deeper look into the darkening forest. An invitation.

The larch hold their needles longer, holding them all the way to the bitter end of autumn. The broad leaves of the other deciduous trees flap and twist and rattle in the wind and are wrested free, day after day, but the larch needles hang in there, until their cool gold wave is all the color — besides the blue-green of the spruce, fir, pine, and cedar — that is left.

The larch have been gold now for so long that you have almost become accustomed to the beauty, have almost come to believe it is your unending due. A few trickle off, steadily, throughout the fall, but for the most part they hold on, these strange, reluctant dinosaurs, with one foot in the prehistoric past of the ancient conifers and another tentative foot in the relatively modern, sunnier, and somewhat daring camp of the deciduous trees.

When they do let go — usually in late October — it is one of the great sights of this landscape.

It will have been increasingly windy, all through October, but finally the wind is too much — or rather, just enough. Sometimes at night you will hear it when it comes roaring through, and the sound and excitement of it will lift you from your bed, just as the needles are being lifted from their branches.

The big wind often brings rain just behind it as well, which helps peel the needles from the trees; but some years the wind is dry, though no matter: still the air is filled, suddenly and finally, with what must be literally tons of flying gold needles, gold needles like darts or tiny arrows; and if you go out on the porch at night, you will be able to feel the needles striking you but will not be able to see them in the darkness. They will land in your hair, though, will coat your arms and feet, and in the morning, when you rise and look outside, the world has been transformed, sculpted in gold, with every sleeping, inanimate shape pasted with gold needles, and all roads and trails paved with gold.

How can any of it be accident — must not all of it be some design? The larch needles, expelled from the larch trees, cast themselves down onto the forest floor, returning nutrients to the soil, but perhaps even more important, in areas that might have burned earlier in the summer or fall, they provide a woven net that helps to stabilize the tender burned soil, minimizing the loss and damage from erosion. The larch needles drape themselves perfectly, democratically, over every aspect of the topography below, and in the manner with which spider webs were once placed over wounds to aid in coagulation, they stabilize the blacked soil, and just in time, as the rains continue. It's the last window of opportunity to lay down such a stabilizing blanket before the snow arrives: snow which, later the next spring, in melt-off, might otherwise carve destructive tunnels and gullies, were it not for the protective mat of gold.

(Some years it is not perfect, or appears to be imperfect, and slightly off-balance, ill timed by a day, or a week. The snow might arrive early one year, so that the larch needles are cast down on top of the snow — a doubly breathtaking sight — though it is still perfect, for those early snows often melt in the subsequent days, are absorbed into the soil, lowering the net, the weave, of needles gently, inch by inch, onto that burned soil.)

It's hard to imagine a species more fitted to and desirous of its place. Those same wildfires that have selected the larch — burning up the weedy competitors but not the larch, with its thicker, fire-resistant bark — also aid the propagation of the larch. Studies at the state experimental forest in Coram, Montana, have shown that larch seedlings regenerating in a newly burned area outcompete other species for the uptake of nutrients in a burned landscape by a factor of *three,* so that it is as if the metaphor of larch as a vibrant, leaping, living flame has become transformed to the real. Surely this is one of the definitions of magic.

The larch trees, with their autumn gold needles blazing, do not just look like candles or flames, birthed long ago of fire, but they have *become* the fire, so enthusiastic in their initial uptake of the soil's fire-rich nutrients that they might as well be burning already, and anyone who will take a walk through the woods in October after the big wind has blown through can see how perfectly they were made for this place, or this place for them — this wet place of fire, this perfect mix and balance of the burning out and the growing old; of rot and char in a duel, a titanic struggle.

How could there not be a tree like the larch?

The snow can be here any day now. One year eight inches fell on the sixteenth of October and we didn't see bare ground again until May. Another year, on the opening day of deer season — the twenty-sixth — it was twenty-six degrees below zero.

Usually it comes slowly, though, in the form of valley rain and fog and mist, the blue-sky days ebbing, and with the highest tops of the mountains receiving an inch or two of rain, rain, rain, soaking and then saturating the summer- and autumn-parched soil so that in the spring water will be available to newly emergent plants even before all the snow has melted. Tucking the earth into bed for the long sleep, is how I think of it: taking care of everything.

So frequent are the rains now that it seems almost as if it is the landscape that is moving rather than the seasons, and the cant of light across this land; as if the landscape is traveling by mechanical conveyance, clicking forward a few gears, over into the northern Rockies and those basins of sunlight, but then sliding backwards — again, as if by mechanical gear works — back into the rainy shade of the Pacific Northwest.

Not all of the alder leaves have been knocked loose by the wind and the rain, so that the branches surrounding my cabin still have a few individual leaves left, like lone decorations, weather tattered.

When the steadier, later rains of October beat down on these frost-fatigued, blood brown remainders, it knocks them loose, finally, but as they fall, they descend much more slowly than the steady rain that is drumming now on my tin roof. And in my cabin, hunkered next to the stove, listening to the sleepy sound of that hard rain against the roof, it seems to me that there's a dissonance, a disparity, between what I'm hearing and what I'm seeing. If the rain's coming down so hard, how can the leaves be falling so slowly, so gently?

In my morning trance, and perhaps my winter-coming-on trance, it seems somehow that the physical distance between those two senses — the sound of the fast rain, and the sight of the slow-falling leaves — contains the same space, the territory, in which lies the short story, the fiction I am pursuing — that there is a crack, a niche in which the story is hiding — but that I cannot quite figure out how to work or earn my way into that space but can instead only see it, as if across the lateral distance of the rainy marsh, on the other, farther side of the marsh.

I think that to achieve that place in fiction, which seems to be some lateral distance, you really have to descend: that this perception of a farther, lateral shore is an illusion, and is a vertical distance, really; that you have to go down a set of damp stair steps, into another place, as if lying down to sleep in winter, for all the rest of winter, perhaps.

A turning away from the sun, with the days and nights chilling slowly, gradually, half a degree at a time, and the snow line creeping down out of the mountains a few hundred feet each night, is how it goes most years, until one morning, finally, the snow is down in town, and we feel a joy and relief that the waiting is finally over, though a bit of regret too, at the loss of the lovely autumn, and at the responsibility of winter. How much easier it would be to sleep, or leave, than to stay.

One sunny morning I'm sitting at the picnic table, in the fading alder bower, writing, when I feel the barometer dropping. The sky is blue and unchanging, and there's no wind, but I feel nonetheless an onrush of invisible pressure, like the breath of something, a pressure so dense that brown and red and yellow leaves begin falling from the alders and aspen despite being unbidden by any stirring of breeze — *leaping* from the branches, it seems, and tumbling straight to the dank and rotting black earth, obeying autumn.

Or perhaps the moisture in the air has so saturated them that they are now too heavy to retain their tenuous, lingering hold on the branches. Whatever the reason, they are all falling, melting, with no breeze, just falling, and it is like watching snow fall in a silent, windless storm, this same motion a preface to the coming months: as if there is always only one story, one pattern, in all of nature, but that it is too vast and complex for us to ever see anything but glimpses and edges of that penultimate answer, or knowledge.

Answer is not quite the right word, for that implies there is a question, which there isn't. There is only one beautiful day after another. One awakens, draws breath, and moves forward into each new day like a deer venturing into the tall waving marsh grass.

Later in the day, when I've moved back into the cabin and am working, the wind does return, and it blows more leaves down, swirls them dancing in all directions, with the brief collections and assemblages of leaves taking on in their descent once more the shapes and forms of living creatures, so that it appears as if there are ghosts moving across the marsh. And so many dry leaves are landing on the tin roof of the cabin that it sounds like rain; and even though it is a dry rain, a ghost rain, I hunch up and edge in closer to the wood stove.

Which is greater, joy or peace?

My own peculiar dilemma, I think, is that peace *brings* me joy; that from peace, I soon enough escalate into euphoria. Which is lovely enough. But then, coming back down can be a frightening feeling, this descending from euphoria. It's absolutely a feeling like falling.

Perhaps I should hold on to the one thought, in the descent, a mantra — something like *Only beauty; Only beauty* — and in that manner, slow or relax in my descent, traveling and landing wherever the breeze and my own weight take me, and remembering always that I am but one among billions, that there are as many of us as there are leaves in this forest.

Still, I can't help it. I stare out at the beauty of those swirling leaves, and the white trunks of the aspen, the gold pastel of their remaining leaves, the butterscotch of larch regal against the coming purple storm sky in the north and the great brooding mountains beyond — the leaves scurrying across the marsh now — and I get too far out there, into joy, too quickly, and then I don't know what to do with that joy, don't know how to process such beauty, and I feel a touch of panic or even sorrow, without having a clue what it's about.

Do you know what I mean? Is it this way for others of us, in the autumn? Why is it this way?

One more year. And one more. And one more. Always, one more.

One of the sweetest things about October, finally, I think, is the hush that comes right before the start of hunting season. Some of us will have been out hunting birds in September and early October, and might even have gone out with the bow, hoping to call in an elk. But for most of the state, and most of the culture, hunting season does not begin until late October, with the start of rifle season — the ultimate opportunity for bounty gathering — and I wonder if part of the hush that precedes the season's start — kind of a soft spot in time, in which time seems disinclined, for once, to move forward — might come because almost all of us have finally made our peace with the human decision to push on and reach for more even as most of the rest of the world is lying down and going to sleep.

For the next five weeks, we will be more active, physically, than we have been all year. We'll run ourselves ragged, rising hours before dawn and hauling ourselves up one mountain and down another, traveling always to the deeper, farther reaches, the back sides of places, following tracks and scent and intuition and landscape. And perhaps in this exhaustion, we will reach the dream-state, the descent or immersion that is required of the season after all. Perhaps the hunt is our own migration, and our own fit in the world, and in this rank and bountiful place.

I have to say something here that I'd really rather not say. For all of my penchant for navel-gazing, I still think it's easier to walk your way into a fit with landscape than to think your way into such a fit.

I do not mean to alienate intellectuals, or overly glamorize wood-chopping and rock-toting. And I need to remember not to offer my own thoughts as prescription, but rather simply as my own obser-vations and predilections. But for my own volatile, mood-tenuous, drifty self, any assurances or resolutions about the world and my place in it that I have gotten by thinking or pondering — the ab-stract — have almost always been second rate, compared to the physical, tangible specificity of fit that seems to happen most often when I'm not even aware of searching for such a fit: near the end of a long hike, or at the top of a mountain, leaning winded against a big rock and staring out at the valley below.

Or hunting: following a deer, or an elk, all day long. Adjust-ing my pace to his, and seeing the landscape — topography, precipi-tation, substrate, temperature, wind direction, *everything* — with an intensity that matches his. A stepping-up of hunger and its broader, wider, perhaps more interesting cousin, desire.

I love the intellectual world — the life of the mind, which is to me sometimes like a shadow life, the shadows and echoes and mem-ories of other things. Such a landscape seems to possess infinite depth. But what I like about the physical world, the life of the body, is how much the world craves, it seems — despite our strange drift-ing, and our physical awkwardness — to make a fit with all things.

Every hunt is different, every hunt is special and wonderful: but one that I am remembering right now involved a big bull that I tracked through a mix of rain and falling snow. I followed him all day, into and through a place in the valley where I had never been before, until finally, I think, he himself came to a place he too was unfamiliar with: a gnarly tangle of lodgepole blowdown.

When I caught up with him, near dusk — sneaking as silently as I could, in the soft new snow, and the fog, and the dim blue light, both of us drenched — he was looking back, knowing that I was somewhere out there, and the reason he had paused was that he had boxed himself in: had hopped over a wind-felled girder work of lodgepole and found himself in the equivalent of a small corral.

He could have gotten out; he wasn't entirely trapped. But he was weary, like me, and was just standing there in the hard rain and blue fog, coat drenched, antlers gleaming, breathing hard.

Of all the thousands of trees that had blown over in this one stretch of forest, he had found the sixteen or so that had toppled four-square into a small corral, a roofless cabin. It seemed to me almost as if he had decided to go no farther; and though he was not ceding any of his wildness — was in no way yielding to domesticity — he was nonetheless, finally, in a sort of wild corral, and I felt that I was meant to find and take this animal.

Some days — many days, in this wild blue snowy valley — the world's grace and desire for order (despite what physicists say about the world craving disorder) seems to shout its message, over and over again, until you see it, that order, in every glimpse and glance. Infidel that I am, I do not always want to quite accept the enormity of the idea that some one person, or some one deity, could make all of this, or that it could be so elegant, and I want to instead propose some certain dry mathematical formula, $y\ '\ m\ 1/x\ X\ r\text{-}1/3\ (V\text{-}1/m)$, or something of that nature, by which all things will suddenly fit, evident in all shapes. And all movements — this one formula capturing even the laminar flow of the wind itself, the invisible ribbons of air that might be the pulse and breath of a God, perhaps: nothing less, one thing, only one thing.

You see it in the daily rhythms of things — this sameness, this sacredness — not just in the cycle and whirl and repetition of seasons.

Twenty years ago, when I first wandered into this marsh, I found a set of fresh wolf tracks, not hours old, in the October mud, behind some willows. I never saw that wolf — indeed, wolves were not thought to even be here, back then — but this October, as I was staring out the window, daydreaming, a black wolf emerged from those very willows, paused, and then struck out across the marsh, traveling through the precise place where I had seen those rare tracks long ago.

Twenty years is a long time, to us. To the world, of course — as well as to any gods or God, much less any mathematical formula — it is so insignificant as to perhaps be unnoticeable. Even though it could not have been the same wolf, perhaps that is a distinction known only to you and me, across time's vast landscape.

In the front yard, there was for a long time a log that we'd felled, a big leaning green but beetle-infested pine that, until we felled it, had been in a position where it could fall over onto the house.

For years, the girls and I used it for a crude balance beam, playing follow the leader on its knotted, tapering spine. When the log finally cured, we had it sawn into lumber to make a bookshelf (which might one day hold a children's book I'd like to write, about, among other things, tightrope-walking along the spine of a fallen tree).

The log lay there for nearly three years, drying, and changing, ever so slightly, the chemistry and compaction and vegetation of the soil just beneath it — forming a kind of invisible shadow, in that manner.

And when this year's first snow arrives in the valley, the rain turning one night to slushy white, in the morning the front yard is blanketed, perfectly white, and we think, *All right, it's here again, already.*

A strange thing happens though, later in the morning. A mild sun appears, and by noon some of the snow is melting — as if time, and the seasons, are reversing direction, pulling back to reveal some earlier time again.

The first place to melt is the ghost shadow of where that log was. For whatever reason, that space warms faster, so that even a year later we can see precisely where that log — the ghost log, now a bookshelf — rested.

Are the shapes and paths of all ghosts so very nearly the same — indeed, often exactly the same — as those of the living? Call it the unbreakableness of things, and know, almost surely, that again this must be at least partly designed, cannot be fully accidental. And whether designed by us, or Another, or some collaboration of force between the two — between all — make no mistake: some kind of effort is being made, and it is in the fullness of the year, perhaps, that we sometimes get our best chance, our best shot, at seeing this.

NOVEMBER

....

WHAT MAKES A SEASON? What is the nature of time? How much of time's passage is a mathematical abstraction, and how much of it, if any, is a living, breathing organism, a life process, stirred and generated in part by our passage through it — a symbiotic relationship, or perhaps even at times a parasitic one, but a relationship nonetheless, in which two forces act and are acted upon by each other?

The way an injury to us on a certain date, years ago, can mar the shape or path of a subsequent year — that same date becoming as specific to the body of a year, of subsequent years, as might an injury to one's kidneys, or ribs. It's been ten years since my mother died young, died too early — dying in November — and yet each year thereafter, a heaviness enters my spirit around that time, and my dreams are filled with a sadness I seem unable to control.

And this year I find myself injured again, around that same time: not in anywhere the same fashion, or with even a fraction of the same grief, but strangely, near the same point in the year.

Less than a full day after the date on which my mother died, a stranger comes driving down our long driveway, lost, and drives over our old blind and deaf Homer-dog, killing her. Neither the grief I feel nor the circumstances of it have anything to do with the loss of my mother; it is merely another, infinitely smaller loss, at that same point in time.

Elizabeth was down in Missoula, visiting friends, and the girls were in school. I was out hunting in the rain, and when I came home at lunch, I didn't even see Homer, who was laid out next to Point and Superman's kennel. Instead, there was a note on the table, expressing how sorry the driver was, how he didn't see Homer, yadda yadda — and my mind froze, not knowing what the note was talking about and yet also knowing somehow immediately.

I went out and looked for Homer, called her name, whistled in the high pitch that sometimes she could still barely hear. Certain she would come bounding around the corner — still spry, for sixteen and a half — and would shatter, as if with the force of the myth, the stranger's ragged note.

There was only the sound of hissing rain. The other dogs whining a little in their kennel, watching me.

The note had said she was laid out by a stump alongside the driveway. I went to the stump and she wasn't there; and again, it seemed to me that by her not being there, the myth of the note could be broken, that time itself could be reversed, as if in a river's eddy, if even only for an hour or two, or for however long it took to get her back upright, standing, and alive.

I found her by the other stump, the one at the corner of the driveway, laid out neatly enough, but soaking, sodden in the cold damned rain.

The driver had been gone only a few hours. Homer was still not yet as cold as the rain and snow around her. Not warm, but not yet cold or stiff. I kept thinking, desperately, of how she might yet be saved; how I could rush her down to the miracle vet in town, who had on so many occasions before rescued her from one calamity or another.

I picked her up to carry her back into the house. There was a certain way she would lean into you when you bent to pick her up that was meant to assist you in the act; and without it, I scarcely knew how to lift her.

I laid her on her bed and wrapped her in an old jacket. Her lips were curled back, as if she had been in pain, and her hindquarters were torn from the gravel, and again I felt desperate, felt that I had let her down. I had picked her and her twin sister, Ann, up on the side of the road in Mississippi, back in late May of 1985 — indeed, there'd been a third pup with them, already dead, struck by a car or truck — and though part of me was aware that I had saved her, had given her sixteen and a half great years, there was another part of me that knew she deserved much better, that she deserved for me to be there with her, comforting her, and that she deserved a painless death. She was the most loyal and affectionate dog I'd ever had, and I was angry at the carelessness of the pilgrim who had not been more cautious, coming down a strange driveway out in the country, and angry at the unthinking disrespect of trespass, but angriest of all that after all those years together, I had been unable to give Homer even that one small dignity of a natural death, that one small comfort, at the end: that instead, after all those years of service, she had known at the end only pain and confusion.

She was not yet decrepit. She still enjoyed being a dog: being fed and cared for, and wandering her well-worn route, her territory. Being dressed up in bows and dresses by the girls — surely the only coonhound in the world to wear frills. Even now, I'm sad and angry about the injustice of it, the unfairness, though I am also struck by the possibility that the odds were stacked against her from the beginning — that she began her life as an orphan, road dumped along the highway, and that there was or is a force in the world that asked her to end it that way, too, though for whatever purpose or reasons I cannot begin to fathom.

The strangeness of the world, and all its murmuring cycles, both beautiful and dangerous: she had died not five feet from where her twin sister, Ann, had died, also beneath an automobile, several years earlier, so that it was as if their blood was together again. Ann was buried beneath a grove of aspen trees, beneath a stone in which we had etched the word *Bravery* — it had been Ann who was always getting into tussles with coyotes, defending hearth and home — and long ago we had decided that when it was Homer's time to go, we would lay her next to Ann, with the word *Loyalty* scratched on the stone.

The bridge they build across our hearts: for parts of three decades, that bridge had been crafted, a living and specific thing, like a path or a process. And now that she is gone, the bridge still remains, as ornate and beautiful as ever, though it is no longer living, has forfeited the supple mystery of life, and has instead assumed the durable calcification of myth and memory — the residue of where our love was, the residue of the love we had for her, the residue of sweetness, of loyalty, the residue of a great dog who lived once upon a time.

I remember a November up here not too long ago in which a young friend of mine, Travis Shearer, son of the great Texas man of letters

Bill Shearer, who died from a brain tumor at the age of forty-two — as good and honest and loyal a man as there ever was — decided to come up and visit us over Thanksgiving, the first year after Bill died. There is a particular mountain that is special to me in this valley, a place to go to in times of sickness and sorrow as well as in joy and celebration, a beautiful mountain, and while Bill was sick, I had made many trips up that mountain, thinking of him. I would write to Bill and describe these hikes, and would send him things I'd found on those walks — a feather, a stone, a shed antler, a jar of jam made from huckleberries growing on that mountain — and it was, and is, a powerful and yet reassuring place to think about death, and cycles, surrounded by all the many cycles of wild nature that can still be found in such places. It is a comfort to go into such a place as far as you can, on foot, and no matter whether only fifty or a hundred yards in or all the way to the center, simply knowing that there is a center, and a vastness too, a vastness that will be here longer than any of us, is the comforting thing, not the amount of miles traveled into such a wild place.

It was Travis's desire to see the mountain I'd been describing to Bill. (It had been one of Bill's desires to see the mountain, and to climb it; to take a picnic on it, with his wife and two daughters and Travis.) And being from the hill country of Texas, Travis was interested also in stomping around in the lowlands, looking for white-tailed deer. He had not been able to get a hunting license in time for this trip, but I still had not yet been gifted with a deer, so that he would be able to participate in that manner: the two of us looking for and hopefully finding a deer, which I might then be able to take and which the two of us could then pack out.

He's a tall, handsome, intelligent young man, with a politeness and a consideration of others that exceed even his father's own substantial courtesy. I believe he was fifteen at the time of this trip, and that it was in '96 — the year of the record snow, snow beginning on October sixteenth and falling steadily, heavily, lasting all the way deep into May — twenty feet of snow, here in the Yaak, and a brutal winter on big game, as well as upon the spirits of men, women, and children.

In November, however, it was still all wonderful, still all bright and new. I picked Travis up in Kalispell — he was flying in from Washington, D.C., where he and some of his classmates had participated in the Close-Up program — and we drove out east, up and over the snowy Divide, and along the incredible Front Range, and then farther east, far out into the prairie, toward Great Falls, where we hunted for pheasants the next afternoon in a howling wind with a chill factor of twenty below. I had neglected to tell Travis what kind of clothes to bring — particularly boots — and so the cold was pretty wretched. The heater in my truck didn't work either, and so for warmth as we drove we took turns sharing my gaunt and shivering great hound, Colter, nudging our frozen feet under his quivering, bony frame.

At one point we visited with a rancher in one of his outbuildings, where he had a coal fire burning in a metal drum; and hunkered over that fire, still shivering, while the storm raged outside, Travis was astounded that even though he could see the fire and was holding his bare hands as close to it as he dared, he was receiving no warmth from it. I could see in his eyes the surprise, the revelation, that there could be a cold so intense and massive that it could — for a while — defeat even the miracle warmth of spark and flame, and that this was, for him, an almost frightening realization.

We saw only one pheasant that day, a rooster, which leapt up into the swirling storm about a hundred yards in front of us and then vanished into the storm like a ghost, and at dusk we turned right around and headed back toward the mountains, up and over the pass and into their heart.

Near the summit of our valley, around three a.m., we encountered a young man wearing only jeans and a jean jacket, shoveling feebly at the snow that had swallowed the front half of his truck. We could tell from his skid marks that he had almost gone over the cliff and down into the Moose Hole, but fate or chance had turned his skid and sent him into the uphill side, into the snowbank where he was now half buried.

He had been drinking — we could smell the rank, stale odor of all-night liquor on his skin, and in his clothes and his vaporous, volatile breath — and with our truck and tow rope we pulled him free of the snowbank but then told him to sit this one out for a while, to take a nap before attempting to head on down the hill, back into the town of Libby, not just for his own sake but for the sake of anyone else who might be coming his way in those early hours. But he could not be dissuaded and set off again on his foolish way while we headed north, saddened and sobered by his recklessness, and by the waste of his hours.

The next day, we packed a little lunch and headed up toward the mountain — Bill's mountain — where more than a foot of new snow had fallen. We started up the trail on snowshoes — Travis using them for the first time in his life — and as we trudged upward, I was reminded of what it was like to be fifteen, of what an amazing confluence of strength and inexperience that is, a time and place at which you're physically and intellectually capable of doing almost anything in the world and yet at which almost everything is still — somehow fairly new, if not brand new. A time when every day brings a first. First wild pheasant seen. First look at the Front Range. First snowshoeing trip, first blizzard. And on and on and on. I remembered that, and while I may be mistaken and do not intend or claim to be speaking for Bill, it seemed to me strongly, there on the mountain, that Bill was remembering it too. And again, I could be completely mistaken — this could be only all my own emotion, with no other or outside communication going on whatsoever — but the feeling I got was that Bill was watching, or knowing, and remembering; and that the remembering was causing him something like sadness. Not quite sorrow or sadness, or futility, but something along those lines.

It might not have been that way at all. It might have been just me feeling that — all me. But I don't think so.

The relationship doesn't end with death. Anyone who's ever lost someone knows this. The terms of the relationship simply change dramatically — the scale and amplitude, once compressed into the moment of life, are suddenly expanded, as if in a big bang spreading out. A larger cycle of going away and returning is entered, in the relationship. I do believe that we will all see each other again, and that there will always still be, even in the brief compression of life, moments in time as well as places on the landscape — unpredictable, and certainly, ungovernable — at which we the living pass through pockets of time or place where the relationship sparks again in a way that impresses itself upon us; that it can be like ascending or descending into a different place, where it is almost as if the departed has never gone away, or as if the departed has returned.

I hesitate to say this next part, but the feeling I was getting was that Bill wasn't ready for us to get to the top of that mountain; that he had been planning on going up there himself with Travis and the rest of his family for so long that it did not fit the cycle or pattern of — how to say this? — what was *right* for Bill not to be making this trip, not just in spirit, or in the flesh of his son, but in his own physical body.

The snow got deeper and deeper. The powder was so deep and cold and dry that our snowshoes weren't working and Travis's Texas boots weren't working, either — his socks kept filling with snow, which the heat of his feet melted, so that the wet socks were sliding then to the bottom of his boots. At one point we sat down on the mountain (dry snow up to our chests), and Travis pulled off his boots and sopping wet socks — his feet were blue and pained — and put on a new dry pair I had in my pack, and I was struck by the strangeness of the image, this young man from Texas sitting barefooted in four feet of snow high in the mountains of northern Montana, in a blizzard. And while we could have pushed on and gained the peak, I asked him if he would mind overmuch waiting and coming back another time — he had his whole life ahead of him — and though he would have pushed on, blue feet and all, he agreed to descend.

I didn't tell him that I didn't think Bill wanted us to go up there yet, or that I felt like the spirit of Bill was having some mixed feelings, as was I. We just headed back down, frigid and caked with snow, eyebrows rime-crusted and toes and fingers and ears and lips numb: back down to the snow-shrouded truck far below, and then back home, to the warm yellow squares of light and the fire burning in the wood stove.

The next day was Thanksgiving. Travis and I were up early, making our breakfast and getting a fire going in the wood stove, while the rest of the house slept. It was still snowing hard. We dressed warmly and then went out the back door and walked off into the woods, heavy flakes falling wet against our faces. For a couple of years, I'd been seeing the tracks and scrapes and rubs of a big whitetail down at the bottom of the hill, in another series of marshes similar to the one next to my writing cabin; and not far into our journey, we cut the big buck's tracks and caught the dense, rank smell that told us he was in full rut.

It wasn't even daylight yet — we were still using our flashlights through the woods — and as we passed through the vertical bars of the old lodgepole forest, following that wandering buck's path, our lights illuminated vertical columns of spinning snowflakes.

So fresh were the tracks, and so heavy the falling snow, which had not filled or even yet obscured his tracks, that we knew we were right upon him. We hunkered down under the spreading branches of a big spruce tree and waited for the woods to grow light enough to see without a flashlight, and then we started out after him again. The tracking conditions were perfect: we were able to walk quickly but silently.

For a while, the buck's tracks had snow in them — representing those five or ten minutes we'd sat quietly, waiting for dawn — but then they grew sharp and distinct again and we knew that we were right behind him once more. The slight breeze was in our face, and because we were being silent, and because his tracks were still wandering and unhurried, we were certain that he had no idea we were behind him.

We were certain that while he was out lollygagging around, wandering through the forest, wearing his great crown of antlers, looking around in the snowstorm for a doe to breed, we would be able to slip right in behind him and take a nice clean shot, and have a big fat buck to drag home on Thanksgiving Day, with the end of the hunting season only a few days away.

It was incredibly exciting, believing that with each next, silent step we would see him just ahead of us, either paused and looking around, or perhaps simply wandering unaware; and as we followed him farther and deeper into the forest, the tension continued to build and I was very glad that Travis was getting to experience this.

We followed the deer for nearly two hours and were beginning to learn, even if only subconsciously, the shape and rhythm of him — ducking under the same branches he ducked under, and picking the exact same routes, the same paths and passages that he had chosen — our steps in his steps, like a stream following the valley grooves cut by a glacier, our bodies and our movements adapting to the forest as had his, always following his lead, and in that manner, perhaps, beginning to assume or understand likewise some of his thoughts, or at least his general mood and disposition. And thus it was sometime early into our third hour of trailing him, still only and always but a few moments behind him, that we finally came to understand that which we had heretofore been denying: that he knew we were back there and that we were after him.

It's one of the oldest lessons in the world: just because a thing cannot be seen, or even heard or smelled or touched or tasted, does not mean it does not exist.

Gradually we came to understand in following that buck (he was beginning to lead us in wide circles now) that it was a game of cat and mouse; that although he was still out cruising, still looking for does, he was leading us through small open areas so that once he was safely into the woods on the other side he could look back and glimpse us. We began to see from his tracks where he had sometimes ascended a small knoll and paused to look down on us before whirling and bounding off. There would be a telltale divot of snow, or even black earth, in each of these places; but still we pushed on, despite having our cover blown — and again and again, he would eventually slow to a walk, almost a saunter.

The snow was beautiful. I very much wanted to catch up with this buck. I very much wanted Travis to see this magnificent buck taken, wanted Travis to participate in that.

I had followed such bucks before and knew that what they often eventually did under such pressure was the not-very-nice thing of searching out another of their kind — a younger buck, usually — and crossing paths with that deer so that the pursuer might then become confused, or even tempted, and follow the new tracks rather than the initial tracks. Bull elk do the same thing, under the same kind of pressure. I whispered to Travis that we might see that happen soon — he looked at me dubiously — but five minutes later, that was what happened, and the realization by Travis of this animal's intelligence, as well as its cool cunning, and its supreme predisposition to keep on living, astounded him.

We followed him as long as we had time for — another hour, still only moments behind him, but never seeing him — and with a growing sense of frustration, I began to beseech Bill above, whom I was certain was looking down and watching this hunt with extreme interest, for help. I asked him, silently and repeatedly, to use any new intercelestial clout he might have obtained in the afterlife to help deliver this deer to us, for Travis's benefit — for Travis, for Travis — and as we continued on through the snowy forest, hot on the trail of that buck, I felt certain that that wish would be delivered; that as the suspense of this wonderful hunt continued to build, with the smart old buck turning us inside out, our endurance would eventually be rewarded and the hunt would culminate with our being granted an opportunity to take the animal — that the animal himself, under some understanding with Bill, might even finally present himself, or at least the opportunity, to ourselves.

That was not how it happened. Sometimes it happens in that manner, but not this time. We ran out of time — we had pushed the buck a couple of miles south — and we finally had to turn around and head back through the falling snow to our Thanksgiving feast. I was a little bummed that we had not even *seen* the deer — toward the end, I had negotiated downward so that all I'd been beseeching Bill for was just a glimpse, so we could see what kind of antlers the big deer was carrying — but still, it had been one of the most rewarding and satisfying hunts I'd been on, and I knew the same was true for Travis; and I supposed it was a great lesson for him, as well, that even when everything seems to be in your favor, you don't always get the deer. That, in fact, you rarely get the deer.

We took a shortcut through the woods, triangulating toward home, and got there shortly before the meal was ready. We had other friends staying with us too, and had a big feast, and afterward whiled away the dusk and then the evening lying in front of the fire reading and playing board games while the snow continued to fall. Was it wrong to ask so fervently for that deer when we already had so much — a turkey in the oven, biscuits and sweet potatoes baking, and a chocolate pie on the counter? Perhaps not *wrong;* but I could see, even then, that the hunt itself rather than the animal had been the great blessing. And that Travis was going to do what his father, his parents, most wanted him to do: to continue living a full and engaged life. The deer didn't matter in the least. Even I could see that.

We saw the deer the next day. We had packed up and I was driving Travis to the airport in Kalispell. I might be plain wrong about this, but what it felt like to me — and I still believe this — is that it was an echo of my prayer, my beseechment, and that the delivery of it was filled with irony, and something else, not quite prankster-ish, but something along those lines. Something I don't think there's a word for, but it certainly got my attention, and reminded me — not that I had ever doubted it — that Bill still had an eye on his boy, would always have an eye on his boy.

Travis had witnessed a good way to hunt, a fair and honest way — an engaged way — the way Bill liked to hunt, and the way Bill liked to do everything, with muscular force and passion, and now he, Travis, got to see the other way too: the lesser way.

I'd been asking for even a glimpse of that big old deer, asking for it fervently, and when we came around a bend in the road not two miles into our journey, crossing the bridge that spanned the creek where we'd turned back the day before, we got to see him.

He was in the air when we saw him, as if flying. His antlers were huge, almost supernaturally so — dark and long-tined — and his body likewise was dark and long. And so spectacular a deer was he that the strange sight of it almost made sense, for a moment; of course such an amazing animal should be flying, just like Pegasus.

He was huge and graceful and flying through the air, right in front of us. He landed awkwardly, however, slipping on the icy road, and then lay there on his side, kicking, slipping each time that he tried to rise, as if the ice was getting the better of him: as if there existed, within his great power, some sort of Achilles' heel whereby the force generated by his body was too great to focus itself upon the ice, constrained as he was by his delicate black hoofs, which seemed so useless now, failing him each time he tried to stand. As if there was simply too much torque for the ice.

I stopped the truck and we sat there, staring in amazement. The deer was only thirty feet in front of us, and like the deer itself perhaps, I felt strangely off-balance: as if I had run into some fracture of time, some disynchronous chasm where yesterday's hunt had not ended but had only been paused, and was now continuing. There seemed also to be a similar break in space, so that it was as if our truck had struck the deer and knocked him to the ground, even though we had stopped thirty feet short. As if we had run into a glass wall and stopped, but as if something else — the motion, through time and space, of how things might have been — had carried on through that glass wall.

The deer lay his head down on the ice as best as he could, encumbered as he was by his antlers, and lay there, gasping; and it was only then that I focused beyond the deer and saw at the bottom of the icy hill, about sixty yards distant, the tilted skew of a hastily stopped truck, with its doors flung wide open, and two hunters — excuse me, two shooters — crouched out in the middle of the icy road, rifles in hand, out-of-state license plates.

Such were the slightly-behind-real-time synapses of my mind that I perceived the wide-eyed, quick-stopped crouching shooters to be only now spying the fallen, ice-slipping deer, as were Travis and I, but that unlike Travis and I, they intended to try to shoot it, right there in the middle of the road. And realizing this, or believing it, Travis and I were severely discomfited, with that deer (which was growing strangely, slowly becalmed) directly in front of us, and us directly in the line of fire.

One of the hunters had his rifle raised and was watching the deer through the scope — watching us through the scope, is what it seemed like — and angrily, we waved him off, and it was only as he, an Elmer Fudd–looking character, lowered his gun that I understood which side of the glass wall we were on and which side the deer was on.

The deer lay there dying, already shot — "Pigs," I said — and we drove around him slowly, sadly, as if around the scene of an accident, and on past the road hunters without looking at them or stopping, with the unspoken obvious: that if they had missed that leaping, running deer, the bullet would quite likely have gone into our windshield just as we came around the corner. That although it was not quite this way, it might as well have been, and in one sense, was true: that that deer had leapt in front of us and blocked, with its body, the bullet that might otherwise have struck us.

It was that simple, and that complicated. We ourselves, in seeking to end the deer's life, to take the deer's life, had set it into motion the day before, like the winding of some vast and complicated mechanism, pushing the deer, with our relentless trailing, out of the care of his home territory, and here, only a day later, my wish, my prayer, my request to Bill — *at least let us see this deer* — was being delivered, though in what tone or manner, I was unsure. Hard irony, perhaps?

These things, I know: That Bill loved Travis, loved all of his family fiercely. That Bill and Travis should have seen that mountain together, should have hunted Montana deer together.

What were the trip's successes — what did I have to offer Travis, on both Travis's and Bill's behalf? I was glad for all that Travis had seen: the moronic, deadly attempts to drive under the influence of alcohol; the joy of a good hunt, and the ugliness of a bad hunt.

Any other conclusions beyond that would be conjecture: notions such as the idea that there is another world beyond this one, or rather, a spirit world that accompanies this one. And whether that world on the other side is like a shadow cast by the short days of our lives or our lives themselves the shadows, cast by those spirits, none can say for sure. I do know that he, Bill, was there with us, on that hunt, and that I think he will always be there with his son, his family.

The day opened up, after that, as if some pustule had been lanced. We drove on toward the airport through bright blue sky and gold-lit forests, with sunlight everywhere: as rare an occurrence, in November, as an eclipse. There were only three days left in the season, and the road hunters were frantic — even on U.S. Highway 2, we saw trucks pulled hastily to the side of the road and parked crookedly, errantly, doors flung open, and older gentlemen in blaze orange hurrying across the right-of-way, rifles in hand, laboring to straddle their way over sagging barbed-wire fences and then disappearing into the forest in pursuit of any rut-wandering buck that happened to cross the highway — and Travis and I could laugh about it, finally, because it was funny, like some sort of campy zombie movie, all those old fellows in orange suddenly being summoned from and abandoning their vehicles and rushing off into the forest, mouths agape and arms outstretched . . .

We saw the most amazing thing, halfway to the airport: perhaps the most amazing image of a short and amazing trip.

A deer had been struck and killed some time ago, crossing the road, and there on the embankment, its carcass was being attended by the usual assemblage of ravens — at least a dozen beautiful shining black ravens, thick-billed and broad-winged, hopping and flapping over their laid-out bounty, as if gathered at some Thanksgiving feast.

There was an immense bald eagle sitting some distance from the carcass too, his snowy head more brilliant than even the new snow; but the sight that stopped us and then made us turn around and go back, even if it meant being late to the airport, even if it meant possibly missing the plane, was the giant golden eagle sitting atop that pecked-over carcass, trying to defend it against a coyote that kept sneaking in, trying to steal a bite.

The golden eagle had one set of talons locked into the open rib slats of the deer's skeleton and was using his other talons to claw and feint at the coyote whenever the coyote darted in for a quick bite. The golden eagle's wings were spread high and wide to their full seven-foot span, and even grounded as the eagle was, its powerful wingbeats and awkward ground hops were dragging the carcass of the adult deer, a doe, along on the ground. And as it did so, the coterie of ravens, like the rise-and-fall fluttering of a kite tail, followed, and so did that stalking coyote, ducking the eagle's one-clawed swipes while snarling and baring his teeth, hackles raised. There wasn't much deer left to share among all of them.

We sat on the other side of the road and watched. Sometimes the coyote would run around to the back side of the carcass, so that the eagle — one talon still locked into those slatted, hollowed ribs — would have to whirl around, spinning the carcass as it did so and lifting it partially free of the ground so that it gave the impression of some wild helicopter trying to become airborne.

There were no other cars on the road, during that time, and we watched for several minutes. Finally, the coyote's winter hunger, its winter boldness, was overcome by its fear of man, and it skittered off into the woods; and likewise the ravens scattered and flew a short distance away, cawing and croaking, unsure of our intent. The bald eagle, which had been watching this battle, left too, leaving only the gigantic golden eagle, which, strangely enough, or so it seemed to us, did not lower its head to eat but simply remained atop the weathered carcass, still gripping it and looking around as if still ready, or even eager, for another defense. Studying us, even, on the other side of the road, as if to say, *You want a piece of this?*

We were late to the airport, then, and had to leave, had to hurry on. Travis was ecstatic; we both were.

"It's not always like this," I told him.

Unsettled. That's the word I'm looking for, about the feeling I got that Bill, or the spirit of Bill, might have been with us that day we went up on the mountain, in the blizzard. Like new snow on a steep slope early in the winter, before the passage of time and the accrual of more snow weight settle that first snow.

By and large, the sun vanishes in November. In addition to spring's ceaseless blood tide of mosquitoes and the summer's tide of wildfires, there is this aspect of the landscape that I'm compelled to remind the gentle reader of — the daunting gloom, and the descent of the cold rain. In November, out in my writing cabin, my candles waver in the night, stirred now it seems not by any breezes but simply from the weight of winter descending. On the plywood floor of my cabin, the treaded boot prints of snow remain Vibramed across the floor, unchanged from their initial deposition more than three hours ago, despite their proximity to the wood stove by which I sit huddled.

It's a beautiful wintry view at my window, all fog and crystal frost and ice rime, and for the first time this season, I'm having to write with gloves on, so that I'm holding the pen clumsily, gripping it in my gloved hands like chopsticks in the hands of a first-time user. As such, I can barely read my own writing, which is often barely legible even under the best conditions — and further complicating the act of writing in this weather, the rhythm and pace of it, is the fact that the page before me is obscured momentarily by the large smoke-cloud of fog formed with each exhalation of my breath, the page vanishing for a few seconds, then reappearing, as if through an opening in the clouds, only to disappear again. And there is very much the disorienting sensation that I am flying along through the clouds, trying to peer down through brief openings at a landscape far below.

My feet are blocks of ice, and I'm shivering, ignoring these things as much as I can and trying carefully to follow the path of my own sentences, as if trailing the tracks of some elusive quarry through the woods.

The rut is coming. It's only days away, and might even be already starting. As I stare out the window at the marsh, grieving Homer, there is the hunter's part of me, the physical part, that responds nonetheless with a deep joy at the sight of the purple-gray storm sky to the south, with its impending promise of the sweet coming betrayal of fresh snow, upon which the comings and goings of no animal, neither prey nor predator, will any longer be kept a secret.

One day while the girls are at school, I carry the Great Pumpkin and his entourage of Great Cucumbers off the porch, where they have been slipping daily into deeper and deeper senescence, collapsing in on themselves as each night's frost breaks them down further — as if breathing, through some cold bellows, the allure of rot into them, rather than the spark of life — already, they retain only mere vestiges of their former glory. And I take the sad pumpkin, and the sad cucumbers, far out into the forest to decompose in peace and feed the larch trees as they do so, carrying them out to the forest as I would carry the dogs' bowls of food to them, out in their kennels: feeding the Great Pumpkin to the larch trees, whose needles, in another eleven months, will be as orange as the pumpkin itself.

The twisted stalk vine of the jack-o'-lantern's lid, the vine-handle, looks exactly like the base of a buck's antlers.

Earlier in the day, I had seen a nice big buck, strips of orangish alder bark hanging from his antlers, cruising through the marsh, where he had been marking his territory. Perhaps later in the evening — at dusk — he will come investigate the cucumbers and pumpkin. Perhaps he will even chew on them, a bit — becoming, in that manner, the Great Pumpkin, like the larch trees, like us, like everything that is still connected up here. The pumpkin top that looks like the deer's antlers *becoming* the deer's antlers.

Who needs any more magic? Isn't it already everywhere, and not just in the color orange, but in every color, every shade, every pulse, and every stirring of a taut and full world?

The girls notice the pumpkin's absence, of course. "Where did he go?" they ask.

"Ah," I tell them, looking out at the treetops, "I believe he has flown away."

My youngest brother, B.J., born when I was fifteen, is coming out for Thanksgiving this year, and I'm hoping to be able to take him on a good hunt. He's only going to be here for a couple of days, but I'm hoping to be able to spend one of those days going far into the backcountry and seeing whatever we might see. I understand completely the Native American practice of being careful about speaking aloud the name of one's quarry, in the belief that such casualness would be a form of disrespect, implying a taking-for-grantedness, and an act little different from saying, "I'm going to run down to the store for some oranges."

I understand completely the greater respect afforded by a statement such as "I am going to go into the woods to see what I might see" — and, cursed at times with my past history of having been a scientist, first a biologist with a timber company and later an oil and gas geologist — there is often a part that tries to analyze the selective evolutionary advantages of various behaviors and adaptations rather than simply or solely reveling in the mystery of a thing.

I am not saying a thing is any less beautiful for being examined or studied or better understood; in my experience, in fact, the contrary holds true.

But as a scientist, there can become a habit of believing that just because there is usually a logical and interconnected reason for anything you care to examine, then there must therefore be a logical and interconnected reason for *everything;* and that mysteries such as love and honor and respect can become subtly devalued, not by knowledge but by the accruing arrogance of beginning to believe that everything in the world can and must somehow justify itself.

From such a pattern or mindset, it is but a short hop to the belief that everything in the world must somehow have the potential, and sometimes even the obligation, to serve mankind through the mere virtue of that object's existence and through mankind's knowing.

Nonetheless, like any miner, I push on, probing and picking, grasping and handling the objects that interest me: wanting, often, to know them more deeply. I can examine such a beautiful emotional truth as the fact that hunters in native cultures preferred not to speak the name of their quarry out loud, and I can sense and celebrate the beauty and mystery of that truth even as the scientist part of me — almost sacrilegiously, it feels — is musing how for those native hunters, a constant acknowledgment of the grace and luck involved in hunting could have a selective evolutionary advantage. It's possible that those individuals — and therefore a culture that supported the presence of such individuals — could be more successful in that by reinforcing their respect for their quarry, and the extreme luck and grace required to kill or capture their quarry, they might move more carefully and cautiously through the forest, more respectfully, more observantly, perhaps, than a hunter who entered with any lesser degree of respect. And that it could be, then, that those extra-cautious, extra-respectful hunters ended up with more game-taking opportunities.

I can think that way as a scientist even while knowing as a hunter and an artist the deeper emotional truth, that it is the landscape or sometimes even the animal itself that usually gives the animal to the hunter; and that although there are exceptions, particularly with our brute technology, the land once rewarded (and still sometimes rewards) hunters who were able to enter the woods in that state or zone of a respect so deep and honoring and respectful as to approach a trance. Connections between the woods, the hunter, and the quarry, and every other thing in the woods, animate and inanimate, were established under such conditions, with a complexity that surely exceeds any electronic circuitry or schematic wirings of man's design.

And for whatever reason, it is still in the backcountry — in the biotic integrity of wilderness not yet damaged, the wilderness still intact — where such connections are most likely to still be deeply felt.

The scientist part of me can wrestle with this piece of cultural anthropology even as the hunter part of me understands it intuitively without having to explain or defend or deconstruct it.

Writing on the etiquette and rights of hunters of the Déné people — a nomadic hunter society of Athapaskan Indians, living in the interior of British Columbia and Alaska, once including as part of their southernmost range the Kootenai-Salish country of the Yaak — a 1953 monograph prepared by the Provincial Museum of British Columbia informs us that when

> any Déné hunter made a kill, custom prevented him from using the meat himself. If he had a companion, he gave the animal to him. If hunting alone, he would skin the carcass, hang it in some safe place, and, on returning to camp, would tell someone where it was cached and that they might have it. Among certain bands this custom was modified to the extent of the hunter making a distribution of the meat among all members of his band.
>
> Another aspect of Déné hunting etiquette was for the hunter to minimize or belittle his success. If, on returning to camp, he was questioned by his companions or by his family, he invariably professed complete failure, or at least very poor luck. After some time of such stalling, he told the women of the band, or the person to whom he intended giving the meat, that there was some insignificant amount cached in the forest. This disparaging nonchalance was always expressed, even though the hunter might have made the best catch of the season.

Not only would such a tradition reinforce constantly the need to avoid, at all costs, hubris and the inevitable clumsiness that would follow such self-awareness, but it would also serve to prevent the closure of the hunt and to provide almost constantly the hunter with the tribe's gratitude and support; and to keep in place a system in which the hunter was encouraged to always keep hunting, never ending.

And further in this spirit of avoiding arrogance at all costs was the practice of rewarding the observation skills of a group. "Game shot during the course of the day's traveling always belonged not to the person who brought it down, but to the one who first sighted it."

Hunters who failed to abide by this etiquette were ridiculed by the tribe.

This is kind of a cruddy thing to say — particularly since I'm mired as deep in technology as almost any of the other six billion of us — but I keep thinking about those out-of-state hunters that Travis and I saw, the pigs of the Kootenai.

People — hunters — have always needed game. At what point in our culture, however, did technology supplant the once steadfast requirements that a hunter show utmost respect for his or her quarry?

Yet again I find reason for the protection of our last roadless lands — these last crumbs and corners of the fabric of an American landscape in which respect for the animals and their habitat, whether one is a hunter or nonhunter, remains relatively uncompromised by the buzz of snowmobiles, motorcycles, cars, and trucks.

I am not demonizing that technology: I have accepted it myself, am complicit in fossil fuel use. But I don't think such complicity prevents me from celebrating the notion that it's healthy to have as many wild places available to us as possible, places where we will always have the choice, the opportunity, of stepping away from that other, crowded, rushing, noisy world. And whether for only an afternoon, or for months at a time, no matter: places where it might even still be one of the necessary components of a culture.

I mean for this to be a journal of the seasons in a slow, quiet place — a place blessed with the rarity of still possessing four distinct seasons. A place where — as once existed in the not-so-distant past — every inhabitant knows the identity and character of every other inhabitant, every other neighbor, for forty or fifty miles in any direction. I know that someday a place like this is liable to exist only as a myth or memory; and as such, I want to chronicle it, while it lives, and celebrate it. It is not my intent to return again and again in this book to the premise of the necessity of wilderness.

But again and again, in considering the one, I find myself led inescapably to the other. It seems to me to be such an obvious solution of how to best protect the wild character of this place — those dark forests where we have not yet built roads, and where mystery still resides, emanating from those cores like steam from a river on a foggy morning. I can see nothing but the need for wilderness — as much as we're able to protect and nurture. The wilderness itself no longer reaches to the curve of any horizon, not in this country — but the need for it continues at least that far, anytime I pause to consider the question.

Wilderness does not need to be a refutation of the twenty-first century, does not need necessarily to stand in glaring contrast to a time of disease and terror and crowding and confusion. It certainly has that ability. But I like to think of wilderness as complementing rather than opposing the new century; of wilderness enriching our culture. Wilderness is not a cost, or a burden, or even a silent moral judge witnessing the awkward movements of man. It can be those things, but above all it is its own thing, and the more of it we can protect and retain, the richer and more secure we become.

Blessed with an elk early in the year, I have been able to afford the luxury of passing up bucks on the occasions that I am fortunate enough to see any, and I have to confess, it is halfway in my mind that I would like to wait until B.J. is with me before possibly being presented with the opportunity to see and perhaps even take an animal. It certainly does not work that way — the hunter never does all of the choosing, and is never capable of determining in advance on which date, if any, an animal might be taken — but still, it's in my mind that *if* it works out that way, it would sure be nice for B.J. to participate in a good backcountry hunt; and so I've been passing up shots in order to not yet kill the one deer allowed to me by permit each year. This makes me a little uneasy, with the season winding down, knowing that each little buck I see might very well be my last opportunity — only seven days left in the season, and then six, and then five.

Our plan calls for B.J. to fly up from his home in Austin, Texas, to Spokane, arriving the night before Thanksgiving, and to then wait six hours in Spokane before catching a one a.m. Amtrak that will travel east to Libby, arriving about five-thirty Thanksgiving morning. I'll drive over the summit and pick him up, and since he can only stay two days, we'll leave straight from the train station, Thanksgiving morning, to go hunt.

I pack our lunches the night before and gather gear for both of us, and clean the rifle, the bone saw, and the meat pack, should we be fortunate enough to take an animal. I go to bed excited and wake up at three-thirty the next morning and drive up and over the snowy summit, with my excitement building — perfect tracking weather — and sure enough, B.J. gets off the train, and it's great to see him.

The trouble is, however, that he hasn't slept in thirty-six hours. His house in Texas flooded that week, and he's been working around the clock nonstop, moving stuff out, and ripping up old carpet, and so forth; and furthermore, once he arrived in Spokane, having six hours to kill last night, he went to a local watering hole for much of that six hours, so that when I pick him up, he's still a little green around the gills, and going straight from the flood/plane/bar/train continuum into a daybreak assault on a snowy mountain in near-blizzard conditions does not sound particularly relaxing to him, this Thanksgiving vacation day, or especially therapeutic for what ails him.

In the train station, he stares blearily down at my hunting boots and tries to rally. He goes into the restroom and splashes water on his face, comes back out, looks out the dark window at the snow-storm, and tries to summon the desire for a dawn hunt. But it's not there, and I feel like a crazy person, a fanatic, for having even dreamed that it might be.

It's just that I'm so anxious to get him into the winter back-country, and we have so little time.

"Do you think we could go out later this afternoon?" he asks.

"Absolutely," I tell him. And driving back up and over the summit, driving through the night while he sleeps, finally sleeps, in the front seat, I know we've made the right choice, and I'm just thrilled that he's come all this way. There's nothing like having family home for Thanksgiving.

I drop him off at the house at dawn, build a fire anew in the wood stove, and get his bed set up; and then, knowing that he'll probably sleep until at least noon, I head back into the woods, for now there are only four days left in the season, and the tracking snow will be perfect, with the movements of all animals today revealed inescapably. If I should be so fortunate to find and follow and catch up with and take an animal today, B.J. can come help me pack it out in the afternoon.

There is an extraordinary fullness and sweetness to taking an animal on or around Thanksgiving, and I'm hoping that's how it will turn out this year. We have friends coming over for dinner, and I've told Elizabeth I'll help her cook, in the middle of the day — but in the meantime, the whole day stretches before me, and it's snowing steadily, perfect hunting weather, and I leave the house quietly, with everyone in it still asleep, and head up toward the high country, where the snow will be even deeper.

For the last several years I've been fortunate enough to take a white-tailed deer, which we find delicious, particularly when hung and aged for about a week. This year I have been wanting a mule deer, and have spent a fair amount of time in the upper elevations where they are occasionally found. That's what I'm looking for, this morning, and I head into one of those last wild unprotected roadless areas.

All of the nation's roadless areas in the national forests — our public lands — were briefly protected, earlier this year, for the space of a few weeks, until George Bush (the second one) took office. One of the first things he did, along with his chief of so-called justice, John Ashcroft, was to strip that protection away from the public roadless areas. (The Clinton-Gore administration had spent three years studying and then establishing that protection.) And as I move up the snowy trail in the dim dawn light, it's an uneasy feeling, knowing that although the physical character of the mountain is unchanged, the policy regarding the mountain's future, and that of others like it, has reversed completely, in the blink of an eye, even as the mountain lay sleeping beneath last winter's snow.

Is this what it's like, I wonder, for all those warring countries under Communist control, lands of ceaseless revolution and injustice, where governments, philosophies, policies, and even the names of the countries themselves, change yearly?

I'm daydreaming, walking through the early morning blue light, not really hunting, and as such, I'm surprised when, only halfway up the mountain, I spy a large mule deer back in the timber, watching me.

I think it's a buck, but I can't be sure — the light is still dim and he's back in a tangle of brush, the leafless branches of which also look like antlers — and we watch each other across a distance of perhaps a hundred yards or more, and then he breaks into a trot and I see that it is a buck, and a very big one, and then he disappears into the dense forest and the rest of the herd follows him.

I am not a careful hunter. Any animal I ever get is almost always by luck alone.

I set off up the hill after the herd, following their new tracks. I follow them for the rest of the morning, up and down and all around the mountain. I spy the nervous herd twice more, including a smaller buck, but never again that big one — and then it is time for me to head back home and cook; and weary from all the tracking, I'm glad for the break.

When I return, the house smells incredible. There's a fire going in the wood stove, beside which I can dry my wet boots and clothes, and there is the fragrance of pies and rolls baking, fresh coffee, citrus being zested for the evening recipe. Spiced tea and roasting garlic. The snow still slanting past all the windows. Music playing on the CD player, cooking music; and such domesticity helps ease me toward the necessary transition of the end of hunting season. Three and a half days left.

Peel the potatoes, slice and seed the jalapeños, dice the onions — prep work, mostly, leaving the real cooking to Elizabeth, but I do mix up some pastry dough for the dessert and set it aside to rise — and then it's time to go back up onto the mountain again, and this time, B.J., who is feeling one hundred percent better, is able to accompany me.

This is the pace I like, at this time of year — the cresting and the building. It makes no sense — the equinox has come and gone long ago, all harvest should pretty much be laid in, and any sane or balanced individual would be taking it easy, altering his or her rhythms to adjust to the foreclosure of both the days' light as well as the disintegrating year itself — but I love to keep pushing on, filling the shorter days with more energy and motion than it seems they should be able to hold. The glutton.

It seems astounding to me that yesterday B.J. was mucking around, up to his ankles in Texas floodwaters, pulling carpet and stacking boxes and making calls to the landlord, and so on, and that since that time he has flown halfway across the country and then had a night out on the town, then taken a train through the snowy darkness, across the northern tips of three states, and ridden up and over the summit, and has napped at my house, and is now getting out of the truck, high in the silent mountains, with no traffic out anywhere, and that we are starting up the trail, hunting our way toward the wilderness. Or in what passes for wilderness, in this day and age. What should remain wilderness, now and forever more.

We find fresh buck tracks less than five minutes into our walk. They are huge tracks, and I recognize them from the deer that I followed all morning. The last I had seen of him, he was on the back side of the mountain; and to find his tracks all the way down here, in so short a period of time — I've only been gone a few hours — is a little unsettling, as if, after I turned to leave earlier this morning, he followed me all the way back out, as if escorting me, as if being sure that I truly was leaving after having harassed him and his herd so much.

As with the deer that Travis and I followed a few years before, this buck's tracks are so new and fresh that we cannot be more than a few minutes behind him. He must have been standing here in the forest and heard us drive up and get out; must have heard our truck doors opening and closing, must have heard our voices.

His tracks turn around and head back up the mountain, disappearing into the dense forest; except that now he cannot disappear, not entirely, and we follow him, disappearing ourselves into that seemingly impenetrable forest, passing through snowy fronds of cedars and slipping sideways between the upright bars of lodgepoles, laboring up the hill, invisible now to the rest of the world, and as if having entered another world, the way a key enters the gears and tumblers of any one lock, and this is what I wanted B.J. to see. My Thanksgiving is already complete.

We hurry along behind the deer, as silent in the new snow as ghosts. Maybe the buck thinks we will not find his tracks. Maybe he will think that we are not going to follow him — and never mind that I followed him hard for four hours already, earlier this morning. As long as he does not hear us or scent us, maybe he will not know that he is prey.

He is not running, he is only walking, and for a while, we're excited, thinking we've got the drop on him, because he's passing through some fairly open areas — places where, if we were close enough behind him, I might be able to have a shot.

The wind is breezing from south to north, from our left to our right, and so like casters or weavers, we try to follow his tracks and yet at the same time tack northerly, to help prevent him from slipping downwind of us. We can't assume that he's just going to keep climbing straight up; and so we keep drifting to the right of his fresh tracks, trying to get out ahead of him and look back into the wind, hoping to catch a glimpse of him standing stock-still in all that timber, watching us, even if only for a couple of seconds.

That's all we need; and scanning the forest ahead for such a sight, and reading the crisp unblemished signs of his tracks — we can still be no more than two or three minutes behind him, if even that far — we are intensely alive.

The fantasy we have of possibly sneaking up on him undetected, as if coming upon him while he is merely out for a stroll in the woods, this fine stormy day, lasts for about six minutes. He must have heard a stick snap, perhaps, or the thumping of our hearts, or felt the heat of our living bodies radiating through the falling snow.

His trail soon veers directly into the gnarliest tangles of lodgepole blowdown and cedar thrash available to him — ridiculous obstacles of wind-sprung root wads, and the bristling dry spires and branches of trees long-ago dead. There are those who view our forests as but compartments of agriculture, and who believe that only a tidy, upright grove of young and quickly growing trees is of use to man and wildlife; but in trying to manage for such forests, or so-called forests, the agrarians would take away yet another of the mysteries or tools that has helped craft such rare but durable individuals as the spiny-antlered old deer that is leading us confidently on this game of cat and mouse, just a hundred yards ahead of us.

We play his game anyway. He has led us already into a black hole of blowdown where the only way out would be to turn around and go back down the mountain; and so we follow him, trying to be as quiet as we can, climbing over and under and through, but unavoidably snapping little twigs as we do so, and making little slithering leafy and brushy sounds — and yet even though we know now, beyond certainty, that he knows we're following him, we persist in the myth of the stalk, as if following some extraordinarily formal code of manners.

We continue to whisper, as if our presence — our pursuit — is still a secret; and likewise, as if obeying that same strict and formal code, up ahead of us, the deer does not panic, does not break and run but instead continues to calmly thread us deeper and deeper into the matrix of the most difficult route available to him.

Is it a waste of a sentence to say that I know we are not going to sneak up on him — that he is playing us like a yo-yo at the end of his string, even choosing the different melodies of stick-crunch and branch-snap to send us through, as if composing some kind of tune to be played on this mountainside xylophone of sticks?

It's wonderful, anyway. I want B.J. to see the inner workings of this deer's mind, incontrovertibly. The deer is smarter than we are, and stronger, and more graceful. Of course we want it.

What would it look like — perhaps seen from above, or a great distance — to see that huge deer threading his way silently over blowdown, and only fifty yards ahead of us now, but so completely in control of the situation that perhaps he is even stopping from time to time to look back and listen to our earnest but awkward pursuit?

The deer calmly evaluating the mountain around him — *knowing* the mountain around him, knowing each crevice and gully as well as if it were his own body, or his own mind, magnified a million-fold.

Our mother died when I was thirty-three, when B.J. was seventeen. I feel that I'm often aware of a breath, a pulse, of her in me, encouraging me to help keep an eye on him, to help finish the job — to help her finish the job, the job that is never finished — and though I can feel that she doesn't care in the least whether we get this deer or not — what do such things matter, anymore, if they ever did? — I can feel also that she is looking down with pleasure at the sight or knowledge of two of her boys trailing that deer through the snowy wilderness on a Thanksgiving afternoon while the entire rest of the world, perhaps, sits at the table, at the feast: two of her boys threading their way through the nearly impenetrable wilderness, as unseen to the rest of the world, in that forest jungle, as she is now to us: but again, no less real, for the not seeing.

What it is like, sometimes, is that the hunt becomes like a living thing itself, breathed into a brief life of its own there on the mountain, or in the forest, in the space between the hunter and the hunted. And that is what happens this day as we labor, to the best of our abilities, to stay up with the big deer just ahead of us — there is still no snow filling his casual, steady steps — this deer that is so clearly our physical and intellectual superior, on this mountain at least.

We hang with him nonetheless, and the hunt, or the space within the hunt, shifts and changes.

A young mountain lion slips in between us somehow, coming in from downwind — catching the scent of mule deer buck, and of the humans climbing right behind him.

The tracks suddenly before us show where the lion has come in from the north and joined in the stalk, maneuvering itself into that compressed space just behind the deer, but just ahead of us: the new tracks' heat glistening in the pressed white snow. The lion belly wriggling under the low boughs of yew and cedar and hemlock, and with its big padded feet, and the litheness of its spring-steel muscle, surely as silent as any single strand or current of water within a larger river.

For a while, the lion follows the deer directly, riding silently in that space between man and deer like an upturned leaf riding raft-like on that flowing river; but then the lion appears to make up its mind about something — as if having adjusted itself to the pace of both the pursued and the pursuers — and shifts its route out to the side, downwind, and lengthens its stride; and it seems clear to us, with the back knowledge of the tracks beneath us (as if we are read-ing time backwards, or even, briefly, as if time itself is moving back-wards), that the lion is trying to capitalize on the deer's focus on us.

The tracks are so fresh. We strain, listening for the possible sounds of struggle just ahead. A big deer, two men, and a lion are all jammed in together, all gathered within a fifty-yard sphere on this mountain, and none of them can see one another; and three of the four parties know of the existence of all the others, though it seems certain, by the deer's casual gait, that he does not yet know of the lion.

The lion's tail twitching, perhaps, as it skulks along — being sure to stay ahead of us, whom it fears, and yet using us too as a sort of decoy or stalking horse.

Seen from above, would it look like a parade? The great deer, with his huge crown of antlers like a king, and behind him, the lion, threading the same course, and behind the lion, the two men?

And behind us, what? A single raven, perhaps, following silently, flying coal black and ragged through the falling snow?

It's easy to see when time, or the river, fractures, like placid water stretching suddenly over a span of stony riffles. The great buck never panics, but he must have finally glimpsed or scented or heard or somehow sensed the lion, for he suddenly abandons his leisurely, wandering game of cat and mouse with us and begins as-cending the mountain directly, climbing straight up the steep face not like a deer now but like a mountaineer. Not lunging or running, but climbing straight up and out, traveling up a mountain face so steep that no trees grow from it; climbing through waist-deep snow, belly-deep snow; and the tracks before us indicate that, once busted, the lion follows for but a short distance before abandoning the hunt, choosing instead to conserve its calories and to try again at a later time, once it has again gathered the element of surprise.

B.J. and I, however, indulge in the luxury of not being bound by any such limitations — of being able to be ceaseless in the pursuit of our desires — and we continue on up the steep slope, warming now in our exertions, and with hearts hammering and breath coming hard: and again, I wonder what it would look like, wonder what it *does* look like, with the immense deer now staking out across the sheer mountain face, completely exposed to the world — up above timberline now — though still unseen.

We follow the deer for the rest of the afternoon. We push hard, floundering in the deep snow, thinking always that just over the next ridge we will see him, even if only briefly; and we're all the more excited by the fact that he is out in the open now, passing across wide, steep-tilted parks and meadows. Still his tracks are new cut in the storm, still he is no more than a minute or two ahead of us; and we surge to rejoin him, to connect and coincide with him; to close the distance, like one river seeking perhaps the confluence of another.

But the land, and time, will not yet have it.

Our spirits lift at one point, when, nearing the top, the buck's ascent begins to flatten out, as if he is finally growing weary of climbing straight up — as we certainly are — and I find myself remembering all the many miles I chased him around on the mountain earlier in the day. How wonderful it would be if all that work ended up having some incremental effect of fatigue on him, which might result in B.J. and I being able to finally get up on him.

He begins side-hilling, clearly tiring; but still, like a magician, he always keeps the perfect distance between us and him. The snow is coming down harder, so that he's granted extra protection beneath that cloak, and he heads around to the southern end of the mountain and then climbs up and over the final windy ridge and travels straight down the back side, back down into the dark timber of his home, as if trying now not just to escape but to break our spirit — we cannot help but think of how hard our climb back out will be, and with a Thanksgiving dinner engagement awaiting us, shortly after dark. But still we follow him, almost as if hypnotized now, betranced by some mesmerizing braid of falling snow, and our own desire, and the strange weave of the deer's daylong path.

It's as if some obsession has come over us, to be following him down the back side like that — into the deeper timber, and into the darkness. Back on the ridge, he had done the same thing Travis's deer had done — had headed straight into a herd of other deer, trying to mix his tracks among theirs — and it was this last act that gave us increased confidence that he was wearying and that he might soon make a mistake, or we would never have continued on.

We must have closed the distance considerably, over the course of our afternoon-long pursuit — thirty seconds behind him now? — because his tracks show where, for the first time all day, he has begun to run, bounding straight down the nearly vertical slope in the high-legged prance of his species: and we follow, like wolves, as quiet as we can, down a slope so steep that the snow barely even clings to it. To lower ourselves down it, we grip leafless alder and willow with our gloved hands, as if rappelling.

Perhaps, in so doing, we call his bluff. There is only half an hour of light left, and a dim cold blue light, at that — but finally, he ceases in his descent and begins angling to the north and side-hilling his way slowly back up to the ridge.

His tracks continue to pass through those of other deer — fresh tracks there too, even in the falling snow, so that we are tempted to follow those herd tracks — but his are so much larger than any of the others that it is easy to stay with him. To stay on message, as a businessperson might say.

We are a long way from our truck.

We're getting tired and sloppy, and losing our hunter's edge, I think, at a time when it should be growing sharper, with only a very few minutes left in the day. We're looking off into the dark canyon below, and at the snowy wild crags in the blue distance, as night slides in over the wilderness. And it seems to us, in the way that the icy spots of snow are striking our face, and in our exhaustion, that we are somehow in a much wilder place than when we started out, and it is all the more beautiful for that extra or added wilderness. We stop and rest, looking out at the horizon, pausing to admire the sight of such country before the night takes it away.

We can see where the buck has stopped to rest, also, and even where he must have sighted us, for his walking tracks will suddenly disappear, punctuated by long leaps, the only possible explanation for which, particularly given the state of his own fatigue, can be that he waited, looking back, to see finally in blue dusk the face or name of the thing that was following him, and glimpsed it, two upright creatures moving slowly through the dimness, and through the falling snow, only fifty yards behind . . .

Walk and run, walk and run; we close the distance with our brute endurance, and he opens it back up again, stretches it farther once more. We never see him — only the places where, looking back, he has seen us — and finally, though it is not quite yet dark, it is time to head on back, so far are we from our truck, and home. It's been a great hunt, with every single minute of it filled with the possibility of making game — *saturated* with the possibility, and at times even the likelihood, of making game — and we have no regrets.

We pause one more time to look out at the mountains, as they sink beneath the darkness — it would take us a week, in these conditions, I think, to reach even the next mountain — and then we turn back toward home, no longer hunting but merely trudging through the deep snow, passing through a forest, and in my mind, there is a feeling like I have released the buck, as if, in my letting go, I have snipped some thread or leash that has connected us all day long.

I have gotten what I needed; I have gotten what I came for.

It's snowing harder. We pass out of a grove of dark lodgepole and into a small opening, and I look downslope and see in the dimness, nearly two hundred yards away, a doe mule deer peering out from behind a tree — she too is about to pass on into the same clearing — and then I see the buck just behind her.

He is facing us, looking upslope, and has his head lowered, in the way that big mule deer bucks will sometimes do when evaluating something.

Unthinkingly — as if with the echo or momentum of desire rather than the previous burning essence of it — I raise the rifle to put the scope on him. Even at this distance, I can tell he's big — that it's the deer we've been following — but I can't find him in my scope. I've forgotten to keep it clean in the fog and snow, and now I've got to lower it quickly and rub it clear with my sleeve.

I do so, then lift the gun again, quickly — desire has now resumed its path with mine, has reentered my steps — and even at this distance, he looks immense, and I squeeze the trigger.

He is gone, vanished immediately. The doe that was standing next to him is still there, prancy now — she whirls and trots away — and the snow begins coming down harder, as if the sound of the rifle shot punctured some reserve or restraint, some previous withholding, and I watch and wait, wondering where the buck went.

There is the chance that the bullet struck him and that he is poleaxed, sleeping already the sleep of eternity — but there is the chance too that I missed him cleanly. And there is the chance also, regrettable but ever present, that he is only wounded — perhaps fatally, perhaps not — and that if B.J. and I wait quietly he will lie down to rest, unpursued, and will die quietly in the falling snow.

I don't have a clue.

Under normal conditions, we'd sit down and wait. Rushing down there isn't going to change anything: if he's dead, he's dead.

But if he's hurt, I want to know it. In this falling snow, we're not going to have the luxury of letting him lie down to die quietly. We'll have to stay with him, following him, and any spotted trail of blood he might leave, through the night, before the falling snow can obscure the blood sign of his path.

As if we might be destined to follow him forever, like the wheeling revolutions of some one set of constellations, following eternally another set, across the autumn or winter skies, night after night, and with their distance never varying.

We wait about five minutes to see if he might come back out into the opening — sometimes a startled or even slightly injured deer will retreat to the edge of the woods and then stand there for a long while, as if in a trance, before finally resuming whatever he had been doing before the shot, as if intent on completing his goals — and as we walk, I measure the distance, counting the paces.

It is a hundred and seventy-five yards to the place where he was standing — farther than I'd realized. We examine his tracks — the doe ran north, while he turned and bounded down the mountain, to the west — and I can find not even a fleck of blood, or even any hair.

Always, when a bullet exits a deer, it will cut hair on the way out. There'll almost always be a fine spray of blood, bright on the snow; but always, there is hair, long, hollow deer hair that always reminds me of larch or pine needles.

There is no hair here, no blood, only air, space, snow, absence.

I thought my aim was good; I had felt good about the shot.

I examine the tracks more closely. They look awkward to me, in a way I can't explain: not the usual choreographed dance steps of whirl-and-bound alarm, but with something else, some indecision or confusion charted in the snow — or so it seems to me, or to my subconscious. Or perhaps only to my desire.

We follow the tracks down the hill. Even though I saw nothing in the blink that followed my shot, I feel as if I should have hit this deer. That I did hit this deer.

Out in the middle of the steep clearing, there is one lone bush, a large leafless willow, its limbs and branches stark against the snowy evening.

"Look," B.J. says, pointing to the base of the tree, where there are more branches, wide branches beneath the other branches, and a dense, dark sleeping body that is being covered already with snow: vanishing already now except for the memory, our memory, of the hunt.

He's heavy. It takes both of us to pull him into the woods, where I gut him quickly and peel the cape of his hide back to help cool him down. The bullet struck him in the neck, right where I was aiming, but his neck was so massive that it absorbed the bullet so that it never exited, which is why I never found any hair or blood.

We tuck the deer in tight beneath a big lodgepole so that he won't be buried by snow overnight. I wrap one of my jackets around him so that lions and coyotes and lynx and wolverines will be less likely to fool with him — hopefully the bears are all sleeping, this late in the year — and I scrub my hands in the snow, wipe them on the green bough of a lodgepole, thank the mountain and the deer for one of the best hunts ever, thank B.J. for being part of it, and for helping with the tracking, and for spotting the big old deer, dead under that willow tree — and then, in the darkness, we start up the long slope to the ridge, and back down the mountain toward our truck.

The next day, we will sleep in until eight o'clock, and then return to quarter and debone and pack out the heavy deer, both of us struggling beneath fully loaded packs, and each dragging a deer shoulder behind us like a sled — and the day after that, B.J. will return to Texas and I will begin butchering and wrapping the deer for the freezer; but that evening, even though we have many more chores ahead of us, the hunt feels wonderfully complete, almost magically so; and all the way down the mountain in the darkness, I keep exclaiming to B.J., "Man, what a wonderful hunt that was!" and, alternately, "I so love to get an animal on Thanksgiving!" until I'm sure he must wonder if perhaps I haven't turned into a bit of a simpleton, living so far out in the wilderness, to be made so euphoric by such a simple act, the taking of one animal.

And except for the fact that he was there, he might think it so: that I was overreacting, with my pleasure. But he was there, and saw it, and felt it, and though he cannot know of the other 364 days, he knows of this one; and he understood, by the way I kept repeating it, that it wasn't just the one day I was grateful for, in being presented with that deer at dusk on Thanksgiving, but instead, the whole year: the entire year that just passed by, and the whole year to come, as we eat on that deer. Everything.

Here is what greeted us on our return to the warm, dry, well-lit house, ten minutes before dinner was to be served.

A houseful of friends, already happy and smiling, laughing, joyful, even before the news of our wonderful hunt — Tim and Joanne, and Todd and Mollie — and the girls shrieking and playing, chasing each other around the house on roller skates, and all the mixing fragrances of our Thanksgiving meal.

Someday when we are all dead and gone, not just this season's deer and elk, but this generation of mankind — someday soon enough, when we are all dust — these words will be all that is left from that evening, and for that reason, it seems important to me to put down the names of some of the dishes that night, to bear witness to some of the bounty, as I might also seek to celebrate the existence of a wild country — entire mountain ranges — no less imperiled than the foreshortened moments of our own lives, nonnegotiable against time.

The mountains, the wilderness, should be beyond that. They should be marked and measured on another scale, if on any scale at all.

The wilderness — unlike our own lives — should not be compromised, should never grow diminished: should be as immortal as we are mortal.

Whipped Yukon potatoes, grilled salmon with fennel. Spicerubbed organic free-range turkey with sage gravy, stuffed with garlic and leeks. A second free-range turkey, with a honey-lime-orange citrus glaze, and chipotle gravy. Venison backstrap, cooked rare on the grill. Southwest cornbread stuffing with corn and green chilies. Mango-cranberry chutney with Parker House rolls. Pear tarts with caramel sauce. Chocolate chess pie.

Each day is another growth ring secreted by the shell of the nautilus, or the cambium of a tree, in each and every tree in the forest. These layers of beauty, so available to the residents of this incredible place — a new concentric ring accreting in our lives with each passing day, and each passing night — anchor us, and keep us so grounded at this one level, in this one life, that there are times when suddenly it seems like a magic trick, and that although we know there are other levels, and other lives beyond our own brief existence, the specific presence of beauty in this valley seems so durable as to achieve a kind of permanence beyond our own participation in that beauty.

Our soft bodies will be in the ether soon enough, but the nacreous oyster shell residue of where we were, what we saw, who we loved and were loved by, beneath these mountains, and in these forests, and at the edge of these marshes, seems finally so durable as to become like a polished fossil, or even a gemstone: again a jade nautilus, perhaps, with a thousand or ten thousand chambers.

What it seems like, on certain evenings such as this one — our friends waving goodbye, walking out to their trucks with armfuls of food, a week's worth of leftovers, walking out to their trucks in the falling snow, calling out their good wishes, and warm and contented and sleepy and happy — is that in our lives here in this valley, surrounded by such grace and bounty and beauty and mystery, not even the voracious animal of time can eat away at this residual beauty: beauty being laid in like a store of firewood against the longest winter imaginable, but enough, more than enough, so that after winter is gone, some firewood will still remain.

And that after the soft bodies of our lives are gone, these shells, polished and worn, will somehow remain, swirling and rattling around in the currents at ocean's bottom, and making a sound, occasionally, like the clinking of fine china.

As if we filter the wilderness through us, through our lives and experiences, and that these shells we leave behind are but more pure expressions of the breath of the wilderness, as much a product of this place as the shed antler of a deer, or a feather, or even the entire skeleton of a deer, quartered and rendered and left up on a mountain while the meat and hide we carried home.

More lasting than those things, though, somehow. Not as lasting as the wilderness itself, perhaps — or as lasting as the wilderness should be — but almost.

And if not quite as lasting, or durable as shell or stone, then as enduring, perhaps, as the great larch trees, with their own slow-growth rings, which live sometimes to be six or seven hundred years and then take another hundred years or more to die, and which then after life has fully left them still remain standing for another hundred or more years; and which, after finally falling over — perhaps one millennium has passed, since they were a first seedling — might take another century or more to rot, as they become covered slowly with the shedding needles of those that follow them.

It feels that way, on nights such as this one, with the year's meat secured and our friends waving goodbye and good night: that there does not need to be any other level, or any other life before or after this one; that there is no need for the concept of eternity, for it already exists, and has as its proof the chinaware sound of those little shells, sprung from the wilderness, clinking together.

Two births: the organic birth of our lives, and then the inorganic birth, the accretion, of our shelled lives; the physical residue of whatever kind of world and breath surrounds us.

Not long after the grace of Thanksgiving, I'm due to gather with friends at the Forest Council office for a regular monthly board meeting — trying, as ever, to figure out how to raise some funds to keep our two wonderful part-time staffers hanging on, and to strategize about various upcoming community service projects, and how to best achieve wilderness protection for our wildest backcountry.

Elizabeth is out of town, and I've got the girls with me. The plan is for me to drop them off at Bill and Sue's, nearby, while I attend the meeting. Elizabeth will be home before the meeting is over and can pick them up.

And that's the way it goes, just as planned, except for a little alteration. On the steep drive down to Bill and Sue's, my slick summer tires spin on the ice and snow, and when I try to ascend the hill to their driveway above the river, my tires spin again, so much so that I must stop and back up and then try it again, with more of a running start; and even then, we barely gain the crest of that little hill.

I'm a few minutes late, and so although the thought occurs to me that I might really have trouble ascending the steep hill on the way out, I file the thought quickly away so that it's really just a little grass bur of a thing.

I drop the girls off at Bill and Sue's — the girls are delighted to get to play with Wendy and Tyler on a school night — and then hurry on to the meeting. In typical gluttonous fashion, wanting to have my cake and eat it too, I have made plans to fix a fancy supper for Elizabeth's return, but have run out of time. On my way out the door, however, I scooped up my preparations in all their varying stages of half readiness — diced onions, diced jalapeños, grated Monterey Jack cheese, sliced avocados, toasted cumin seeds, chopped cilantro, and so on — in the hopes of perhaps being able to work on the dish (black bean huevos rancheros) at the little gas stove in the Forest Council office, while attending the board meeting.

I've tossed the pots and pans I'll need into a paper grocery bag, as well as our fancy twenty-dollar metal spatula with its sleek cherry-wood handle: a spatula that makes you want to fry an egg.

I hurry on into the meeting, where, of course, there's no time to cook — the discussion is too intense, the issues too clamant to receive anything other than the undivided attention of each of us — and just about the time the meeting ends, Elizabeth arrives to pick up the girls.

I'm a little off-balance. Part of me is still clinging to the dreamy, snowy suspension of the deer hunt, and part of me is rattled, agitated by the brittle demands of the activist. Part of me is wanting to get home and cook that meal too — as if that might be some way of establishing a transition between dreamland and reality — but part of me remembers also that little grass bur of momentary tire spin on the way in, and so I tell everyone else to drive on out ahead of me, so that if I get stuck I won't be blocking anyone else's path, and for the girls to ride in Elizabeth's truck, which already has on its studded snow tires, rather than in mine, which does not yet. (Ever the cheapskate, I was hoping to get a couple more weeks' wear out of my old tires, and to save a couple of weeks' wear on my studded tires.)

Not quite uneasy, but feeling *something* — some kind of imbalance — I have the prescience, at least, to go grab some more firewood to toss in the back of my truck, for added weight over the rear axle, to give me better traction on my way up the long hill: the tilted hill that hugs the cliff that hangs out over the river so far below.

It's snowing hard, and even though the snow is piling up on the ice skin of the road, making it even more treacherous, I'm glad to see it. Except for the one year we got way too much snow, we can hardly ever get enough. Rain doesn't count — it washes away, into the Yaak River below, and then to the Kootenai, and then the Columbia, and then the Pacific. Only snow counts, as true protection against the greenhouse heat of summer, and the apocalyptic dry winds that seem to increase in both aridity and vigor each year.

I wave goodbye to my fellow board members as they drive off into the snow and up that steep, icy hill, disappearing safely into the night, secure in their four-wheel-drive trucks and Subarus, secure with their newly studded snow tires; secure in their wisdom for not having scrimped or hoarded but having instead put their snow tires on right away. Secure in their having stepped forward resolutely into winter; having turned their back, finally, on autumn, rather than lingering any longer.

I ask Elizabeth and the girls to wait for me at the top of the hill, just in case I have trouble; in case I can't get up the hill and have to back down and leave the truck overnight. I hope that's not how it turns out, for it will mean having to come back and jack the truck up and take the summer tires off and put my set of studded tires on — wrestling around in the snow rather than in a dry garage — and I'm hoping fervently to get just one more run out of those old summer tires, those old street tires.

As I start up the hill, I'm pretty acutely aware that I'm in that land of feeling two things: pleased, partly, with my wisdom, my maturity, at having sent everyone else safely on ahead of me, but uneasiness also, that niggling little grass bur of a feeling that's trying to tell me, *Bass, you're about to step in deep shit again. Why can't you be more careful?*

There is an impulsive recklessness in me, and there is an overriding and unbearable caution, a hesitancy.

The truck makes it about halfway up the hill, wheels spinning before it can go no farther. It's not stuck, in the traditional sense — it just can't go any farther; the rubber-slick tires are spinning shrilly, whining, against the sheet of ice beneath them.

Tilted up as I am on the steep pitch of the hill, I can't even see the road in front of me. I feel like an astronaut buckled in for a space launch.

There's nothing to do but back down. I'll just take it real slow and easy, touching the brake lightly, and ease back down to where I started from. There's no rush. I'll come back tomorrow, change those tires out, and start all over.

Up to this point, I have neglected to tell the reader that there is a bend in the road, a sharp bend, right there at cliff's edge. The truck has just managed, wheels spinning, to make it around this bend, and to start slowly up that final grade, so close to the top.

It'll be a little tricky, backing down around that sharp corner, but again, I'll take it as slow as is humanly and mechanically possible.

I am not unmindful of the cliff just on the other side of my truck, or the river below.

For a little while, things work fine. I back up a few inches, stop; back up a few inches, stop. Safety first. I'm hugging the inside edge, the uphill-tilted edge, trying to catch a bit of roadside snow with my left tires for some wee bit of traction, and just about the time I think I've got it whipped, the truck begins to slide, or worse than slide, really — more of a skate or a glide — with a cleanliness of movement so completely void of friction that for the tiniest of moments I am impressed by its beauty.

There is terror too, of course: the sickening, total kind, one I-can't-believe-this-is-happening kind, and a powerlessness that is absolute and astounding, as the thing that once seemed an advantage — the great workhorse weight of a big machine — is suddenly reversed to become deadweight liability, a two-ton skateboard, an avalanche, a virtual free fall.

There's no sound, only that frictionless, steady backwards skate. Ridiculously, I try to turn the wheel to navigate the sharp bend above the river. The truck is moving along backwards at a pretty good clip now, things are happening fast and then faster, and when the truck doesn't change direction at all despite the wheel being turned, I decide completely, unambiguously, to part company with it, in one of the cleanest decisions I can ever remember making.

I unbuckle and jump out just as the truck is sliding over the edge — my truck door is spread open like a bird's wing, and I have to hurry away from it to keep from being swept over the edge like some last crumb being scooped along by a dustpan — and then, just like that, I am standing unsteady on the steep sheet of glare ice, and the big truck is going over the edge backwards, being swallowed into the quiet of the night.

It looks like the *Titanic* going down, twin high-beam headlights piercing the sky vertically, illuminating the spinning spirals of snowflakes above — and what I feel, standing there clean and uninspired on the ice, is not financial remorse at having just severed myself from such an expensive piece of machinery, but instead, strangely and perhaps illogically, liberated: as if I have just shed two tons of weight, a two-ton burden. I feel light and clean and whole and imminently alive; and the grating, rasping, bouncing sound of the unpiloted truck rolling down the cliff, scraping rock and earth, seems only to accentuate this alive-ness.

I'm not there. I'm here.

After a while, the crashing stops — the night is almost immediately, instantly, peaceful again, with giant snowflakes falling softly and steadily — and almost casually, as if approaching some scenic overlook, some natural landmark of interest, I walk over to the edge and look over it and see that the truck has stopped about a hundred feet downslope, pinned on its side against an immense and ancient and unmoving Doug fir. The crazy, plowed-up trail of snow looks like the staggering last steps of some great heart-shot mythic beast, and because the headlights are still on, I climb down the slope carefully and crawl into the side-tipped truck (opening the driver's side door as if lifting the hatch to a submarine), and turn the lights off.

In a little while, I know, Elizabeth will come driving back down the road, worried, and will see where my new-snow tracks leave the road and vanish over the edge, and will be further worried, perhaps even alarmed, and I hurry back up the slope so that I can walk out to the upper road before that happens.

The tracks, the furrows of black earth and stone, are already being covered, so heavily is the snow falling, and all over the hillside, I'm finding various Ziploc bags and pots and pans from the dish I'd intended to cook, which spilled out as the truck went down the slope.

How fiercely we cling to the mundane; how stubbornly we grasp at ritual and routine! Like some hillside berry harvester, I pause, trying to gather all of the spilled accouterments — the bag of smashed Roma tomatoes, which were meant to be diced anyway, and the avocados, which at a dollar nineteen a whack are not to be left behind, if possible; and I search in vain for my twenty-dollar spatula, casting up and down the hill for it, and going back into the submarine of a truck to search for it, all to no avail; and when Elizabeth comes creeping back down the hill in her truck, peering over the edge to see me climbing back up, hand over fist, that is the first thing I say to her: "I'm okay, but I can't find the damn spatula."

There's certainly nothing to be done tonight. The back of the truck bed is wrapped around that old Doug fir like a crumpled-up gum wrapper — the word *unpeel* comes to mind when considering possible extrication — though what kind of machine might be capable of setting up on the glare-ice road above and hoisting the truck up a hundred feet of cliff, I can't imagine — some sort of military helicopter, perhaps, next spring — and I'm fairly certain that this is going to be the final resting place for my truck, that here it will lie forever, with birds eventually building nests in the engine block, and wild roses sprouting up through dusty cracked windows. Though again, what concerns me in the moment is that wonderful spatula.

It's snowing so hard that if I don't find it quickly, it'll be buried until March or April, and so I take a flashlight from Elizabeth's truck and once more canvass the cliff, though again with no luck.

I ascend the hill one last time, climb into her nice warm dry truck, safe, and we drive quietly home, through swirling snow. I do not try to explain to her about how liberated I feel — though she knows what I mean about the spatula, and laments its possible loss too.

"It'll be there in the spring," she says. "It's got to be around there somewhere."

The girls are pretty quiet, asking to be sure I'm okay.

"I wouldn't have gone up that hill if y'all had been in the truck," I tell them. "We'd have walked up."

"You're sure you're okay?" they ask.

"Absolutely," I tell them. "Just fine." But they're quiet, all the way home, thinking things over, even if I am not, quite yet.

In the morning, after we drop the girls off at school, Elizabeth takes me back over to the cliff. The truck is still there — the great hulk of the Doug fir has not somehow decided in the middle of the night to release it, like an angler turning a caught fish back into the river — though because of all the snow that has fallen, it appears at first that the truck has vanished, that it is no different from any of the other hillside boulders, snow shrouded, as if sleeping. Only the black tires, two of which are up in the air, like the hoofs of some recently expired and newly stiffening ungulate, draw notice to the fact that there is a truck down there in the woods, at the bottom of the cliff.

I'm worried that we might have to saw that magnificent tree down to get the truck out. I don't see how any engine of man can pull that truck back up over the cliff, and am thinking a lane, a path, may need to be cut through the woods, for a distance of fifty or sixty feet, to reach the little dirt road farther below, the little river road that is my neighbor Monroe's driveway.

I've called Monroe, have asked if he can take a look at the situation and come up with any ideas. Monroe has both a snowplow and a backhoe, and he does much of the valley's heavy work. He's a large, bearded man who sometimes dresses as a werewolf at Halloween and Santa Claus at Christmas, fitting each part equally well. Monroe is perhaps most recognizable to us in the valley from a distance not by any certain silhouette or bushiness but because he will be the one not wearing a coat.

Almost always, only jeans and a T-shirt. In the most inclement weather, perhaps some kind of long-sleeve canvas shirt. But ninety-nine winter days out of a hundred, just a T-shirt.

Elizabeth heads on home — she'll come back and check on me later in the afternoon, when she comes back to pick the girls up — and I walk down the snowy drive to Monroe's. The roads are icier than ever, which last night I would not have thought was possible, and several times, even in the simple act of walking, walking on flat and level ground, I slip and fall so hard that I bounce back up into the air, hitting so hard that my teeth are jarred — it's a bad time of year for vertebrae — and yet I keep getting up cheerfully, the residue of my luck from the night before still so fully upon me that I still feel light and unburdened, liberated, even almost untouchable. The snow world around me seems to be vested with the full potential of its almost unbearable and overwhelming beauty — that is to say, on this day, this day after, the fullness of the beauty that must surely be always present but which is for whatever subtle reasons of plaque, accrual, and routine too often obscured from us. And unless it is only my imagination, other people I encounter on this day after, friends, seem to be feeling or witnessing this same common little revelation of how clean and fine and wonderful the world is: as if it did not have to be any of them who leapt from the plunging truck and was saved but that merely hearing or knowing of the story is enough to remind them of that larger beauty.

Like most of us, I hate asking for things, if only because I hate in particular hearing the word *no*. I don't even like to say the word myself, but I sure don't like taking the risk of putting myself in a position where someone else can say that word. This isn't a particularly admirable trait, I know, but there you have it. And to my small credit, I'm getting better.

Asking Monroe for help, for instance: knowing, even as I do, that like all of us, he is overloaded with deadlines. It's not unusual to wake up on a winter night and look out the window and see him plowing your driveway in the middle of the night, rooster tails of sparks flying from his chains and snowblade as he scrapes back down to the grit and gravel, sparks flying like fireworks even in the midst of a swirling snowstorm.

Monroe greets me in his tool yard. Today he's wearing his navy blue T-shirt. "I looked at it this morning," he says. "We can get it out. There's a lot of different options we can try, a lot to choose from, but we can get it out. It just might take a while," he says. He tells me that he had planned to drive over the mountain to go to town today — to put studded tires on his own truck, in fact, in addition to other chores and jobs and errands — but that what the heck, he's already running late anyway, so it won't hurt as bad to put it off another day: a Yaakish kind of logic that makes perfect sense to me.

I'll spare the reader a blow-by-blow description of the various methods we attempted, but it was like a magic trick, the way an entire morning vanished simply to the logistics of digging cables here and there under the snow, attaching chains and cables here and there, going back down the hill to look for more cables, setting up sawhorses to close the icy road, sliding off the road in Monroe's big truck two or three times (though never, fortunately, over the big cliff). At one point, we came around the corner in Monroe's truck (we'd driven into Yaak to see if the gravel pit was open, to get gravel to spread on the icy road for better traction before beginning our labors) only to encounter a little tiny two-wheel-drive car coming up the driveway, the kind of vehicle that a car rental company would call a subcompact, or maybe some newer classification denoting a craft even more minuscule than that.

The little car was coming up the hill and around that corner at a pretty good clip — *I think I can, I think I can* — and Monroe hit his brakes, and the other driver hit her brakes, right at the spot where I'd gone off.

Since they were coming uphill, they were able to stop; Monroe's heavy truck, on the other hand, locked up and began sliding down the hill.

I could see the people in the little car making horrified faces. It was a family of three generations, all on their way to Bible school — grandma, daughters, and itty-bitty baby, half a dozen people squeezed into that little sled of a car — and, certain that Monroe's big truck was going to slide right into them and thump them over the cliff like a well-placed cue ball smacking its target into some corner pocket, I jumped out again and ran alongside Monroe's twisting, skating truck, running toward the petrified occupants of the tiny car, holding out my arms and saying, "Give me the baby! Roll down the window and give me the baby!"

Ridiculous stuff.

Monroe's truck bumped theirs, and sure enough, knocked it lightly backwards, but only a short distance; so slow had been his skid that there wasn't quite enough mass and momentum to send them (and perhaps Monroe, likewise) over the cliff. Baby, mama, auntie, grandmother, sisters — all were safe. Or so it seemed.

Everyone climbed out of the vehicles and congregated around the scene: ashen and terrified and joyful all over again. Everyone checked to be certain everyone else was all right, and then Monroe got in his truck to back it up to the top of the hill, which wasn't so far away.

He was only able to go about ten feet, however, before his tires began to spin, as mine had the night before — and like in some eternally damned time loop, he began sliding back down the hill once more, heading straight for the little car, and the whole gaggle of us, baby and all.

Like alarmed deer, we leapt in all directions — some down the hill, others of us up the hill — while the owner of the little car rushed out and waved her arms at Monroe's sliding truck, as if trying to ward it away with hoodoo.

Once again, his truck slid into the little car; and once more, miraculously, it held its ground.

There was nowhere to go but down. Like an astronaut, Monroe climbed into their little car and backed it down the hill, one inch at a time, and was able to safely reach the bottom, where the family rejoined their car and decided to turn around and go back home rather than attempting the hill, and church, that day.

It's at that point that we give up on all our various plans. "Let's just go home and call it a draw," I say, "and try again in a few days, when the ice isn't so bad." It's impossible to even stand up without holding on to a tree, or the side of a truck. But just as we have reached that agreement, another neighbor, Chuck, who has heard all the commotion, comes wandering down to investigate.

Chuck has a big old skidder that he sometimes uses for logging, a machine even bigger and more powerful than Monroe's backhoe, and with the hopeful arrogance of a man who might think his racehorse is a little faster than it really is — or so it seems to me — Chuck says, "I believe I can get that truck out."

Trees and deer: the fabric as well as the foundation of our lives up here. With a jury-rigged assemblage of mismatched chains and hasps, we fashion Chuck's belching skidder to a giant Doug fir that leans out of the slope above us. The tree will serve as Chuck's anchor, it is hoped, to keep him from being pulled over the edge of the cliff during his labors. I ask out loud the question for which Chuck does not have an answer — "What if it pulls that leaning tree out of the ground?" — but his opinion is that it probably won't, that the power of roots, even on a steep hillside, is significant: sufficient for the task, if not quite the miracle requested.

The machine disgorges a clatter of ancient valves and a burst of black diesel smoke, and Chuck lowers the stabilizing legs onto the ice, planting them two-square, like the abdominal dabbing of some arachnid, probing the ice, positioning itself for some kind of predatory excavation, or settling in for a war of besiegement.

From the skidder, we unwind a long choker cable, to which —

surprise! It's not quite long enough — we have to knot another one, and attach it to the back end of my truck.

The plan is simple: elegant to me in its shocking reliance on brute strength.

In the first phase, Chuck will pull the tail end of my truck up the hill, unwrapping it from the tree's clutches and lining it up so that it's aiming straight down the cliff, dangling from the end of the skidder's winch cable like a plumb bob; and after reeling the truck in a few feet, to make sure it's hanging straight, Chuck will employ a kind of reverse Yaak logic, unspooling the cable, letting the weight of the truck and the cliff grasp of gravity pull the truck slowly (one spool click unwinding at a time, hopefully) down the cliff, weaving its way through the trees, over stumps and boulders, to the lower road, farther below.

And that's how it works. Once he gets the back end pulled off the tree and the truck is straightened out, I climb in and buckle up, and it's like a carnival ride, one of those Ferris wheels in which the bucket, the cage, spins upside down so that you're staring directly at the ground.

I'm strapped in like a fighter pilot, already pulling G's, even at a standstill. A little audience is gathered at the bottom, watching. If the tree that Chuck's anchored to cracks, or if one of the jury-rigged cable knots breaks, or if the winch fails, or the cable otherwise pulls free of my salt-rusting old truck, things will get more interesting than they already are, and with a river looming below me like the possible landing site for a ski jumper, I've already prepared myself to leap from the truck again, if need be. For the time being, though, I will keep my harness snug around me as I try to help navigate the truck through the forest, down the last of the sixty-degree slope, steering in slow motion around boulder, stumps, and trees.

Far up above, Chuck lets out the first gear click of winch spool, and the truck shudders as it eases roughly down its first foot of terrain. Coins, plastic forks, sections of unread newspaper, gloves, baseball caps, and wrenches all go hurtling past my ear and fall against the windshield, then slide down into various dashboard heater apertures, like small rodents ducking back into their burrows — some perhaps to disappear forever, while others might eventually trickle out through the carriage to the ground below, so that it might be possible, if we ever get the truck out, to come back some years later and track the strange path of our descent as if following the spoor of some wounded animal.

Another spool click and the truck lurches another foot closer to the river, and yet another foot closer to freedom. Like a running back drifting along the line of scrimmage, peering through the seethe of bodies tangled before him, I can see a little lane that has opened slightly to the left, and I crank the wheels that way, and Chuck lets out another length of spool. We slide into that gap successfully, and then, perhaps emboldened by his success, Chuck begins letting the line out more steadily, and it's more frightening that way, and yet it's also bringing us closer to success faster, and so I hang on tightly and try to steer the vertical truck, feeling supremely awkward and yet ridiculously, vaguely hopeful, as when on occasion one might get suckered into playing one of those coin-slot gripping-talon games such as are found at carnivals or in pizza parlors, in which the victim, the sap, tries, through clumsy maneuvering of oversize toggle switches, to direct a three-pronged claw into a pile of purple stuffed teddy bears and other useless clutter, attempting to latch on to one of the those bright objects of desire.

There is no clutter before me, however: only snow and forest and mountains and river. The irony is not lost on me that for much of the last twenty years I've been working hard, along with other local residents and activists, to protect the last public lands where we the taxpayers have not yet built roads on our national forest, and yet here I am, driving anyway, through the forest where there is no road — even if only for fifty feet, and even if only across a little wedge, not of national forest but of private ground, caught between two other roads — a higher one, and a lower one.

Actually, as I get closer to the bottom — closer to safety — it's kind of fun, and it occurs to me that were some of the extreme motorheads to witness this, it might give them new ideas for recreational activities and the national forests: that they might soon clamor to bring cranes and cables to their favorite cliffs and canyons of the public lands and lower themselves spinning over the edge in similar fashion when bored on some certain Sunday afternoon.

The last part is the steepest — a little three-foot sheer ledge, like a ski jump. There's a thumping and scraping beneath me, and I'm traveling faster, careening through brush and dry branches, and then suddenly, like a deer bounding from out of the woods, I'm out onto the icy road and then am crossing it, my brakes useless once again, and out into the snowy field that lies between the lower road and the river.

I reach the end of my tether, though, and now all Chuck has to do is reel me back a bit to that lower road, which he does; and I climb out and unhitch the cable.

Both Monroe and Chuck refuse to accept any payment for their day's labors, saying that they like the feeling of doing a good deed every so often, and so in the end all I can tell them is that I was happy to be of service. (Later that year, on a drive into town, Elizabeth will find Monroe ditch-skidded off the road, and will pull him out.) Another neighbor, Geoff, has helped us shovel a truckload of gravel into Monroe's truck, and the three of us spread it up and down the long icy hill, and then it's time for me to drive home.

It's nearly dusk, and though I've finally changed into my studded tires and we have some of the new gravel on the road, there's still very much the feeling of climbing right back on the horse that has thrown you — but this time the truck makes the corner and climbs right on out, slipping and spinning only a little right at the top. My truck is running a little rough — some crankcase oil evidently spilled into the old worn valves during the night, while the truck rested on its side — but by nightfall, I am safe and warm and dry in my own home, alive and well, and still encased in that cyst or cocoon of shimmering, lucid grace where time slows and, again, the world's full beauty is revealed in every glance, and every moment.

It is a wonderfully light and luminous feeling, one that cannot and will not last forever, it seems, but it is with me that evening, and even for several days afterward; and the distance between what is versus what could have been is both as steep and vast and yet as hairline minute as it ever was. It is only that on this occasion I have been permitted to walk all the way to the edge of that constant gulf and peer down into it — as if into an abyss — and witness, with all of my senses, how narrow the breach is in that gulf, and yet how infinitely deep also the chasm is.

To witness it, but then turn away; to turn back.

Even after the cocoon of grace and heightened awareness has been worn down by the passage of time, traces of it will remain, however — not just on me, but, it seems, on my family. Months later, Lowry will misplace a treasured candy bar in the back of my cluttered truck: one of those big, supremely expensive dark chocolate bars, for which some of the proceeds go to help protect the habitat of this or that endangered species — grizzlies and swans, flamingos, polar bears, manatees — and we search and search for it but cannot find it.

She's disappointed, of course, and so I go back out again and keep looking; it's only been missing for a couple of days. And finally, I find it, and she's elated.

It will have been months since the accident, or near accident, at the time I am speaking of now — we will not have discussed or even mentioned it for weeks — but as if from out of the blue, and overjoyed to have found her candy bar, Lowry will say, "It sure is a good thing you didn't die when your truck went over the cliff, Dad."

At first I laughed, thinking she meant, *Who else would be able to find my candy bar in the back of your truck?* Which is what a six-year-old *should* say.

But now, in the remembering, I think she was just remembering the general upside-downness of things in the truck the day after I returned home. The way some things can change — can be turned completely upside down — even as other things, such as a father, can and must forever, stay constant. And that while for me one lingering story or memory will be my liberating leap from the plunging truck, a story or deep-set memory for the girls might be seeing where my tracks went off the road and disappeared, and yet at the same time that they were witnessing that, they were also seeing me come climbing back up the slope, up through the snow and out of that chasm, illuminated in headlights and swirling, falling snow. *Everything's fine, don't worry. Everything's going to be fine.*

Nothing is ever always fine, of course, but how nice for children, growing children, to believe that story, that myth, so that they are free then to focus their energy and attention on the wonders and beauty of the world, worry-free.

While we adults, likewise — as we come increasingly to understand how impermanent everything is, or almost everything — are similarly helped to focus on the same message, the same understanding, even if coming to that understanding from the other end of the spectrum.

Shyly, Lowry breaks off a piece of her candy bar and hands it to me — and whether as reward or communion, I cannot be sure. I know only that it is delicious, and I remember, for a few moments all over again, what it was like, to be in that cocoon of grace: immersed in the world not just of luck and chance but also of the concern and assistance of my neighbors.

Everything.

DECEMBER

....

DRAMA! ON THE DAY of the school Christmas play, Wendy, who is to play the lead actress, is sick, throwing-up-and-fever sick. Her part in *Santa Claus and the Wicked Wazoo* is that of none other than the Wazoo herself, and as an eighth-grader, it's her last year to be in the play before she graduates and heads on to high school down in Troy. Her classmate, Karen, can't take her part, because Karen is Mrs. Claus, who is often in the same scene as the Wicked Wazoo (whose goal it is, of course, to spoil Christmas).

If Wendy doesn't rally, it'll be up to Mary Katherine to learn the part — not just the forty lines, but the timing, blocking, entrances and exits, the whole structure — in addition to keeping her part as "Martha, a peasant girl." (There are only five girls in the Yaak school this year — the eighth-graders, Wendy and Karen; Mary Katherine in fourth grade; Lowry in first grade; and Cheina in kindergarten.)

Mary Katherine doesn't find out about this until midmorning on the day of the play, but takes right to the task; she and Karen spend the day practicing, and when Mary Katherine comes home that afternoon, she's cool as a cucumber, casual and confident: not arrogant, just confident. If anything, she's subdued, because it's Wendy's last year. But about her lines, and their delivery, she's confident, with neither stage fright nor overconfidence: just another day in paradise.

Either Elizabeth or I would be jittery; and I can't help but think that this low-key nonchalance on Mary Katherine's part — a native durable confidence rather than the affected confidence of bravado — is one of the products of place, one of the myriad benefits of a small school, the two-room log school, in which all the different grades sit together, and interact every day, year in and year out, like family — learning lessons such as responsibility and friendship and loyalty in addition to all the prescribed traditional curricula.

She's not nervous, I think, because she has everyone's support.

And no one else is nervous because there's so much trust and team-work. The two teachers, Jeannette and Bill, have been working with the students for almost a month, and so accustomed have I become to the easy familiarity of the little school — the older students help-ing to teach and take care of the younger ones, and the younger ones benefiting from all that "extra" instruction (and learning the model of leadership that they'll grow into, as the older ones gradu-ate) — that it's easy for me to forget that it's not necessarily like this in other schools. I try not to ever take it for granted, how wonderful this opportunity is for the girls, for all the students, and how much strength it will give them as citizens of the twenty-first century, to have had this log-cabin experience — but still, I've become ac-customed to it, even if I don't take it for granted, and it is moments like Mary Katherine's and the other students' poise that remind me again of the fuller value of that rarity. Her response, and their response — taking confident pleasure in the arrival of a challenge rather than melting down into the jitters — is probably the normal or "natural" one, whereas the self-induced nervousness that Eliza-beth or I would encounter, though common, a less natural re-sponse . . .

It's a big deal, this Christmas play. Every year, the whole com-munity shows up, hermits and all. The plays are always wonderful, and there are cookies and cakes, and after the play, the kids and community sing Christmas carols, there in the log cabin commu-nity center, up near the Canadian line, in the middle of the forest, more than forty miles from the nearest town, and it's just nothing but sweet. Some years there's a hayride afterward.

And this year, like all the other years, goes off perfectly. It's the strangest thing, hearing Mary Katherine's deep, maniacal laugh booming from behind the curtain, preceding the Wazoo's villain-ous entrance. It's like, *Okay, if she's determined to grow up, I can still be proud of her;* and though I knew already how proud of her I am, how proud of both girls, it is a revelation, and a growing-up on my part, to see her come swashbuckling out from behind the curtain, still booming that laugh of the great Wazoo, determined to spoil Christ-mas. It's so strange to see her giving the community, the audience of adults, a gift.

And I feel the same sensation when Lowry, in her pink glittering ballerina suit, comes twirling out center stage, hands poised over her head in graceful, elegant ballerina pose — the Dancing Doll — and cries out, "Help, help!"

Every parent feels it, and every audience member, this most excellent gift by the children to the community that supports them — but for me, with my hermit- or recluse-like tendencies, it's a profound witnessing to see that I don't necessarily have to pass on all of my less-than-wonderful attributes to my children, and that they will likely be better in the world for it; and that already, they have something to give to the world, and are giving it.

All the children are giving it, breathing the breath of Christmas more fully into the community: Mike (whom, as an eighth-grader, and having killed his first deer this year, a monster whitetail buck, we can no longer call "Mikey") as a great Santa Claus; Karen as the calm and confident Mrs. Claus; Jed as the boisterous singing leprechaun, the true star of the show; Kilby, Luke, Levi, and Noah as sly trolls, dressed in camouflage, out to steal Christmas; Kyle as a happy elf; Lowry as the Dancing Doll; Zachary and Cheina as fairies.

Outside, it's snowing hard. The pew benches in the community center are packed shoulder to shoulder, and the wood stoves are popping. Over the course of the coming year, as with every year in small western towns, there will be disagreements among the adults, fears and accusations and misunderstandings, and sometimes the plain old-fashioned chemical imbalances of humanity — disagreements between individuals, between neighbors — but this evening, at least, the beauty and purity of the children fills the cabin with a love so sweet and dense that after the play is over we linger, not wanting it to end; and when we open the door finally and step outside into the falling snow, that love is adhering to us. Some of it goes sliding out the door like warmth spilled, and off into the night, and into the woods, but a lot of it stays with us, I think, and travels home with us, and stays in us for a good long while, I hope. Peace on earth and goodwill to men.

Such are the cycles of our lives — the regularity and repetitions of rhythms, here in this place-that-is-still-a-place, this forested island that still seems to be governed somewhat by its own system of time rather than always mankind's — that the end of one thing can feel also like the beginning. December is that way, as the last of the deer or elk is cut and wrapped and frozen, if a hunter was fortunate enough to receive one: the coming year's meat stored away safely. The snow is always down to the valley floor by December — another beginning — and while the rest of the world, including our relatives in the more civilized places, enter into the full frenzy of the Christmas season, things are so much quieter up here, amid a complete absence of malls, though in that quietness, emotions are no less deeply or passionately felt. It's just quiet and slow, is all — like walking in soft new snow at dusk.

The days are shorter, but with the hunting season behind us and the pressure of making meat lifted, we can sleep later. We can spend any free time we might have skiing too instead of hunting. It's the beginning of rest, of sleep, of play; the beginning of being able to spend even more time with family. We begin wrapping jars of huckleberry jam, for gifts, and take the girls out into the snow for the annual Christmas card picture. Elizabeth gathers boughs of cedar and pine with which to make beautiful wreaths — she and half a dozen other women in the valley gather to spend the days making these wreaths, and then mailing them, fresh-scented, to friends and family in the outside world — and though the days are shorter than ever, and still usually sunless, they feel also brighter and newer, with all the clean white snow.

The children, having warmed up on Halloween, and then Thanksgiving, are fully into the dreaming (Lowry's still a true believer, but Mary Katherine's dubious about Santa — though as the days progress, I notice that Mary Katherine comes back across the line, if even for only one more year, and it is a sweet and wonderful thing to see, made all the more special by the knowledge that surely this is the last year), and their Christmas lists are posted on the refrigerator. I suspect that they're as cutthroat and mercenary as any children anywhere — it's not like they'd be thrilled with but an orange in their stocking and in a good year maybe a candy cane — but I have to laugh at Lowry's list: a pencil and pencil sharpener, a Barbie (I know, I know), and, most curiously, a bottle of whiteout. And even Mary Katherine's list is somewhat of a relief: books and CDs, a new pair of snow boots, and a pair of ski goggles.

Like a cliché of a cliché, or as if in a dream of a dream, the holiday season begins for us, I think, on the day that we go to get the Christmas tree.

For as long as the girls have been able to walk, they've gone into the woods with me each year to find a tree — always a young Doug fir, a species that is overabundant in many of our fire-suppressed forests, and in need of thinning, literally by the millions — but finding the perfect one is never easy. Any tree is beautiful in the forest, but we only had to bring one home one year, pleased with it ourselves, only to hear Elizabeth's considerably more subdued reaction, to vow never again to settle for anything less than perfect.

What once sometimes took us half an hour now takes us an hour, sometimes an hour and a half: and though the pleasure is in the hunt, there is pleasure also each day and night thereafter in admiring the tree all throughout the holidays.

I prepare the girls for it, the cutting, as I would were we to be going on a real hunt; on Sunday night, before they get ready for bed, I tell them that when I pick them up after school on Monday I'll bring their cross-country skis and we'll go out and look for the tree. And the fact that they're as thrilled with this news as if it were Christmas itself pleases me greatly, and though I know they love having regular markers of tradition and security in their lives, I know also that I love it as much as they do, and perhaps more.

It's bitterly cold when I pick them up, about fifteen degrees, but with a rare breeze that makes it feel closer to zero, and the sky is its usual beautiful ragtag mix of purple and gray clouds, with more snow coming any minute. I've brought a thermos of hot chocolate, and on the way home we share a cup of it, drinking it out of the screw-on top like duck hunters, and then we turn into the little road where we always turn, and get out where we always get out.

We engage in a brief snowball fight, and then I buckle on my snowshoes, and they put on their skis, and we start up the rocky ridge, which is now covered with snow.

The skies are beautiful — the color of plums, the color of the back of a seagull, the color of sharks, the color of oyster shells — and we take turns breaking trail through the new snow like explorers, and it pleases me that the girls remember where we are going from all the other years. They're bundled up with as many clothes and coats as they can wear, and I have more of my own larger coats in my backpack, along with the thermos.

It pleases me to see what natural backcountry skiers they are, having grown up on them — such a strange difference from my own south Texas upbringing — and those beautiful skies hanging dense above the somber blue-green mountain, and amid the stark winter forest through which we're skiing, also elevate my spirits, even at a time when biologists or physicians might tell us that they should not be elevated as we enter more fully now the depths of winter and its at times extreme lightlessness — and I can't tell who is happier, me or the girls.

As we move on through the woods, seemingly the only living creatures out and about in this vast snowscape and sleeping forest, there is a spirit that accompanies us, that emanates from the three of us — a *happiness,* to use an old and worn word — that braids together to form a larger whole; and in accompanying my daughters up the ridge, I can sense and at times taste the flavor not just of that new-made happiness but even of their own elemental happiness, which I remember, dimly now, from my own childhood thirty-five years ago.

I fear that I'm not saying it clearly. In my experience, it's rare for an adult to experience, ever again, the happiness of a child. There are a million different sorts of adult happiness, mixed in with perhaps a million different nuances — satisfaction, pride, relief, euphoria — but what I feel, moving up that hill with my daughters in the soon-approaching winter dusk, self-sufficient, for the time being, on our skis and snowshoes, and moving deeper into the woods, is a child's happiness, and I cannot remember having felt that in a long, long time.

Once we reach the ridge, we begin to encounter the young Doug firs growing in between older lodgepoles and larch, and again, the girls are old enough this year to be good judges of physical character: bypassing weaker or asymmetrical trees and judging also which trees are too large and which are too small. Making guesses, and mental notes, about certain trees that we might be able to come back and examine in years hence. But searching, still, for this year's.

We look for a long time. The wind blurs our eyes and sometimes makes far-off trees look better than they really are; we'll ski and snowshoe down into a bowl or ravine and up the other side to some such tree, only to discover upon reaching it that it's not even remotely like what we're after.

For a long time now, we have been bringing back a perfect Christmas tree, one that even Elizabeth will acknowledge is perfect, with every branch, every needle, balanced and symmetrical — a tree with a beauty that is somehow magnified in looking at it, compounded by each tier of branches until surely its beauty exceeds any possible summation of its parts — and though the girls are not aware of any sort of pressure, are unable, I'm sure, to imagine anything other than success, simply because that is all they've ever known, in this one tradition, I'm less secure; and as the dusk deepens, we travel farther, looking hard.

We pass over the stippled, methodical trails of deer, and the seemingly aimless tracks of snowshoe hares; across the tracks of a mountain lion, one that has probably not eaten in a while, and is probably hungry, because we do not hear any ravens squabbling over the remains of a kill nearby, and so I keep the girls close to me.

We're all three beginning to grow chilled, and so we duck down into a little ravine, a windbreak, and huddle beneath the shelter of a big spruce tree, as if in a little fort or clubhouse, and share another cup of hot chocolate. I bundle them further, putting my heavy overcoats on over their own, and make sure their mufflers are snug; and warmed now, they're ready to play again, and climb back up out of the ravine, herringboning on their skis, only to ski right back down, again and again.

They're laughing, shrieking, and I do not want to caution them to conserve their energy, to not tire themselves out; I do not want to counsel moderation to their joy, though I am concerned that we're so far from the truck, and with the hour so late, and the evening so cold.

Carefully, cautiously, trying hard not to disrupt the spirit of their play, I begin to ease and urge them back toward the truck — not following our old tracks, but triangulating. They're still looking up from time to time, evaluating various trees, but in their happiness, and in the fast-fading light, their evaluating skills seem also to be diminishing, and a couple of times they urge me to take a tree that, in my opinion, is less than perfect: recommending one because it is "cute," and another because it is "stately."

We drift on, buoyed by happiness, floating above the snow on our skis, our snowshoes.

We find the perfect tree right at dark. I spy it initially, and at first hardly daring to believe our luck, snowshoe over to it without saying anything, wanting to be sure. I call the girls over, ask them to check it out and see what they think — wanting unanimity — and even though I think they are taking our eventual success for granted, they're very excited by the beauty of the tree, and after double-checking to be sure they're sure this is the one they want, I take my saw out of the pack, tell the tree and the forest thank you, out loud, like a pagan, and then saw through the sweet green bark and sap, and the tree leans over slowly, softly, lightly, and settles into the snow.

We head back to the truck, taking turns pulling it. It's surprisingly hard work, and the tree's needles leave a beautiful wandering feathery trail behind us, completely erasing our tracks.

Unprompted, as darkness settles, the girls begin singing "Jingle Bells," and then, right after that, with no prior sort of communication save that unspoken kind that exists between sisters, they break inexplicably into the chant of a street-side political rally, a protest, really, that we witnessed (all right, participated in) a few years ago: "What do we want? De-moc-racy! When do we want it? *Now!*" And in a strange and silly singsong way, the chant seems to make perfect sense, out in the middle of the unpeopled forest, in the deep cold, beneath the gathering night, unseen and unheard by anyone other than our own selves. It is a catchy chant, fitting perfectly, it seems, the cadence of our progress through the snow, so that it could be the mantra for boot camp marching Marines, or Arctic explorers seeking to make a certain destination just before a storm hits.

By the time we reach the truck, we're all three cold again, and after loading the tree into the back — it fills the bed, and even lying on its side, looks perfect — I warm the truck up and we sit there in the cab, vapor breathing and clouding the windshield, and drink more hot chocolate before turning around and driving the short distance home, where, upon our arrival, Elizabeth comes out onto the porch to inspect that which we have brought home to her.

She looks it over carefully.

"It's perfect," she says, finally.

Long after the tree is gone, and the year, I will remember that afternoon.

When we first moved up here, I used to believe that the people I heard complaining about winter's length, and particularly winter's lightlessness, were malingers, nabobs of negativity — chronic light-weights deeply entrenched in the hapless pattern of seeing the cup as being half empty instead of half full. I looked at them as a callow youth looks at an aging person and believes or at least suspects that the physical diminishment of age must surely be due at least in part to some sort of character flaw, so unimaginable is that diminishment to the youth, in his or her full strength, and having known only its increase, day after day and year after year.

All I saw, my first several winters, everywhere I looked, was beauty.

I still see winter's beauty, in every glimpse, but like those old-timers who pined for the sun and lamented its absence, I too miss it deeply, desperately now, in winter, and have come to believe that winters up here can have a debilitating cumulative effect: that they are like concussions, wherein the first one or two seem to have no lasting or even negative effects, until suddenly — or so it seems — you wake up after your eighth or ninth, or tenth or eleventh, and have difficulty remembering your name, and do not always recognize the face in the mirror.

Scientists, of course, are discovering the neurochemical and physiological causes of these traumas, these debilitations — seratonin disruptions, seasonal affective disorder, and so on — and there are drugs and medicines and treatments that can be prescribed now to try to counter the brute force of the phenomenon — sunlamps, vitamins, Prozac, and strategic trips to the Caribbean.

More and more each winter, however, when I catch myself in the throes of lightlessness — staring slack-jawed out a dusty window at the dim light, unblinking and incognizant of any one coherent thought — I find myself understanding the biological adaptations of not just the species that migrate but the bears, with their deep sleeps of hibernation. It seems to me often, in winter's midst, that I have entered a quasi hibernation myself — a mental hibernation — and I am reminded yet again of how closely we are all wedded to this landscape, shaped and sculpted by it and always at some level attentive to it, as it in turn is attentive to us.

When the sun does come, our spirits surge like those of children, and for the few hours or even minutes that it might be present, we wander out into its beautiful blue embrace, staring up and out at such rare and magnificent illumination, saying things like "Wow!" and "Geezo-peezo!" over and over again; and we can feel deeply, intimately, the puppet-string leap and pull of our bloodstream's chemicals being scrambled and rearranged, bestirred and invigorated, awakening even if only briefly, and become refreshed.

We might invest thirty or forty days in a row of lightlessness in exchange for a few moments of such blue-sky brilliance — sometimes the sun and the blue-sky against the snowy mountains remain visible for a whole afternoon — but it is almost worth it (when the sun's out, it *is* worth it) and I have to wonder if, while slumbering in their ice caves, the bears are aware of that brief appearance: if, even as they sleep, their blood lifts and their spirits surge. I wonder if the sun's appearance somehow makes it down even through the shell of their snow chambers, bathing them in a warmer, golden glow, as opposed to the usual dull blue light of winter. Sometimes the bears will even climb up and out of their snow caves and wander around for a while, like sleepwalkers, even in the dead of winter — no one's really sure why — and I have to wonder if these brief rousings are somehow tied to the infrequent return, or appearance, of the low, cold winter sun.

Daily, like some workaday businessman, I ensconce myself in my own ice cave and attempt to descend into the land of blue dreams, trudging out to my cold cabin at the edge of the marsh, carrying in my arms a stack of papers, a thermos, a coffee cup, and sometimes a load of kindling.

And once in the ice shell of the cabin, and with the cold little fire in the wood stove straining to heat some distance beyond my cold boot, which is propped up on its edge within a foot of the flames, I will find myself staring out at the frozen prairie expanse of marsh for fifteen or twenty minutes, without ever thinking a single thought, so that again, I might as well be hibernating.

On the sunny days, however, it's torture to be inside — I try to work quickly so that I can go outside and play — and I am made agitated, excited, by that rarest of sights and sounds, the sun-filled icicles gleaming, becoming translucent as they warm. They're nearly incandescent, like the glowing filaments in light bulbs, as the sun strikes them — and then, most amazingly of all, *dripping* — and I have to sit there in my chair, at my table, and watch it rather than go out into it.

I try to dive deeply, quickly — to get that day's work done as fast as possible. It's so hard to concentrate, though. Is this how it is for the bears? Do they fight to keep on in their task of hibernating?

Sometimes on such a rare sunny day, I'll have just succeeded in making it to dreamland when the slab of snow that's been resting on either side of my steep-pitched metal roof will suddenly release as the sun warms the top of that metal and the bottommost layer of snow melts. Often I'll be staring out my windows, entranced by both the dream and the lovely gold light, the rare gold light, when that ice sheet suddenly releases above and goes curling past the window, hurtling past the window blocking out the sun, and all light, for an instant, with flashes of gold sunlight shuttering in through the window, piercing little cracks in that tumbling sheet of snow — and then the snow will have all passed and once more there will be a steady stream of gold light shining into my eyes — during this whole event, this whole collapse, I will not have blinked. I feel that gold light, that new gold light, shining somehow deeper into the back of my brain, after having witnessed or been primed by those erratic flash-camera shutterings of only a few seconds ago — and always, when that happens, I will arise as if hypnotized, or rather, as if having awakened, and remembering what really matters, what's really important. I will close my notebook and cap my pen and tamp down the fire and leave my cabin, then, and will step back out into the light.

Such clear days usually bring clear nights, which means cold nights, as the day's warmth escapes back to outer space. On these nights, I put new hay in the dogs' insulated kennels, for them to burrow into, and must knock the ice from their watering bowls. And the next day, if we should be so fortunate for the sun to be out again, it's common to hear sawyers working all around the valley, cutting more firewood in that new winter light, bestirred to action by the previous night's harshness, and by its demands on the woodpile; and yet again, the link, the connection, between landscape and the individual, is immediate and direct, forming a strength of bond between the two that is not so common, anymore, rarer, even, perhaps, than December sunlight, and in a way that I cannot prove or explain, our country, our nation, somehow the poorer and more diminished for that rarity.

I am not arguing against or even criticizing big cities, or cities and towns of any size, when I say such a thing — only reminding myself of that which poets and philosophers have been telling us for several centuries now, that the American wilderness is one of our great and unique treasures, and that it is not renewable. And that if it becomes diminished, then so too must we.

Part of me wants to stay home every hour of every day, in every season, but particularly in December, the holiday season — to burrow into the snow, to sink down into the idyll of childhood with the girls — but up here, bird season ends in December too, particularly for pheasants, which are the species that most thrills and jazzes my sweet and big-running pointers, Point and Superman, the former speckled like a pale Appaloosa, strong as a bull, and mischievous, and the latter chocolate-colored, mellow and obedient, and one of the most graceful, athletic dogs I've ever seen work.

It cannot be called work, of course. I love it — perhaps I was made for it, destined the moment my DNA twined the way it did — but the dogs love it too, and for certain, they were made for it: the scents and pursuit of the gallinaceous birds is a breeze that blows oxygen into the glimmering embers of their soul.

The nearest pheasants are half a state away, in eastern Montana, up and over the Continental Divide, out on the plains, and generally I take the boys out there at least two or three times in the autumn for multiday hunts, but then I more or less disappear into the woods myself, deer and elk hunting in November, so that they must wait until December to hunt again.

I want to be both places: hunting pheasants on the east side, and slowly settling into Christmas on the west side, cooking cinnamon rolls, hanging wreaths, reading Dickens, writing Christmas cards.

In typical gluttonous compromise, I attempt both. We get the girls ready for bed, read to them, and then I lie down for a short nap before awakening to the alarm clock at two-thirty. In good weather it's five hours to pheasants; a heavy snow is falling, however, and the roads are icier than ever, so I know it'll take at least eight hours. My plan is to hit pheasant-land by noon, hunt till dusk, then turn around and drive back into the storm that night, getting home within twenty-four hours. One day. There is a sweetness, a tapering knife edge where a season's satisfaction lies on one side and a lament that it is ending on the other side.

These dogs deserve all the birds the world can throw at them, I tell myself, particularly in light of the long and impending off-season. Given a choice of extra sleep or giving your dogs one more hunt, only a cretin would choose sleep.

"All I want," I explain to Elizabeth and the girls, aware of how much I sound like a child petitioning Santa Claus, "is the sight of one rooster against blue sky, with new snow behind him. I don't even need to hit it: I just want a good point, and the sight of a brilliant rooster against the snow, and then rising higher, into that blue sky."

Elizabeth and the girls have been out with me and know what I mean. They do not hold this image as intensely as I do (just as I in turn do not hold it as intensely as, say, the dogs), but they know what I mean. They've seen it, and though Elizabeth in particular shakes her head and says it's crazy to work so hard for such a brief image — one I've already seen, countless times, and will surely see again and again — she does not think it's so crazy as to try to argue me out of it, and instead only cautions me to drive carefully.

I get off to a slow start, creeping down the untracked roads, sipping coffee, the dogs warm and excited in the front seat, and the snow still falling so heavily, and in such large flakes, that peering through the windshield, it feels to me as if we are suspended in one of those little glass globes that you can shake up to agitate the artificial snow within, and I wonder idly if it's possible to construct one of those little globes so that bright roosters likewise flutter through the snow, rising from thick cattails even as all the snow is descending.

Memories are strong, photographs are beautiful, but nothing will do for me but the real thing.

I have traveled less than a dozen miles in solitary wonder before encountering another pilgrim, a traveler less fortunate than I who has plowed headlong into a snowdrift sometime earlier — his truck is shrouded with a night's worth of snow — and as I pass, believing his vehicle's misfortune to be days old, I'm surprised to see him step from the truck, rumple-haired, flagging me down.

I'm the first person that's gone past, he says; he's been here five hours. For a couple of hours he tried digging out, clawing at the snow with his hands, lacking a shovel, but finally he became drenched and decided to quit and change into a dry set of clothes so that he didn't become hypothermic, and to wait for someone to pass by.

He's a Bible salesman from New Jersey, it turns out, wandering down from out of Canada on some convoluted and lonely-sounding sojourn. He's all out of Bibles but still has a few boxes of grapefruit and oranges, which he offers me as repayment for the bother of my time. I thank him but tell him that where I'm going, they'd freeze for sure.

I crawl under his truck, and then mine, fastening my old tow rope — he's all but clueless about such matters — but tugging his back end uphill, as the cant of his truck forces me to do (the front is swallowed almost entirely by the snowdrift), I'm unable to get enough bite and torque to free him, though I snatch and jerk again and again until we're both risking whiplash. I can almost get him out, but not quite.

Neither of us has a shovel — it's still too early in the year for us to be fully equipped; always, winter catches me by surprise, as if, by my not fully preparing, I can somehow stall its arrival — so we're clawing with sticks and empty coffee cans at the snow in front of his truck, with the resigned hopelessness of prisoners trying to dig an escape tunnel with nothing more than a soupspoon, when the headlights of another truck appear.

I've been fooling with the salesman's truck for about an hour by this point — an hour I don't have to spare — so I'm extra chagrined when the truck passes by us without even stopping to inquire whether we need help or not. For some strange reason, however, I hold off from making a judgment — so unlike me — and my virtue is rewarded a few moments later when the truck, its occupants perhaps having reconsidered, turns around and comes driving back down the hill.

It's a truck full of lion hunters — they don't have time to spare, either — but they get out and visit for a while. They've got several hounds in the back of their truck, and it strikes me as an odd juxtaposition, the three groups of us moving around on the mountain beneath the cover of darkness and snowfall, as if in some netherworld, while the rest of the citizenry sleeps: a Bible salesman with his crates of grapefruit in Montana, and two trucks filled with hounds. As if only in the middle of the night, and in the midst of a blizzard, are such travelers willing to emerge from that lower, secret world and move about in the realms of the upper world . . .

By hooking their chain to the back of my truck, and then my yellow tow rope to the back of the salesman's truck after connecting it to a longer chain owned by the lion hunters, we're able to generate enough pulling power in tandem like that to ease him out of the drift, although in the process, my tow rope has gotten knotted and is cinched so tight from the force generated by our pulling that we have to cut the knot where it was fastened to the lion hunters' chain. This leaves a scrap of bright yellow embedded in their rusty chain, like a marker, a memento, of their good deed.

We part ways, then — the lion hunters heading north and west, and me and my bird dogs, south and east — and though I would rather have not had to stop, it's a code of the north, and, I suspect, a code of any place that still has any kind of identity at all, that when someone's in trouble, you stop and help.

It's slow going, even slower than I'd planned. I have to stop for gas in Libby — what a recent miracle the twenty-four-hour gas pumps are, the ones that accept credit cards, even at gas pumps far out in the hinterlands; in the old days, not so long ago, night travelers in the outback had to plan their gas stops around big cities — and then, twenty miles farther, I have to stop again to let the dogs exercise and void, lest their rumbling, hissing flatulence asphyxiate me.

They take their sweet time wandering around in the hard-falling snow before finally settling into the obligatory hunker, like twin yard ornaments, and then we are on our way again, later than ever; and after only twenty more miles, my oil pressure drops — evidently some leaked through the valves the other evening while my truck was perched lightly on the side of the cliff — and twenty miles beyond that, I must stop yet again to retighten the lug nuts, which are nearly unspun, causing all four wheels to wobble lugubriously, and it is clear to me now that the party, the dawn party of bright roosters, moving at first light, will be starting without me — without us.

By midmorning we are nearing the Divide, traveling along the eastern boundary of Glacier National Park, and making pretty good time — the road is plowed and sanded — and as I pass through the town of West Glacier, I notice the Amtrak cars idling there, offloading a few passengers and taking on a few new ones, and I have the wish, not for the first time, that Amtrak would travel directly to my hunting place, and that the dogs could travel on it with me, so that we could sleep, or so that I could ride in relaxation, reading a paperback, perhaps, and looking out the window at the beautiful winter scenery without having to worry about staying on the road.

For the next fifty miles or so, the train and I seem to engage in a push-and-pull game of tag — the train catching and passing me occasionally, tracking a straighter line along the other side of the Flathead River, though with me usually catching it and then passing it again, on the straightaways — and I cannot help but imagine that there is some passenger on the train who is noticing my truck, with the dogs in the back, thinking, *Aha, the lucky devil is going hunting this beautiful blue winter day,* just as I am thinking of the train's passengers, *Aha, how nice to be simply riding, without worrying about anything.*

And although I recognize it as silly, even immature at best, after a while I discover that there's a part of me that wants to stay ahead of the train, even if only by a minute or two. I know, it's ridiculous! And I'm not going to compromise my safety — our safety (often while driving with the dogs I find myself aware of how they aren't wearing seat belts) — but on the straightaways, well, I don't lolly-gag, but ease down on the accelerator; and if I'm a hundred or so yards ahead of the train, I soon realize that I'm trying to maintain or even increase that distance; and if I'm a hundred or so yards behind, I'm trying — within the limits of safety, certainly — to close that distance.

It's not anything as serious as a competition — I'm not *that* immature. Instead, it's more like a kind of an awareness, is all: something to rouse me from the postdawn torpor of all-night driving.

And on the train, is that hypothetical passenger, or passengers, likewise urging the train on?

Not far from the summit at Marias Pass, we hit another straightaway, the train and I, and I'm able to pull ahead again, and to improve the margin of my lead, so much so that the train isn't even in sight any longer, and I drive along feeling strangely better.

I don't want the season to ever end. I don't like the feeling of being left behind, and I don't like things ending.

I'm so far ahead of the train now — a mile? two miles? — that I can't even see it in my rearview mirror, and soon enough, it's all but forgotten, as if but a trifle. I'm bored again, trying to stay sharp and awake, and begin fiddling with my daughter's CD Walkman, trying to get it to play. (There aren't any radio stations up in the mountains — not even the narcoleptic stock and farm reports — and my truck's tape player hasn't worked for three years now.)

The disc — Gillian Welch's sleepy, wonderful *Time (The Revelator)* — is skipping on the bumpy road, and I glance down for a second to make sure I haven't bumped the Pause button. When I look up again the view through the windshield is of nothing but a wall of snow spraying up over the windshield — immediately, all around me, there's a muffled silence that tells me that although I'm still moving, I'm not on the road anymore. And then we are sinking, descending, and there is blue winter light all around us, and we come to a stop — the dogs, jolted by the impact, rouse themselves from their naps and look at me as if wondering whether it's time to go hunting, finally — and when the snow spray finally clears, I'm surprised at how far off the road I am.

I shift down into four-wheel low and attempt to back out, but it's pointless, I'm buried up to the headlights, and resting atop another four feet of snow, below the wheels — and so I burrow into the snow beneath the truck and begin attaching the tattered yellow tow rope to the frame, so that it will be ready to fasten to the chain of the first Samaritan who happens along.

It's not too long of a wait. The train passes first — though I can see no passengers through the small window portals, I wave anyway — and not long after that, a truck driven by two men working for the railroad passes by, and stops.

One man is my age, the other, much younger, and they're dressed in heavy coveralls and are sipping steaming coffee from insulated cups. Their truck — the Burlington Northern's truck — is a big, new, fancy one, and they've got a super-long new tow rope, which they loop on to mine.

I buckle up, start my truck, put it in reverse, and then experience the strange and resurrection-like feeling of being uprooted from all that snow, tugged free with immense power; and just like that, I'm out, my extraction nearly as smooth and effortless as my entrance.

Once again, my tow rope is knotted inextricably around theirs, and so I saw the rope off again, leaving another little butterfly tuft of gilding on their rope, a remnant marker — like some strange kind of Montana-winter chain letter, I think, on either side of the Divide, so that soon enough, at this rate, many Samaritans will be wearing fragments of this yellow rope on their own tow chains, and their own tow ropes, both the pullers and the pullees — and I thank and shake hands with the two railroad employees and then continue on my way, hoping to make it to the plains now by noon in order that the dogs and I might at least have half a day of hunting before turning right around and heading back.

Eventually, I'm over the pass and sailing down the back side of the Divide, to the Atlantic. The plains are gold below me, bathed in sun, beneath pale blue windy-winter's skies, and the roads are scoured free of snow so that I'm able to make better time, quicker time — stopping only once, to give those cliff-tipped valves another transfusion of thirty-weight — and before I know it, the Sweetgrass

Hills are in view on my left, sugar-topped above the gold stubble that surrounds them, and on my right, the incomparable Front Range, perhaps the grandest view in North America. Bravo to Senator Max Baucus for his attempt to protect it from being developed into yet another oil and gas field; bravo to ex–Lewis and Clark National Forest supervisor Gloria Flora for withdrawing these public lands from oil and gas leasing. How a damaged world needs heroes.

We drive right up to our honey hole of yore, visit with the rancher, Tom, his foreman, Steve, for a while, and their words are like a sweet and rare kind of music — yes, there are plenty of birds this year, but no, there haven't been many hunters, because the hunting was so poor early on that people just stopped trying.

Always, I have to run little Point first. He simply won't tolerate letting Superman hunt first; if I don't take him first, he howls, whirls in circles on the front seat, scent-marks the steering wheel, tears at the upholstery with his claws, then begins biting and tearing the door apart in an attempt to tunnel out to freedom and glory.

This year, the birds aren't there: no scat, no tracks, no scent, though it doesn't even really matter; it's great just to be striding the snowy fields, and for Point to be charging through them, scampering, casting left and right; and with such a modest goal as wanting to see only one bird, one rooster, sky borne, there's always the possibility that we can accomplish that goal at any moment. Just one bird, and no matter whether a cagey old veteran that holds tight, knowing the hunters and dogs sometimes pass on by, or a foolish young bird, believing that because he is hidden, he is safe.

Our next run, at another old-favorite place, is more productive. Superman's not scenting well — he's still got a couple of porcupine quills embedded deep in his gums, left over from an encounter earlier in the fall, and they've formed cysts right against his nasal passage that are temporarily disrupting his usually phenomenal scenting ability — but he manages to put me into a flock of Hungarian partridge, which, perhaps because of the cold — it's about ten degrees, with a stiff wind — are hunkered down in the cattails, just like pheasants.

Amazingly, I'm able to hit one, and while a hunt's success should never be measured by whether game is harvested or not, it's still a wonderful thing to see him go retrieve the bird, and to slip it into the game bags. Tomorrow evening, I think, I'll fix it on the grill — cook it over mesquite coals in the falling snow.

Maybe there's even another one out there.

There is, and Superman finds it on the next run, and then, running Point again, we find a lone sharp-tail — I shoot twice and miss — and then a big flock of Huns, which get up in staggers, sheets of bronzed birds rocketing away on clattering wings, and like Custer, I stand there and blaze away, missing and reloading, missing and reloading, as the waves of birds keep catapulting into the sky. I miss eight times in all without ever moving my feet.

Near the truck, hiking out, Point locks up in the heaviest thicket of cattails I've ever seen, and the two of us stand there for perhaps five minutes, with our tension building.

Every now and then I kick at the cattails, but no bird erupts. Still, Point remains locked up, with the widening flare of his nostrils the only movement.

I kick again, with my gun still on safety, and finally the bird scooches a little — we can hear it struggling to get out of the cattails in which it has embedded itself — and after what seems like a full minute of noise, the bird claws its way up from out of the cattail jungle, right between us, and it is a wild-eyed rooster, rising to eye level with me, close enough to catch in a butterfly net. My goal is achieved, my wish granted. As it peels away to the north, a straightaway lining out, I miss with the first shot, and then the second.

How many hundreds — perhaps thousands — of times have I rewarded the most stellar dog work with the most abysmal shooting?

What is a dog's concept of time, and of things ending? Hopefully it's as nonexistent as it seems, for Point pushes on as if it's no big deal; as if he's certain we're going to get at least one more chance, certain that the season is not ending. Or rather, unaware.

Already, it's the last run of the day; the afternoon, though filled and compacted with strength and wildness, suffused with anticipation and beauty, is still, after all, despite the many miles driven and then walked, only an afternoon. And the sunset over the Rocky Mountain Front — purple storm sky with sheets of Arctic snowstorm, copper and orange firelight piercing through just above that mountain-hanging storm, cold purple and white reefs sculpted by a force of grander design and order than anyone likely ever could have dared dream of or hope for — *all I want is what I got, the sight of one rooster* — reminds me of how precious few minutes the boys and I have left, an hour perhaps, before it's time to turn back around and face the music and head back into that storm.

Earlier in the afternoon, leaving the birdless honey hole of old, I'd seen an old farmhouse on a hill, in the yard of which there were what looked like a hundred pheasants strutting. Such sights are not infrequent, late in the season, as every bird in the area soon learns which property is posted and which is not, and though I was certain such bounty was protected, I'd pulled into the driveway to ask anyway. No one was home, and so I'd driven on; but because that farm is somewhat on the way home, and closer to those beautiful stormy mountains (it's still clear and cold out on the plains), I decide to swing by and see if anyone's in.

Miraculously — like some angelic being who's come down to earth for a few brief moments in that crepuscular hour, the owner is in, and is out in his yard, carrying buckets of feed out to a corral. He's a tall, older man named Ted, and when I introduce myself and ask if he allows hunters on his land — there's an immense swath of wild CRP land stretching beyond his house, traveling what seems like halfway to the horizon — he doesn't really answer directly but instead asks how many pheasants I've gotten today.

Well, I tell him, *not that I'm really counting, but zero.*

He looks at me, and the dogs in my truck, and at that last thirty minutes of light; at that big storm hanging up over the mountains, and at his big damn field, and he says, "All right, I'll tell you what. Why don't you and your dog go back in there and get your supper."

If you hunt enough days, enough years, sometimes it happens like this.

I thank him and am about to go grab Point when he adds a couple of stipulations.

"Don't shoot toward the hay bales, and don't run over my mailbox," he says.

It turns out he hasn't let hunters on his land in almost two years. The last time he did, one of them shot toward the big mound of giant rolled hay bales that was sitting out in the center of his field, and the heated BB burrowed into that tight-packed hay, where the heat and friction of it smoldered through the rest of the day, until later that night it started a bonfire that could be seen fifty miles away, and the heat from which Ted could feel even through the windows of his house.

The hunters before that backed over his mailbox on their way out, he says. They didn't mean to — they were just kids — but it was dusk, they didn't see it, and they came walking back up his driveway carrying the mailbox while Ted was inside having supper and asked if it was his.

"Whose else would it be?" he asks me, still fuming two years later. "There's nobody else out here for a mile in any direction!"

I commit a near fatal gaffe; I tell the truth. "I'm such a poor driver," I tell him, "it sounds like something I would've done."

His eyes widen, and in that instant, I can see him scrutinizing me, wondering how safe his mailbox really is, and then in the next instant casting back in his memory to see if indeed I might have been one of those hunters from years before.

What is it that makes us say the wrong things at the wrong time? What perversity compels me to say, honestly, "That's interesting, about the BBs — I never knew they'd do that." It's all I can do to keep from adding, "I must've fired toward a hundred hay bales in my life — I had no idea!"

"Of course it'll happen," Ted says. "People don't think."

If I had more time, I'd try to explain to him what it's like, to be a dreamer — how it's not willful, but instead, as if you're often a stranger in a strange, albeit beautiful land; of how you become so enamored with the senses of the world that it's like being lifted up by some greater force and carried away some other distance, sometimes near and sometimes far: in the manner, perhaps, of a hunting dog first catching that rank and exquisite scent, or even the hint of scent, of faraway game.

But by now, because there are only about twenty minutes left in which to hunt, I don't say any of that. Instead, I shake my head and say something like, "I can't believe they lit your *hay bales* on fire," and then add, convincingly, I hope, "The numb nuts!"

Anything for my dog!

My last utterance is apparently enough for Ted to release me to the wilds of his fields. He wishes me good luck, picks up his grain buckets, and continues on with his end-of-day chores, while I grab Point and hurry on out into the field, past the hay bales.

The pheasants see us coming, hear us coming, *feel* us coming, and begin leaping up from the field in flocks, a hundred and two hundred yards distant, and flying toward the horizon. I've never seen so many pheasants in my life, and Point's never smelled so much scent. There's so much juice on the ground, fresh juice overlaid on more fresh juice, running juice and sitting juice and roosting juice, that it's impossible for a dog of even his abilities to weave any narrative, and instead we just hurry into the wind, toward the distant bat-flock of pheasants that are still getting up and flushing wild, flushing unendingly. And it seems to me, if not to Point or Ted, that perhaps this unrivaled phenomenon is like some secret, long-hidden gear works of the universe, one rarely if ever witnessed before, and that it is somehow the frantic departure of this near infinity of birds that is setting in motion the coming of darkness, the end of day, like the curtain coming down on some grand play or opera.

Point stops, then creeps, then stops, then creeps, then stops again, jarring me from dreamland. Then he accelerates wildly — the bird he's scented is running hard, and never mind that I can't see him, that he's like a ghost — this is the best part, or the second-best part, next to seeing him — and then Point slams to a stop again and whirls ninety degrees to the right, then is running again, and for the first time that day, I hedge on my earlier goal; I fudge, and amend it, there in day's last light.

I'd really like to hit one. I'd really like to watch one rise, then fall fluttering bright and stone dead back to the prairie, and for Point to retrieve it. When Ted told me to go out and get my supper, I'm sure he was envisioning the limit, which is three pheasants, but all I want is one.

Point's a little too far out, running a little too hard — all right, a lot too hard, and as such, I'm just out of range when the grain-fat pheasant, the lingerer — a rooster — gets up wild and flies.

But he is flying the wrong way, not in the gear works direction of all the other departing thousands, but toward me, pushed there, somehow, by Point, or luck, or choice, and whether the rooster ever realizes his mistake or not I cannot say, for I take him on the first shot — a pleasure infinitely cleaner and more satisfying than that of missing with the first and having to use the noisome second shot — and the bird falls cleanly, just as they do sometimes, in my dreams. Point bounds over to the bird, picks it up, and brings it to me, the two of us a team, and I pet him, rub his big stone head in the gathering dusk, and finally realize for the first time all day how truly cold it is. *Why, it's mid-December,* I realize — as if there has been some part of me, all afternoon, wanting to pretend that because it's still bird-hunting season, it must still be September or October.

I slide the big bird into my game bag, unload my gun, and rise and start back toward my truck, Point capering and whirling in front of me, and with my next goal so simple and elemental: don't run over the mailbox on the way out.

Marias Pass is grimmer than I even imagined it could be, with the road, illumined a couple hours later by my feeble headlights, in the whirling, hallucinogenic disorder of the blizzard so indistinguishable at times from the hills and then mountains around me that I could just as easily be completely lost, and creeping out across some forlorn pasture or meadow, as on a major U.S. highway. My speed slows to fifteen miles an hour, and then to ten, and then five, and then I can see nothing but snow howling against my windshield and must stop completely. I can feel it, hear it, piling up already, immediately against my truck, now as motionless as a boulder, and somewhat horrifically, even though my foot is pressed firmly on the brake and the speedometer reads zero, it seems that I am still moving, still driving into the storm — sliding into the storm, being swallowed into the storm, is what it feels like — and that furthermore my truck, and therefore the road, or rather the landscape beneath it, is tilted at a sixty-degree pitch, like the steep bank of an aircraft entering the final turn of its landing approach; and the snow keeps sweeping past, raging past, carrying me farther along into some strange place equipoised between dream and reality.

Point slumbers on the seat beside me, snoring gently. I press the brake harder, as if that might somehow still or dispel the horrific vision, or even the storm itself.

Sometimes, it seems that the storm has to pause to take a breath — to suck in air, as if in a bellows, if only so that it can blow harder on the out breath — and after a while, I learn that I can creep forward a short distance in those brief and erratic shifts between breaths; and in this manner, I'm able to inch up over the Divide, making the last two miles in thirty minutes. Once I'm off the face of the Divide and more fully into the mountains, things stabilize. It's snowing just as hard, but the terrible winds are more subdued, as if unable to get up much momentum among the icy crags and peaks.

The next several hours pass as if I'm in catatonia — if I see another vehicle on the road, other than in the big city of Kalispell, I don't remember it — and it's well after midnight when I finally turn up the thin mountain road that will lead ultimately into my valley.

Another hour passes like but a minute — it's still snowing — and I pass the trace, the legacy, of Bible man's snow burrow, almost completely obscured already by the storm.

I'm close enough to home to start some serious daydreaming now, and I remember something someone said, Hemingway, or maybe it was someone else, about bird hunting, which was along the lines of *Whatever it ends up costing, it's not enough;* and idly, and suddenly bone tired, I tinker with the math: two dogs, and one hunter, three birds; three birds in six hundred miles; three birds in twenty-four hours.

How do you break it down? You don't. It's a different kind of math. Less is more, and, as if in a dream, you become enriched by the sweet diminishment.

The children, thank goodness, seem fairly immune to the concussively long winters, as if there is some external light in their blood, some vigor percolating almost constantly, that serves as either a preventative shield or an antidote.

One weekend before Christmas, Wendy comes home with us after school and spends the night. After supper (spaghetti and venison meatballs), Elizabeth and I are sitting on the couch, sipping hot chocolate and watching a movie on the VCR, when we hear a tremendous thumping.

I investigate and find the three girls are playing tennis, or some wild variant thereof, in the utility room. They are wearing their bicycle helmets for safety, and the tennis ball is ricocheting in all directions — off not just the walls but the tile floor and ceiling and even the washer and dryer (when it hits either of these two appliances, it gives a pleasing and resounding bass drum). The girls are shrieking and giggling — it's more like tennis defense than tennis — and the unfortunate cat is in that tiny room with them leaping and scooting back and forth like a flying squirrel.

They've got their bicycle helmets on. They're not hurting anything. They're having a good time. I close the door and go back to the movie. Where else are they going to play tennis at this time of year?

The way they hurl themselves at play and pleasure: leaping into snowdrifts for no other reason than to make snow angels — all three girls lying on their backs out in the yard, flapping and kicking, fanning one snow angel after another, until the yard is filled with them.

Ever thoughtful, Lowry runs over to Homer's grave and lies down on top of it and fans one for her too, remembering how she used to love to play and caper in the snow.

The older I get — and the more I learn from my children, learning even as I attempt to teach them some things — the more I remember that, for all my rhapsodic love of nature, and particularly the unaltered and uncompromising wilderness, it is, after all, always friends and family and community that make us most human, and most humane. Just because there are far more humans than there is wilderness, particularly American wilderness, does not diminish the sweetness of friendships, or childhood, or community, and indeed, from an individual's perspective, given the brevity of our time here in the physical world of rock and snow, antler and bone, fruit and meat, sky and sun, these latter pleasures are actually more

ephemeral than even the fast-diminishing and beleaguered unprotected wilderness itself.

Children grow up and move away, friends grow old and
stooped, communities shift and flow, fragment and weave back together. The deliciousness of a moment, and of beauty, is almost always heightened by the consciousness of such brevity. It is a sweetness, an awareness, however, that I sometimes tend to overlook, or
take for granted; and it's good for me, particularly during the holidays, to step back and remember that it is not merely the marsh, or
the natural cycles of things, that give me stability and even peace in
a tumultuous world, but also the braid, the weave, of people passing
all around me — a current of people, friends and others, as ceaseless and interesting as the wind itself, or the currents of some broad
river, or, again, the flow of the seasons themselves, passing around
and around the globe, year after year, bathing us in change, and at
the same time bathing us in regularity, with a constancy that is remarkable, and which in my opinion follows very much in the same
pattern and logic as does the human emotion of love.

It's New Year's Eve, and snowing hard, a true blizzard, with huge,
soft flakes falling by the millions. We're having some friends over
to celebrate, and we've been cooking all afternoon: grilling an elk
ham, slow-roasting a couple of pheasants, and baking desserts. The
Christmas tree is lit up outside, glowing blue and yellow and green
and red in the storm, barely visible, like a lighthouse, and it's seven
p.m, and the phones are all out, and we're waiting, waiting, waiting:
watching out the window, and waiting.

At about eight o'clock, the headlights appear through the trees
and falling snow, coming slowly down the driveway, one truck, and
then another, and another, and then another.

My heart leaps. I couldn't stop it if I wanted. Here they come
again. Here comes everything again, one more time, at least.